Minority Governments in Comparative Perspective

COMPARATIVE POLITICS

Comparative Politics is a series for researchers, teachers, and students of political science that deals with contemporary government and politics. Global in scope, books in the series are characterized by a stress on comparative analysis and strong methodological rigour. The series is published in association with the European Consortium for Political Research. For more information visit
www.ecprnet.eu

The series is edited by Nicole Bolleyer, Chair of Comparative Political Science, Geschwister Scholl Institut, LMU Munich, and Jonathan Slapin, Professor and Chair of Political Institutions and European Politics, University of Zurich.

OTHER TITLES IN THIS SERIES

The Government Party
Political Dominance in Democracy
R. Kenneth Carty

The New Kremlinology
Understanding Regime Personalization in Russia
Alexander Baturo and Johan A. Elkink

Reimagining the Judiciary
Women's Representation on High Courts Worldwide
Maria C. Escobar-Lemmon, Valerie J. Hoekstra, Alice J. Kang, and Miki Caul Kittilson

Coalition Governance in Western Europe
Edited by Torbjörn Bergman, Hanna Bäck, and Johan Hellström

Beyond Turnout
How Compulsory Voting Shapes Citizens and Political Parties
Shane P. Singh

Party System Closure
Party Alliances, Government Alternatives, and Democracy in Europe
Fernando Casal Bértoa and Zsolt Enyedi

Minority Governments in Comparative Perspective

Edited by
BONNIE N. FIELD
SHANE MARTIN

Great Clarendon Street, Oxford, OX2 6DP,
United Kingdom

Oxford University Press is a department of the University of Oxford.
It furthers the University's objective of excellence in research, scholarship,
and education by publishing worldwide. Oxford is a registered trade mark of
Oxford University Press in the UK and in certain other countries

© the several contributors 2022

The moral rights of the authors have been asserted

Impression: 1

All rights reserved. No part of this publication may be reproduced, stored in
a retrieval system, or transmitted, in any form or by any means, without the
prior permission in writing of Oxford University Press, or as expressly permitted
by law, by licence or under terms agreed with the appropriate reprographics
rights organization. Enquiries concerning reproduction outside the scope of the
above should be sent to the Rights Department, Oxford University Press, at the
address above

You must not circulate this work in any other form
and you must impose this same condition on any acquirer

Published in the United States of America by Oxford University Press
198 Madison Avenue, New York, NY 10016, United States of America

British Library Cataloguing in Publication Data

Data available

Library of Congress Control Number: 2022938768

ISBN 978–0–19–287165–7

DOI: 10.1093/oso/9780192871657.001.0001

Printed and bound by
CPI Group (UK) Ltd, Croydon, CR0 4YY

Links to third party websites are provided by Oxford in good faith and
for information only. Oxford disclaims any responsibility for the materials
contained in any third party website referenced in this work.

Preface and Acknowledgments

We are deeply indebted to the many people who made this volume possible. A particular word of thanks to the authors, both for agreeing to contribute and for responding happily to our various requests. This book was written and edited during the Covid-19 pandemic, and the challenges which this posed for everyone makes us all the more grateful.

At Oxford University Press, we are very grateful to Dominic Byatt for his support and encouragement, as we are to Nicole Bolleyer, Susan Scarrow, Jon Slapin, now or recent editors of the wonderful and rightly impactful *Comparative Politics* series. We are grateful to the reviewers, not just for the very positive reception, but also for engaging so fully and deeply with the draft.

Bonnie Field wishes to acknowledge research support from Bentley University. Shane Martin wishes to acknowledge research funds made available by the Department of Government, University of Essex.

The editors' thinking about minority governments has been shaped fundamentally by opportunities to interact and engage with a number of colleagues over the years whose work on the topic has been at the forefront of political science scholarship. For their inspiration, we thank in particular Kaare W. Strøm, Torbjörn Bergman, José Antonio Cheibub, and Bjørn Erik Rasch. On the territorial dimensions of minority government, Bonnie Field's thinking has been greatly influenced by foundational work on Spain by Cesáreo Alguilera de Prat, Jordi Capo, William Heller, and Josep María Reniu. Shane Martin's interest in minority governments underwent a renaissance after reading Field's ground-breaking 2016 monograph *Why Minority Governments Work: Multilevel Territorial Politics in Spain*.

Martin's curiosity about why minority governments form and Field's interest in how they work and how well they perform brought us together to lead this volume. Additionally, we were struck by the absence of a comparative, country-based book on minority governments. The desire to fill this hole strengthened with Field's participation in the research project on *Coalition Governance in Western Europe*, led by Torbjörn Bergman, Hanna Bäck and Johan Hellström. That same project informed our thinking about minority governments.

The core questions of *why*, *how*, and *how well* that structure the volume build on Kaare Strom's classic work *Minority Government and Majority Rule*, which Field also used in her 2016 monograph.

Both editors wish to thank their partners for their unending support and encouragement.

Contents

List of Figures	viii
List of Tables	ix
List of Contributors	xi

I. INTRODUCTION

1. The Politics of Minority Government ... 3
   Bonnie N. Field and Shane Martin

2. The *How*, *Why*, and *How Well* of Minority Governments ... 19
   Bonnie N. Field and Shane Martin

II. WHERE MINORITY GOVERNMENTS ARE PREDOMINANT

3. Minority Governments in India: Party System Federalization and the Emergence of Contract Parliamentarism ... 41
   Csaba Nikolenyi

4. Norway: A Land of Minority Governments ... 66
   Kaare W. Strøm

5. Minority Governments in Romania: A Case of Stable Instability ... 86
   Veronica Anghel

6. Minority Governments in Spain: Government Strengthening Institutions in a Multilevel State ... 108
   Bonnie N. Field

7. Minority Governments in Sweden: Majority Cabinets in Disguise ... 129
   Hanna Bäck and Johan Hellström

III. WHERE MINORITY GOVERNMENTS ARE COMMON

8. Minority Governments in Canada: Stability through Voting Alliances 151
   Jean-François Godbout and Christopher Cochrane

9. Minority Governments in France: A Mix of Presidential and Parliamentary Logics 170
   Olivier Rozenberg

10. Ireland: Minority Government with a Majoritarian Twist 189
    Liam Weeks

11. Minority Governments in Italy: From Structural Stability to Political Change 208
    Daniela Giannetti

12. Minority Governments in Poland: Governing after a Crisis with Ad Hoc Majorities 241
    Radoslaw Zubek

13. Minority Governments in Portugal: Institutions as Solutions to Historical Legacies 262
    Jorge M. Fernandes

IV. WHERE MINORITY GOVERNMENTS ARE EXCEPTIONAL

14. Minority Government in Australia: Lesson Learning and Making It Work 283
    Kate Crowley (with Cath Hughes)

15. Minority Governments in the United Kingdom: Nearly-winning Minorities and Lost Majorities 306
    Andrew Jones and Richard Whitaker

16. Comparative Conclusions on Minority Governments 325
    Bonnie N. Field and Shane Martin

Index 345

List of Figures

1.1.	The rate of minority government, select democracies, 1990–2020	9
1.2.	Proportion of seats held by governments, select countries, 1990–2020	10
1.3.	Proportion of seats held by governments, by government type, select countries, 1990–2020	11
1.4.	Proportion of seats held by governments, by country, 1990–2020	12
3.1.	The effective number of legislative parties in the Lok Sabha, 1952–2019, India	43
9.1.	The use of Article 49.3 in France (1988–1992)	178
10.1.	Independent parliamentarians in Ireland, 1922–2020	194
11.1.	Party policy positions and seats, 1987 showing a non-empty core, Italy (intersection of median lines at the DC position)	219
11.2.	Party policy positions and seats, 1996 showing an empty core, Italy	220
12.1.	Winning coalitions in the 1997–2001 parliament, Poland	246
12.2.	Winning coalitions in the 2001–2005 parliament, Poland	247
12.3.	Winning coalitions in the 2005–2007 parliament, Poland	249

List of Tables

1.1.	Prevalence of minority governments, 1990–2020 (conventional counting rules)	15
1.2.	Party system fragmentation, based on average effective number of parliamentary parties (1990–2019)	15
1.3.	Institutional variation	16
3.1.	Types of government, India, 1989–2020	45
3.2.	Government performance, India, 1952–2019	60
3.3.	Actual and relative duration by government type, India, 1952–2019	61
3.4.	Law production by government type, India, 1952–2019	61
3.1A.	Types of government, India, 1952–1989	65
4.1.	Types of government, Norway, 1945–2020	67
4.2.	Norwegian cabinets by composition and majority status, 1945–2020	69
4.3.	Performance by cabinet type, Norway, 1945–2020 (Mean Values)	81
5.1.	Types of government, Romania, 1990–2020	87
5.2.	Cabinet legislative record and duration, Romania, 1996–2020	102
6.1.	Types of government, Spain, 1977–2020	110
6.2.	Government performance indicators, Spain, 1977–2020	121
7.1.	Types of government, Sweden, 1945–2020	131
7.2.	Swedish governments' performance, 1945–2020	141
8.1.	Types of government, Canada, 1945–2020	157
8.2.	Legislative record and duration, Canada, 1945–2020	165
9.1.	Minority governments in France, 1958–2021	172
9.2.	The rationales of three political forces when a minority government was shaped in 1988, France	175
9.3.	The rationales of two pivotal political forces to occasionally support government bills, 1988–1993, France	182
10.1.	Types of government, Ireland, 1945–2020	191
10.2.	Governments formed with support of independents, Ireland, 1945–2020	195
10.3.	Legislative record and duration, Ireland, 1945–2020	203
11.1.	Types of government, Italy, 1992–2021	211
11.2.	Legislative activity, Italy, 1996–2018	227
11.1A.	Government types in Italy, 1948–1992	232

12.1.	Governments in Poland, 1997–2020	242
12.2.	Party support on government bill votes, Poland	253
12.3.	Party support on government bill votes, Marcinkiewicz I &II, Poland	255
12.4.	Rolls and defeats on final passage votes, Poland	257
12.1A.	Government bills and approval rates, Poland	261
13.1.	Types of government, Portugal, 1976–2022	265
13.2.	Law-making success and duration of Portuguese governments, 1976–2019	273
13.3.	Government performance indicators, Portugal, 1976–2019	275
14.1.	Types of government, Australia, 1987–2020	286
14.2.	Legislative record and duration, Australia, 1987–2020	296
14.1A.	Types of Government, Australia, 1939–1987	301
14.2A.	Legislative record and duration, Australia, 1939—1987	305
15.1.	Types of government, United Kingdom, 1945–2019	308
15.2.	Legislative record and duration, 1945–2019, United Kingdom	320
16.1.	Party system fragmentation and minority governments	328
16.2.	Government formation rules and minority governments	331
16.3.	Opposition influence in parliament and minority governments	332

List of Contributors

Veronica Anghel is Lecturer at the Johns Hopkins School of Advanced International Studies and a Max Weber Fellow at the European University Institute.

Hanna Bäck is Professor of Political Science at Lund University.

Christopher Cochrane is Associate Professor at the University of Toronto.

Kate Crowley is Associate Professor of Public and Environmental Policy at the University of Tasmania.

Jorge M. Fernandes is Assistant Research Professor at the Institute of Social Sciences, University of Lisbon.

Bonnie N. Field is Professor of Political Science in the Global Studies Department at Bentley University.

Daniela Giannetti is Full Professor in Political Science at the University of Bologna.

Jean-François Godbout is Professor of Political Science at the University of Montreal.

Johan Hellström is Senior Lecturer in Political Science at Umeå University.

Cath Hughes is an independent researcher and a past Chief of Staff of the Office of the Tasmanian Greens.

Andrew Jones is Post-Doctoral Research Fellow at University College London.

Csaba Nikolenyi is Professor of Political Science at Concordia University.

Shane Martin is the Anthony King Chair in Comparative Government at the University of Essex.

Olivier Rozenberg is Associate Professor at Sciences Po, Center for European Studies and Comparative Politics.

Kaare W. Strøm is Distinguished Professor of Political Science at the University of California, San Diego.

Liam Weeks is Lecturer in Government and Politics at University College Cork.

Richard Whitaker is Associate Professor of Politics at the University of Leicester.

Radoslaw Zubek is Associate Professor of European Politics at the University of Oxford.

PART I
INTRODUCTION

1
The Politics of Minority Government

Bonnie N. Field and Shane Martin

In parliamentary regimes, governments are responsible to and can be removed by parliament. Nonetheless, *minority* governments are common. These are governments in which the party or parties that hold cabinet posts in the executive do not simultaneously hold a majority of seats in the legislature. This makes minority governments a particularly interesting governing arrangement. This book focuses on the politics of minority government. It analyzes the formation, functioning, and performance of minority governments, what we term the *why*, *how*, and *how well* of minority governments.[1]

Approximately one-third of parliamentary democracies are or are typically governed by a minority cabinet.[2] Moreover, the rate of minority governments appears to have increased slightly over recent decades. Examples abound. The Conservative minority government in the United Kingdom (UK) (2017–19), led by Prime Minister (PM) Teresa May, depended on a small regional party from Northern Ireland. The short-lived Socialist minority government of PM Pedro Sánchez in Spain (2018–19) relied on a combination of radical left and regionally-based nationalist parties to govern. The Socialist minority government in Portugal of Prime Minister António Costa (2015–19) relied on the support of the radical left. The rightist minority coalition government (2016–19) in Denmark, led by PM Lars Løkke Rasmussen, relied on the external support of the radical right.

Very few parliamentary democracies have not experienced minority government, though post-War Germany is a prominent exception. In some countries, minority government is a little-used governing formula, as in the UK and Australia. In others, minority governments are the norm rather than the exception, as in the Scandinavian democracies. Yet, even where minority governments are common, the form they take at a particular time may indeed be novel. While Spain has minority governments more often than not, the government of PM Pedro Sánchez that formed in 2020 was its first post-transition minority coalition government.

---

[1] The core questions of *why*, *how*, and *how well* that structure the volume build on Strøm (1990: 93), which Field also used in her 2016 monograph.

[2] We use the terms parliament, legislature, and assembly interchangeably throughout the volume. By parliamentary system, we mean a form of constitutional design where the government is politically responsible to the legislature, in contrast to presidential systems. We treat semi-presidential systems as a particular form of parliamentarism, although on occasions we will differentiate between semi-presidential and pure parliamentary regimes.

Denmark, in contrast, typically has minority coalitions, but the government's reliance on the far right for support in parliament beginning in 2001 was a departure from prior governing dynamics.

This volume examines minority governments in countries where they occur frequently and where they are rare. Three core research questions guide this endeavor: First, we ask why minority governments form. This includes whether the formation of minority governments (as distinct from majority coalitions) is related to political institutions (such as legislative rules and organization), electoral incentives, the shape or composition of the party system, or something else. Second, we explore how minority governments govern once in office. After all, government formation is normally a relatively short-lived process compared to the actual time the government will spend in office. Questions here include whether minority governments operate with formal agreements with other parties in parliament, their alliance-building strategies within parliament, and the motivations of the non-governing political parties or individual legislators that provide support to minority governments. Third, we explore how well minority governments perform, and where possible and useful compare this performance to periods of majority government in the same country. This includes common indicators of performances—such as legislative productivity and rates of survival in office of minority governments, and what citizens think of the performance of the minority government—as well as more nuanced assessments that contextualize performance in the particular national context.

We seek answers to these questions through the in-depth examination of national minority governments in thirteen countries, with particular emphasis on the period since 1990. As the goals of the book are to address minority government formation, functioning, and performance, we do not include countries where national-level minority governments do not occur. We seek to provide contextualized knowledge of minority governments in different partisan and institutional contexts, and advance our understanding of minority government through cross-national and within-country comparisons. But we also suspect the *why*, *how*, and *how well* of minority governments are interrelated questions in need of concurrent examination rather than, as conventionally done, studied separately in relative isolation from each other.

Cross-national country-level comparative work on the topic of minority governments has not been particularly common in the political science literature. Strøm (1984, 1990) broke new ground on the topic over thirty years ago, helping us understand better why minority governments form, and the lessons of this for our wider understanding of party politics. We otherwise lack a comparative book-length treatment of the topic that explores jointly the causes, nature, and consequences of minority governments.[3] This volume does just that, providing an

---

[3] Comparative, contextualized analyses of minority governments have not kept pace with those of coalition governments (Bergman, Ilonszki, and Muller 2020; Bergman, Bäck, and Hellström 2021).

examination of minority governments in Australia, Canada, France, India, Ireland, Italy, Norway, Poland, Portugal, Spain, Sweden, Romania, and the UK. We selected these countries, in part, to foster new insights regarding how the party system and political institutions *jointly* shape the formation, functioning, and performance of minority governments.

We continue this chapter by exploring, more closely, what a minority government is and is not, and how frequently they occur. We then set out in more detail the context and motivation for this comparative volume on minority governments and our selection of country cases for study.

What minority government is, and is not

A basic definition of a minority government is a government where the party or parties in cabinet do not simultaneously hold a majority of seats in the legislature (e.g. Cheibub, Martin, and Rasch 2021). A number of earlier works can help to clarify what a minority government is, and what it is not.[4] Herman and Pope (1973: 192) helpfully differentiate between a *minority situation* (where no single party controls a majority of seats in parliament), and a *minority outcome* (where the governing party or parties do not control a legislative majority). Because parties can form (majority) coalitions, not all minority situations lead to minority outcomes.[5] Of course, minority governments can be single party or multiparty. A multiparty minority government is a coalition government that has the other characteristics of a minority government (namely the lack of a majority in parliament).

Because various authors have defined minority governments in slightly different ways, the concept is worth discussing in detail. A minority government, in our understanding of the term, has the following characteristics:

First, there is the numerical requirement of being in minority. Perhaps here, Field's (2016: 2) definition is clear, referring to a minority government as "one that comprises ministers from one or more political parties and one in which the party's or parties' legislators do not hold an absolute majority (50 percent +1) of the seats in the parliament." It seems an easy task to link the partisan composition of the cabinet with the partisan composition of a legislature. Observe the parties in cabinet and calculate if, between them, they control a majority of seats in parliament.[6] And importantly, the focus is on the cabinet, and parties represented

---

[4] One of the earliest published works on the topic (Janson 1928) provides no definition of a minority government.
[5] We do not know of a situation where a majority party remains in opposition and a minority government forms instead.
[6] However, at the risk of sounding pedantic, parties do not sit in cabinet, individuals do. And some cabinets have non-party members, either "technocrats" or individuals without a party affiliation, often referred to as independents.

therein—and not on officeholders such as junior ministers or other non-cabinet offices even if appointed by the government.

Rightly, the baseline is not about a simple majority (i.e. more yes than no votes in any given parliamentary vote). In most parliaments, members can abstain from voting, and in some cases can vote to abstain. The difference between simple majority support and absolute majority support is of particular importance because minority governments can be formed and continue because they receive implicit support from other parties who choose to abstain in legislative votes. In most parliamentary votes, outcomes are decided based on those legislators who actually vote, assuming a quorum is met. But a government that wins the support of parliament is still a minority government if the party or parties comprising that government do not hold an absolute majority of the seats in the parliament.

Super majorities are sometimes required in parliaments for certain decisions, but definitions of minority government do not include super majority requirements. For example, constitutional change requires super majority support in many national legislatures, such as in India. In the United Kingdom, between 2011 and 2022, Parliament could only be dissolved by a 2/3 majority (although it would only take a simple majority to change this via legislation, as did happen in 2022). However, definitions of minority government focus on absolute majority rather than super majority. This is because the only thing that guarantees the survival of a government in a parliamentary democracy is the explicit (through voting for the government) or implicit (through abstaining from voting against a government) support of an absolute majority of parliamentarians.[7]

Second, there is the question of which chamber or chambers matter for assessing the numerical requirement. Parliaments have their own internal organization, and many are bicameral in design. Hence, Strøm (1990: 6) describes a minority government as "any cabinet that meets all appropriate constitutional requirements and that is composed of persons acting as representatives of political parties or parliamentary groups" that control less than half of all seats "*in the national legislature, or that chamber of the legislature to which the cabinet is constitutionally responsible*" (emphasis added).

In most parliamentary democracies with a bicameral legislature, the government is responsible to only one chamber, even if both chambers may perform oversight of the executive. Lower chambers in bicameral parliamentary settings tend to have the role of selecting or removing the cabinet. One clear exception is Italy. Both the lower and upper chamber must vote to invest an Italian cabinet, and the Italian cabinet remains constitutionally responsible to both. Thus, according to our definition, any Italian cabinet with a majority in only one of the two

---

[7] It is worth noting that Strøm (1990) argues that a government with exactly half the number of seats in parliament can use executive-favoring parliamentary procedures to function as a majority government and hence governments without a majority are not the same as governments with a minority.

chambers of the Italian parliament is a minority government (although see further, Giannetti, this volume). Romania is another interesting case. The government is responsible to parliamentarians of both chambers—jointly. Thus, according to our definition, a government in Romania is in minority if it does not hold a majority of seats in the parliament as a whole.

More typically, a government remains a majority government if it controls a majority of seats in the lower chamber but not in the upper chamber. The 2019 UK cabinet led by PM Boris Johnson is a good example: it controled a majority of seats in the House of Commons, but a minority of seats in the House of Lords. Despite the latter, it is a majority cabinet because it is not constitutionally responsible to the House of Lords. Conversely, a government is a minority one if the party or parties in government control an absolute majority in an upper chamber, to which it is not constitutionally responsible, yet a minority of seats in the lower chamber to which it is responsible, as is the case of Spain's Socialist-United We Can minority coalition government formed in 2020.

It is also worth noting what a minority government is not. A government is not a minority one if the party or parties that comprise the cabinet have failed to secure a majority of votes in a general election. For example, in the 2019 UK general election, the Conservative Party won 43.6 percent of the vote. This allowed them to gain a parliamentary majority (365 of 650 seats) and thus lead a majority government. Along these same lines, no majority government in Spain since redemocratization in the 1970s won a majority of the vote (Field 2016: 50–1).

Finally, minority governments can, and often do, have the *support* of a majority in the legislature. This majority, however, comprises parties or legislators whose parties do not have representation in cabinet. Again, the key focus of a definition of minority government is not whether the cabinet has the support of a majority of parliament, but whether the party or parties in cabinet between them control a majority of seats in the relevant chamber of the legislature.

As Strøm's definition above reveals, minority governments are in distinct positions in parliamentary compared to presidential regimes. Minority governments in parliamentary regimes, on which this volume focuses, are particularly interesting because the cabinet is responsible to parliament. *Responsibility* differs from the concept of *oversight*—the role of legislatures in keeping tabs on the executive. Responsibility means that a government is *politically* responsible to parliament and can ultimately be removed by parliament if parliament so wishes, typically through a vote of no confidence procedure.

Although our focus in this book is on parliamentary regimes, a few observations about presidential regimes are in order. It is certainly common to equate, in terms of definition, minority governments in presidential and parliamentary regimes. However, the nature and consequences of minority status vary between presidentialism and parliamentarism. A minority government in a parliamentary regime risks parliament removing it; minority presidents do not face this risk, except through the process of impeachment, which typically requires criminal or other wrongdoing on the part of the president. In fact, a leading scholar of presidentialism, Cheibub (2002: 287), differentiates a *minority government* in parliamentary regimes from what he terms a *minority president*, defined as "a president whose party controls less than 50 percent of the seats in at least one legislative house."

The frequency of minority governments

We noted at the beginning of this chapter that minority governments administer around one-third of parliamentary democracies. In this section, we examine the rate of minority governments more precisely, and how this varies over time and from country to country. We limit ourselves to looking at larger democracies around the world and focus only on parliamentary regimes (including semi-presidential sub-types).[8] Our unit of analysis is a cabinet, and here we follow the conventional methods in the comparative politics literature in defining when a new cabinet exists, which includes a change of prime minister, change of the partisan composition of the cabinet, and a general election. This excludes cabinet reshuffles, where the premiership and partisan composition remain the same, or where a sitting government loses its majority in parliament or secures a majority (for example, because of party switching) without a general election.

Let's start by looking at the number of minority governments in early 2020. Of the forty-three countries in our sample, twenty-eight have a majority government and fifteen have a minority government—giving a rate of minority government of 34.8 percent. In this group, Canada is the only non-European example of a minority government. Of the fifteen minority governments, four are single-party governments and eleven are coalition governments. Eight of the minority governments are in pure parliamentary systems while seven are in semi-presidential systems.

But, of course, looking at one point in time only provides a snapshot. Next, we extend our look at the rate of minority government back through 1990. Here the sample reduced to include only countries that were continuous democracies since 1989 (based on Freedom House Scores), leaving twenty-eight countries to explore. In our sample of twenty-eight continuous democracies and looking back at the last thirty years, 31.6 percent of governments have been minority governments (142 minority cabinets compared with 306 majority cabinets). Figure 1.1 reports the rate of minority governments for each of these countries.

Israel has had the largest number of minority cabinets with nineteen, although it also has the largest number of cabinets in our sample. In comparing the

---

[8] We use Freedom House scores to identify democracies, coding a country as democracy if it scored "Free" in the given year. We look only at countries with a population of 0.5 million or more. We thank Andrew Jones for research assistance.

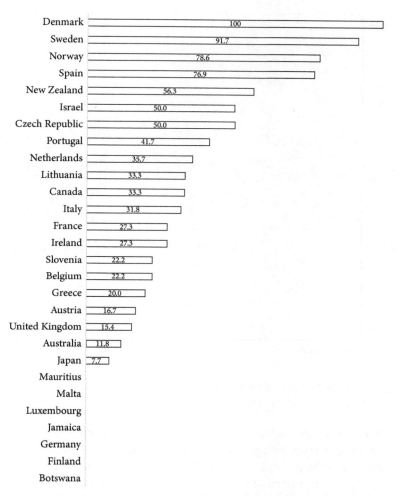

Fig. 1.1 The rate of minority government, select democracies, 1990–2020

proportion of minority to majority cabinets in each country, Denmark has the highest proportion of minority cabinets, at 100 percent. Twenty-one of the twenty-eight countries have had a minority government at least once. Seven countries in this group never had a minority government between 1990 and the start of 2020. These are the European countries of Finland, Germany, Luxembourg, and Malta, as well as Botswana, Jamaica, and Mauritius. Finally, looking at variation between semi-presidential and pure parliamentary regimes, on average 22 percent of semi-presidential cabinets have been minority governments compared with an average of 33.6 percent of cabinets in pure parliamentary systems.

To explore temporal trends in the rate of minority governments, Figure 1.2 plots the proportion of seats held by governments between 1990 and the start of 2020.

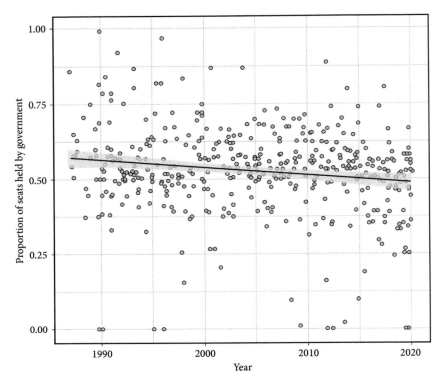

Fig. 1.2 Proportion of seats held by governments, select countries, 1990–2020
Notes: Includes governments in office starting January 1, 1990

We observe here, on average, a modest decrease in the number of seats held by the governing party or parties. Figure 1.3 breaks down the proportions of seats in parliament held by governments by coalition and single-party government. This demonstrates a clear trend of single-party governments to move toward minority administrations since 1990 (as well as showing a downward trend in the number of seats held by coalitions).

Finally, Figure 1.4 breaks this down by country, and it shows nicely which countries are on trend. In Germany, Greece, Italy, Japan, Malta, and Norway, the proportion of seats in parliament held by the cabinets has been, on average, increasing over time. In all other countries, the trend is for governments to get closer to, or below, the 50 percent threshold. We take this as evidence that minority governments are becoming more, rather than less, common.

Undercounted?

In this volume, we offer an important innovation in how cabinet composition and cabinet change is counted by scholars, with implications for how the rate

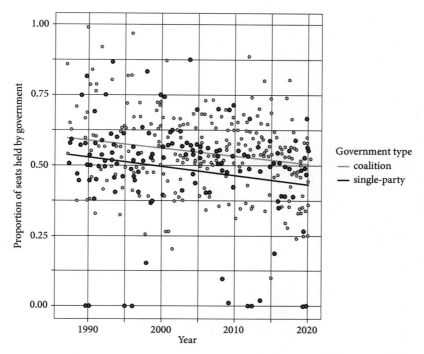

Fig. 1.3 Proportion of seats held by governments, by government type, select countries, 1990–2020

Notes: Includes governments in office starting January 1, 1990

of minority government is calculated. As we noted above, most data on cabinet membership records a change in government as happening when one or more of the following conditions are met: a change in the partisan composition of the cabinet, a change of head of government, or a general election (see, for example, Döring and Manow 2021). This measure excludes a situation where a sitting government loses its majority in parliament or gains a majority in parliament without a general election or without change in partisan composition of cabinet, for example due to the resignation, death, or expulsion of a governing party legislator, or because an MP switches parties.

The Netherlands provides an example. Until October 2019, Prime Minister Rutte's four-party coalition held seventy-six seats in the 150-seat lower house, the *Tweede Kamer*. However, this wafer-thin majority vanished when one of the governing party's parliamentarians was expelled from his parliamentary party group, depriving the governing coalition of its majority in the *Tweede Kamer* and immediately flipping the government from a majority government to a minority government. By not recognizing such situations as a change in cabinet (instead

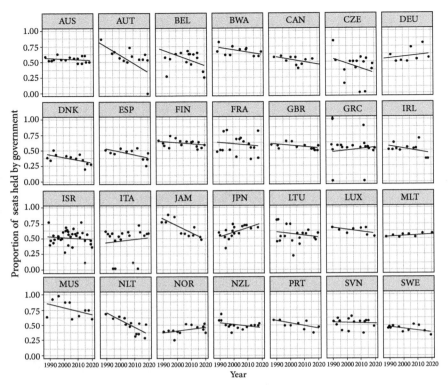

Fig. 1.4 Proportion of seats held by governments, by country, 1990-2020

relying on the status of the cabinet at the government formation stage), conventional counting practices likely undercount minority governments.

We remedy this in our country studies by asking the authors to count a government as a minority one when and if it slides into minority status, even when the partisan composition of the cabinet does not change. Our counting rule has implications beyond the counting of minority governments; for example, a surplus majority coalition could be transformed into a minimal winning coalition. We also ask the authors to determine the majority or minority status of the government in the chamber, chambers, or parliament as a whole that can hold the government responsible. We return to this in the concluding chapter.

Changing contexts

This book provides a comparative study of minority governments in thirteen democracies. But, why do we need this study, and why now?

While there is important research on minority governments, which we discuss in Chapter 2, we still have a lot to learn about why minority governments form, how they operate in office, and how they differ in their performance when compared with majority governments. Much of the recent research on minority governments has a country-specific or regional focus. Simultaneously, research on a small subset of countries has driven theory on minority governments, particularly the Scandinavian democracies (Field 2016: 1). Thus, we know a lot about minority government in certain national contexts, and far less about them in others. This hinders our ability to understand them comparatively. This volume expands the geographic scope of analysis to include countries across northwestern, southern, and eastern Europe and outside of it (Canada, Australia, and India). While it is a big ask for any book, we hope this volume goes some way to progressing answers to the *why*, *how*, and *how well* of minority government through cross-national (and within country) comparisons, and providing contextualized knowledge of minority governments in specific institutional and partisan contexts.

Also, it has been over thirty years since Kaare Strøm's path breaking book, *Minority Government and Majority Rule*, published in 1990. It is no exaggeration to say that the book transformed the study of minority government. It did so, as we will see, because it shed light on the commonality of minority governments and brought intuitive but novel arguments to the question as to why we see minority governments in some countries and not in others. The book and Strøm's earlier work were particularly consequential in arguing that minority governments are a rational cabinet solution, and that minority government does not mean minority rule. Virtually all research we are aware of on minority governments since 1990 has in one way or another built on Strøm's pioneering work.

Still, a lot has changed, and in ways that could affect how we understand minority governments. Strøm examined minority governments between 1945 and the late 1980s, a context that included clear left–right socio-economic cleavages, grounded in social class, and a Cold War bi-polar world. The past three decades, of course, have seen significant developments. We highlight several.

First, a new wave of democratization began in the mid-1970s and dramatically expanded with the fall of communism in Europe beginning in 1989. Therefore, the southern European democracies of Portugal, Spain, and Greece were very young democracies in the 1980s, and the central and eastern European democracies had yet to come about. Many of these countries subsequently joined the European Union (EU). Democratization also increased the number of semi-presidential regimes, where a popularly elected president co-exists with a government responsible to parliament. More recently, parts of central and eastern Europe, such as Hungary and Poland, have experienced democratic backsliding.

Second, while left–right socio-economic divisions still structure party competition, a second dimension of party competition has emerged or strengthened, particularly in the wealthy capitalist democracies. Scholars variously refer to it as the libertarian–authoritarian or liberal–conservative dimension (among other terms) (Evans, Heath, and Lalljee 1996). Of course, some countries have other, significant political cleavages, such as center–periphery (Alonso 2012).

Third, and related, party systems have changed in composition, and, in many countries, fragmented (De Vries and Hobolt 2020; Hopkin 2020). Voters have also become less attached to a particular political party and electoral volatility has increased (Drummond 2006). The large governing parties of the left, in particular social democratic parties, have been challenged by new left parties, particularly green parties (Kitschelt 1994). Communist parties declined in the aftermath of the fall of the Soviet Union, and radical left parties emerged, strengthened, or became relevant for government formation in recent years (Olsen, Koss, and Hough 2010), for example in southern Europe in the aftermath of the Great Recession (approximately 2007–9). Starting in the 1980s, radical right parties also began to grow in importance, posing challenges to mainstream right parties (conservative, Christian democratic, and liberal parties) (Norris 2005; Mudde 2007; Bale and Rovira Kaltwasser 2021), and others.

Fourth, while federalism and political decentralization of state authority to regional institutions have existed in countries such as Canada and India, other countries have set up new federal or decentralized state institutions, such as Spain and the UK (Hooghe, Marks, and Schakel 2010). Simultaneously, many European states gave up a degree of sovereignty to the European Union, and in one case, the UK, took it back.

Therefore, minority governments govern in very different political and institutional contexts, allowing us to examine why they were formed, how they have worked, and how well they have performed in the period since the 1990s. These changes potentially influence not just the political landscape within which governing takes place, but the incentives and barriers that political parties face when deciding whether or not to enter government, support it, or attempt to bring it down.

Country studies

Three considerations guided the selection of the thirteen country studies. First, the countries vary in terms of the prevalence of minority governments between 1990 and 2020. *Using the conventional counting rules* and the *number* of governments (as opposed to the amount of time in office) (see Table 1.1), minority governments were predominant (more than half of governments) in Romania, Norway, Spain, India, and Sweden. They were common (between 25 and 50 percent) in Poland, France, Canada, Ireland, and Portugal; and exceptional in Australia, the UK, and Italy. We think a strength of our approach is to examine minority governments in countries where they occur frequently and infrequently.

Table 1.1 Prevalence of minority governments, 1990–2020 (conventional counting rules)

Predominant (> 50%)	Common (≥ 25 ≤ 50%)	Exceptional (< 25%)
Romania[a] (64%)	Poland[b] (25%)	Australia (12%)
Norway (79%)	France (27%)	United Kingdom (15%)
Spain (80%)	Canada (33%)	Italy (16%)
India (82%)	Ireland (42%)	
Sweden (91%)	Portugal (50%)	

Notes: The calculations do not include caretaker governments.
[a] Romania includes governments since 1996.
[b] Poland includes governments from 1991.
Sources: ParlGov (Döring and Manow 2021) and our calculation for India based on Nikolenyi, this volume.

Table 1.2 Party system fragmentation, based on average effective number of parliamentary parties (1990–2019)

Low (< 3.0)	Moderate (≥ 3.0 < 4.0)	High (≥ 4.0)
United Kingdom (2.4)	Spain (3.1)	Poland (4.1)
Portugal (2.7)	Romania (3.4)	Sweden (4.4)
Australia (2.7)	Ireland (3.6)	Norway (4.6)
France (2.8)		India (4.8)
Canada (2.9)		Italy (5.1)

Notes: Average effective number of parties, using elections between 1990 and 2019, inclusive, except Romania (1996 through 2019).
Sources: Who Governs (Casal Bértoa 2021); ParlGov (Vaishnav and Hintson 2019; Döring and Manow 2021).

Second, because we want to better understand the politics of minority governments in different partisan contexts, we selected countries that vary in terms of the number of parties in parliament (Table 1.2). As an indicator, we use the average effective number of political parties in parliament between 1990[9] and 2019, which weights parties in terms of size (Laakso and Taagepera 1979). Our country studies have highly fragmented party systems, indicated by four or more effective parliamentary parties (Italy, India, Norway, Sweden, and Poland); moderately fragmented party systems, with between three and four parties (Spain, Romania, and Ireland); and low fragmentation party systems with fewer than three effective parties (UK, Portugal, Australia, France, and Canada). This is, of course, a blunt categorization that masks some changes over time—such as the recent increase in fragmentation in Spain, Sweden, Ireland, and Australia, or its

---

[9] Or the first year of democracy, as measured by a Freedom House rating of Free. This only affects Romania, whose data begins in 1996.

Table 1.3 Institutional variation

	Strong opposition powers	Average opposition powers	Weak opposition powers
Lower hurdle formation		Portugal (0.67) Sweden (0.62) France (0.59)[a] Norway (0.45)	*Australia* (0.42) *Canada* (0.43) *India* (0.29)
Higher hurdle formation	*Italy* (0.87) Romania (0.76)	Poland[b] (0.73) Ireland (0.55) UK[c] (0.51)	*Spain* (0.40)

Notes: Italics indicate a powerful tier of regional government. All have a Regional Authority Index (RAI-Region) score above 18.0 in 2018 (Shair-Rosenfield et al. 2021).
Lower hurdle = there is no investiture vote in the legislature or a negative investiture vote; higher hurdle = there is a positive investiture vote. The latter includes *ex ante* and *ex post* votes. Categorized by the authors based on Rasch et al. (2015).
Opposition powers based on Wegmann (2022). Opposition powers: range 0 to 1, with 0 being weak opposition power. In the study of 50 countries, the average was 0.588 with a standard deviation of 0.157. For classification purposes, strong opposition power = more than one standard deviation above the mean; average opposition power = within one standard deviation of the mean; weak opposition means more than one standard deviation below the mean.
[a] France was not included in Wegmann (2022). The average opposition powers statistic was calculated following the study's methodology. (We thank Hatim Tapory for research assistance, and Simone Wegmann for her advice and feedback.)
[b] An investiture vote is not required if a sitting prime minister reshuffles the cabinet or loses their majority. See Zubek, this volume.
[c] With regard to regional government power, the UK is an unusual case in that its overall level of regional authority is low, but high for Scotland, Wales, and Northern Ireland.

decrease in Poland—and differences within categories, such as the sheer number of distinct parties in India. The countries also allow us to incorporate various types of possible or actual support parties, such as populist radical right (e.g. Sweden), radical left (e.g. Portugal), regional (e.g. India), and ethnic (e.g. Romania) parties.

Finally, our country cases capture a rich variety of institutional arrangements that have been important in the study of minority governments: First, the rules for forming governments (Strøm 1990; Bergman 1993; Cheibub, Martin, and Rasch 2021) that may present lower or higher hurdles; second, those that affect the influence of parties who are not part of the government (Strøm 1990), such as the strength of legislative committees, and the powers of parliament compared to government (Rasch 2011; Field 2016); and, third, the existence of a powerful regional tier of government or not (Reniu 2002; Field 2016). Table 1.3 provides a categorization of our country studies based on these institutions.

Conclusion

Parliamentary forms of government require that the executive somehow come from, and remain politically responsible to, the national legislature. As such, one could reasonably expect that the governing party (or parties) would need the support of a majority in the legislature to form the government and to govern. Nevertheless, as we have seen in this chapter, approximately one-third of governments in parliamentary democracies are minority governments. This chapter discussed the nature and frequency of minority governments, and set out our country selection strategy, which focused on variation in the prevalence of minority governments, in the party system, and in political institutions. The next chapter discusses our three research questions in greater detail, and in doing so explores existing research.

References

Alonso, Sonia. 2012. *Challenging the State: Devolution and the Battle for Partisan Credibility.* Oxford: Oxford University Press.

Bale, Tim, and Cristóbal Rovira Kaltwasser, eds. 2021. *Riding the Populist Wave: Europe's Mainstream Right in Crisis.* Cambridge: Cambridge University Press.

Bergman, Torbjörn. 1993. "Formation Rules and Minority Governments." *European Journal of Political Research* 23 (1): 55–66.

Bergman, Torbjörn, Hanna Bäck, and Johan Hellström, eds. 2021. *Coalition Governance in Western Europe.* Oxford: Oxford University Press.

Bergman, Torbjörn, Gabriella Ilonszki, and Wolfgang C. Muller, eds. 2020. *Coalition Governance in Central Eastern Europe.* Oxford: Oxford University Press.

Casal Bértoa, Fernando. 2021. Database on WHO GOVERNS in Europe and Beyond. Available at: https://whogoverns.eu/

Cheibub, José Antonio. 2002. "Minority Governments, Deadlock Situations, and the Survival of Presidential Democracies." *Comparative Political Studies* 35 (3): 284–312.

Cheibub, José Antonio, Shane Martin, and Bjørn Erik Rasch. 2021. "Investiture Rules and Formation of Minority Governments in European Parliamentary Democracies." *Party Politics* 27 (2): 351–362.

De Vries, Catherine E., and Sara B. Hobolt. 2020. *Political Entrepreneurs: The Rise of Challenger Parties in Europe.* Princeton, NJ: Princeton University Press.

Döring, Holger, and Philip Manow. 2021. Parliaments and Governments Database (ParlGov): Information on Parties, Elections and Cabinets in Modern Democracies. Development Version.

Drummond, Andrew J. 2006. "Electoral Volatility and Party Decline in Western Democracies: 1970–1995." *Political Studies* 54 (3): 628–647.

Evans, Geoffrey, Anthony Heath, and Mansur Lalljee. 1996. "Measuring Left-Right and Libertarian-Authoritarian Values in the British Electorate." *The British Journal of Sociology* 47 (1): 93–112.

Field, Bonnie N. 2016. *Why Minority Governments Work: Multilevel Territorial Politics in Spain*. New York: Palgrave Macmillan.

Herman, Valentine, and John Pope. 1973. "Minority Governments in Western Democracies." *British Journal of Political Science* 3: 191–212.

Hooghe, Liesbet, Gary Marks, and Arjan Schakel. 2010. *The Rise of Regional Authority: A Comparative Study of 42 Democracies*. London: Routledge.

Hopkin, Jonathan. 2020. *Anti-System Politics: The Crisis of Market Liberalism in Rich Democracies*. Oxford: Oxford University Press.

Janson, Florence E. 1928. "Minority Governments in Sweden." *The American Political Science Review* 22 (2): 407–413.

Kitschelt, Herbert. 1994. *The Transformation of European Social Democracy*. Cambridge: Cambridge University Press.

Laakso, Markku, and Rein Taagepera. 1979. "'Effective' Number of Parties: A Measure with Application to West Europe." *Comparative Political Studies* 12 (1): 3–27.

Mudde, Cas. 2007. *Populist Radical Right Parties in Europe*. Cambridge: Cambridge University Press.

Norris, Pippa. 2005. *Radical Right: Voters and Parties in the Electoral Market*. Cambridge: Cambridge University Press.

Olsen, Jonathan, Michael Koss, and Dan Hough, eds. 2010. *Left Parties in National Governments*: Palgrave Macmillan.

Rasch, Bjørn E. 2011. "Why Minority Governments? Executive-Legislative Relations in the Nordic Countries." In *Parliamentary Government in the Nordic Countries at a Crossroads*, ed. Thomas Persson and Matti Wiberg, 41–61. Stockholm: Santérus Academic Press Sweden.

Rasch, Bjørn Erik, Shane Martin, and José Antonio Cheibub, eds. 2015. *Parliaments and Government Formation: Unpacking Investiture Rules*. Oxford: Oxford University Press.

Reniu, Josep María. 2002. *La formación de gobiernos minoritarios en España, 1977–1996*. Madrid: Centro de Investigaciones Sociológicas.

Shair-Rosenfield, Sarah, Arjan H. Schakel, Sara Niedzwiecki, Gary Marks, Liesbet Hooghe, and Sandra Chapman-Osterkatz. 2021. "Language Difference and Regional Authority." *Regional & Federal Studies* 31 (1): 73–97.

Strøm, Kaare. 1984. "Minority Governments in Parliamentary Democracies: The Rationality of Nonwinning Cabinet Solutions." *Comparative Political Studies* 17 (2): 199–227.

Strøm, Kaare. 1990. *Minority Government and Majority Rule*. Cambridge: Cambridge University Press.

Vaishnav, Milan, and Jamie Hintson. 2019. *India's New Fourth Party System*. Carnegie Endowment for International Peace. Available at: https://carnegieendowment.org/2019/08/19/india-s-new-fourth-party-system-pub-79686.

Wegmann, Simone. 2022. "Policy-making Power of Opposition Players: A Comparative Institutional Perspective." *The Journal of Legislative Studies* 28 (1): 1–25.

2
The *How*, *Why*, and *How Well* of Minority Governments

Bonnie N. Field and Shane Martin

This chapter further develops the three core research questions that guide this volume: why minority governments form, how they operate, and how well they perform. In discussing each of these in the following sections, we acknowledge existing work on the topic as well as unanswered questions and outstanding puzzles. We conclude the chapter by introducing the thirteen country case studies.

Our literature review and analyses focus on national-level minority governments. Nonetheless, there is a growing body of literature on minority and other forms of government at the subnational level.[1] And we note that national and subnational governing formulas can differ in the same national context. For example, Germany has not had a post-war minority government at the national level, but minority governments have formed at the subnational level (Ganghof et al. 2019; Matthieß 2019).

We begin with the question of why minority governments form.

Why minority governments form

The first research question we ask our contributors to address concerns why minority governments come into existence in their country of study. We want to understand why some government formation processes result in minority governments rather than majority governments. This allows the contributors to evaluate existing hypotheses, and, where relevant, offer new explanations. It also allows us to explore potential multiple pathways to minority government in our conclusion to the volume. As we discuss below, a rich literature exists on why minority governments form, but findings are often contradictory, leaving many of the fundamental questions unanswered. Before discussing this literature, a few points are worth noting.

---

[1] See, for example, (Ștefuriuc 2009, 2013; Cairney 2011; Palmer 2011; Falcó-Gimeno and Verge 2013; Lundberg 2013; Crowley and Tighe 2017; Martínez-Cantó and Bergmann 2020).

Bonnie N. Field and Shane Martin, *The How, Why, and How Well of Minority Governments*. In: *Minority Governments in Comparative Perspective*. Edited by Bonnie N. Field and Shane Martin, Oxford University Press.
© Bonnie N. Field and Shane Martin (2022). DOI: 10.1093/oso/9780192871657.003.0002

The first, rather simply, is that we would only expect to find a minority government in a minority situation (a situation where no single party controls a majority of seats in the national legislature). So-called *office-seeking* theories (though more on this later) of party behavior stress the desire of parties in parliamentary systems to secure membership in the cabinet and enjoy the spoils of ministerial office (Riker 1962). Thus, it would seem unthinkable that a party that won a majority of seats in a general election would not wish to form the government. The alternative would be for that majority party to cede the government formation opportunity to opposition legislators. We know of no such case and we do not expect minority governments to form in such circumstances.[2] Of course, most parliamentary elections today do not produce a clear winner, requiring parties in the legislative arena to bargain with each other over who gets to form the cabinet, though clearly there are exceptions.

The second point, and a significant motivation for this study, is the fact that the formation of a minority government represents something of a puzzle in parliamentary systems of government. In other words, from a basic understanding of what parliamentary government is, we would not expect it to be possible for a minority government to exist at all. The defining feature of a parliamentary system is that the government operates in the presence of a very simple but fundamental principle: a cabinet must have, or be able to rely on, the confidence of a majority of the national legislature. This "confidence" is tested through the responsibility requirement. Given the responsibility requirement inherent in parliamentary government, a coalition to reach majority support in the legislature seems not just an obvious outcome but also a necessary outcome. Alongside the mechanical requirement to reach sufficient support in parliament, the above discussed motivation of parties to hold cabinet positions means that parties should bargain to form the government, with a majority government the equilibrium outcome. If being in government is the prize, why would a majority of the legislature allow a minority of the legislature to take that prize? Or as Strøm (1984: 200) puts it: "one would not expect minority administrations to be viable or effective solutions in parliamentary democracies, where the political life of the cabinet is, at all times, in the hands of the parliamentary majority."

Third, while we draw on insights from the literature that attempt to explain the cross-national variation in the frequency of minority governments, we are interested in why minority governments form in countries where they are predominant, for example Norway, as well as in countries where they are exceptional,

---

[2] Features of a polity such as the electoral system or party system, by shaping electoral outcomes, shape the propensity for minority governments. If a country has a two party system or electoral system that is winner takes all in nature, minority situations become less likely, making minority governments less likely. Of course, minority situations may be a necessary but are not a sufficient condition for the emergence of minority governments.

for example Australia. This allows us to identify multiple pathways to minority government that may receive less attention in studies that employ a quantitative approach to explain frequency.

Given this, under which circumstances are minority governments likely to form, according to existing research? Three primary sets of answers dominate the literature: the first focuses on what motivates political parties and in particular whether membership in the government is the real prize that scholarship on government formation has long assumed. The second set highlights characteristics of the party system. A third set focuses on how the design of political institutions may shape the formation of minority governments. While these sets of explanations are not necessarily mutually exclusive, we discuss each in turn.[3]

The goals that motivate political parties likely influence their interest in joining a government, with consequences for the formation of minority governments. As discussed above, it was once assumed that all parties were office seeking (Duverger 1959), meaning that they compete in elections in order to win political offices, and cabinet is the ultimate political office to hold in parliamentary systems (Laver and Schofield 1998). Such theories had a difficult time explaining the existence of minority governments because parties choose to stay out of government, or at least allowed a minority one to form or govern without coalescing to attain power. Later scholarship recognized that parties have multiple goals (Strøm 1990a). Policy, office, or votes are often competing goals and parties may have to make hard decisions when determining priorities (Müller and Strøm 1999). Thus, different parties may have distinct goals, which can help account for minority government formation.

Our country studies provide insight into party goals in distinct national contexts. Why would some parties or indeed legislators choose to forego a share of the spoils of office? One answer is that they are policy- or vote-seeking. Strøm's (1990b) rational theory of minority government formation incorporates parties' desire to affect public policy and their willingness to stay out of government if it is possible to have policy influence outside of it, especially via strong parliamentary committees. Strøm (1984, 1986, 1990b) also refers to "deferred gratification." Merely being in government may cost a party votes at the subsequent general election—what is now termed the "electoral costs of governing." Thus, parties may decide not to enter government to avoid these future costs, helping to account for minority governments, everything else being equal.[4] Based on a theoretical model that combines the importance parties place on ideology (policy) and office goals, Bassi (2017) argues that minority governments form when there exist some

---

[3] As Potrafke (2021: 510) notes "[t]here seem to be no studies to date examining the economic conditions under which minority governments take office."
[4] On the goal of party cohesion, see Bergman (1995).

(external support) parties that prefer to support the minority government rather than to vote against it and form an alternative coalition.

While much of the earlier work on minority governments and party goals focused on Scandinavia, their examination in multilevel states shows that parties may pursue distinct goals in different territorial arenas (Reniu 2002; Field 2016). Reniu (2002, 2011) explores how bargaining over government formation in Spain is impacted by the fact that some parties represented in the parliament have a regional basis—where they also have distinct goals—and are involved in negotiations at multiple state levels (local, regional, national), which helps account for minority government formation.

A second line of research explores the impact of party system characteristics on the formation of minority governments. We highlight two strands of this literature. A suggestion is that minority government is associated with a large central party (Crombez 1996; Laver and Shepsle 1996), meaning that it contains the median legislator on the primary dimensions of party competition. This is because a large, central party has a strong bargaining position vis-à-vis other parties—it therefore does not need to offer other parties cabinet portfolios. In this scenario, it is not necessarily that parties *opt out* (as in much of the prior body of literature) of government but rather that they are *kept out*. Similarly, based on an examination of the Nordic democracies, Rasch (2011) finds that minority governments are more likely in systems with one centrally located, relatively large party. Bergman, Ersson, and Hellström (2015) also find that the presence of a large party or a dominant party increases the probability of a single-party minority government.

A second strand of the literature posits that party system polarization may also matter. Greater policy differences on the primary dimensions of party competition—whether socioeconomic, cultural, or center-periphery—may make it more difficult for majority multiparty coalitions to form (Dodd 1976), and indeed some parties may be considered "pariah" parties with which mainstream parties refuse to ally (Downs 2012). Kalandrakis (2015: 321) posits a positive probability of minority government "when policy disagreement or polarization is significant, or when utility from cabinet posts is relatively small compared with partisan policy disagreement." He notes this may be because of the tradeoffs potential partners face—if they don't support the proposed (minority) government, the alternative may be even worse in terms of policy. Thürk et al. (2021: 296) suggest that the degree of party polarization interacts with legislative organization to shape the propensity for minority governments to emerge: "[l]egislatures with a high degree of party system polarization and a low number of veto points are associated with an increased likelihood of forming minority governments, whereas highly polarized party systems with many veto points tend to form surplus coalitions."

As mentioned in Chapter 1, the party systems in many countries have fragmented and challenger parties, on the radical left and right ends of the spectrum, have emerged or strengthened. However, radical parties have not been consistently excluded from governing. Using the example of radical right parties, while they have served as support parties for minority governments (e.g. in Denmark), they have also joined government coalitions (e.g. in Italy, Austria, the Netherlands, and Norway) (De Lange 2012; Twist 2019).[5] This suggests that radical parties can be mainstreamed (Akkerman, De Lange, and Rooduijn 2016; Bale and Rovira Kaltwasser 2021), and that they have at times have sufficient bargaining power to attain office, if they want it.

Finally, of course political institutions may shape behavior at the point of government formation. To complicate matters, a defining feature of parliamentarism is that the government somehow comes from and remains responsible to parliament. The term "comes from" may imply some form of parliamentary investiture—a vote to select the government or confirm an already-in-place government. Strøm (1990b) suggests that a minority government is more likely to form when a parliamentary vote to select the government is not required. Bergman (1993) distinguishes between "positive parliamentarism" (a situation where a parliament needs to explicitly support an incoming government) and "negative parliamentarism" (a situation where parliament must only "tolerate" the government) and finds that minority governments are more likely in countries with negative parliamentarism. Relatedly, others argue that investiture rules tend to create a bargaining environment in which majority coalitions form more often (Bergman, Ersson, and Hellström 2015).

But not everyone is convinced. Golder, Golder, and Siegel (2012) suggest that minority governments should not necessarily correlate with the absence of an explicit parliamentary investiture votes. Rather, no confidence procedures, they suggest, mitigate the impact of investiture because any government must be capable of surviving a test of parliamentary confidence. Cheibub, Martin, and Rasch (2021) find that parliamentary democracies that have an investiture requirement are no less likely to experience minority governments than those where governments come to power without an investiture vote. However, they find that the specific form of the investiture vote affects whether minority governments are likely to form. Therefore, much uncertainty continues to surround the impact of parliamentary investiture rules on the type of government that forms.

If political parties have at least some interest in policy, then, all else equal, the incentive to enter a government reduces as the capacity of political parties to influence public policy outside government increases. And political institutions affect the degree to which political parties outside government can influence policy. As mentioned previously, how parliament operates, Strøm (1984, 1990b) suggests, determines policy influence outside of government, and in particular whether or not there are strong standing committees in parliament that enable

---

[5] Support parties are parties that do not hold seats in the cabinet but that provide support within parliament for the government (for example, through voting with the government in parliament).

non-government parties to influence policy. However, Rasch (2011) notes that while the Scandinavian democracies of Denmark, Norway, and Sweden frequently have minority governments and also "strong parliaments" that give opposition parties considerable influence, so do Finland and Iceland where minority government is not prevalent. To our knowledge, there has not been further cross national testing of this proposition. And, the role of parliament in public policy, and the capacity of committees to influence policy is not static. Committee systems do become more or less powerful (André, Depauw, and Martin 2016).

Finally, we draw attention to the literature on the institutional structure of the state, and in particular whether there is a powerful regional tier of government (Reniu 2002; Ştefuriuc 2009, 2013; Field 2016). The same parties are often in negotiations in multiple parliaments (Colomer and Martínez 1995), sometimes simultaneously, and at times at multiple state levels. Various studies argue that the territorial structure of the state can affect party goals, discussed previously, and provide incentives to link government formation strategies at different levels (Reniu 2002; Deschouwer 2009; Falcó-Gimeno and Verge 2013; Ştefuriuc 2013), though variation in territorial structures, party systems, and party organizations also impact coalition bargaining.

In summary, we hope the in-depth analyses in the country studies that follow provide additional insight that helps us better understand why minority governments form. Nonetheless, once minority governments form, they need to govern. It is to this question that we turn next.

How minority governments govern

The country chapters seek to elucidate how minority governments govern. This includes whether they govern with formal agreements with other parties in parliament and their alliance-building strategies within parliament, and the political parties that provide support to minority governments from parliament or the individual independent legislators who do so.

While there are several typologies of minority government, we know less about their frequency, why different types form, and their consequences (though see Thürk 2021; Krauss and Thürk 2022). The country studies identify and discuss the types of minority governments and their support parties, where relevant. A support party provides parliamentary support for a minority government to reach legislative majorities and/or remain in office, without holding cabinet positions.

Scholars make a key distinction between minority governments that have explicit support from non-governing parties in parliament and those that do not (see, for example, Herman and Pope 1973; Strøm 1990b; Bale and Bergman 2006a). Strøm's (1990b) typology distinguishes *formal* and *substantive* minority government. The former have an explicit agreement with a political party or parties in parliament that is negotiated prior to government formation, provides more than a short-term commitment to the government's agenda and survival, and brings the government's support to a majority. Substantive minority governments do not.

Grounded in Sweden and New Zealand, Bale and Bergman (2006a) argue that *contract parliamentarism* is a new type of minority government. Such a government has written agreements with political parties (or party) that provide it with support in parliament, and the relations between them are highly institutionalized, to the degree that it resembles majority government. They also argue that contract parliamentarism was becoming more common at the time they wrote. Along these lines, Christiansen and Damgaard (2008) show that support parties in Denmark, Norway, and Sweden have become highly integrated into the policy process. In contrast, Boston and Bullock (2012) identify the variety of arrangements minority (and majority coalitions) governments use, which allow for various levels of (dis)agreement. Even support agreements permit varying degrees of room for agreement and opposition (Otjes and Louwerse 2014; Field 2016: ch. 6).

Once a minority government assumes office, it needs to pass bills through parliament and legislate. Parliament also needs to reach majorities to accomplish its business. The country chapters discuss how they do so and whether some strategies work better than others. There is, of course, research in this area upon which our contributors build. Strøm (1990b) identified different majority building strategies. At one extreme, majorities in parliament have consistent membership, that is, the same parties repeatedly ally. At the other extreme, governments can build majorities with ad hoc or shifting majorities. He also linked the type of minority government with its majority building strategy, namely that formal minority governments rely on consistent legislative coalitions.

However, the degree to which the type of minority government and majority building strategies are linked remains an open question empirically. For example, substantive single-party minority governments in Spain at times repeatedly built majorities with the same set of parties, without a formalized support agreement (Field 2016); at other times, they shifted allies (Field 2009). And both strategies have worked. In Denmark, there is evidence that formal minority coalition governments use different legislative strategies than substantive ones; the former are more likely to use a logrolling strategy to attract support parties, "paying its support party off with concessions on issues not regulated by the coalition agreement" (Christiansen and Pedersen 2012).

Other scholars have sought to explain which parties join legislative coalitions and why they may not. Is it based on support party status (as above), ideological or policy positions, electoral or office considerations, or a combination thereof? Ganghof and Bräuninger (2006) caution that parties' policy preferences are not their only consideration. Because parties' electoral and office goals also matter, a party may reject a government's policy proposal even if it is closer to its preferences than the status quo. Examining Canadian minority governments, Godbout and Høyland (2011) point to parties' proximity, on ideological and territorial issues, and electoral considerations. In the context of Spain's decentralized state, Field (2014) also shows that parties' office goals at the regional level affect their willingness to ally with the government in the central parliament—parties that need support to govern at the regional level are more likely to vote with the party governing Spain.

Finally, the chapters examine the role of support parties, and whether there are differences in how minority governments operate due to distinct types of support parties, or indeed of support legislators. Research on support parties has examined their motivations for supporting a minority government, their behavior during minority governments and the benefits and costs of being a support party (Bale and Dann 2002; Heller 2002; Bale and Bergman 2006b; Artés and Bustos 2008; Reniu 2011; Field 2014, 2016; Thesen 2016; Anghel and Thürk 2021). Such parties are not fully in the opposition, nor are they in government; rather, they have a hybrid status.

The extant research has examined regional parties (Heller 2002; Artés and Bustos 2008; Reniu 2011; Field 2014, 2016), green parties (Bale and Dann 2002; Crowley 2003; Bale and Bergman 2006b; Crowley and Moore 2020), and ethno-regional compared to mainstream parties (Anghel and Thürk 2021). It is not only parties that provide support for minority governments. Kefford and Weeks (2020) investigate the support role that independent parliamentarians play in Australia and Ireland. In this volume, the country studies provide additional understanding of support parties and support parliamentarians in their national contexts.

How well minority governments perform

Finally, we come to the *how well* question. Does it matter if there is a minority government or majority government in terms of government performance? And, why might some minority governments govern better than others?

Where possible, the country studies provide and discuss common indicators of success to help answer this question, such as government duration, the number and share of government bills approved, and/or the degree to which the electorate rewards or punishes governing parties in the subsequent election. We recognize that these are blunt, imperfect indicators, which may not be the best way to assess performance. Number or share of government bills approved does not tell us about their importance. Government durability perhaps measures something different in Sweden, where the government cannot call early elections, than in Spain, where the PM has a great deal of discretion to do so. Therefore, we encouraged our authors to go beyond standard indicators, where fruitful, to contextualize performance. Many chapters also examine how well minority governments govern compared to majority (single-party or coalition) governments *in the same country*.

There is a growing literature on minority government performance upon which to draw. Once presumed to be a particularly problematic form of government, research of the past several decades shows that minority governments can be effective, though they are not necessarily so (Artés and Bustos 2008; Field 2016; Thürk 2021; Krauss and Thürk 2022). Strøm (1990b) and his earlier work was particularly influential in changing the perception of minority governments to being considered rational cabinet solutions.

Do minority governments govern better or worse? It is difficult to conclude that there is consensus on this question, particularly when we compare minority governments to majority coalitions—the most plausible alternative. There is cross-national evidence that minority governments, single-party and coalition, do not last as long as their majority counterparts (Strøm 1990b; Saalfeld 2008). However, the (crisis) circumstances surrounding their end were no more troubling than those of majority coalitions in the period Strøm (1990b) analyzed. Furthermore, recent research that examines 471 cabinets in 30 countries finds that formal minority governments are as stable as majority ones, while substantive minority governments are less stable than majority governments (Krauss and Thürk 2022).

Minority governments do not appear to have any greater difficulty than majority coalitions in passing their legislation (Cheibub, Przeworski, and Saiegh 2004; Cheibub 2007; Saiegh 2011). There is also evidence that they are often able to carry out their electoral promises (Artés 2013; Moury and Fernandes 2018) [on pledge fulfillments more generally, see Naurin, Royed, and Thomson (2019) and Thomson et al. (2017)] and controversial policy reforms (Alexiadou 2013).[6]

The research on budgeting and fiscal discipline has produced mixed findings (De Haan, Sturm, and Beekhuis 1999; Artés and Jurado 2015; Potrafke 2021). However, research on 197 governments in 21 parliamentary democracies indicates that the legislative success of substantive minority governments (and not formal minority governments) is lower than that of majority governments (Thürk 2021).

What about electoral performance and public support? There is evidence that (parties in) minority governments perform better than those in other cabinets in electoral terms (Narud and Valen 2008). However, this may indicate that the public faces greater difficulty holding minority governments accountable (Powell and Whitten 1993; Vowles 2010).

---

[6] Evidence from subnational studies is more mixed: Looking at subnational governments in Australia, Brenton and Pickering (2020) find that minority governments keep fewer of their pledges—64 percent of their promises, compared with 80 percent for majority governments. In the German subnational case, Matthieß (2019) finds similar pledge fulfillment performance between minority and majority governments.

We hope to contribute to this debate about performance by asking the contributors to assess performance within their national context and, when useful, compared to majority governments in the same country. There is, of course, some research on particular national contexts, though the evidence is also mixed. Examining Canada, Pickup and Hobolt (2015) find that minority governments are more responsive to the median voter than majority governments, though less effective at passing legislation. Similarly, Thomas (2007) concludes that compromise and deliberation, executive accountability and opportunities for private member bills increased during Canadian minority governments. However, efficiency, government stability, and accountability declined. Based on an analysis of Spain between 1982 and 2011, Field (2016) finds little difference in performance between single-party majority and minority governments when considering government duration, policy success, or electoral performance.

Why might some minority governments perform better than other minority governments? The hypotheses overlap, in some instances, with the literature on how they operate. Research examines several hypotheses. For example, does the type of minority government matter? In addition to the cross-national quantitative studies cited previously (Thürk 2021; Krauss and Thürk 2022), Fernandes, Magalhães, and Santana-Pereira (2018) argue that contract parliamentarism facilitated strong government performance in Portugal. On the other hand, Field (2016) shows that both substantive and formal minority governments have governed well in Spain. Do distinct majority-building strategies matter, or are they simply alternative tools that can be used (in)effectively in different circumstances? In Denmark, both changing coalitions and left (or right) bloc politics have worked (Green-Pedersen 2001; Green-Pedersen and Hoffmann Thomsen 2005).

Another line of research investigates the government's bargaining position, such as its median or central positioning in the party system or ideological proximity to potential allies. Using evidence from the Danish and Swedish cases, Klüver and Zubek (2018) test whether the central location of the government or its ideological proximity to opposition parties account for legislative effectiveness, and find more support for the latter. Also in Denmark, different patterns of portfolio allocation in minority coalitions is also related to the policy effectiveness of the government (König and Lin 2021).

Building on some of this literature, Field (2016) develops an analytical framework for understanding minority government performance, which includes the design of political institutions, the partisan bargaining circumstances and the reconcilability of party goals. Minority governments are expected to perform better where institutions strengthen the government, where it is in a strong partisan bargaining position, and where parties' goals are more easily reconciled.

In sum, the country studies in this volume provide additional insight into the *why*, *how*, and *how well* of minority governments. Of course, these questions may be interrelated. Let us explain briefly.

Interconnected questions

Such potential connectivity gave rise to the desire to examine the questions simultaneously and concurrently in each of the country studies rather than separately or exclusively as has been common in the study of minority governments. For example, how minority governments govern may be shaped by why the minority government formed in the first place. The performance of specific minority governments (for example in terms of productivity, survival, and subsequent electoral success) may be shaped, in part, by how the minority government operates. And in turn, the performance of the incumbent (or past) minority governments may shape the next government formation process (or perhaps the next involving similar political actors). Political actors may learn and calculate whether a governing arrangement works for them when they next face a government formation process.

Chapter outline

We group our country studies according to the prevalence of minority governments, measured in terms of the share of all governments. We determine prevalence using our counting rules discussed in Chapter 1. Thus, we count a change of majority/minority status as a change of government. The majority or minority status of the government refers to the chamber, chambers, or parliament as a whole depending on who can hold the government responsible. Part II includes countries where minority governments are predominant (India, Norway, Romania, Spain, and Sweden). Part III covers countries where minority governments are common (Canada, France, Ireland, Italy, Poland, and Portugal). Part IV includes countries where minority governments are exceptional (Australia and the United Kingdom). Below we provide a summary of each country chapter. In the final chapter, we draw comparative conclusions and outline what we think are important pathways for further research.

We turn first to India, where minority governments are predominant. After four decades (1947–89) of single-party majority governments, India experienced two decades of minority governments (1989–2014), all multiparty coalitions. Nikolenyi argues that an adequate account of why minority governments form requires taking into account pre-electoral alliances and the federalization of the party system. Regional parties have become more relevant in national politics, and they retained an ambivalent attitude toward formal participation in national government. The chapter also traces the development of contract parliamentarism as an arrangement to foster government stability in the highly fragmented party system. Comparing different types of minority government, the chapter shows near-majority-sized minority governments and those that include a strong centrally-positioned party perform significantly better than minority governments with fewer seats in parliament. Notably, near-majority minority governments outperform single-party majority governments in terms of their duration and law production.

Norway has one of the highest incidences of minority government among parliamentary democracies. Coalition and single-party minority cabinets are common. Formal minority governments are rare, and when they occur they are a sign of weakness rather than strength. Strøm argues that the predominance of minority governments is due to several characteristics of Norwegian politics. A permissive institutional setting provides the opportunity to form minority governments. A highly electorally competitive pattern of two-bloc politics constrains coalition bargaining and motivates parties to eschew coalitions with uncomfortable partners. And a consensual political culture characterized by high levels of interpersonal trust allows party leaders to take longer-term views of their political interests and avoid more conflictual forms of political contestation. These traits allow minority cabinets to sustain themselves in office and build a reasonable record of policy accomplishment.

More than half of governments since Romania's transition toward democracy in 1990 have been minority governments. Most have been minority coalitions. Anghel argues that party system and institutional features help explain the prevalence of minority governments. The former includes the presence of dominant parties, polarizing electoral competition, and the strategies of small parties. The latter relates to the importance of the president in this semi-presidential regime and of the informal institutions of corruption and clientelism. While there are exceptions, Romanian parties use informal support arrangements between party leaders and vague commitments rather than detailed agreements. Anghel attributes this to the parties' disinterest in the implementation of specific policies and short-term strategies. The chapter posits that the absence of a thorough written commitment is associated with shorter cabinet durability, and highlights how party switching and corrupt practices affect alliance-building strategies. While minority cabinets are among the most and least durable, they are no different than majority cabinets in terms of legislative success.

Minority governments are predominant in Spain. Spain had either single-party majority or minority governments between its transition to democracy in the mid-1970s until a minority coalition formed in 2020. Field argues that contextual factors during the transition to democracy and historical legacies from the 1930s encouraged single-party minority governments in the early years of the new regime. Political actors also established institutions and practices to make single-party minority governments a viable governing formula. The formation, functioning, and performance of minority governments are also intertwined with the relevance and nature of regional parties and the decentralized state. Regional parties have little interest in governing Spain, yet want to receive policy concessions, further state decentralization and political support to govern their regions. The chapter explains why Spain's minority governments have often performed as well as their majority counterparts. It highlights three factors: political institutions, the government's partisan bargaining position, and the reconcilability of party goals.

Minority governments also predominate in Sweden, accounting for over 70 percent of post-war governments. In their chapter, Bäck and Hellström note the lack of a need for parliamentary investiture, unidimensional left–right political conflict and the historically dominant position of the Social Democrats as factors contributing to the high propensity for minority administrations. They note also the role of contract parliamentarism in how minority governments function—formal agreements between the government and the party or parties which support it, resembling in many ways a majority coalition cabinet. Bäck and Hellström find no systematic difference between how minority and majority governments perform in Sweden.

We now turn to countries where minority governments are common. In the post-war period, Canada has never had a coalition government. Instead, single-party governments differ based on their majority or minority status, and the latter are common. Minority governments have also resisted formalized support agreements. Godbout and Cochrane argue that this is due primarily to the structure of the party system. Canadian parties prefer single-party governments. The party system, with national and regional parties, facilitates the formation of ad hoc voting coalitions and makes minority government relatively effective. A majority can always be built on at least two types of issues: left–right ideological and center–periphery regional. While minority governments have a shorter lifespan and are less productive than their majority counterparts are, they provide more opportunities for opposition party members to influence the legislative process and are more responsive to public opinion.

France experiences two very different types of minority government: regular minority governments but also one-month minority governments. In his chapter, Rozenberg suggest that minority governments are facilitated by the absence of a compulsory investiture vote and need for an absolute majority for the government to be removed. Three factors facilitate minority governments in office: the "rationalized parliamentarianism," the party system—which provided potentially two supporting groups, and "good relations" between the government and some opposition MPs, due in part to constituency-oriented particularism. On performance, Rozenberg notes a major contrast between the policy achievement of the minority government and the lack of electoral support.

Ireland has experienced a number of minority governments, with some controlling only a small percentage of legislative seats. In his chapter, Weeks explores how the fractionalization of the party system has made minority governments more likely, and (majority) coalition governments less-likely. The chapter points to the crucial role of non-party (independent) legislators in the Irish parliament in facilitating and enabling minority governments—in return for office, policy, but also constituency-focused particularistic spending by the government. On performance, Weeks finds that minority governments in Ireland are generally as productive, survive as long, and are no less electorally unsuccessful as majority counterparts.

Political reforms in Italy in the 1990s led to a reduction in the number of minority governments. In her chapter, Giannetti explores how structural instability of the policy space explains the sharp decrease of minority governments in the Second Republic, suggesting that the presence or absence of a centrally located large party is the most important factor explaining the occurrence (or lack) of minority governments. Non-cabinet seat spoils of office to supporting parties remain an important inducement to support the government. On performance, Giannetti finds that minority cabinets in Italy do not differ substantially from their majority counterparts, at least in terms of duration and legislative effectiveness.

Most Polish minority cabinets emerge after an incumbent majority cabinet breaks down and the government moves into minority status. As Zubek notes, this is possible because incumbent cabinets can shift between majority and minority status without having to face an explicit investiture vote in parliament, and a constructive no-confidence vote makes removing a government difficult, even if a party leaves the cabinet and withdraws parliamentary support. Minority cabinets have typically governed by building ad hoc legislative coalitions. Office payoffs beyond cabinet seats act as an important inducement for parties to support a minority government. Zubek suggests that Polish minority cabinets have had a mixed record in legislative performance, with supported minority cabinets and unsupported cabinets formed by disciplined core parties demonstrating higher effectiveness.

Minority governments are a common governing arrangement in Portugal. They are particularly prevalent on the left. Fernandes argues that political actors designed political institutions at the outset of democracy to permit the emergence of minority governments because of the impossibility of a coalition between the Socialists and the parties to its left. This historical rift and the policy-seeking and outsider nature of the latter leftist parties create incentives for the formation of minority governments. The norm has been for minority governments to govern without formal support. However, the chapter explains why the Socialist Prime Minister António Costa's minority government (2015–19) departed from this pattern. It also presents evidence that minority governments perform (at least) as well as majority governments. Importantly, minority governments allow for a more inclusive democracy by promoting the fulfillment of the opposition's pledges.

In our last two country cases, minority governments are exceptional. In Australia, single-party majority governments have dominated. Crowley argues that the two major parties—Labor and the Coalition—expect to govern alone and are resistant to executive power sharing, despite greater fragmentation of the party system. The chapter examines in depth how the federal minority government of Labor Prime Minister Julia Gillard (2010–13) built on experience with minority government in the subnational states and territories. The near-majority government negotiated formal support agreements with the policy-seeking Greens and independents, in contrast with the short-lived Coalition minority government (2018–19) that relied on ad hoc support. The Gillard government performed comparably to majority governments in Australia; however, its achievements were undersold and Labor lost the next election. These experiences provide lessons for possible future minority governments in this more fragmented Australian party system.

The United Kingdom is not a country one usually associates with minority government, but as Jones and Whitaker point out in their chapter, minority administrations do come about, sometimes following an indecisive general election, but also when an incumbent majority government loses sufficient MPs. They note that with the UK's changing territorial politics, devolution has increased the likelihood of minority government and makes flexible support arrangements more attractive than formal coalitions. They conclude that the performance of minority governments has been affected at least as much by governments' difficulties in building majorities within their own parties as by their relationships with support parties.

References

Akkerman, Tjitske, Sarah L. De Lange, and Matthijs Rooduijn, eds. 2016. *Radical Right-wing Populist Parties in Western Europe. Into the Mainstream?* London: Routledge.

Alexiadou, Despina. 2013. "In Search of Successful Reform: The Politics of Opposition and Consensus in OECD Parliamentary Democracies." *West European Politics* 36 (4): 704–725.

André, Audrey, Sam Depauw, and Shane Martin. 2016. "'Trust Is Good, Control Is Better': Multiparty Government and Legislative Organization." *Political Research Quarterly* 69 (1): 108–120.

Anghel, Veronica, and Maria Thürk. 2021. "Under the Influence: Pay-Offs to Legislative Support Parties under Minority Governments." *Government and Opposition* 56 (1): 121–140.

Artés, Joaquín. 2013. "Do Spanish Politicians Keep Their Promises?" *Party Politics* 19 (1): 143–158.

Artés, Joaquín, and Antonio Bustos. 2008. "Electoral Promises and Minority Governments: An Empirical Study." *European Journal of Political Research* 47 (3): 307–333.

Artés, Joaquín, and Ignacio Jurado. 2015. "Fiscal Deficits and Type of Government: A Study of Spanish Local Elections." In *The Political Economy of Governance: Institutions, Political Performance and Elections*, ed. Norman Schofield and Gonzalo Caballero, 363–376. New York: Springer.

Bale, Tim, and Torbjörn Bergman. 2006a. "Captives No Longer, but Servants Still? Contract Parliamentarism and the New Minority Governance in Sweden and New Zealand." *Government and Opposition* 41 (3): 422–449.

Bale, Tim, and Torbjörn Bergman. 2006b. "A Taste of Honey Is Worse than None At All? Coping with the Generic Challenges of Support Party Status in Sweden and New Zealand." *Party Politics* 12 (2): 189–202.

Bale, Tim, and Christine Dann. 2002. "Is the Grass Really Greener? The Rationale and Reality of Support Party Status: A New Zealand Case Study." *Party Politics* 8 (3): 349–365.

Bale, Tim, and Cristóbal Rovira Kaltwasser, eds. 2021. *Riding the Populist Wave: Europe's Mainstream Right in Crisis*. Cambridge: Cambridge University Press.

Bassi, Anna. 2017. "Policy Preferences in Coalition Formation and the Stability of Minority and Surplus Governments." *The Journal of Politics* 79 (1): 250–268.

Bergman, Torbjörn. 1993. "Formation Rules and Minority Governments." *European Journal of Political Research* 23 (1): 55–66.

Bergman, Torbjörn. 1995. *Constitutional Rules and Party Goals in Coalition Formation: An Analysis of Winning Minority Governments in Sweden*. Umeå: Umeå Universitet.

Bergman, Torbjörn, Svante Ersson, and Johan Hellström. 2015. "Government Formation and Breakdown in Western and Central Eastern Europe." *Comparative European Politics* 13 (3): 345–375.

Boston, Jonathan, and David Bullock. 2012. "Multi-party Governance: Managing the Unity-Distinctiveness Dilemma in Executive Coalitions." *Party Politics* 18 (3): 349–368.

Brenton, Scott, and Heath Pickering. 2020. "Trustworthiness, Stability and Productivity of Minority Governments in Australia." *Parliamentary Affairs* 75 (2): 308–339.

Cairney, Paul 2011. "Coalition and Minority Government in Scotland: Lessons for the United Kingdom." *The Political Quarterly* 82 (2): 261–269.

Cheibub, José A. 2007. *Presidentialism, Parliamentarism, and Democracy*. Cambridge: Cambridge University Press.

Cheibub, José Antonio, Shane Martin, and Bjørn Erik Rasch. 2021. "Investiture Rules and Formation of Minority Governments in European Parliamentary Democracies." *Party Politics* 27 (2): 351–362.

Cheibub, José A, Adam Przeworski, and Sebastian M. Saiegh. 2004. "Government Coalitions and Legislative Success under Presidentialism and Parliamentarism." *British Journal of Political Science* 34 (4): 565–587.

Christiansen, Flemming J., and Erik Damgaard. 2008. "Parliamentary Opposition under Minority Parliamentarism: Scandinavia." *The Journal of Legislative Studies* 14 (1/2): 46–76.

Christiansen, Flemming J., and Rasmus B. Pedersen. 2012. "The Impact of the European Union on Coalition Formation in a Minority System: The Case of Denmark." *Scandinavian Political Studies* 35 (3): 179–197.

Colomer, Josep M., and Florencio Martínez. 1995. "The Paradox of Coalition Trading." *Journal of Theoretical Politics* 7 (1): 41–63.

Crombez, Christophe. 1996. "Minority Governments, Minimal Winning Coalitions and Surplus Majorities in Parliamentary Systems." *European Journal of Political Research* 29 (1): 1–29.

Crowley, Kate. 2003. "Strained Parliamentary Relations: Green-supported Government in Tasmania." *Australasian Parliamentary Review* 17 (2): 55–71.

Crowley, Kate, and Sharon Moore. 2020. "Stepping Stone, Halfway House or Road to Nowhere? Green Support of Minority Government in Sweden, New Zealand and Australia." *Government and Opposition* 55 (4): 669–689.

Crowley, Kate, and Megan Tighe. 2017. "Where Greens Support Conservatives: Lessons from the Rundle Minority Government in Tasmania 1996-98." *Australian Journal of Politics & History* 63 (4): 572–587.

De Haan, Jakob, Jan-Egbert Sturm, and Geert Beekhuis. 1999. "The Weak Government Thesis: Some New Evidence." *Public Choice* 101 (3–4): 163–176.

De Lange, Sarah L. 2012. "New Alliances: Why Mainstream Parties Govern with Radical Right–Wing Populist Parties." *Political Studies* 60 (4): 899–918.

Deschouwer, Kris. 2009. "Coalition Formation and Congruence in a Multi-layered Setting: Belgium 1995–2008." *Regional and Federal Studies* 19 (1): 13–35.

Dodd, Lawrence C. 1976. *Coalitions in Parliamentary Government*. Princeton: Princeton University Press.

Downs, William M. 2012. *Political Extremism in Democracies: Combating Intolerance*: New York: Palgrave Macmillan.

Duverger, Maurice. 1959. *Political Parties: Their Organization and Activity in the Modern State*. London: Methuen.

Falcó-Gimeno, Albert, and Tània Verge. 2013. "Coalition Trading in Spain: Explaining State-wide Parties' Government Formation Strategies at the Regional Level." *Regional & Federal Studies* 23 (4): 387–405.

Fernandes, Jorge M., Pedro C. Magalhães, and José Santana-Pereira. 2018. "Portugal's Leftist Government: From Sick Man to Poster Boy?" *South European Society and Politics* 23 (4): 503–524.

Field, Bonnie N. 2009. "Minority Government and Legislative Politics in a Multi-level State: Spain under Zapatero." *South European Society and Politics* 14 (4): 417–434.

Field, Bonnie N. 2014. "Minority Parliamentary Government and Multilevel Politics: Spain's System of Mutual Back Scratching." *Comparative Politics* 46 (3): 293–312.

Field, Bonnie N. 2016. *Why Minority Governments Work: Multilevel Territorial Politics in Spain*. New York: Palgrave Macmillan.

Ganghof, Steffen, and Thomas Bräuninger. 2006. "Government Status and Legislative Behaviour: Partisan Veto Players in Australia, Denmark, Finland and Germany." *Party Politics* 12 (4): 521–539.

Ganghof, Steffen, Sebastian Eppner, Christian Stecker, Katja Heeß, and Stefan Schukraft. 2019. "Do Minority Cabinets Govern More Flexibly and Inclusively? Evidence from Germany." *German Politics* 28 (4): 541–561.

Godbout, Jean-François, and Bjørn Høyland. 2011. "Coalition Voting and Minority Governments in Canada." *Commonwealth & Comparative Politics* 49 (4): 457–485.

Golder, Matt, Sona N. Golder, and David A. Siegel. 2012. "Modeling the Institutional Foundation of Parliamentary Government Formation." *The Journal of Politics* 74 (2): 427–445.

Green-Pedersen, Christoffer. 2001. "Minority Governments and Party Politics: The Political and Institutional Background to the 'Danish Miracle'." *Journal of Public Policy* 21 (1): 53–70.

Green-Pedersen, Christoffer, and Lisbeth Hoffmann Thomsen. 2005. "Bloc Politics vs. Broad Cooperation? The Functioning of Danish Minority Parliamentarism." *The Journal of Legislative Studies* 11 (2): 153–169.

Heller, William B. 2002. "Regional Parties and National Politics in Europe: Spain's Estado de las Autonomías, 1993 to 2000." *Comparative Political Studies* 35 (6): 657–685.

Herman, Valentine, and John Pope. 1973. "Minority Governments in Western Democracies." *British Journal of Political Science* 3 (2): 191–212.

Kalandrakis, Tasos. 2015. "A Theory of Minority and Majority Governments." *Political Science Research and Methods* 3 (2): 309–328.

Kefford, Glenn, and Liam Weeks. 2020. "Minority Party Government and Independent MPs: A Comparative Analysis of Australia and Ireland." *Parliamentary Affairs* 73 (1): 89–107.

Klüver, Heike, and Radoslaw Zubek. 2018. "Minority Governments and Legislative Reliability." *Party Politics* 24 (6): 719–730.

König, Thomas, and Nick Lin. 2021. "Portfolio allocation patterns and policy-making effectiveness in minority coalition governments." *European Journal of Political Research* 60 (3): 694–715.

Krauss, Svenja, and Maria Thürk. 2022. "Stability of Minority Governments and the Role of Support Agreements." *West European Politics* 45 (4): 767–792.

Laver, Michael, and Norman Schofield. 1998. *Multiparty Government: The Politics of Coalition in Europe*. Ann Arbor: University of Michigan Press.

Laver, Michael, and Kenneth A. Shepsle. 1996. *Making and Breaking Governments: Cabinets and Legislatures in Parliamentary Democracies*. Cambridge: Cambridge University Press.

Lundberg, Thomas C. 2013. "Politics is Still an Adversarial Business: Minority Government and Mixed-Member Proportional Representation in Scotland and in New Zealand." *British Journal of Politics & International Relations* 15 (4): 609–625.

Martínez-Cantó, Javier, and Henning Bergmann. 2020. "Government Termination in Multilevel Settings. How Party Congruence Affects the Survival of Sub-national Governments in Germany and Spain." *Journal of Elections, Public Opinion & Parties* 30 (3): 379–399.

Matthieß, Theres. 2019. "Equal Performance of Minority and Majority Coalitions? Pledge Fulfilment in the German State of NRW." *German Politics* 28 (1): 123–144.

Moury, Catherine, and Jorge M. Fernandes. 2018. "Minority Governments and Pledge Fulfilment: Evidence from Portugal." *Government and Opposition* 53 (2): 335–355.

Müller, Wolfgang C., and Kaare Strøm. 1999. "Coalition Governance in Western Europe: An Introduction." In *Coalition Governments in Western Europe*, ed. Wolfgang C. Müller and Kaare Strøm, 1–31. Oxford: Oxford University Press.

Narud, Hanne M., and Henry Valen. 2008. "Coalition Membership and Electoral Performance." In *Cabinets and Coalition Bargaining*, ed. Kaare Strøm, Wolfgang C. Müller, and Torbjörn Bergman, 369–402. Oxford: Oxford University Press.

Naurin, Elin, Terry J. Royed, and Robert Thomson, eds. 2019. *Party Mandates and Democracy: Making, Breaking, and Keeping Election Pedges in Twelve Countries*. Ann Arbor: University of Michigan Press.

Otjes, Simon, and Tom Louwerse. 2014. "A Special Majority Cabinet? Supported Minority Governance and Parliamentary Behavior in the Netherlands." *World Political Science Review* 10 (2): 343–363.

Palmer, Rosanne. 2011. "Coalition and Minority Government in Wales: Lessons for the United Kingdom." *The Political Quarterly* 82 (2): 270–278.

Pickup, Mark, and Sara B. Hobolt. 2015. "The Conditionality of the Trade-off between Government Responsiveness and Effectiveness: The Impact of Minority Status and Polls in the Canadian House of Commons." *Electoral Studies* 40: 517–530.

Potrafke, Niklas. 2021. "Fiscal Performance of Minority Governments: New Empirical Evidence for OECD Countries." *Party Politics* 27 (3): 501–514.

Powell, G. Bingham, and Guy D. Whitten. 1993. "A Cross-National Analysis of Economic Voting: Taking Account of Political Context." *American Journal of Political Science* 37 (2): 391–414.

Rasch, Bjørn E. 2011. "Why Minority Governments? Executive–Legislative Relations in the Nordic Countries." In *Parliamentary Government in the Nordic Countries at a Crossroads*, ed. Thomas Persson and Matti Wiberg, 41–61. Stockholm: Santérus Academic Press Sweden.

Reniu, Josep María. 2002. *La formación de gobiernos minoritarios en España, 1977–1996*. Madrid: Centro de Investigaciones Sociológicas.

Reniu, Josep M. 2011. "'Spain is Different': Explaining Minority Governments by Diverging Party Goals." In *Puzzles of Government Formation: Coalition Theory and Deviant Cases*, ed. Rudy B. Andeweg, Lieven De Winter, and Patrick Dumont, 112–128. London: Routledge.

Riker, William H. 1962. *The Theory of Political Coalitions*. New Haven: Yale University Press.

Saalfeld, Thomas. 2008. "Institutions, Chance, and Choices: The Dynamics of Cabinet Survival." In *Cabinets and Coalition Bargaining: The Democratic Life Cycle in Western Europe*, ed. Kaare Strøm, Wolfgang C. Müller, and Torbjörn Bergman, 327–368. Oxford: Oxford University Press.

Saiegh, Sebastian M. 2011. *Ruling by Statute: How Uncertainty and Vote Buying Shape Lawmaking*. Cambridge: Cambridge University Press.

Ştefuriuc, Irina. 2009. "Introduction: Government Coalitions in Multi-level Settings— Institutional Determinants and Party Strategy." *Regional & Federal Studies* 19 (1): 1–12.

Ştefuriuc, Irina. 2013. *Government Formation in Multi-Level Settings: Party Strategy and Institutional Constraints*. New York: Palgrave Macmillan.

Strøm, Kaare. 1984. "Minority Governments in Parliamentary Democracies: The Rationality of Nonwinning Cabinet Solutions." *Comparative Political Studies* 17 (2): 199–227.

Strøm, Kaare. 1986. "Deferred Gratification and Minority Governments in Scandinavia." *Legislative Studies Quarterly* 11 (4): 583–605.

Strøm, Kaare. 1990a. "A Behavioral Theory of Competitive Political Parties." *American Journal of Political Science* 34 (2): 565–598.

Strøm, Kaare. 1990b. *Minority Government and Majority Rule*. Cambridge: Cambridge University Press.

Thesen, Gunnar 2016. "Win Some, Lose None? Support Parties at the Polls and in Political Agenda-Setting." *Political Studies* 64 (4): 979–999.

Thomas, Paul E.J. 2007. "Measuring the Effectiveness of a Minority Parliament." *Canadian Parliamentary Review* 30 (1): 22–31.

Thomson, Robert, Terry Royed, Elin Naurin, Joaquín Artés, Rory Costello, Laurenz Ennser-Jedenastik, Mark Ferguson, Petia Kostadinova, Catherine Moury, François Pétry, and Katrin Praprotnik. 2017. "The Fulfillment of Parties' Election Pledges: A Comparative Study on the Impact of Power Sharing." *American Journal of Political Science* 61 (3): 527–542.

Thürk, Maria. 2022. "Small in Size but Powerful in Parliament? The Legislative Performance of Minority Governments." *Legislative Studies Quarterly* 47 (1): 193–224.

Thürk, Maria, Johan Hellström, and Holger Döring. 2021. "Institutional Constraints on Cabinet Formation: Veto Points and Party System Dynamics." *European Journal of Political Research* 60 (2): 295–316.

Twist, Kimberly A. 2019. *Partnering with Extremists: Coalitions between Mainstream and Far-Right Parties in Western Europe.* Ann Arbor: University of Michigan Press.

Vowles, Jack. 2010. "Making a Difference? Public Perceptions of Coalition, Single-Party, and Minority Governments." *Electoral Studies* 29 (3): 370–380.

PART II
WHERE MINORITY GOVERNMENTS ARE PREDOMINANT

3
Minority Governments in India
Party System Federalization and the Emergence of Contract Parliamentarism

Csaba Nikolenyi

India provides a puzzling case for the study of minority governments. In a country that was used to the regular recurrence of single-party majority governments for four decades (1947–89), the sudden shift to two decades of minority governments (1989–2014) is surprising. Moreover, unlike other adversarial Westminster democracies, such as Canada or Ireland, where hung parliaments normally lead to the formation of a single-party minority government[1] (Herman and Pope 1973: 195; Strøm 1990: 237, 244), almost all of India's minority governments were multiparty coalitions, often formed by an extremely large number of parties, by comparative indicators (Sridharan 2012). The era of minority governments seems to have come to an end with the general elections of 2014 and 2019, which once again led to majority governments. However, given that these governments were also multiparty coalitions, we can conjecture that the era of minority governments constituted an important transitional stage in the evolution of the Indian party system from a period of single-party government (1952–89) to one where governments by multiparty coalition have become the norm.

This chapter puts forward three arguments about the formation, operation, and performance of minority governments in India. First, the formation of minority governments is consistent with several comparative theories of minority governments—such as an increase in party system fragmentation (Taylor and Laver 1973; Dodd 1974, 1976), the presence of a strong centrally positioned party (van Deemen 1989, 1991; van Roozendaal 1992a, 1992b; Crombez 1996), the institution of negative parliamentarism (Bergman 1993), and the combination of high electoral costs of governing with an increase in policy benefits that opposition parties can acquire from the development of a new, albert comparatively still weak,

---

[1] Historically, the British tradition favors single-party governments to coalitions as "Disraeli is famed for saying: 'England does not love coalitions'" (Herman and Pope 1973: 195). It is important to stress, however, that coalitions have become increasingly more acceptable in both Ireland and Britain. In the former, all minority governments since 1989 were minority coalitions and a majority coalition government was formed even in the latter in 2010. Canada thus truly remains the only mature Westminster democracy without coalition governments since the end of the Second World War.

Csaba Nikolenyi, *Minority Governments in India*. In: *Minority Governments in Comparative Perspective*. Edited by Bonnie N. Field and Shane Martin, Oxford University Press.
© Csaba Nikolenyi (2022). DOI: 10.1093/oso/9780192871657.003.0003

legislative committee system (Strøm 1990). Nonetheless, an adequate account of Indian minority government requires taking into account the federalization of the party system (Arora 2003). As a result of this process, regional parties have become increasingly more relevant in national party politics, although they have retained an ambivalent attitude to formal participation in national government. The role that federalism, or multilevel politics in general, can play in producing minority governments has been noted in only a few comparative works so far (Field 2009, 2014; Sridharan 2012). Second, similar to a few Western democracies, the functioning of minority governments in India was also marked by the development of contract parliamentarism (Bale and Bergman 2006). Searching for a modality that would ensure government stability in the context of a highly fragmented party system, India's political parties gradually adopted increasingly more formal and sophisticated practices to retain the support of both coalition members and the external supporters of the coalition (Arora and Kailash 2018; Kailash 2007, 2014). Third, consistent with a long tradition of research on government duration and stability (Herman and Pope 1973; Taylor and Laver 1973), the Indian data show that near-majority sized minority governments and governments that include a strong centrally positioned party perform significantly better than smaller minority governments in terms of their duration and law production.

The Indian political system

India is a parliamentary federal republic with a bicameral national parliament and an indirectly elected President serving as the head of state. Representatives in the lower house of parliament, the House of the People (Lok Sabha), are elected in single-member districts using the first-past-the-post electoral system while members of the second chamber, the Council of State (Rajya Sabha), are elected indirectly by the state assemblies (Vidhan Sabha) using the single transferable vote system according to a staggered schedule. Although legislative bills can be introduced in either chamber, India follows the Westminster tradition in that money bills can be introduced only in the lower house. Furthermore, it is the Lok Sabha that holds the government of the day accountable through the mechanisms of votes of confidence and no confidence. The two chambers have a little more co-equal status only when they meet in a joint session to decide about constitutional matters, however, the far greater size of the Lok Sabha (543 versus 245 seats) ensures that it will always prevail.

For the first four decades (1947–89) following independence, India's national party system was dominated by the Indian National Congress Party that won legislative majorities in all but one of the national parliamentary elections.[2] The Lok

---

[2] The exception was the general election of 1977.

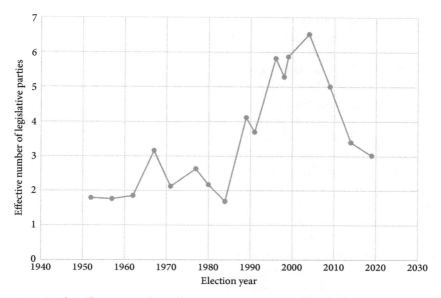

Fig. 3.1 The effective number of legislative parties in the Lok Sabha, 1952–2019, India

Sabha elections of 1989 opened a new chapter, in the evolution of the country's political and party system, which was characterized by three features. The first was the sudden and sharp increase in the effective number of parties (see Figure 3.1), fragmentation, and a concomitant recurrence of hung parliaments.

Second, minority governments, and especially minority coalition governments, were the norm between 1989 and 2014. In stark contrast to the pre-1989 era when every national election was followed by a majority government, all seven national elections during this second period led to minority governments. Third, pre-electoral alliances assumed a central role in organizing Indian elections and presenting the electorate with competing government alternatives. Although the number of individual parties contesting elections and entering the Lok Sabha significantly increased, the number of partisan blocs and alliances remained quite stable, between three and four (Nikolenyi 1998, 2010).

The general elections of 2014 and 2019 led to a return to majority parliaments (Schakel, Sharma, and Swenden 2019). However, unlike before 1989, the majority party, the Hindu nationalist Bharatiya Janata Party (BJP), opted to form surplus majority coalition governments with its electoral allies instead of single-party majority governments after both of these elections.

There are no formal investiture rules in India. The constitution assigns formal power to the president to appoint the council of ministers (Nikolenyi 2015). However, during the first decade of minority parliaments (1989–98), when electoral verdicts were particularly unclear, presidents asked the new governments to pass a vote of confidence on the floor of the lower house. By the second decade of the minority governments (1999–2009), with national elections producing near-majority victories by the largest electoral alliance, this was no longer necessary.

Table 3.1 provides an overview of India's types of governments following the 1989 general election, the first national poll to produce a hung parliament, to December 31, 2020. Detailed information about governments prior to 1989 is provided in the Appendix. Both Table 3.1 and the Appendix Table 3.1A adopt the counting rule for governments used in this volume. Accordingly, a government is considered to have ended, and the new government to start, when one of the following conditions holds: (a) the legislature is dissolved and a new election is held; (b) there is a change of prime minister; (c) there is a change in the party composition of the government; or (d) the majority/minority status of the government changes. Table 3.1 points to an important shift in the nature and stability of minority governments over time. In the first decade of minority governments (1989–99) a change in the prime minister and an early election were the main causes of government change. In the second decade of minority governments (1999–2009), however, the leading cause for government change was a shift in the party composition of the government. As a result, Prime Minister Vajpayee (1999–2004) and Manmohan Singh (2004–09, 2009–14) were able to stay in power for the full duration of their five-year terms, even though the partisan composition of their coalitions changed significantly.

Why minority governments form

The formation of minority governments in India is consistent with several explanations proposed in the literature, particularly those related to the traits of the party system and institutional features, such as negative parliamentarism. However, in India the existence of minority governments may have encouraged the strengthening of parliamentary committees, and not the reverse as Strøm (1990) hypothesized.

First, there is a clear correlation between minority governments and a sudden increase in the degree of *party system fragmentation*. The demise of the Congress Party was followed by a sharp increase in the effective number of parliamentary parties, which lasted between the elections of 1989 and 2014. Indeed, political parties failed to find majority government solutions during this period. As soon as the effective number of parties returned to pre-1989 levels in 2014 and 2019, the general elections also produced a majority winner.

A second important factor that explains Indian minority governments is that they are overwhelmingly rooted in *pre-electoral alliances* (Sridharan 2012) Specifically, minority coalitions were always formed by parties that contested the

Table 3.1 Types of Government, India, 1989–2020

Parliament	Prime Minister	Start date	End date	Government parties	Coalition (yes/no)	Minority (yes/no)	If minority formal or substantive	Support parties if any
9	VP Singh	02–12–1989	10–11–1990	Janata Dal, TDP, Congress (S)	Yes	Yes	substantive	**BJP, Left Front**
9	C Shekhar	10–11–1990	21–06–1991	SJP	No	Yes	substantive	Congress
10	Rao	21–06–1991	16–05–1996	Congress	No	Yes	substantive	—
11	Vajpayee-I	16–05–1996	01–06–1996	BJP, SHS, SAD	Yes	Yes	Substantive	—
11	Gowda	01–06–1996	21–04–1997	Janata Dal, TMC, SP, DMK, TDP, CPI, C(T), AGP, MGP	Yes	Yes	Formal	CPI(M), RSP, AIFB, Congress
11	Gujral	21–04–1997	19–03–1998	Janata Dal, TMC, SP, DMK, TDP, CPI, C(T), AGP, MGP	Yes	Yes	Formal	CPI(M), RSP, AIFB, Congress

Continued

Table 3.1 Continued

Parliament	Prime Minister	Start date	End date	Government parties	Coalition (yes/no)	Minority (yes/no)	If minority formal or substantive	Support parties if any
12	Vajpayee-II	19–03–1998	20–04–1998	BJP, AC, SMT, BJD, PMK, SAD, SHS, AIADMK, LS, AC 2 Independents	Yes	Yes	Formal	NC, TDP, HLD, SDF, MSCP, BSMC, CCF, RJP, **WBTC, HVP, MDMK, 2 Independents**
12	Vajpayee-III	21–04–1998	14–04–1999	BJP, AC, SMT, BJD, PMK, SAD, SHS, AIADMK, LS, AC 1 Independent	Yes	Yes	Formal	NC, TDP, HLD, SDF, MSCP, BSMC, CCF, RJP, **WBTC, HVP, MDMK, 2 Independents**
12	Vajpayee-IV	14–04–1999	13–10–1999	BJP, AC, SMT, BJD, PMK, SAD, SHS, LS, AC 1 Independent	Yes	Yes	Formal	NC, TDP, HLD, SDF, MSCP, BSMC, CCF, RJP, **WBTC, HVP, MDMK, 2 Independents**

13	Vajpayee-V	13–10–1999	05–02–2001	BJP, WBTMC, SHS, SAD, JD(U),DMK, MDMK, NC, MSCP, PMK, BJD, 1 Independent	Yes	Yes	Formal	**TDP, INLD, SDF, HVC, ABLTC, MADMK, IFDP**
13	Vajpayee-VI	05–02–2001	15–03–2001	BJP, WBTMC, SHS, SAD, JD(U), DMK, MDMK, NC, MSCP, BJD, 1 Independent	Yes	Yes	Formal	**TDP, INLD, SDF, HVC, ABLTC, MADMK**
13	Vajpayee-VII	15–03–2001	22–07–2001	BJP, SHS, SAD, JD(U), DMK, MDMK, NC, MSCP, BJD, 1 Independent	Yes	Yes	Formal	**TDP, INLD, SDF, HVC, ABLTC, MADMK**

Continued

Table 3.1 *Continued*

Parliament	Prime Minister	Start date	End date	Government parties	Coalition (yes/no)	Minority (yes/no)	If minority formal or substantive	Support parties if any
13	Vajpayee-VIII	22–07–2001	01–07–2002	BJP, SHS, SAD, JD(U), DMK, MDMK, NC, MSCP, BJD, 1 Independent, RLD	Yes	Yes	Formal	TDP, INLD, SDF, HVC, ABLTC, MADMK
13	Vajpayee-IX	01–07–2002	23–12–2002	BJP, SHS, SAD, JD(U), DMK, MDMK, NC, MSCP, BJD, RLD, PMK	Yes	Yes	Formal	TDP, INLD, SDF, HVC, ABLTC, MADMK, 1 Independent
13	Vajpayee-X	23–12–2002	23–05–2003	BJP, SHS, SAD, JD(U), DMK, MDMK, MSCP, BJD, RLD, PMK	Yes	Yes	Formal	TDP, INLD, SDF, HVC, ABLTC, MADMK, 1 Independent
13	Vajpayee-XI	23–05–2003	08–09–2003	BJP, SHS, SAD, JD(U), DMK, MDMK, MSCP, BJD, PMK, IFDP	Yes	Yes	Formal	TDP, INLD, SDF, HVC, ABLTC, MADMK, 1 Independent

13	Vajpayee-XII	08-09-2003	21-12-2003	BJP, SHS, SAD, JD(U), DMK, MSCP, BJD, PMK, IFDP, WBTMC	Yes	Yes	Formal	TDP, INLD, SDF, HVC, ABLTC, MADMK, 1 Independent
13	Vajpayee-XIII	21-12-2003	30-12-2003	BJP, SHS, SAD, JD(U), MDMK, MSCP, BJD, PMK, IFDP, WBTMC	Yes	Yes	Formal	TDP, INLD, SDF, HVC, ABLTC, MADMK, 1 Independent
13	Vajpayee-XIV	30-12-2003	12-01-2004	BJP, SHS, SAD, JD(U), MSCP, BJD, PMK, IFDP, WBTMC	Yes	Yes	Formal	TDP, INLD, SDF, HVC, ABLTC, MADMK, 1 Independent
13	Vajpayee-XV	12-01-2004	22-05-2004	BJP, SHS, SAD, JD(U), MSCP, BJD, IFDP, WBTMC	Yes	Yes	Formal	TDP, INLD, SDF, HVC, ABLTC, MADMK, 1 Independent
14	M Singh-I	22-05-2004	24-07-2004	INC, NCP, IUML, PMK, DMK, JMM, TRS, LJP, RJD	Yes	Yes	Formal	Left Front, SP, BSP, AIMIM, SDF, JKPDP, MDMK, KC

Continued

Table 3.1 Continued

Parliament	Prime Minister	Start date	End date	Government parties	Coalition (yes/no)	Minority (yes/no)	If minority formal or substantive	Support parties if any
14	M Singh-II	24–07–2004	23–06–2006	INC, NCP, IUML, PMK, DMK, TRS, LJP, RJD	Yes	Yes	Formal	Left Front, SP, BSP, AIMIM, SDF, **JKPDP, MDMK, KC, JMM**
14	M Singh-III	23–06–2006	22–05–2009	INC, NCP, IUML, PMK, DMK, LJP, RJD	Yes	Yes	Formal	Left Front, SP, BSP, AIMIM, SDF, **JKPDP, MDMK, KC, JMM**
15	M Singh-IV	22–05–2009	28–05–2009	INC, WBTMC, NCP	Yes	Yes	Formal	SP, BSP, RJD, JD(S), SDF, NPF, AUDF, JVM(P), BVA, 3 Independents, **JMM, AIMIM, BPF, KC, VCK**
15	M Singh-V	28–05–2009	18–12–2011	INC, WBTC, NCP, DMK, NC, IUML	Yes	Yes	Formal	SP, BSP, RJD, JD(S), SDF, NPF, AUDF, JVM(P), BVA, 3 Independents, **JMM, AIMIM, BPF, KC, VCK**

15	M Singh-VI	18-12-2011	18-09-2011	INC, WBTC, NCP, DMK, NC, IUML, RJD	Yes	Yes	Formal	SP, BSP, JD(S), SDF, NPF, AUDF, JVM(P), BVA, 3 Independents, **JMM, AIMIM, BPF, KC, VCK**
15	M Singh-VII	20-03-2013	18-09-2011	INC, NCP, DMK, NC, IUML, RJD	Yes	Yes	Formal	SP, BSP, JD(S), SDF, NPF, AUDF, JVM(P), BVA, 3 Independents, **JMM, AIMIM, BPF, KC, VCK**
15	M Singh-VIII	26-05-2014	20-03-2013	INC, NCP, NC, IUML, RJD	Yes	Yes	Formal	SP, BSP, JD(S), SDF, NPF, AUDF, JVM(P), BVA, 3 Independents, **JMM, AIMIM, BPF, KC, VCK**
16	Modi-I	05-07-2016	26-05-2014	BJP, LJP, TDP, SHS, SAD, RLSP	Yes	No	—	**PMK, SP, AINRC, NPP, NPF, RPI(A), AD**

Continued

Table 3.1 Continued

Parliament	Prime Minister	Start date	End date	Government parties	Coalition (yes/no)	Minority (yes/no)	If minority formal or substantive	Support parties if any
16	Modi-II	05-07-2016	17-03-2018	BJP, LJP, TDP, SHS, SAD, RLSP, RPI(A), AD	Yes	No	—	**PMK, SP, AINRC, NPP, NPF**
16	Modi-III	17-03-2018	10-12-2018	BJP, LJP, SHS, SAD, RLSP, RPI(A), AD	Yes	No	—	**PMK, SP, AINRC, NPP, NPF**
16	Modi-IV	10-12-2018	30-05-2019	BJP, LJP, SHS, SAD, RPI(A), AD	Yes	No	—	**PMK, SP, AINRC, NPP, NPF**
17	Modi-V	30-05-2019	(11-11-2019)	BJP, SHS, LJP, SAD, RPI(A)	Yes	No	—	**AIADMK, JD(U), AD(S), AJSU, NDPP, RLP, IND.**
18	Modi-VI	11-11-2019	01-01-2020	BJP, LJP, SAD, RPI(A)	Yes	No	—	**AIADMK, SHS JD(U), AD(S), AJSU, NDPP, RLP, IND.**

Notes: Entries in italics indicate parties that join the government as post-election allies. Bold entries indicate pre-electoral allies that chose to stay outside the governments.
Share of minority governments 1952–2020: 64%.
Share of minority governments 1990–2020: 82%.
Source: Kailash (2014), Nikolenyi (2010, 2015), Sridharan (2012) and author's compilation from media reports.

election as pre-electoral allies, although it was not always the case that every member of a pre-electoral alliance would join the government. Such alliances either took the shape of a series of coordinated seat-adjustments, that is, the nomination of jointly supported candidates in the country's single-member electoral districts, among formally independent parties (as in 1989) or a broad institutionalized front that contested the election together under the same banner (e.g. the NDA or the UPA). Pre-electoral alliances facilitated the formation of minority governments in India's rapidly fragmenting party system, as long as none of the competing alliances won a legislative majority, because they encouraged political parties effectively to pre-commit themselves to a specific coalition at the electoral stage already. Although breaking ranks with a pre-electoral alliance was technically possible, it carried the prospect of electoral backlash and, therefore, most parties refrained from doing so.

The interaction between the plurality electoral system and federalism always provided a strong institutional base that conditions the dynamics of party competition in India. On the one hand, the electoral system pushed toward the emergence of two-party or bi-polar party systems in the different parts and regions of the country while, on the other hand, federalism promoted the territorial diversification of this pattern, leading to geographically diverse "multiple bipolarities" (Yadav 1996). In the post-1989 party system, party competition has been structured by competition among pre-electoral alliances that would bring together national and regional, or state-specific, parties with territorially different bases of electoral support. This, in turn, promoted the formation of minority governments because a number of regional and state-based parties often found it more advantageous to remain formally outside the national government while leveraging their membership in the pre-electoral alliance that supported its formation to demand and receive more regional autonomy. As McMillan (2005: 33) notes "a federal electoral system can confound theoretical expectations. The balance between state-specific and national interest can lead to apparently sub-optimal outcomes ... Coalitions may be oversized, and coalition partners may not take part in the direct distribution of ministerial benefits, in return for autonomy ..."

Third, Congress as a large centrally positioned party shaped the patterns of minority governments in a significant way (Nikolenyi 2010). As long as the non-Congress parties did not coordinate against it, Congress was able either to form a government on its own (Prime Minister Rao) or determine which alternative coalition to support from the outside (Prime Ministers Shekhar, Gowda, and Gujral). Congress lost its pivotal role after the 1998 elections when the party system became dominated by the two competing blocs, the NDA and the UPA, headed by the BJP and Congress, respectively.

Fourth, minority governments were also encouraged by negative parliamentarism (Bergman 1993; Nikolenyi 2015; Rasch, Martin, and Cheibub 2015). Even when presidents resorted to calling for votes of confidence in a newly appointed government, these were optional and never required more than the demonstration of a simple relative majority support.

Fifth, the formation of Indian minority governments is also consistent with the argument that attributes such outcomes to the high electoral cost associated with being in government (Strøm 1990). Since 1989, incumbents were re-elected to power on only two occasions: in 1999 and in 2009. Finally, there is some support for Strøm's (1990) proposition, which attributes the formation of minority government to strong legislative committees. In 1989, the Indian Parliament created the first three subject-based standing committees, eventually leading to the creation of a new system of Departmentally-Related Standing Committees (DRSCs) in 1993. The adoption of the new the committee system was the result of Congress Prime Minister Rao's recognition that it was important to provide the opposition with a formalized way to make input into legislation and government oversight. Scholars agree that DRSCs have remained comparatively weak legislative institutions according to most measures of committee strength. These include a large asymmetry between the number of DRSCs and government departments; the lack of a binding committee stage in the legislative process; and an absence of dedicated professional staff and resources (Singh 2010; Singh 2015). Therefore, while there is a temporal co-occurrence between minority governments and the development of relatively stronger systems of legislative committees, the causal arrow actually points in the opposite direction compared to Strøm's proposal, that is, it was the shift to minority governments that led to the adoption of the DRSC system and not vice versa. Also, there is no evidence that these DRSCs can offer the kind of policy and legislative influence that would incentivize potential coalitionable parties to stay outside and exert their influence from the committees.

Minority governments at work: Contract parliamentarism

Over time, Indian minority governments came to rely on an increasingly more formal and institutionalized mechanism of coalition management. By 1999, India seemed to have adopted the model of *contract parliamentarianism*, which was earlier documented only in Western parliamentary democracies (Bale and Bergman 2006). As the Indian party system was becoming more fragmented, these contract institutions played a crucial role not only in binding together the members of India's increasingly more fractured governing coalitions but also in cementing the support of the government's external partners. Indeed, even though coalition minority governments were theoretically considered to be a very unstable form of government, Indian parties managed to use these institutions of coalition governance to keep her fractured minority governments together for gradually longer periods and, eventually, for full, or near-complete, parliamentary terms.

The first minority government (Prime Minister VP Singh) formed after the 1989 elections was based on very general support that the Left Front and the BJP lent to the National Front's electoral manifesto which centered on defeating and replacing the Congress Party in power. Ideologically and policy-wise, the two external supporters of the government were as opposed to each other as they were to letting Congress continue in office. Although the National Front government experimented with the formation of issue-specific cabinet panels to coordinate common positions, the absence of a regular mechanism of consultation between the government and its supporters played an important role in failing to diffuse tension and conflict over the two key issues (job reservation for members of the Other Backward Castes that was championed by the Prime Minister's party and the temple construction movement Ayodhya that was advocated by the BJP) that ultimately led to the BJP withdrawing its support, and the defeat of the government.

The single-party minority government that the centrist Congress formed after the 1991 election managed to stay in office by carefully balancing its ideological rivals on the right and the left. The party was able to secure the support of the BJP for its ambitious economic reform package, which the National Front and Left Front parties opposed, in exchange for tolerating the communal politics of the BJP-run state governments in key states of the north Indian Hindi heartland: Madhya Pradesh, Rajasthan, Himachal Pradesh, and Uttar Pradesh (Malik and Singh 1994: 91). The support that the National and Left Fronts extended to the Congress rested on their shared commitment to secularism, which the rise of the BJP increasingly threatened. The ability of the Rao government to navigate the middle ground between the communal and secular camps in the Lok Sabha was severely challenged in the wake of the violent communal riots at Ayodhya. Yet, given its near-majority size, the government managed to survive by securing the ad hoc support of small parties and engineering defections in the ranks of others before, and often on the days of, key votes in parliament.

The short-lived BJP government that formed after the 1996 elections did not have time to develop any mechanism for governance. In stark contrast, however, the Gowda government, which was the first complex minority coalition government in which regional and state parties played a key role, rested on a network of interconnected institutional mechanisms of coordination that had never been tried before at the national level.[3] This coordination involved three groups of political parties: (a) those members of the United Front that chose to enter the executive coalition; (b) those members of the United Front that chose to stay outside the executive coalition, for example the CPI(M); and (c) the Congress Party that offered carefully negotiated external legislative support to the government. At the core of the management of the Gowda government's coalition stood

---

[3] It is worth mentioning that the two states where coalition politics had been well entrenched since the 1960s (Kerala and West Bengal) served as important models for these national-level experiments.

the Common Minimum Programme (CMP), a document that identified areas of agreement in the election manifestos of the member parties of the United Front. Although the Congress was not a signatory to the CMP, it prepared its own document outlining its support for government policy in areas of "broad national consensus" and its expectation that the new government would continue to pursue policies "which have acquired the imprimatur of history," for example those that were put in place by past Congress governments (Kailash 2007: 315). This document was also taken into account by the CMP which outlined a broad program of government action focusing on political and economic decentralization, secularism and support for minorities, economic redistribution and the encouragement of the small-scale sector of the economy to drive economic growth, employment creation, and import-substitution (*India Today* June 15, 1996: 25).

The United Front parties further established a Steering Committee that was in charge of coordinating the legislative strategies of the Front members. Parties that declined to enter the government formally, most conspicuously the CPI(M), were also given representation and a voice in the Committee's decision-making (*India Today* June 15, 1996: 25; Kailash 2007: 310; Roy 1996: 254). Five months after the formation of the Gowda government, the leaders of the eleven most influential members of the Front formed another coordinating committee, the Standing Committee of the Steering Committee. The two committees met regularly and played a key role in maintaining the cohesion of the coalition. The third and final pillar in the architecture of the management of the Gowda government's coalition was the interaction between the prime minister and the president of the Congress Party. Since the survival of the government fundamentally rested on the legislative support extended by the Congress Party, the personal rapport between the head of government and the Congress president was of utmost importance. The initial positive tone that characterized the relationship between Congress president, and former Prime Minister, Rao and Prime Minister Gowda quickly changed for the worse when the former was replaced by Sitaram Kesri as the new president of the Congress Party.

A key shortcoming of the Gowda government's coalition management was that it remained confined to the national level of party and legislative politics (Kailash 2007: 311). In the context of a federalizing party system where state-level party competition was becoming increasingly more relevant for national dynamics, this proved to be a fatal error. Specifically, the Gowda government was never able to reconcile the contradiction between its own reliance on the support of the Congress Party in the Lok Sabha, while a number of regional and state party members of the United Front, for whom the state party system was much more important than the national party system, were locked in a bipolar competition against the same Congress Party in their respective home states. This contradiction led to the inability of the United Front to support the Congress in key state elections, most notably in Uttar Pradesh, the largest state of the country, in exchange for the latter's legislative support in New Delhi, which ultimately paved the way to the Congress withdrawing its support from the Gowda government.

The successive Vajpayee governments further improved on the coalition management techniques of the United Front coalition in a number of ways. First, similar to the CMP, the BJP and its allies in the NDA also agreed to a common program, known as the National Agenda for Governance (NAG), which formed the basis of their cooperation in the national government and parliament. Second, the NDA also formed a Coordinating Committee (CC), however, learning from the negative lessons of the United Front coalition, this committee was also replicated in the states where the BJP and coalition partners were active. In these state-level committees, the BJP deferred the senior position to its local partner if the latter was in a stronger electoral position. Unlike the United Front Steering Committee, the CC was explicitly used to handle inter-party matters in order to make sure that they would not have a spill-over effect in the national NDA government. Indeed, several state-level political conflicts involving NDA partners were effectively resolved in these state-level CCs with no adverse effect on the national government (Kailash 2007: 316).

Third, on policy issues where consensus was lacking in the NDA, such as the reservation of legislative seats for women, or where the BJP genuinely wanted to build a broad national consensus, such as the improvement of India's subsidized food distribution to the poor, the so-called public distribution system, the prime minister convened all-party meetings in parliament and canvassed for support outside the narrower framework of the coalition and its external supporters. Finally, the Vajpayee government also introduced a new system within the government, the Group of Ministers (GoM), which deepened cooperation within the executive coalition (Arora and Kailash 2018). The GoMs brought together a small number, three to six, government ministers, both senior and junior, to work out a coordinated position on issues before they reached the cabinet. Unlike the more conventional inter-ministerial panels, GoM membership was much more loosely defined and such groups would often include senior bureaucrats but, importantly, also state ministers and even state chief ministers if the issue at hand was particularly important to specific states. This framework helped the BJP use the institution of government to broaden its appeal to a greater number of regional and state parties in an effort to enhance its overall strategy of electoral alliance formation. Moreover, this technique not only insulated the cabinet from potentially explosive issues, which could be resolved in the GoM, but also allowed the smaller regional and state parties to acquire jurisdictional "property rights" over the key issues that mattered to them (Arora and Kailash 2018).

The two UPA minority coalition governments added further layers to these earlier coalition management mechanisms. Unlike the NDA governments, they also had a negotiated support agreement with the four-member Left Front in the Lok Sabha. The Left Front was consulted on the preparation of the UPA's CMP, however, the two blocs also "agreed to disagree" on the government's economic policy and its position on the creation of the new states in the Indian Union. Sticking to its traditional commitment to supporting secular national governments, which meant that the Left Front would primarily want to prevent the BJP from forming another national government, the Left Front pledged that it would not use these areas of contention as a reason to withdraw its support from the government (Kailash 2007: 312). The UPA also created a new body, the National Advisory Committee (NAC), chaired by Congress Party President Sonia Gandhi and tasked to help the government implement the CMP by bringing together social actors and groups in a non-governmental framework for cooperation and coordination. The UPA also continued with the practice of GoM in order to facilitate the active participation of its regional allies in government (Arora and Kailash 2018).

Coordination among the coalition partners and the Left Front took place in a number of arenas. The UPA formed its own Coordination Committee that primarily served the purpose of bringing together the UPA members who took on government portfolios; however, on occasion it also included non-governmental members of the alliance and even the Left Front. The Left Front established its own committee to coordinate the work of its four member parties towards ensuring that the government remained supported. Finally, the UPA government parties and the Left Front set up a brand new mechanism, the UPA Government-Left Coordination Committee (UPLCC), which for the first time in the history of national coalitions provided for the formal consultative framework between the government and its external supporters. Given the initial agreement between the two sides to "disagree" on certain policies and issues, this formal mechanism played a particularly important role to help the government forecast and strategically prepare for votes where it would not be able to count on the legislative support of the Left.

The performance of Indian minority governments

India's minority governments can be clearly divided into two groups based on the size of their support in parliament. On the one hand, Prime Minister Rao's single-party Congress government as well as the last three minority coalitions led by Prime Ministers Vajpyaee (1999–2004) and Manmohan Singh (2004–9 and 2009–14) were near-majority governments. Although the Rao government was a substantive minority government without any pre-negotiated support propping it up from the outside, the latter three were formal minority governments (Strøm 1990) based on a majority-size legislative coalition that included both pre-electoral allies and other parties. The second group is made up of all other minority governments that not only fell much more significantly below the majority mark but also were substantive minority governments. In this section, I demonstrate that the difference in the size of their support made a crucial difference in the performance of the respective minority governments. To evaluate the performance of a minority government, I use indicators of their duration, stability, and law production. Near-majority minority governments outperformed single-party majority governments on all of these indicators. In stark contrast, small minority governments were noticeably less durable, less stable and far weaker in their ability to pass legislation and, as a result, to carry out their program. For the present purposes, minority governments with 40 percent or more of the parliamentary seats under their control are considered near-majority while those with less than 40 percent of the seats are considered small minority governments.

Table 3.2 summarizes the values of these indicators for each of India's twenty-three governments between 1952 and 2019. For the purposes of this table, I do not consider every change in the partisan composition of the government as a new government but rely, instead, on the remaining three indicators of government change: a new election, a change in prime minister; a change in the government's majority/minority status. Doing so shows the tremendous differences that separate near-majority from other minority governments. As mentioned in connection with Table 3.1, several near-majority minority coalitions suffered a large number of changes in their partisan composition without any effect on the survivability of the government and the prime minister in office. If we were to consider the entry or exit of individual coalition partners to constitute a new government then, for example, the first Manmohan Singh government would have to be considered, inaccurately, to be one of the least durable minority governments.

Actual government duration is simply the count of the number of days between the prime minister's entry and his/her exit from office (Woldendorp, Keman, and Budge 1998), while the relative duration of each government is calculated by dividing the actual number of days by the maximum the number of days that the government could have lasted. Relative duration corrects the bias against mid-term governments that is inherent in the measure of actual duration. While we would expect that relative duration should not exceed 1, the Indira Gandhi-3 did exceed it because of the government's invocation of Emergency Rule that extended its normal term.

Table 3.3 groups Indian governments into three categories: majority, near-majority, and small minority governments. The table shows that near-majority governments outperform the other two types on both indicators: on average, they last longer in both actual and relative terms. Evidently, the Gandhi-IV government was the most durable on both counts thanks to the effect of Emergency Rule. Apart from this unusual case, however, it is striking to find that the near-majority M Singh-1 and M Singh-2 governments are actually among the top three most durable in all of India's history. This is *prima facie* evidence that some minority governments, even in the context of an extremely fragmented party system, can last and provide a durable government solution. Conversely, we also find that the

Table 3.2 Government performance, India, 1952–2019

	Government	Government bills introduced (N)	Government bills approved (N)	Government bills approved (%)	Days in office	Relative duration (ratio)
1	Nehru-1	351	160	45.6	1800	0.98
2	Nehru-2	330	312	94.5	1810	0.99
3	Nehru-3	153	132	86.3	787	0.43
4	Shastri	101	85	84.2	581	0.57
5	I Gandhi-1	65	42	64.6	413	0.96
6	I Gandhi-2	195	153	78.5	1466	0.80
7	*I Gandhi-3*	*194*	*173*	*89.2*	*2198*	*1.20*
8	Desai	178	128	71.9	856	0.47
9	*C Singh*	*0*	*0*	*0.0*	*170*	*0.18*
10	I Gandhi-4	339	309	91.2	1752	0.96
11	R Gandhi-1	0	0	0.0	61	0.81
12	R Gandhi-2	355	308	86.8	1797	0.98
13	*VP Singh*	*66*	*34*	*51.5*	*343*	*0.19*
14	*Shekhar*	*29*	*24*	*82.8*	*223*	*0.15*
15	Rao	344	272	79.1	1791	0.98
16	*Vajpayee-1*	*0*	*0*	*0.0*	*16*	*0.01*
17	*Gowda*	*59*	*46*	*78.0*	*109*	*0.06*
18	*Gujral*	*34*	*16*	*47.1*	*332*	*0.22*
19	*Vajpayee-2*	*88*	*65*	*73.9*	*573*	*0.31*
20	*Vajpayee-3*	*293*	*211*	*72.0*	*1681*	*0.92*
21	*M Singh-1*	*307*	*238*	*77.5*	*1826*	*1.00*
22	*M Singh-2*	*291*	*179*	*61.5*	*1830*	*1.00*
23	Modi-1	237	166	70.0	1830	1.00

Note: Minority governments are indicated in bold italics.

MINORITY GOVERNMENTS IN INDIA   61

Table 3.3 Actual and relative duration by government type, India, 1952–2019

	Average actual duration (in days)	Average relative duration
All governments (N=23)	1054.1	0.66
Majority governments (N=12)	12,795.5	0.84
Near-majority governments (N=4)	1782	0.97
Small minority governments (N=7)	252.3	0.16

Table 3.4 Law production by government type, India, 1952–2019

	Average number of government bills introduced	Average number of government bills passed	Percentage passed
All governments (N=23)	174.3	132.7	64.6
Majority governments (N=12)	208.2 (227)	164 (178.9)	71.9 (78.4)
Near-majority governments (N=4)	308.7	225	72.5
Small minority governments (N=7)	39.4 (55.2)	26.4 (37)	47.6 (66.7)

seven small minority governments, all of which were also substantive minority governments, are the seven least durable governments of all.

These findings have important implications for Strøm's distinction between formal and substantive minority governments. The Indian data show that substantive minority governments are much less durable than formal minority governments, unless they are formed by the ideologically centrist party, that is, Congress (Gandhi-III and Rao). Furthermore, the durability of a formal minority government is strongly affected by the size of the governing coalition, and hence its vulnerability: minority governments that are both formal and close to the majority threshold are more durable than narrowly-based formal minority governments.

Table 3.4 provides summary information about the record of law production by India's governments. Once again, near-majority governments outperform both majority and small minority governments not only by introducing but also by passing more government bills. The numbers in brackets indicate values that are obtained by excluding from the relevant categories the three short-lived governments (C Singh, R Gandhi-1, Vajpayee-1) that did not have time to submit a single bill.

The finding that India's near-majority governments had the best performance in terms of duration and law production is consistent with an important line of the theoretical work in the literature on minority and coalition governments that stresses the power of a centrally positioned party. The centrist Congress Party (Rao, M Singh-1, 2) formed and led three of the four near-majority governments. As we saw in the previous section, its centrist position allowed Congress either to make ad hoc deals with parties to its left and to its right (as it did during the Rao government) or to enter into a pre-negotiated support framework with the Left parties (M Singh-1, 2). The fourth case (Vajpayee-3) was different in that the BJP was able to form and sustain a near-majority government in spite of its extreme ideological position because it could exploit the unique legislative dynamics generated by the pivotal presence of regional and state parties. As Sridharan (2012) notes, several parties that remained outside the executive coalition were actually locked-in to support the Vajpayee-3 government because of their competitive relationship vis-à-vis the main national opposition party (Congress) in their home states.

Conclusion

A key finding of this chapter is that the formation and performance of Indian minority governments are consistent with the predictions of several comparative theories. Similar to other adversarial Westminster democracies, minority governments formed in India when elections failed to produce a clear winner. However, unlike other Westminster cases, most minority governments were formed by multiparty coalitions that were often rooted in the pre-electoral alliances that parties forged under the conditions of a federalizing party system. Another important comparative lesson that emerges from the Indian data is the importance of a strong centrally positioned party. Congress is the party with the unique capability to form a stable minority government without any pre-negotiated legislative support coalition or any formal executive coalition partners, and the only one that can have the potential to determine the viability of other coalitions of which it is not a part.

Finally, the Indian case also shows that minority governments have provided important opportunities for the development of contract parliamentarism. Through careful institution building, Indian parties mastered the art of coalition governance, in spite of a very high degree of party system fragmentation, and build minority coalitions that have proven to be more effective both in terms of survival in office and implementation of their program than majority party governments have been. The general elections of 2014 and 2019 seemed to have ended the era of minority governments. Yet, the fact that the majority party opted to form surplus-majority coalitions with its regional electoral allies and that it still continues to employ mechanisms of coalition governance that were developed in the previous decades of minority government rule suggests that the legacy of the minority government may be quite durable and lasting still.

References

Arora, Balveer. 2003. "Federalisation of India's Party System." In *Political Parties and Party Systems*, ed. Ajay K. Mehra, D. D. Khanna, and Gert W. Kueck, 83–99. New Delhi: SAGE Publications.

Arora, Balveer, and K. K. Kailash. 2018. "Political Innovation in the Working of Indian Democracy: A Study of the Group of Ministers Device (1999–2014)." In *Exploring Indian Modernities*, ed. Leila Choukroune and Parul Bhandari, 81–106. Singapore: Springer.

Bale, Tim, and Torbjörn Bergman. 2006. "Captives No Longer, but Servants Still? Contract Parliamentarism and the New Minority Governance in Sweden and New Zealand." *Government and Opposition* 41 (3): 422–449.

Bergman, Torbjörn. 1993. "Formation Rules and Minority Governments." *European Journal of Political Research* 23 (1): 55–66.

Crombez, Chrisophe. 1996. "Minority Governments, Minimal Winning Coalitions and Surplus Majorities in Parliamentary Systems." *European Journal of Political Research* 29 (1): 1–29.

Deemen van, Ad. 1989. "Dominant Players and Minimum Size Coalitions." *European Journal of Political Research* 17 (3): 313–332.

Deemen van, Ad. 1991. "Coalition Formation and Centralized Policy Games." *Journal of Theoretical Politics* 3 (2): 139–162.

Dodd, Lawrence. C. 1974. "Party Coalitions in Multiparty Parliaments: A Game Theoretic Analysis." *American Political Science Review* 68 (3): 1093–1117.

Dodd, Lawrence. C. 1976. *Coalitions in Parliamentary Government*. Princeton: Princeton University Press.

Field, Bonnie N. (2009) "Minority Government and Legislative Politics in a Multilevel State: Spain under Zapatero." *South European Society and Politics* 14 (4): 417–434.

Field, Bonnie N. (2014) "Minority Parliamentary Government and Multilevel Politics: Spain's System of Mutual Back Scratching." *Comparative Politics* 46 (3): 292–312.

Herman, Valentine, and John Pope. 1973. "Minority Governments in Western Democracies." *British Journal of Political Science* 3 (2): 191–212.

Kailash, K. K. 2007. "Middle Game in Coalition Politics." *Economic and Political Weekly* 42 (4): 307–317.

Kailash, K.K. 2014. "Institutionalizing a Coalitional System and Games within Coalitions in India (1996–2014)." *Studies in Indian Politics* 2 (2): 185–202.

Malik, Yogendra K. and V. B. Singh. 1994. *Hindu Nationalists in Isndia: The Rise of the Bharatiya Janata Party*. New Delhi: Vistaar Publications.

McMillan, Alistair. 2005. "The BJP Coalition: Partisanship and Power-Sharing in Government." In *Coalition Politics and Hindu Nationalism*, ed. Katherine Adeney and Lawrence Sàez, 13–36. London: Routledge.

Nikolenyi, Csaba. 1998. "The New Indian Party System: What Kind of a Model?" *Party Politics* 4 (3): 367–380.

Nikolenyi, Csaba. 2010. *Minority Governments in India: The Puzzle of Elusive Majorities*. London: Routledge.

Nikolenyi, Csaba. 2015. "Government Investiture in India: Formal Rules and Informal Practices." In *Parliaments and Government Formation: Unpacking Investiture Rules*, ed. Bjorn-Erik Rasch, Shane Martin, and Jose Cheibub, 275–292. Oxford: Oxford University Press.

Rasch, Bjørn Erik, Shane Martin, and Cheibub José Antônio, eds. 2015. *Parliaments and Government Formation : Unpacking Investiture Rules*. Oxford: Oxford University Press.
Roozendaal van, Peter. 1992a. "The Effect of Dominant and Central Parties on Cabinet Composition and Durability." *Legislative Studies Quarterly* 17 (1): 5–35.
Roozendaal van, Peter. 1992b. *Cabinets in Multi-Party Democracies: The Effect of Dominant and Central Parties on Cabinet Composition and Durability*. Amsterdam: Thesis Publishers.
Roy, M. 1996. *India Votes: Elections 1996*. New Delhi: Deep and Deep Publications
Schakel, Arjan H., Chanchal Kumar Sharma, and Wilfried Swenden. 2019. "India after the 2014 General Elections: BJP Dominance and the Crisis of the Third Party System." *Regional and Federal Studies* 29 (3): 329–354.
Singh, Devender. 2010. "Of Laws and Law Making in India." *Indian Journal of Public Administration* 56 (2): 271–284.
Singh, Mahendra Prasad. 2015. "The Decline of the Indian Parliament." *India Review* 14 (3): 352–376.
Sridharan, E. 2012. "Why Are Multi-Party Minority Governments Viable in India? Theory and Comparison." *Commonwealth and Comparative Politics* 50 (3): 314–343.
Strøm, Kaare. 1990. *Minority Government and Majority Rule*, New York: Cambridge University Press.
Taylor, Michael, and Michael Laver. 1973. "Government Coalitions in Western Europe." *European Journal of Political Research* 1 (3): 205–248.
Woldendorp, Jaan, Hans Keman, and Ian Budge. 1998. "Party Government in 20 Democracies: An Update (1990–1995)." *European Journal of Political Research* 33 (1): 125–164.
Yadav, Yogendra. 1996. "Reconfiguration in Indian Politics: State Assembly Elections, 1993–95." *Economic and Political Weekly* 31 (2–3): 94–105.

Appendix

Table 3.1A Types of Government, India, 1952–1989

Parliament	Prime Minister	Start date	End date	Government parties	Coalition (yes/no)	Minority (yes/no)	If minority formal or substantive	Support parties if any
1	Nehru-I	13–05–1952	17–04–1957	Congress	No	No	—	—
2	Nehru-II	17–04–1957	01–04–1962	Congress	No	No	—	—
3	Nehru-III	01–04–1962	27–04–1964	Congress	No	No	—	—
3	Shastri	09–06–1964	11–01–1966	Congress	No	No	—	—
3	I Gandhi-I	24–01–1966	13–03–1967	Congress	No	No	—	—
4	I Gandhi-II	13–03–1967	16–11–1969	Congress	No	No	—	—
4	I Gandhi-III	16–11–1969	18–03–1971	Congress (R)	No	Yes	substantive	PSP, CPI, CPI(M)
5	I Gandhi-IV	18–03–1971	24–03–1977	Congress	No	No	—	—
6	Desai	24–03–1977	28–07–1979	Janata Party, SAD	No	No	—	—
6	C Singh	28–07–1979	14–01–1980	Janata Party (S), AIADMK	Yes	Yes	substantive	Congress
7	I Gandhi-V	14–01–1980	31–10–1984	Congress	No	No	—	—
7	R Gandhi-I	31–10–1984	31–12–1984	Congress	No	No	—	—
8	R Gandhi-II	31–12–1984	02–12–1989	Congress	No	No	—	—

Notes: See Table 3.1.

4
Norway
A Land of Minority Governments

Kaare W. Strøm

Ever since national independence was gained in 1905, Norway has been a land of minority governments, with one of the highest incidences of such cabinets in the world of parliamentary democracies. Over the entire post-1945 period, close to two-thirds of all cabinets have lacked a parliamentary majority. Since the Labor Party lost its majority in 1961, the proportion of minority cabinets has been even higher. Indeed, there have been only two periods of sustained (meaning a full parliamentary term or more) majority government: 1965–71, under Per Borten's broad non-socialist coalition, and 2005–13, under Jens Stoltenberg's "red-green" coalition of the Labor Party, the Center Party, and the Socialist Left.

This chapter examines Norway's high incidence of minority governments and shows that it reflects several characteristics of Norwegian politics. A permissive institutional setting provides the opportunity to form viable minority governments. A highly electorally competitive pattern of two-bloc politics has constrained coalition bargaining and motivated parties to eschew coalitions with uncomfortable partners. And a stable, inclusive, and prosperous society characterized by high levels of interpersonal trust has allowed party leaders to take longer-term views of their political interests and avoid more conflictual forms of political contestation. This "low-key" version of parliamentary democracy has allowed outwardly vulnerable cabinets to sustain themselves in office and build a reasonable record of policy accomplishment.

The cabinet record

Norway has seen a succession of different governments, but their most striking characteristic has been that so many of them have lacked a parliamentary majority. Out of thirty-six post-World War II governments through 2020, twenty-three have been minority cabinets. Only thirteen cabinets, or just over one-third, have thus included parties controlling a majority of the seats in the *Storting* (the Norwegian Parliament). Over the same period, Norwegian cabinets have broken down almost equally between coalitions and single-party formats: there have been nineteen

Kaare W. Strøm, *Norway*. In: *Minority Governments in Comparative Perspective*. Edited by Bonnie N. Field and Shane Martin, Oxford University Press. © Kaare W. Strøm (2022). DOI: 10.1093/oso/9780192871657.003.0004

Table 4.1 Types of government, Norway, 1945–2020

No.	Prime Minister	Assumed office	Cabinet parties	Parlia-mentary seats	Cabinet type	Support parties
1	Gerhardsen I	25-06-1945	A, H, V, SP, KRF	147/150	Surplus majority coalition	
2	Gerhardsen II	05-11-1945	A	76/150	Majority single-party	
3	Gerhardsen III	10-10-1949	A	85/150	Majority single-party	
4	Torp I	19-11-1951	A	85/150	Majority single-party	
5	Torp II	12-10-1953	A	77/150	Majority single-party	
6	Gerhardsen IV	22-01-1955	A	77/150	Majority single-party	
7	Gerhardsen V	07-10-1957	A	78/150	Majority single-party	
8	Gerhardsen VI	11-09-1961	A	74/150	Minority single-party	
9	Lyng	28-08-1963	H, SP, V	74/150	Minority coalition	
10	Gerhardsen VII	25-09-1963	A	74/150	Minority single-party	
11	Borten I	12-10-1965	SP, H, KRF, V	80/150	Minimum winning coalition	
12	Borten II	07-09-1969	SP, H, KRF, V	76/150	Minimum winning coalition	
13	Bratteli I	17-03-1971	A	74/150	Minority single-party	
14	Korvald	18-10-1972	KRF, SP, V	39/150	Minority coalition	
15	Bratteli II	16-10-1973	A	62/155	Minority single-party	
16	Nordli I	15-01-1976	A	62/155	Minority single-party	
17	Nordli II	11-09-1977	A	76/155	Minority single-party	
18	Brundtland I	04-02-1981	A	76/155	Minority single-party	

Continued

Table 4.1 Continued

No.	Prime Minister	Assumed office	Cabinet parties	Parlia-mentary seats	Cabinet type	Support parties
19	Willoch I	14-10-1981	H	53/155	Formal minority single-party	KRF, SP
20	Willoch II	08-06-1983	H, KRF, SP	79/155	Minimum winning coalition	
21	Willoch III	09-09-1985	H, KRF, SP	78/157	Minority coalition	
22	Brundtland II	09-05-1986	A	71/157	Minority single-party	
23	Syse	16-10-1989	H, KRF, SP	62/165	Minority coalition	
24	Brundtland III	03-11-1990	A	63/165	Minority single-party	
25	Brundtland IV	13-09-1993	A	67/165	Minority single-party	
26	Jagland	25-10-1996	A	67/165	Minority single-party	
27	Bondevik I	17-10-1997	KRF, SP, V	41/165	Minority coalition	
28	Stoltenberg I	17-03-2000	A	65/165	Minority single-party	
29	Bondevik II	19-10-2001	KRF, H, V	62/165	Minority coalition	
30	Stoltenberg II	17-10-2005	A, SP, SV	87/169	Minimum winning coalition	
31	Stoltenberg III	14-09-2009	A, SP, SV	86/169	Minimum winning coalition	
32	Solberg I	16-10-2013	H, FRP	77/169	Formal minority coalition	KRF, V
33	Solberg II	11-09-2017	H, FRP	72/169	Formal minority coalition	KRF, V
34	Solberg III	18-01-2018	H, FRP, V	80/169	Formal minority coalition	KRF
35	Solberg IV	22-01-2019	H, FRP, V, KRF	88/169	Minimum winning coalition	
36	Solberg V	24-01-2020	H, V, KRF	61/169	Minority coalition	

Notes: Party of Prime Minister listed first.
Share of minority governments 1945–2020: 64%.
Share of minority governments 1990–2020: 78%.
Party abbreviations:
A: Labor Party; FRP: Progress Party; H: Conservatives; KRF: Christian Democrats; SP: Center Party; SV: Left Socialists; V: Liberals.

Table 4.2 Norwegian cabinets by composition and majority status, 1945–2020

	Minority governments	Minimum winning governments	Surplus majority governments	Sum
Single-party governments	13 (36%) 36% of time	6 (17%) 21% of time	Not applicable	**19 (53%)** 57% of time
Coalition governments	10 (28%) 20% of time	6 (17%) 22% of time	1 (3%) 0.4% of time	**17 (47%)** 43% of time
Sum	**23 (64%)** 56% of time	**12 (33%)** 44% of time	**1 (3%)** 0.4% of time	**36 (100%)**

Note: As of December 31, 2020.
Sources: Rasch and Strøm (2019); regjeringen.no; Björnberg (1939).

single-party administrations and seventeen coalitions (see Table 4.1). Minority governments have similarly been divided between coalitions (10) and single-party administrations (13).

Table 4.2 summarizes the Norwegian cabinet record since 1945. As the table demonstrates, minority governments constitute just under two-thirds of all Norwegian cabinets over that period and an even larger share of those in power since 1990 (78 percent). Measured as a proportion of time, the overall post-war share is slightly lower, but still well above half (56 percent). Among minority cabinets, single-party administrations outnumber coalitions almost exactly two to one, whether measured in pure numbers or proportion of time in office. Moreover, since 1945 Norway has had only one surplus majority coalition: a grand coalition of national reconstruction in office only from the end of World War II hostilities in Norway until the first post-war elections. Whereas the international literature traditionally portrayed minority governments as crisis solutions (e.g. von Beyme 1970), in Norway it is thus surplus majority coalitions that have formed in such circumstances, whereas minority governments reflect more relaxed political times.

Why minority governments form

Though lower than in neighboring Denmark, the incidence of minority governments in Norway is among the highest in the world's parliamentary democracies (and higher than in the other Nordic countries). How can we explain this record? One facilitating condition lies in a permissive institutional environment. More specifically, the Norwegian Constitution, statutes, and conventions regarding cabinet formation are unrestrictive, and they contain no provisions that by design or accident generate hurdles or disincentives for minority cabinet formation. A second causal factor has to do with the party system, which since 1945 has exhibited a pronounced two-bloc format, and in which electoral competition between the two blocs has become increasingly sharp. The rigidity of two-bloc politics has rendered the construction of cross-bloc majorities difficult, and intensifying electoral competition with escalating incumbency losses has made party leaders wary of coalitions with partners that might demand costly policy compromises. Finally, the high interpersonal trust of Norwegian political culture and its commitment to consensus solutions has made policy influence available even to opposition parties and limited any concern about majority tyranny. In the following sections, we shall expand on each of these causes.

The institutional setting

Like all major Western European states except Switzerland, Norway is a parliamentary democracy, whose constitutional chain of governance is comparatively simple. Under the Constitution (Article 49), all legislative authority is vested in Parliament: "The people exercise the Legislative Power through the Storting." Norway also conforms to the ideal type of Westminster parliamentarism in the sense that Members of Parliament (the *Storting*) are the only national agents directly elected by the people. Around the 1950s, Norway also came very close to the Westminster model in the sense of having a singular chain of democratic delegation, running through Parliament and controlled by political parties (see Strøm 2000).

Yet, Norway is a peculiar parliamentary democracy. Much of this peculiarity has to do with the Norwegian Constitution of 1814, the oldest codified constitution of any contemporary parliamentary regime. The 1814 Constitution was written before the evolution of many modern parliamentary institutions, notably concerning the powers and responsibilities of the cabinet. Dating back to the end of the Napoleonic Wars, the 1814 Constitution was born in a spirit of nationalism, egalitarianism, and Madisonianism. James Madison was president of the United States in 1814, and although he did not personally influence the drafting of the Norwegian Constitution, his ideas and the American example certainly did. The 1814 Constitution was Madisonian in its commitment to separation of powers and limited government. It contained a multitude of checks and balances and gave no recognition to political parties.[1] Also, its provisions concerning legislative powers and operations were effectively a carbon copy of those that Madison had written into the American Constitution.

The Norwegian cabinet is still officially known as the King's Council, and the Constitution gives the monarch broad formal discretion to appoint its members. In practice, however, the King always follows the advice of the leaders of the parliamentary parties. There is no provision for a *formateur* and no constitutional

---

[1] Yet, the Norwegian Constitution departed from Madison's legacy in rejecting religious liberties, federalism, and bicameralism.

regulation of the formation process.[2] The use of *informateurs* similarly has no codified place in the Norwegian Constitution and has occurred only once since 1945.[3] Because of this absence of formal rules and *formateur* provisions, Norwegian government formation is best described as "free-style bargaining." Such free-style bargaining has left ample room for minority solutions.

In practice, the choice of a prime minister has rarely been difficult. And the initial attempt at cabinet formation has rarely been inconclusive.[4] Bargaining over cabinet formation deals mainly with policy, and much less time is spent on portfolio allocation, other offices, or governance mechanisms. When the red-green coalition parties negotiated the Soria Moria agreement in 2005,[5] for instance, only the party leaders were involved in portfolio allocation negotiations, while in the center-right Sundvolden negotiations in 2013, portfolio issues were discussed mainly after the policy document had been agreed upon.

A defining characteristic of parliamentary democracy is ministerial responsibility, or the parliamentary majority's power to censure and dismiss cabinet members for virtually any reason. In Norway, the cabinet's accountability to the parliamentary majority dates back to 1884, when the Liberal Party gained control of Parliament and impeached the members of the incumbent cabinet, who had been appointed by the king. Norway thus became the first Nordic country to adopt parliamentary democracy, although a government's obligation to step down in the event of a parliamentary vote of no confidence was not firmly accepted until Norway seceded from the dual monarchy in 1905 (Nordby 2000). Though variously amended, however, the Constitution was not revised to formally acknowledge ministerial responsibility. It was only in anticipation of the constitutional bicentennial of 2014 that Parliament launched a project to revise the Constitution and update its formal provisions to conform to conventions that had evolved since the 1880s. Thus, since 2007 the new Article 15 (Constitutional Amendment No. 364) has formally required cabinet members to resign in the event of a successful parliamentary no-confidence vote.

Yet, minority cabinets could still survive in office if their opposition is divided and unable to agree on a joint motion of no confidence. Moreover, unlike, for example, Germany, Spain, or Poland, Norway does not have a constructive vote

---

[2] Note also that an outgoing Norwegian cabinet does not resign until the next administration is ready. Resignation and installation thus happen in a single day, and there is no interregnum or caretaker cabinet.

[3] In 1971, when a bourgeois majority coalition had just broken down over the European Community issue, Storting President Bernt Ingvaldsen, a Conservative, was asked to explore the feasibility of another non-socialist coalition. Ingvaldsen's role was purely that of an *informateur*.

[4] One exception is the bargaining in 2001 that led to Kjell Magne Bondevik's second government, when negotiations initially broke down over the prime ministership. After a break in the negotiations, however, the coalition parties agreed that the Christian Democrat Party would get the PM, while as "compensation" the Conservatives, as the largest party, would get *both* Finance and Foreign Affairs.

[5] As is customary with such accords in Norwegian politics, this agreement was named after the conference center in which it was negotiated.

of no confidence. This facilitates the formation of minority governments, since the bar for forming a constitutional government has been set lower than in other parliamentary regimes (Bergman 1993).

Norway is also unique among European parliamentary regimes in having fixed parliamentary terms. The Storting is elected every four years on the second Monday of September, and there is no constitutional provision for its early dissolution. This lack of an electoral safety valve has facilitated the survival of minority cabinets when otherwise early elections might have seemed a preferred alternative. In the process of updating the Constitution in the early 2000s, one reform proposal that was debated but ultimately rejected would have introduced a mechanism of parliamentary dissolution. The Norwegian Constitution is thus in several ways permissive, in the sense of facilitating minority government formation and survival.

The party system and two-bloc politics

A second factor facilitating minority governments in Norway is the two-bloc format of its party system, a feature long shared with neighboring Sweden and Denmark. But two-bloc politics is definitively also party politics. Independents and non-partisans have been rare among members of parliament and virtually non-existent in the cabinet. Norwegian parties date back to the 1880s and the divisive constitutional debates that gave rise to the mobilization of Liberals vs. Conservatives. Liberals represented the egalitarianism and nationalism of the Constitution, Conservatives its Madisonianism. Bipartism quickly faded, however, as the Norwegian Labor Party rapidly grew to be a dominant party between the early 1900s and the 1920s. With the adoption after World War I of proportional representation, an Agrarian (later Center) Party gained parliamentary representation, along with a splinter Labor Party faction which became the Norwegian Communist Party (NKP). The NKP rapidly lost support from the 1950s on and eventually merged into the Socialist Left Party. A Christian Democrat Party emerged on the national scene after World War II.

Whereas from the 1920s to the early 1970s the Norwegian party system was one of the most stable in Western Europe, it has since fragmented and destabilized. In 1961, a left-wing splinter group broke off from the Labor Party and formed the Socialist People's Party, which in 1975 merged with other left-leaning (and anti-EU) forces to form the Socialist Left. In 1973, a populist right-wing party which eventually became the Progress Party formed in protest against high taxes and public expenditures.[6] The same year saw the formation of a small extreme-left Marxist-Leninist party, currently known as the Red Party. Finally, a Green (Environmentalist) party (MDG) was founded in 1988, but did not gain parliamentary representation until 2013.

---

[6] The Progress Party was originally Anders Lange's Party, named after its founder.

The Norwegian party system was defined around political cleavages rooted in economic, geographical, and cultural circumstances (see Rokkan 1967 and 1970; Valen and Rokkan 1974). The major division, however, has traditionally run along a left–right axis between socialists and non-socialists. Roughly from left to right the present parliamentary parties are: the Red Party (*Rødt*, R), the Socialist Left (*Sosialistisk Venstreparti*, SV), the Labor Party (*Arbeiderpartiet*, A or DNA), the Greens (*Miljøpartiet de grønne*, MDG), the Center Party (*Senterpartiet*, SP), the Christian Democrat Party (*Kristelig Folkeparti*, KRF), the Liberals (*Venstre*, V), the Conservatives (*Høyre*, H), and the Progress Party (*Fremskrittspartiet*, FRP). The first three are clearly identified with the center-left bloc, whereas the last four are conventionally considered to constitute the center-right bloc. The Center Party was until the 1990s part of the center-right bloc, whereas Greens have not yet played any role in national coalition politics.

Norwegian cabinets have been roughly equally divided between socialist (or center-left) and non-socialist (or center-right) cabinets: there have been eighteen socialist administrations, fifteen non-socialist ones, and only three that have straddled the divide. Between 1945 and 2005 all Norwegian cabinets could be clearly identified as either socialist or non-socialist. For a long time the Norwegian Labor Party was the only major social democratic party in Western Europe never to have governed with any non-socialist party.[7] From 1945 until 1961, Labor was predominant and won four consecutive parliamentary majorities. However, the 1961 emergence of the Socialist People's Party eroded Labor's support, while the non-socialist parties gained in strength and cohesion. Labor also eschewed coalitions with any party to its left and all its cabinets between 1961 and 2005 were therefore single-party minority governments. From the early 1960s until the early 2000s, center-right coalitions alternated with Labor governments. However, the latter party's massive 2001 electoral losses provoked a policy change. After the general election of 2005, Labor joined the Center Party and the Socialist Left in the first majority cabinet since 1985—a "red-green" coalition that straddled the socialist–non-socialist divide. Since 2005, it is therefore more appropriate to label the two competing blocs center-left and center-right, respectively.

Center-right cabinets have tended to be coalitions, and twelve of fifteen have included at least three parties. There have been three types of non-socialist governments: broad center-right coalitions, center-right coalitions excluding one or more of the centrist parties (the Center Party, the Liberals, and the Christian Democrats), and two centrist coalitions consisting of the latter three parties but not the Conservatives. Both of the latter (Korvald and Bondevik I) formed

---

[7] The exception here was a short-term grand coalition (Gerhardsen I) led by the Labor Party from the end of hostilities in Norway in May 1945 until after the first post-war elections in September the same year.

when dissent over European integration precluded coalescence between Conservatives and the other non-socialist parties, and specifically the Center Party (see Rommetvedt 1984).

Two-bloc politics has been a critical factor shaping cabinet politics in Norway and contributed to the high rate of minority governments. Until the 1990s especially, the blocs were extremely evenly balanced. Most elections saw a close contest between the two blocs, and the result was frequent alternation between them, such as in 1963 (twice), 1965, 1971, 1972, 1973, 1981, 1986, 1989, 1990, 1997, 2000, 2001, 2005, and 2013. Since the 1990s, the center-right has gradually gained ground over the center-left. At the same time, however, the center-right bloc has become less cohesive, and the Center Party has abandoned the center-right in favor of the center-left.

Due to the two-bloc format, party cohesiveness, and transparency of Norwegian coalition politics, coalition bargaining rounds have failed on only four occasions, including both of the two most recent parliamentary elections (2013 and 2017) prior to 2020. Conservative PM Erna Solberg had a strong wish, in 2013 as well as in 2017, to build a four-party coalition with the Progress Party, the Christian Democrats, and the Liberals. In 2013, the two latter parties pulled out simultaneously after the initial talks, but signed a comprehensive support agreement with the coalition parties. The negotiations following the 2017 election were by far the longest in history, lasting 128 days. Once again, the four-party coalition that the PM wanted proved impossible, mainly because the Christian Democrat leader, Knut Arild Hareide, had committed his party not to govern with the Progress Party. Early in 2019, Solberg finally succeeded in uniting the Conservatives, the Liberals, the Progress Party, and the Christian Democrat Party, in a majority, center-right coalition. The four-party majority coalition that formed lasted only a year, however, as the Progress Party decided to go into opposition in January 2020.

Two other important policy dimensions in Norwegian politics are correlated: the urban–rural dimension and the center–periphery axis. Thus, the parties that most favor rural interests are also the strongest defenders of the peripheries, and vice versa. The Progress Party has traditionally been the most pro-urban party and the Center Party the most pro-rural one. The Conservatives are fairly close to the Progress Party, whereas the Christian Democrat Party tends to be pro-rural. The other parties, including Labor, hold more centrist positions on this dimension (see e.g. Valen and Narud 2007a). Thus, the parties in the center-right camp, who are neighbors on the left–right axis, are highly polarized along the urban–rural dimension. This dimension is therefore particularly inimical to center-right cooperation.

These dimensions were mobilized most dramatically during the European Community/European Union (EU) campaigns in the early 1970s and again in the 1990s. On these occasions, the established two-bloc politics weakened. Indeed, disagreement on the urban–rural dimension has led to the termination of two coalitions and facilitated the formation of Norway's numerically weakest minority government, headed by Lars Korvald and supported by only 47 out of 150 parliamentarians (Narud 1995). It has also caused great internal strain in the Labor Party and among the Liberals. The urban–rural policy dimension can be powerfully mobilized even when no EU issue is on the agenda, as in 2017 when the Center Party almost doubled its vote share, largely due to rural resistance to the government's efforts to merge many small Norwegian municipalities and reduce the number of provinces from nineteen to eleven.

The most dramatic party system changes since the 1990s have been the rise and subsequent decline of the two most prominent "flank" parties: the Progress Party and the Socialist Left. Long considered fringe parties with little governing potential, both parties have entered coalition governments in the 2000s: the Socialist Left from 2005 to 2013 and the Progress Party from 2013 to 2020. Another striking development is the rise of electoral volatility—voters changing parties between elections. Through the 1960s Norway had one of the most stable electorates in Western Europe, with gross volatility rates of 15 to 25 percent. From the early 1970s, however, about one out of three voters began changing parties from one election to the next. In 1993, volatility reached almost 44 percent, a proportion that has since remained virtually unchanged. In addition, the number of "late deciders" has increased substantially. In 1997 and 2001, about half of all voters reported deciding which party to support during the election campaign itself (Aardal 2007). While this number has since declined, it remains much higher than it was until the late 1980s.

These trends have contributed to a highly competitive party system, in which incumbency in executive office has carried a high price. Parties holding cabinet office have tended to lose large vote shares at subsequent elections. These setbacks have been particularly high for broad coalition governments and rising over time. The rigidity of the coalition options (at least until the twenty-first century) and the highly competitive elections have imposed costs on governing parties and particularly on broad coalitions. Herein lies part of the explanation of Norwegian minority cabinets: the net costs of gaining executive office can be high, and at times these costs outweigh the short-term benefits of being in office.

A consensus culture

A third factor that has facilitated minority governments in Norway is the country's culture of consensus and inclusiveness. These features of Norwegian, and broadly Scandinavian, politics have been widely recognized (e.g. Arter 2016). They foster minority government by lessening the importance that politicians place on holding executive office, since political adversaries are trusted not to abuse their power. The parties have little to fear by remaining in opposition and tolerating minority governments—the political environment is largely benign and opposition parties generally do not have to fear harassment or government power grabs (Strøm and Leipart 1993).

Consensualism has cultural foundations but is also and importantly reflected in political institutions and their operations. Like other Scandinavian countries, Norway is characterized by high levels of interpersonal trust. It is also a country in which confidence in various political institutions is among the highest in the world. These characteristics of Nordic societies are commonly associated with their traditionally close-knit communities, their cultural homogeneity (for example, the virtual absence until recent times of racial or religious divisions), their lack of feudal traditions, and also with the fragility of social communities under near-Arctic conditions and the social interdependence it generates.

In the Norwegian parliamentary arena, this is interestingly reflected in seating patterns in the chamber, in which representatives are seated according to electoral district, and within districts according to the rank of the seat they occupy. Due to the multiparty nature of Norwegian politics and the fact that it virtually never happens that the same party wins two consecutive seats in the same district, Norwegian parliamentarians will in the great majority of cases sit next to representatives of other parties on both sides. During long plenary sessions in particular, this has often given rise to social interaction and camaraderie across unpredictable party lines and occasionally also to romantic engagements.

But there is also a more institutionalized side to this inclusiveness, as reflected in the Scandinavian process of remiss, in which important bills are rarely introduced in parliament until they have been vetted. This typically means that a cross-partisan commission of inquiry, consisting of government and opposition politicians as well as independent experts and representatives of social interests, has been appointed to recommend action on the topic. Groups representing affected interests and ordinary citizens are then also granted a statutory right to comment on the commission's report before it is submitted to parliament. In parliament, the relevant bill will then be deliberated on in the relevant permanent committee, in which all parties are proportionally represented and where the chairships are similarly proportionately distributed among the parliamentary parties. Since Norwegian parliamentary committees are relatively small and conduct their business behind closed doors, they are arenas conducive to legislative compromise. All of this constitutes a policy process that is predictable and transparent, where at each step of the process there is incentive and often a normative commitment to find consensus (Strøm 1990; Narud and Strøm 2011). In this context, minority governments can perform in ways that are not so different from those with a parliamentary majority behind them.

Minority governments in office

Given the frequency of minority governments, Norwegian cabinets have needed to attend carefully to their relationships with formal opposition parties (Strøm 1990). The simple calculus of parliamentary decision-making has required most governments to seek outside support for their most important decisions. Majority-building in Norway has mostly been ad hoc.

Only four governments, all led by Conservative prime ministers (Kåre Willoch and Erna Solberg) have had stable and pre-negotiated support from parties outside the cabinet. The fact that only center-right minority governments have had such support reflects weakness rather than strength. Prior to its cabinet entry in 2013, the populist right Progress Party had been an unpredictable and uncomfortable ad hoc partner for center-right minority governments. The often uneasy relationship between the Progress Party and the centrist parties was exacerbated by the latter's moral (or moralistic) opposition to many of the populist appeals of the Progress Party. In three successive governments between 2013 and 2019, Solberg therefore brought the Progress Party into formal cabinet membership, while concluding formal support agreements with two centrist parties.

Coalition governance, including minority coalitions, in Norway is characterized by compromise, consensus, collegiality, and a lack of anything approaching a prime ministerial dictatorship. Constitutionally speaking, the cabinet[8] is a collegial organ of at least seven members (in addition to the PM) (Constitution, Art. 12), in which the prime minister does not have an elevated position compared to his ministers. Overall, the constitutional powers of the Norwegian cabinet are comparatively weak. The relevant regulations permit individual cabinets fairly wide latitude in designing their internal operations. Yet, most Norwegian governments since 1945 have functioned in similar ways. The prime minister heads the cabinet. She has the formal right to appoint ministers and set the agenda for Cabinet conference meetings. She can demand any kind of information from cabinet colleagues and their civil servants (Prime Minister's Office 1969). Yet, the Norwegian prime minister's power is low compared to her opposite numbers in many other countries. She cannot formally dismiss individual cabinet members, veto cabinet decisions, or call elections of any kind. The collegial nature of the cabinet also extends to the ministers themselves, as none of them enjoy full autonomy in their own jurisdictions.

There are two forms of cabinet meetings, the weekly (every Friday) and formalized Council of State meetings in which the King presides, and cabinet conferences (once or twice a week), without the monarch's presence.[9] Cabinet conferences are

---

[8] In their operation, Norwegian governments have to abide by the Constitution and the Cabinet Rules (Regjeringsinstruks 1909), first passed in 1909.
[9] Whereas Solberg's first cabinet met just once a week, cabinet conferences were held twice a week under Bondevik and Stoltenberg.

not regulated in the Constitution and their decisions are not official, though binding for members of the cabinet (Prime Minister's Office 2018: 5). According to existing guidelines (Prime Minister's Office 2018: 8), matters that have to be discussed in cabinet conferences include "issues that have significant financial and administrative implications, issues that are politically difficult and cases where there is disagreement among ministers."

Coalition agreements

Coalition governments need mechanisms to resolve interparty as well as intraparty conflict. Since the first such post-war administration in 1963, Norwegian multiparty governments have governed on the basis of a coalition agreement, occasionally also based on agreements with support parties, as was the case with Solberg I in 2013. The size of coalition agreements has grown steadily, from about 3,000 words under Lyng in 1963 to about 40,000 words in Erna Solberg's third cabinet (2019). Coalition agreements are almost exclusively policy documents; they normally contain very few procedural rules and hardly any commitments concerning the allocation of cabinet portfolios or other government posts.

No coalition agreement has specified any particular conflict resolution mechanisms, as these documents have almost without exception been about policy. Yet cabinets since at least the 1980s have had such conflict resolution mechanisms at their disposal, and many involve meetings and consultations. Ministers spend around two-thirds of their time on matters related to their own ministry (Christensen and Lægreid 2002: 70). Yet, the collegial nature of Norwegian cabinets means that the ministers attend cabinet meetings several times a week: "To be a minister is to love the Meeting," wrote Skjeie (2001: 159). In addition to the cabinet conferences, there are cabinet lunches (prior to the cabinet conferences), as well as meetings in various ministry committees. These different meetings, and the extensive contact between ministries as well as between senior and junior ministers, are ways to avoid intra-coalition conflict.

The relative importance of these conflict resolution mechanisms has varied. Narud and Strøm (2000: 178–179) found the cabinet conference itself to be the most common forum, while the most serious policy conflict had been dealt with in intra-cabinet committees. Thus in 1983, when Kåre Willoch formed his coalition (at first a majority, later a minority government), he simultaneously created an inner cabinet comprising the three party leaders (including himself) and the finance minister. From then on, all coalition cabinets have adopted a similar intra-cabinet body, called the sub-committee, to deal with more serious policy conflicts. From 1990 onwards, the cabinet conference and the sub-committee have been the two key arenas of conflict resolution (see Kolltveit 2013 and 2014).

The period after 1990 has also witnessed an interesting shift in junior minister appointments. Nearly every cabinet has increased the number of junior ministers from a party that is not holding the cabinet ministership, so-called cross-partisan appointees (CPA). This has gone along with an increase in the overall number of junior ministers.[10] While Bondevik II had CPAs only in the PM's office and in the Ministry of Finance, Erna Solberg had twelve in her first government (2013–17). Analysts have identified four different roles that cross-partisan appointees can play, depending on whether they are expected to perform monitoring functions and/or give cross-partisan advice to their respective ministers: watchdog, liaison officer, regular political appointee, and coalition advisor (Askim et al. 2018: 4).[11] Across all cabinets from Bondevik I through Solberg V, the cross-partisan appointees have taken on all of these roles. Askim et al. (2018) argue that a majority of Norwegian cross-partisan appointees have served as coalition liaison officers, that is, combining the watchdog role with that of providing cross-partisan advice.

Alliances and majority building in parliament
Communication and coordination with the Storting is of paramount importance for the cabinet and especially for minority cabinets. Cabinets have organized their formal contacts in similar ways: Every week individual ministers will meet with their own party's MPs in the parliamentary party group meeting. Additionally, ministers meet with all the coalition's representatives from their respective parliamentary committees in so-called "fraction meetings" (fraksjonsmøte). For ministers serving in minority cabinets, nurturing relationships with other parties' representatives in the relevant committee is reportedly also a special priority. Such contact is often informal and can take the form of grabbing a cup of coffee, or meeting over dinner.

The cabinet's relationship with the Storting was particular under Solberg's first three (minority) cabinets (2013–19). Solberg I (formed 2013) had a formalized agreement between the government and its two support parties in parliament: The Christian Democrats and the Liberals. The four parties cooperated in parliament, as expressed in their Cooperation Agreement (Samarbeidsavtalen 2013). This agreement obligated the PM to invite the support parties' leaders to meetings about important matters and stipulated that the parliamentary party leaders were to meet regularly to discuss pending matters.

Even though coalition agreements include no formal rules concerning parliamentary voting, there is a strong expectation that the coalition MPs will vote with

---

[10] Before 1990 each Norwegian ministry generally had only one junior minister (Narud and Strøm 2000: 183).
[11] A watchdog minister is not expected to give cross-partisan advice, for example provide information about his/her own party to the minister, but to monitor the minister and report back to party superiors. A liaison officer is expected to both monitor and to give cross-partisan advice, while a coalition advisor provides cross-partisan advice, but does not monitor. Finally, a regular political appointee neither provides cross-partisan advice nor monitors (Askim et al. 2018: 4).

their cabinet, as indeed they almost invariably do. Party cohesion is very strong in the Storting, which has been related to the parties' strict control over ballot access and state funding (Narud and Strøm 2000: 180). Exceptions are made only in matters of deep personal commitment, such as abortion policies, or in matters of strong constituency (regional/local) importance. Adherence to the coalition line is also expected in other parliamentary behavior, for example in parliamentary questions. Discipline in parliamentary behavior was in fact perfect in Bondevik's second and Solberg's first cabinet.

Of course, minority governments need also to attend carefully to their relationships with the formal opposition parties (Strøm 1990). Contrary to Denmark, where formal—though often substantively limited—accommodations have been common, most majority-building in Norway has been ad hoc. Labor minority governments in particular have felt relatively secure in playing their left socialist opposition off against the center-right parties in order to reach acceptable agreements (and typically throwing in their lot with the left socialists on welfare issues but with the center-right parties on economic issues). Center-right governments have often needed to accommodate the Progress Party, which at times has been an unpredictable or opportunistic partner (Strøm 1994).

One critical occasion for majority-building is the annual budget process, which typically goes on continuously through the fall session (October through December), with budget agreements often reached just before the Christmas recess. From the early 1970s to 2005, such budget negotiations were particularly challenging and high-profile. Especially in the early part of this period, minority governments would often employ the so-called "slalom" method, which meant darting from one legislative coalition to another on different budget issues. The result, however, was often low overall coordination and weak fiscal discipline. To avoid these problems, the Storting adopted a series of procedural reforms aimed at streamlining the budgetary process and imposing a specific budget ceiling. While these reforms have had some success, they have (predictably) not solved such underlying problems as the numerical weakness of minority governments, or weakness of will on the part of politicians.

While there is variation in budget coalitions (see Narud and Valen 2007: 223), one interesting regularity is that minority governments typically prefer to negotiate their budgetary support from the political right. Thus, Labor governments have much more often reached budget agreements with the centrist parties (especially the Christian Democrat Party) than with the Left Socialists. Non-socialists have tended not to reciprocate this favor. Centrist coalitions have tended to coalesce with the Conservatives, and center-right coalitions (including the Conservatives) with the Progress Party. Deviations from this regularity have been driven more by the government's need to maintain credibility ("we are open to cooperation with any opposition party") than by the incumbents' true inclinations.

Minority government performance

Minority governments in Norway have been able to sustain themselves in office and build a reasonable record of policy accomplishment. There are many ways to judge the performance of minority governments. One is to examine their legislative productivity. Over time, there has been a continuous and nearly monotonic increase in the measurable activity level in the Storting. The number of private members' bills increased from 15 in 1984–85, to 80 in 1993–94, and 156 in 2001/2002 (Rommetvedt 2003: 47). It has since plateaued at this high level. Measured in terms of separate proposals, the increase in private members' bills has been even greater. The frequency of minority governments seems to have had little impact on this trend.

Another measure of government performance is their duration, and the circumstances under which they are terminated. Norwegian cabinets have tended to be durable, in the sense that most have served out their maximum constitutional term of four years. In most cases, the cause of termination for Norwegian cabinets has thus been regular parliamentary elections. Recall that all parliamentary elections in Norway are regular, since there is no provision for early parliamentary dissolution. Only four of twelve cabinets formed since 1990, all minority administrations, have failed to serve out their term: Brundtland IV in 1996 because of the prime minister's voluntary retirement, Bondevik I in 2000 on a failed confidence motion, and Solberg III and IV because new parties entered or left the coalition.

Table 4.3 gives a summary of the performance of Norwegian cabinets since 1945 broken down by cabinet type. Minority governments, regardless of composition, have been somewhat less durable than majority governments. While the differences in mean duration are not dramatic, majority coalitions have been the most durable, whereas minority coalitions have been the least long-lived. Interestingly, however, the performance advantage of coalitions over single-party governments that exists for majority governments is reversed for minority governments.

Table 4.3 Performance by cabinet type, Norway, 1945–2020 (mean values)

Cabinet type	Coalition survival (%)	Duration (months)	Aggregate electoral success (% of total vote share)
Majority party	83	25.2	1.4
Majority coalition	50	33.3	−2.3
Minority party	42	27.3	−2.6
Minority coalition	14	19.3	−2.6

These comparisons should be taken with a grain of salt, however, and the first column of Table 4.3 shows why. This column (coalition survival) presents the percentage of cabinets in each category that were succeeded by a cabinet with the same party composition. As Table 4.3 clearly shows, majority party governments (83 percent) have in this respect been much more successful than any other cabinet type, whereas minority coalitions have a particularly depressed score (14 percent). What these two columns jointly reflect is that single-party governments with only one exception have been Labor Party administrations and that the Labor Party has had a tendency to replace its party leaders (and prime ministers) in mid-term. In our figures, this tendency exaggerates the coalition survival numbers, while depressing mean duration.

A final measure of government performance is its success at the polls in the next parliamentary election. Since the 1970s, it has become common in Norwegian journalism and political parlance to refer to governments suffering "wear and tear" (slitasje). While this term is rarely precisely defined, electoral loss of support is surely a major factor. The general recognition of this phenomenon has developed along with, and no doubt partly as a result of, a growing tendency for incumbent parties to suffer at the polls. Table 4.3 shows the electoral gains and losses of incumbent parties between 1949 and 2017.

Overall, there is a moderate adverse incumbency effect: a slight tendency for governing parties to lose votes. The mean net loss between 1949 and 2017 amounts to 2.0 percent of the total national poll, which is not significantly worse than for most comparable countries. Yet, there are differences across cabinet types and parties. Single-party majority governments (all 1945–61 and Labor) are the only category to have had positive electoral numbers on average. This clearly reflects period as well as party effects. Labor actually gained votes in its first three postwar elections, but has since lost ground on most of the occasions it has been in office. In coalition cabinets, it is rare for all parties to suffer the same fate. This has happened only in 1985 and 2017, when all the coalition parties suffered setbacks. In 1985, the overall losses were substantial, whereas in 2017 they were more modest. However, all coalition governments have experienced net losses in subsequent elections.

Yet, the scariest aspect (for party leaders) of electoral performance is the striking temporal trend. From the 1940s until the 1970s, governing parties were actually more likely to gain than to lose vote shares. Thus, Labor gained vote shares in its first three post-war elections. Since that time, however, the prospects for governing parties have gotten progressively worse, and for every decade from the 1950s to the 2000s, the average vote share lost by incumbents grew monotonically. Since 1977, the election of 1993 is the only one in which incumbents gained ground in aggregate vote share. The two most dramatic losses occurred in two consecutive elections: 2001 and 2005. In each case the governing parties jointly slipped more than ten percentage points in the popular vote. By national or international standards, these are huge losses. In the two elections in the 2010s, the average losses declined slightly compared to the previous decade, but it is too early to know whether this constitutes any reversal of the downward trend. Thus, in 2001, 2005, and 2013, the governing parties suffered massive losses. In 2009 and 2017 the incumbent losses were much smaller, but even in the latter year every one of the four parties supporting Solberg I registered a net loss of vote shares.

Conclusion

Norway remains a country experiencing a high incidence of minority governments. While Jens Stoltenberg's red-green majority coalitions of 2005–13 were designed to bring greater numerical strength to the executive, and while Prime Minister Erna Solberg has consistently been attempting to construct a broad and durable center-right coalition, the fact remains that six out of the nine cabinets formed since 2000 have been minority governments. The most novel feature of post-2000 cabinets has been that eight out of the nine have been coalitions.

The high incidence of minority governments in Norway has several causes. One is the permissive nature of the 1814 Constitution, which was drawn up to establish a very different kind of regime: a separation-of-powers system. Central parliamentary principles, such as the cabinet's obligation to inform the Storting and to resign after a vote of no confidence, were not included in the Constitution until 2007. There is no constructive vote of no confidence. And the constitution still contains no parliamentary dissolution powers. The general effect of these constitutional peculiarities is to facilitate the formation and survival of minority governments.

Minority governments have also been facilitated by two-bloc politics and close electoral competition. Until the 1990s at least, two-bloc politics greatly constrained the set of feasible coalitions, and highly competitive elections with increasing volatility and a rising electoral cost of governing has meant that coalitions with uncomfortable partners often have not been worth their costs. Finally, the consensual and inclusive nature of Norwegian politics lessen the costs and risks of being out of executive office and hence raise the willingness of party leaders to accept opposition status for themselves and to tolerate minority governments.

The high incidence of Norwegian minority governments does not translate into a lack of stable governance or a growing susceptibility to political crises. On the contrary, Norwegian cabinets have remained laudably stable, as eight out of ten cabinets formed since 1990 have served out their maximum term. The leaders of the major parties have also since 2005 succeeded in incorporating two growing "fringe" parties (the Socialist Left and the Progress Party) that had previously been considered non-coalitionable. As new parties have thus been incorporated and the incidence of coalitions has increased, new mechanisms of governance have evolved and existing institutions (such as junior ministers) have been strengthened.

The only development likely to disturb the Norwegian political establishment is the growing tendency for governing parties to be severely punished at the polls. Despite unprecedented prosperity, political stability, and political leaders most of whom have avoided even a whiff of political scandal, Norwegian voters have grown increasingly critical and fickle in their partisan attachments. While these trends have so far generated no systemic crisis, it remains to be seen to what extent Norwegian politicians will be able to respond to this challenge.[12]

References

Aardal, Bernt, ed. 2007. *Norske velgere. En studie av stortingsvalget i 2005*. Oslo: Damm forlag.
Arter, David. 2016. *Scandinavian Politics Today*. 3rd edition. Manchester: Manchester University Press.
Askim, Jostein, Rune Karlsen, and Kristoffer Kolltveit. 2018. "The Spy Who Loved Me? Cross-Partisans in the Core Executive." *Public Administration* 96: 1–16.
Bergman, Torbjörn. 1993. "Formation Rules and Minority Governments." *European Journal of Political Research* 23: 55–66.
Björnberg, Arne. 1939. *Parlamentarismens utveckling i Norge efter 1905*. Uppsala: Almqvist & Wiksell.
Christensen, Tom, and Per Lægreid. 2002. *Reformer og lederskap: Omstilling i den utøvende makt*. Oslo: Universitetsforlaget.
Kolltveit, Kristoffer. 2013. "Concentration of Decision-making Power: Investigating the Role of the Norwegian Cabinet Subcommittee." *World Political Science* 9: 173–195.
Kolltveit, Kristoffer. 2014. "Concentration of Power in Cabinets: Exploring the Importance of the Party Political Context." *Acta Politica* 49: 266–285.
Narud, Hanne Marthe. 1995. "Coalition Termination in Norway: Models and Cases." *Scandinavian Political Studies* 18 (1): 1–24.
Narud, Hanne Marthe, and Kaare Strøm. 2000. "Norway. A Fragile Coalitional Order." In *Coalition Governments in Western Europe*, ed. Wolfgang C. Müller and Kaare Strøm. Oxford: Oxford University Press, pp. 158–91.
Narud, Hanne Marthe, and Kaare Strøm. 2011. "Norway. From Hønsvaldian Parliamentarism Back to Madisonian Roots." In *The Madisonian Turn*, ed. Torbjörn Bergman and Kaare Strøm. Ann Arbor: University of Michigan Press, pp. 200–50.
Narud, Hanne Marthe, and Henry Valen. 2007. *Demokrati og ansvar. Om politisk representasjon i et flerpartisystem*. Oslo: Damm forlag.
Nordby, Trond. 2000. *I politikkens sentrum: Variasjoner I Stortingets makt 1814-2000*. Oslo: Universitetsforlaget.
Prime Minister's Office. 1918. *Regjeringsinstruks* [Cabinet Rules].
Prime Minister's Office. 1969. *Regjeringsinstruks* [Cabinet Rules].

---

[12] I am grateful to Torill Stavenes, Bjørn Erik Rasch, and the late Hanne Marthe Narud for their most valuable contributions to previous research on which this chapter builds.

Rasch, Bjørn Erik. 1994. "Question Time in the Norwegian Storting—Theoretical and Empirical Considerations." In *Parliamentary Control in the Nordic Countries: Forms of Questioning and Behavioural Trends*, ed. Matti Wiberg. Jyväskylä: The Finnish Political Science Association, pp. 247-75.

Rasch, Bjørn Erik, and Kaare W. Strøm. 2019. "En mindre særegen parlamentarisme? Utviklingstrekk og reformforsøk." In *Makt og Opposisjon*, eds. Elin Haugsgjerd Allern, Jo Saglie, and Øyvind Østerud. Oslo: Universitetsforlaget, pp. 117-33.

Rokkan, Stein. 1967. "Geography, Religion and Social Class: Crosscutting Cleavages in Norwegian Politics." In *Party Systems and Voter Alignments*, ed. Seymour Martin Lipset, and Stein Rokkan. New York: Free Press, pp. 367-444.

Rokkan, Stein. 1970. *Citizens, Elections, Parties*. New York: David McKay.

Rommetvedt, Hilmar. 1984. *Borgerlig samarbeid*. Stavanger: Universitetsforlaget.

Rommetvedt, Hilmar. 2003. *The Rise of the Norwegian Parliament*. London: Frank Cass.

Skjeie, Hege. 2001. "Inne i 'beslutningsmaskinen'. Regjeringen som kollegium." In *Den fragmenterte staten: Reformer, makt og styring*, eds. B.S. Tranøy and Ø. Østerud. Oslo, Norway: Gyldendal, pp. 157-189.

Strøm, Kaare. 1990. *Minority Government and Majority Rule*. Cambridge: Cambridge University Press.

Strøm, Kaare. 1994. "The Presthus Debacle: Intraparty Politics and Bargaining Failure in Norway." *American Political Science Review* 88 (1): 112-127.

Strøm, Kaare. 2000. "Delegation and Accountability in Parliamentary Democracies." *European Journal of Political Research* 37: 261-289.

Strøm, Kaare, and Jørn Leipart. 1993. "Policy, Institutions, and Coalition Avoidance: Norwegian Governments 1945-1990." *American Political Science Review* 87 (4): 870-887.

Valen, Henry, and Hanne Marthe Narud. 2007a. "The Conditional Party Mandate. A Model for the Study of Political Representation." *European Journal of Political Research* 46 (3): 293-318.

Valen, Henry, and Stein Rokkan. 1974. "Norway: Conflict Structure and Mass Politics in a European Periphery." In *Electoral Behavior: A Comparative Handbook*, ed. Richard Rose. New York: Free Press, pp. 315-70.

Von Beyme, Klaus. 1970. *Die Parlamentarischen Regierungssysteme in Europa*. Munich: Piper.

5
Minority Governments in Romania
A Case of Stable Instability

Veronica Anghel

Romanian politics is defined by stable instability. In thirty years of democratic experience (1990–2020), seventeen prime ministers chaired thirty-four cabinets. Cabinets had an average lifespan of less than a year. Minority cabinets are also a fixed feature of Romanian politics. Among post-communist states, the country tops the charts at more than double the amount of minority cabinets compared to runner-up Latvia (Bergman et al. 2019: 6). Between 1990 and 2020, over half of Romanian cabinets were minority cabinets (18/34, 53 percent). Among these, six were single-party minority cabinets (see Table 5.1). What explains the preference of Romanian parties to form minority cabinets? Does their minority status affect stability or cabinet performance? If so, under what conditions does either cabinet duration or cabinet performance improve?

An analysis of the formation and lives of these cabinets provides a rare chance to observe politicians learning the merits of strategic behavior in a young multiparty environment. In doing so, we can also trace how institutions shape elite behavior in a new democracy and test some of the theories developed for Western Europe on new cases. I find empirical evidence in favor of the important role of the semi-presidential regime structure, and of party and party system features in minority cabinet formation. In particular, the role of the president in nominating the prime minister provides the president with formal and informal power over cabinet composition. Such power was often used to design minority cabinets in favor of the president's party. Party and party system features refer to the presence of dominant parties, polarizing electoral competition, and the strategies of small parties. We also find that individual political goals and informal institutions—such as corruption and clientelism—play a fundamental role in making and breaking parliamentary alliances. These latter phenomena often shape legislative majorities, making individuals highly dependent on state resources and loosely bonded to a specific party. I posit that this encourages minority cabinet formation, as individual payoffs do not require cabinet membership for the whole party.

Table 5.1 Types of Government, Romania, 1990–2020

Cabinet	Start date	End date	Duration (in days)	Government parties	Coalition (yes/no)	Minority (yes/no)	Support agreement (yes/no)[a]	Support parties (if any)
Roman	28-06-1990	26-09-1991	455	FSN	No	No	—	—
Stolojan	17-10-1991	27-09-1992	346	FSN, PNL, MER, PDAR	Yes	No	—	—
Văcăroiu I	20-11-1992	18-08-1994	636	FDSN	Yes	Yes	No	PUNR
Văcăroiu II	18-08-1994	03-09-1996	747	PDSR, PUNR	Yes	Yes	Yes	PSM, PRM
Văcăroiu III	03-09-1996	03-11-1996	61	PDSR	No	Yes	No	NO
Ciorbea I	12-12-1996	05-12-1997	358	PNTCD, PNL, PDL, UDMR, PSDR, PNLCD	Yes	No	—	—
Ciorbea II	05-12-1997	02-02-1998	59	PNTCD, PNL, PDL, UDMR, PSDR	Yes	No	—	—
Ciorbea III	11-02-1998	30-03-1998	47	PNTCD, PNL, UDMR, PSDR, PL, PAR	Yes	Yes	Yes	PD
Vasile I	17-04-1998	27-10-1998	193	PNTCD, PNL, PD, UDMR, PSDR, PAR	Yes	No	—	—

Continued

Table 5.1 Continued

Cabinet	Start date	End date	Duration (in days)	Government parties	Coalition (yes/no)	Minority (yes/no)	Support agreement (yes/no)[a]	Support parties (if any)
Vasile II	27-10-1998	13-12-1999	412	PNTCD, PNL, PD, UDMR, PSDR	Yes	No	—	—
Isărescu	22-12-1999	26-11-2000	340	PNTCD, PNL, PD, UDMR, PSDR	Yes	No	—	—
Năstase I	28-12-2000	19-06-2003	903	PSD, PSDR, PC	Yes	Yes	Yes	PNL, UDMR
Năstase II	19-06-2003	28-11-2004	528	PSD	No	Yes	Yes	UDMR
Popescu-Tăriceanu I	29-12-2004	04-12-2006	705	PNL, PD, UDMR, PC	Yes	Yes	No	NMC
Popescu-Tăriceanu II	04-12-2006	05-04-2007	122	PNL, PD, UDMR	Yes	Yes	No	NMC
Popescu-Tăriceanu III	05-04-2007	30-11-2008	605	PNL, UDMR	Yes	Yes	No	NMC, PSD
Boc I	22-12-2008	01-10-2009	283	PDL, PSD	Yes	No	—	—
Boc II	01-10-2009	13-10-2009	12	PDL	No	Yes	No	No
Boc III	23-12-2009	20-04-2010	118	PDL, UDMR	Yes	Yes	No	UNPR
Boc IV	20-04-2010	06-02-2012	657	PDL, UDMR, UNPR	Yes	Yes	Yes	NMC

Ungureanu	09-02-2012	27-04-2012	78	PDL, UDMR, UNPR	Yes	Yes	Yes	NMC
Ponta I	07-05-2012	09-12-2012	216	PSD, PNL, PC	Yes	Yes	Yes	UNPR, NMC
Ponta II	21-12-2012	26-02-2014	432	PSD, PNL, PC, UNPR	Yes	No	—	—
Ponta III	26-02-2014	05-03-2014	7	PSD, PC, UNPR	Yes	Yes	Yes	NMC
Ponta IV	05-03-2014	17-12-2014	287	PSD, UDMR, PC, UNPR	Yes	No	—	—
Ponta V	17-12-2014	04-11-2015	322	PSD, UNPR, PC, PLR	Yes	No	—	—
Cioloș	17-11-2015	11-12-2016	390	Non-partisan	No	No	—	—
Grindeanu	04-01-2017	21-06-2017	168	PSD, ALDE	Yes	No	—	—
Tudose	29-06-2017	16-01-2018	201	PSD, ALDE	Yes	No	—	—
Dăncilă I	29-01-2018	27-08-2019	575	PSD, ALDE	Yes	No	—	—
Dăncilă II	27-08-2019	11-10-2019	45	PSD	No	Yes	No	—
Orban I	04-11-2019	05-02-2020	93	PNL	No	Yes	Yes	PMP, ALDE, USR, UDMR, NMC
Orban II	14-03-2020	06-12-2020	267	PNL	No	Yes	No	No
Cîțu I[b]	23-12-2020	06-09-2021	257	PNL—USR—UDMR	Yes	No	No	No

Share of minority cabinets (1990–2020)   *53 percent*

Notes: [a]Support agreement distinguishes cabinets that signed any type of document sealing the promise of support, regardless of its level of detail or whether it individually brings the government to majority support in parliament, and those that had none. [b]The Cîțu Cabinet is not included in counts outside Table 5.1. The eight days during which PM Cîțu governed in December 2020 are not consequential for the analysis that covers the period from 1990 to 2020.

The Romanian political system

Romania formed part of the Eastern European communist block of countries after World War II. It formally started its transition to democracy with the Revolution of December 1989 and became a member of the European Union (EU) in 2007. According to the 1991 constitution, Romania is a semi-presidential regime, combining a popularly elected president with a prime minister and a government accountable to parliament. In situations of cohabitation, this architecture may lead to conflict because of the dual legitimacy it allows (Shugart 2005; Gherghina and Mișcoiu 2013).

If a single party wins an absolute majority, the constitution compels the president to nominate that party's proposal to fill the position of prime minister (PM). The PM designate thus becomes the *formateur*, charged with the task of concluding the formation talks. If no party has an absolute majority, the president can select whichever candidate they desire for the position. This sets the framework for an ex-post investiture vote, with parliament being asked to confirm the choice made by the president (for more details see Chiva 2015). How much leeway the president has in making this nomination has been a constant source of political conflict. The Constitutional Court has been called upon several times to mediate such disputes. Most recently, weighing in on a 2020 conflict between the legislature and the executive, one ruling stressed the need for the president to nominate only that candidate with a reasonable chance of acquiring parliamentary support (Romanian Constitutional Court Decision, February 24, 2020).

The Romanian parliament is bicameral, consisting of the Senate and the Chamber of Deputies. The 1991 constitution tasked the chambers with similar responsibilities, reflecting the principle of equal (or symmetric) bicameralism (Lijphart 1999). Some constitutional amendments adopted in 2003 only slightly differentiated between areas where each has a definitive say. The system is one of positive parliamentarism (Bergman 1993). The PM and the cabinet assume office if they receive the vote of an absolute majority (50 percent+1) of the deputies and senators. If the proposed cabinet does not receive the vote of the majority, the formation procedure starts all over again. After 60 days following a first failed nomination, and only after at least two such unsuccessful attempts at receiving the parliament's vote of confidence, the president can dissolve parliament and call early elections after consulting the speakers of the two chambers and the leaders of the parliamentary groups (Romanian Constitution, Art. 89). Romania has never experienced the dissolution of parliament or the organization of early elections.

The parliament has been elected using proportional representation since the first elections of 1990. A 5 percent threshold was introduced in 2000 to limit party system fractionalization. In the early days of democracy, the party system had high levels of fragmentation and electoral volatility, but it has gradually institutionalized and reached continuity and greater stability (Enyedi and Casal Bértoa 2018).

Historically, parties differed in terms of institutionalization and personalization (Anghel 2019; Coman 2015; Soare and Gherghina 2017; Ștefan 2019), yet with time they have become more predictable in how they choose to build alliances (Anghel 2017; Gherghina and Chiru 2018; Chiru 2015).

Six to seven parties on average win representation in the Chamber of Deputies. Nevertheless, only three parties have had a continuous presence in the legislature from 1990 to 2020: the Social Democratic Party (PSD),[1] the National Liberal Party (PNL), and the Democratic Alliance of Hungarians in Romania (UDMR). Another significant player was the Liberal Democratic Party (PDL). The PSD and PDL share a common origin in the National Salvation Front (FSN), from which they split in 1992. The FSN, a political organization that governed Romania in the first weeks after the fall of the communist regime, registered as a party soon after. It was mostly led by communist officials who also took over the reins of successor parties. The PSD and PDL are both communist successor parties and inherited the party structures and some of the human resources of the Romanian Communist Party (PCR), the PSD more so than the PDL. The PDL developed under different names from the early 1990s and merged with the PNL in 2014. These parties have also been in government for most of the period analyzed here. Apart from the PSD, which identifies as center left, the other main parties mentioned identify as center right. The major differences lie in their positioning in terms of economic policies. All parties represent different degrees of socially conservative positions and employ national-populist rhetoric.

Eighteen national minorities (not including the Hungarians) are also represented in parliament where they form the National Minority Caucus (NMC). This group of deputies is not unlike that of a united, disciplined, and institutionalized party and has decisively influenced cabinet formation outcomes on multiple occasions. As in other studies, the NMC can be examined in a similar way to parties (Anghel and Thürk 2021). Non-institutionalized parties that have had temporary roles in minority cabinet coalitions are the Romanian Humanist Party/Conservative Party (PUR/PC),[2] the Union for the Progress of Romania (UNPR), the Romanian National Unity Party (PUNR), and the Alliance of Liberals and Democrats (ALDE).

Why minority governments form

Institutions are credited with substantial effects on political outcomes and types of cabinet. Yet, considering the high number of minority cabinets, the Romanian

---

[1] The Social Democratic Party (PSD) operated under different names in the 1990s. I will refer to it as the PSD henceforth.
[2] To be referred to as the PC.

case provides no evidence that positive parliamentarism inhibits their formation. And, contrary to previous findings (see Cheibub et al. 2019), absolute majority investiture rules did not limit the frequency of minority governments in Romania. This section identifies party system attributes and institutional features that help explain why minority cabinets form so frequently. The first refers to the presence of dominant parties, polarizing electoral competition, and the strategies of small parties. The second highlights the importance of the president in this semi-presidential regime and of the informal institutions of corruption and clientelism.

Party system attributes

Party behavior evolved in the highly volatile social and economic context of post-revolutionary Romania. The effects of the institutional design of the 1991 constitution were not immediately evident. The first PM, Petre Roman, chaired a single-party majority cabinet. At that time, the power of the FSN seemed incontestable. Its leader, Ion Iliescu, also won the presidency in 1990 with 85 percent of the vote. The need for multiparty arrangements to govern only arose once the FSN lost its absolute majority in the 1992 elections. Party system attributes help explain the formation of minority governments, in particular the existence of dominant parties and bipolarized electoral competition. In the case of Romania, political divisions are not ideological (i.e. parties do not align according to clear left–right distinctions), but are issue based. I discuss this distinction below.

According to Laver and Schofield (1998), the presence of a dominant party (albeit without majority legislative support) makes it more likely that a minority government will emerge. Coupled with the immaturity of smaller parties in coalition bargaining, this was also true in the Romanian case. The transition from a monolithic and seemingly everlasting communist regime was sudden and favored the communist successor party. The asymmetry in political professionalization and organizational might between the successor party and the revitalized historical or new parties was profound. Under such conditions, the PSD, a party that split from the previously dominant FSN, cemented its dominant role and was able to limit significant power sharing.

In 1992, the PSD formed a single-party minority cabinet with a technocrat PM, Nicolae Văcăroiu, and acquired parliamentary support from the extreme nationalist Romanian National Unity Party (PUNR). The PUNR did not obtain cabinet membership, but constantly negotiated and threatened to withdraw support unless given subcabinet positions of junior/deputy ministers and county prefect positions, which are appointed to represent the government (see Field 2016 for a rare discussion on subcabinet office concessions). Given the difference in size and authority between the two parties and that the democratic game was still new to all party leaders, these demands remained unanswered for the following two years. In the meantime, the PUNR and other smaller parties started to realize their bargaining power and pushed for cabinet membership.

However, the PSD continued to be the strongest party and exhibited sufficient authority to have the upper hand in all negotiations. This explains why, even under constant threat of a loss of support from their legislative partner, the Văcăroiu I cabinet had an above average duration of 636 days. While at first the PUNR was considered a minor hindrance, the dominant PSD finally grew to understand its value and the risk of losing parliamentary support.

By contrast, the coalition cabinets that came following a turnover of power in 1996 were not dominated by a single party and were oversized cabinets. Apart from a short forty-seven-day interval in which the ministers of one of the main parties temporarily resigned (Ciorbea III), the 1996–2000 period had surplus coalitions of up to six historic or new parties.

The role of the dominant party in forming minority cabinets was once again relevant during the 2008–12 electoral cycle. At that time, the Liberal Democrat Party (PDL) governed with the active support of the president in a minority coalition that included the UDMR. Independent parliamentarians and the National Minority Caucus (NMC) provided the needed additional support in parliament. President Băsescu dominated the PDL, and its coalition potential was closely linked to the president's political health. When Băsescu's approval ratings declined, the PDL's appeal followed a similar trend. The last minority cabinet created around the PDL (Ungureanu) was brought down once it lost the support of the National Minority Caucus and several of its own parliamentarians switched sides. The UNPR and the NMC provided legislative support to the new dominant force that would sweep the 2012 elections, the PSD-led Social Liberal Union (USL).

In addition to having dominant parties, polarization between two competing blocks encouraged minority governments. In this context, small parties adopted a hinge strategy of keeping their options open to both left- and right-leaning alliances. Issue-based bloc alignment defined Romanian electoral strategies, and were the main source of voter polarization. For each electoral cycle, the opposition challenged the incumbent parties based on:

(a) their communist legacy (1990–96),
(b) poor economic performance (1996–2000),
(c) corruption (2000–2008/9),
(d) presidential allegiance (2009–12/14),
(e) undermining the rule of law (2014–20).

These campaigns produced polarized voting patterns that most often led to an alternation of cabinets formed around the center-left PSD or the center-right

PDL/PNL. According to Arter (2016), such party system circumstances are likely to favor a hinge party strategy. Smaller parties such as the PC, UDMR, UNPR and the national minority caucus switched between supporting one of the two main parties based on strategies to assure their own political survival or other office or policy goals.

Parties' office, policy, and vote goals

In the context of widespread and regular coalition volatility in Romania, smaller parties often calculate that the electoral cost incurred in shifting alliances is small, while cabinet participation correlates almost perfectly with a decrease in electoral support. Consequently, smaller parties often decide to keep a lower profile by providing legislative support instead of remaining or becoming members of unpopular cabinets.

On many occasions, junior coalition or support parties quit the cabinet only months prior to elections, adding to the number of minority cabinets in my count. The minority cabinets of Văcăroiu III and Dăncilă II came about after the withdrawal of junior coalition partners, the PUNR and ALDE, respectively. The parties decided to withdraw as local and legislative elections approached and the government was losing public appeal. Dăncilă II was taken down through a motion of no confidence shortly afterwards. The Ungureanu minority cabinet also lost the support of the National Minorities Caucus (NMC) and was defeated in a motion of no confidence. The minority cabinet of Ponta I formed immediately after this, with the support of parties that switched sides, the UNPR and the NMC.

As mentioned previously, electoral competition is single-issue based and highly polarizing. However, parties do not have strong ideological profiles. With few exceptions, most Romanian parties have been self-styled center parties along a left–right dimension. The pursuit of centrism as a political strategy provides an optimal path to political office (Arter 2016). Centrist small parties, the PC, UNPR, and ALDE, have constantly pursued goals to achieve office. Newer parties, such as Save Romania Union (USR), Pro-Romania (PRO), and the Popular Movement Party (PMP), are also not fleeing the center, but overpopulating it with similar mainstream programs. Such parties are mostly office seeking and participate in the general instability of Romanian coalitions and the creation of short-lived minority cabinets. These parties agree to support minority cabinets temporarily, in view of gaining office payoffs in future cabinets. When they withdraw from cabinets, fragile minority cabinets form.

On the other hand, the Democratic Alliance of Hungarians in Romania (UDMR) is an ethno-regional party that strategically pursued a balance between office and policy goals. According to a former UDMR minister, "the UDMR only has to deliver results to certain communities. We are not big players in politics."[3] Indeed, the UDMR qualifies as a small, center-right party in the Romanian multiparty system, winning on average 6 percent of seats. Nevertheless, it often had a kingmaker role in the largely bipolarized Romanian multiparty system. The National Minority Caucus (NMC) never pursued cabinet positions.

Formal and informal institutions

Romania is often included in studies of semi-presidentialism and shown to present favorable conditions for "presidential activism" (Samuels and Shugart 2010; Köker 2017; Raunio and Sedelius 2020). Among former communist European Union members, Romania scores highest on the president's constitutional powers (see PRESPOW2 in Doyle and Elgie 2016). In the EU, only Cyprus, France, and Portugal surpass it. The president wields significant power in government formation, having the exclusive prerogative to nominate the PM and being seen as a power-broker in the negotiations for future governments. The constitution dictates that the president should shed political *parti pris* once in office; yet, in practice, bias towards their party of origin is common. This briefly makes the president's party the informal driving force behind coalition formation, with added bargaining power. However, the success of this control is subject to the actual seat share of the president's party and its coalition potential (Anghel 2018). The president's influence in cabinet composition also increases under the conditions of a unified government (Bucur 2017).

On several occasions, the power to nominate the prime minister proved to be an important formal and informal bargaining chip. Presidents used such powers to limit office distribution to other parties and maximize office payoffs for the president's party. In doing so, they prioritized minority cabinet formation. President Traian Băsescu (2004–14) actively used this power after both of his electoral victories to shape investiture majorities in favor of his preferred choice for prime minister, shaping minority cabinets in the process (Popescu Tăriceanu I, Boc II). President Klaus Iohannis (2014–24) also shaped a fragile legislative majority in favor of his party's PM candidate and a minority cabinet after he won a second mandate in 2019 (Orban II). The intention to maximize cabinet seat share for the president's party under conditions of minority cabinets underpinned other presidential interventions (Popescu Tăriceanu I, Boc IV, Orban I). On each occasion, the PM candidate favored by the president chaired a party with high coalition potential, and which commanded alone or in an alliance a comparable number of seats to the main opposition Social Democratic Party.

---

[3] Member of the UDMR leadership and former cabinet member. Personal interview with the author, Bucharest, June 4, 2013.

Informal institutions also matter. Informal institutions are unwritten, unofficial, widely-known practices that organize individual behavior. The pervasiveness and resilience of such informal institutions are common features of post-communist regimes and are studied from different perspectives to map state capture, client–patron relations, and corruption risk (Grzymala-Busse and Jones Luong 2002; Ledeneva 2006). Resilient informal institutions such as corruption and clientelism lead to lower quality governance (Volintiru 2015), impede democratization (Fazekas and Tóth 2016), and result in underdeveloped rule of law (Ristei 2010). I argue that informal institutions may also affect power-sharing arrangements and are a conditioning factor in minority cabinet formation. In a context where each member of parliament prioritizes her individual goals over her party's goals, in exchange for providing legislative support, the party's bargaining potential for cabinet membership diminishes. This also circles back to corruption practices.

In Romania, there are numerous paths of discretionary access to state resources and public procurement. Most often, they require proximity to the center of executive decision-making. Consequently, choosing which government to support can involve high personal stakes in economic terms as well. At times, such interests influenced the bargaining process for government formation. The 2004 Calin Popescu Tăriceanu I cabinet formation is such an example. Once elected in 2004, President Băsescu aimed to break the victorious electoral alliance between the Romanian Social Democrat Party (PSD) and the Conservative Party (PC), and form a cabinet around the political alliance he chaired, the Truth and Justice Alliance (Alianța D.A.). He leveraged his presidential influence to bargain with the PC, the political vehicle of media mogul Dan Voiculescu. To break its alliance with the PSD, the PC was given the Ministry of Economy, six junior minister positions, and the directorship of ten state agencies.

Voiculescu's corrupt practices were notorious and influenced other cabinet outcomes. According to an interview with a member of the PC leadership at the time, in his 2004 bid for the presidency, the then PM Năstase (2000–04) also took on the PC as an electoral ally because of Voiculescu's ability to use the media for political ends through *kompromat* (i.e. smearing campaigns with compromising information aimed at political rivals) and advertorials (i.e. promotion of positive content in support of allies). PM Năstase had also included the PC in his minority cabinet (Năstase I). In 2014, Voiculescu was sentenced to 10 years in jail for corruption linked to the sale of state assets.

Beyond notorious businessmen, proximity to public office is a coveted means for personal enrichment more generally. According to the annual reports from the National Anti-corruption Agency, the number of ministers, parliamentarians, local representatives, and directors of national companies who are sent to trial yearly under corruption charges are in the high teens (National Anti-Corruption Directorate Activity Report 2019). Being in government is not an absolute necessity to access resources, but proximity to state institutions is. Nevertheless, further studies are necessary to connect corruption directly to a preference for (or indifference to) minority governments.

Minority governments in office

This section examines Romanian minority governments in office. It shows that half of the minority governments governed with at least one explicit agreement with a support party. Yet, on average, Romanian parties value informal support arrangements between party leaders and vague commitments rather than detailed agreements. The UDMR, an ethno-regional party, departs from this rule.

The absence of explicit agreements is a sign of parties' disinterest in the implementation of specific policies and short-term strategies. Though more research is required to establish a causal connection, the absence of a thorough written commitment is associated with shorter cabinet durability (Krauss and Thürk 2021). This section also highlights alliance building strategies, in particular how they are affected by party switching and corrupt practices in achieving individual (rather than party) goals.

Minority government types

According to Strøm (1990: 62), a formal minority government has legislative support that "(1) was negotiated prior to the formation of the government, and (2) takes the form of an explicit, comprehensive, and more than short-term commitment to the policies as well as the survival of the government." In Romania, some support agreements were formalized after government formation, and most are not comprehensive or explicit. Because of the highly volatile context, I adopted a less restrictive criteria. I distinguished between those cabinets that signed any type of document sealing the promise of support, regardless of its level of detail or whether it individually brought the government to majority support in parliament, and those that had none. The more inclusive classification is a reflection of Romanian coalition patterns where agreements are often simply expressions of a willingness to govern together or support the government. This allows us to better understand key distinctions between types of minority governments in the Romanian context.

Using this criteria, nine cabinets had at least one signed agreement of support, and nine did not. In terms of size and explicitness, the most elaborate agreement was between the governing party PDSR and the UDMR for support for the Năstase I cabinet. It included clear objectives (which mostly targeted the Hungarian minority), designated deadlines and was renewed every year. As I show later, this correlates with cabinet durability and performance. The document also set a new organizational standard for future agreements; it even became a model for the coalition agreement signed by the parties that joined the subsequent minority cabinet of Popescu Tăriceanu I. Yet, while it became a model for coalition government agreements, no other support party ever signed an equally elaborate document. Other support agreements, such as the ones signed by the Ponta I cabinet with the UNPR and the NMC, average 170 words and only served the purpose of signaling support. The content of such superficial deals reveals their temporary character.

Nonetheless, having no support agreements, however thin, is often a sign of impending no confidence motions. Single-party minority cabinets with no support are almost always defeated through motions of no confidence. Boc II and Dăncilă II are the clearest examples. In the case of the single-party minority cabinet of Văcăroiu III, the short two months before legislative elections made the introduction of a motion pointless.

Building alliances in parliament

In the case of Romania, it is important to stress the role of party switching in making and breaking governments, more than day to day alliances on legislation. Party switching can both undermine and shore up minority governments. Personal ambitions led party leaders and individual members of parliament to switch parties at key moments. Boc II and Boc III famously formed as a result of individuals from different parties defecting to create another parliamentary group, the UNPR. During the Ungureanu cabinet, PDL parliamentarians switched sides to the PSD or PNL. They later voted to bring down the Ungureanu cabinet and supported the formation of the minority cabinet of Ponta I. During the time PM Ponta chaired his first cabinet, his party (PSD) and his coalition partner, the PNL, received tens of parliamentarians from what became opposition parties. Dăncilă II formed with the official withdrawal of ALDE, but individual PSD parliamentarians were already fleeing to other parties as elections approached and participated in bringing down the cabinet.

According to Klein (2016), every fifth legislator defected from their party between 1996 and 2012. This informal practice ensures the continuation of some individual payoffs—electoral, office, or policy—or greater ones, a strategy Schlesinger (1966: 10) refers to as "progressive ambition." Party switching to provide support for minority cabinets is also a strategy to prevent early elections, as many parliamentarians are usually concerned with the prospects for their re-election and are rarely interested in risking their jobs. Such extreme intra-party politics shows the fallacy of considering coalition politics the exclusive result of strategic actions by unified actors (Gianetti and Benoit 2009).

Party switching has so far not been directly connected to instances of corruption. Although allegations exist, the exchange of material benefits is difficult to prove. Nevertheless, while still in opposition and after a failed motion of no confidence, Victor Ponta expressed his disappointment that "those who received what they had asked for and promised to vote down the government reneged on their promises" (Ponta 2010). PM Boc, the target of the motion, declared the statement was self-incriminating and merited a criminal investigation. Such accusations are common among high-level politicians in all parties. According to local media, PM Călin Popescu Tăriceanu made similar accusations of vote buying and transactional party switching during the motion of no confidence against the Dăncilă II minority cabinet (Popescu Tăriceanu 2019). The Ungureanu minority cabinet was also voted down after many of his party's parliamentarians switched sides and supported another minority cabinet, Ponta I. In an interview with the author, PM Mihai Răzvan Ungureanu also stressed that he had information that parliamentarians were bought by the opposition and heard of such transactions, though he was not in a position to prove the claims.

Support parties

Support parties can be differentiated into two main categories that also reveal their priorities. Mainstream parties are office seeking and sign temporary agreements with a view to later joining the cabinet. Ethno-regional parties, particularly the UDMR, pursue policy and office goals. As in the case of the UDMR, the goal of the National Minority Caucus (NMC) is always to have a foot in and ensure support for minority rights. As coalition bargaining became even more disputed and differences in legislative support became razor thin, the role of the NMC grew. It started to attend coalition meetings in 2010 and signed support agreements with the minority cabinets of Boc IV (center-right), Ponta I (center-left) and Orban I (center-right).

Despite being in government some of the time, office seeking is not a UDMR priority. This ethno-regional party is also committed to achieving group-specific policies. The UDMR's strategy is to alternate government membership with legislative support. The implication here is that office comes with superior access to resources, but this is not the only strategy pursued by the UDMR. In terms of ideological preference, the UDMR preferred to govern with other center-right parties and was a cabinet member in 1996–2000, 2004–08, 2008–12, and joined the last center-right coalition cabinet formed in December 2020. It provided legislative support for center-left minority governments constructed around the PSD in 2000–04, 2012–16, and 2016–20. It only briefly entered the center-left Ponta IV government in 2014.

On more than one occasion, the National Minorities Caucus (NMC) in the Chamber of Deputies was also a kingmaker in minority cabinet formation and termination. This is a cohesive, united group that commands on average about eighteen votes. Each member is a representative of one of the national minorities recognized in Romania. Their election is not bound by getting over a specific electoral threshold. The Armenian representative, Varujan Pambuccian, has been the leader of this group since 1996. He upheld the group's ideological neutrality and strives to keep the NMC out of political disputes. In a 2017 interview, he declared "Our purpose has always been to stay in the game, not to win. We are not in the position to play differently" (Pambuccian 2017). Thus, the NMC has always backed the party or alliance that appears more likely to win (for more details, see Anghel and Thürk 2020).

Minority government performance

To assess how well minority governments in Romania perform, this section analyzes government duration, legislative activity, and electoral and policy success. It shows that minority cabinets are the most stable form of government in Romania, and this is particularly true of minority governments that have the support of the main ethno-regional parties. Comparing minority government to one another, cabinet performance—measured by legislative record and cabinet duration—correlates with detailed support agreements.

Cabinet duration

There is no single way to measure cabinet performance. Looking at the duration of the government in office (Saalfeld 2008; Krauss 2018) is one approach. In Romania, the average cabinet lifespan is less than a year (see Table 5.1). The high rate of cabinet volatility makes durable cabinets stand out. Therefore, minority cabinets such as Năstase I, Văcăroiu II, Popescu Tăriceanu I, Boc IV, Văcăroiu I, and Popescu Tăriceanu III are notable for lasting double or triple that amount of time in office (see Table 5.1). However, the least durable four cabinets were also minority cabinets. Surplus and minimum winning coalitions fall somewhere in between. Such extreme variation warrants further investigation of minority cabinet performance beyond duration.

The temptation to automatically associate high cabinet turnover with minority cabinet instability is not justified in this case, as the most durable governments in Romania were minority cabinets. From among minority cabinets, those with the formal support of the main ethno-regional parties were more durable (see Năstase I and II). Nevertheless, minority coalitions that had electoral incentives not to sign formal agreements with a support party also worked well (see the case of Popescu Tăriceanu III, discussed below).

Regardless of their duration, a closer examination of some of these longer-serving cabinets also reveals fragility and narrow victories in motions of no confidence. Văcăroiu II provides the best example of a long but tenuous life. The government recorded steep GDP growth from 8.8 percent in 1992 to 6.2 percent in 1995, confirming the correlation between stability and economic performance (Aisen and Veiga 2013). However, small support parties constantly threatened the government with motions of no confidence and kept important laws hostage to office payoffs, such as subcabinet positions. According to one interview with a cabinet member: "Civil servants were always unsure of their positions and did not work properly. ... This constantly blocked the work of the government. The partnership did not work well at all."[4] The hardest fought battles were over the yearly state budget law and resource distribution. A united opposition defeated the PSD in the 1996 elections.

Popescu Tăriceanu III is an example of fragile stability based on a secret, unwritten deal between the governing PNL and the main opposition party, the PSD. The arrangement put the government in a very delicate position. Despite no official role, PSD leaders met regularly with the PM and his cabinet, participated in cabinet meetings, and received financial and office benefits at the national and local level. This deal was confirmed by several witnesses to negotiations, who also stated that the unorthodox nature of the alliance was too difficult to explain publicly. At that time, the PSD and PNL were perceived as natural political rivals with separate electorates. A common goal to impeach the president united them.

Electoral and policy performance

All of the main parties in governments suffered from incumbency induced electoral erosion, despite successes in terms of major promises kept (Alexiadou 2013; Artés 2013) or the introduction of fiscal discipline (Artés and Jurado 2015). Minority cabinets are no different. Table 5.1 shows the opposition obtains power after most elections. The PSD is the only party to make a successful comeback in government in 2016, from Ponta V to Grindeanu. However, Ponta did resign in 2014 following major anti-corruption protests and was replaced by a technocrat cabinet, Cioloș, for a year. That year spent in opposition was enough for the PSD to win back popular support and sweep the 2016 elections. The PNL returned to power after the December 2020 elections, but included the PSD in a grand coalition less than a year afterwards to avoid losing that power.

[4] Junior (Deputy) Member of the Văcăroiu Cabinet, personal interview with the author, Bucharest, April 13, 2013.

Table 5.2 Cabinet legislative record and duration, Romania, 1996–2020

Cabinet	Government bills presented (N)	Government bills approved (N)	Government bills approved (%)	Relative duration of government (ratio)
Ciorbea I	252	245	97.2	0.24
Ciorbea II	51	50	98.0	0.05
Ciorbea III	**27**	**25**	**92.5**	**0.04**
Vasile I	187	176	94.1	0.20
Vasile II	409	382	93.3	0.54
Isărescu	513	497	96.8	1.00
Năstase I	**1165**	**1139**	**97.7**	**0.63**
Năstase II	**712**	**687**	**96.4**	**1.00**
Popescu Tăriceanu I[a]	669	652	97.4	0.49
Popescu Tăriceanu II	109	105	96.3	0.16
Popescu Tăriceanu III	486	469	96.5	1.00
Boc I	273	262	95.9	0.19
Boc II	**69**	**67**	**97.1**	**0.01**
Boc III	**43**	**41**	**95.3**	**0.10**
Boc IV	**489**	**457**	**93.4**	**0.68**
Ungureanu	**37**	**36**	**97.2**	**0.25**
Ponta I	**110**	**105**	**95.4**	**1.00**
Ponta II	325	306	94.1	0.30
Ponta III	**8**	**5**	**62.5**	**0.007**
Ponta IV	154	138	89.6	0.28
Ponta V	210	197	93.8	0.45
Cioloș	175	163	93.1	1.00
Grindeanu	94	84	89.3	0.1
Tudose	135	115	85.1	0.16
Dăncilă I	319	273	85.5	0.53
Dăncilă II	**66**	**42**	**63.6**	**0.52**
Orban I	**68**	**38**	**55.8**	**0.32**
Orban II	**175**	**105**	**60.0**	**1.00**
All cabinets	*7,330*	*6,861*	*93.6*	*0.43*
Minority cabinets	*4,233*	*3,973*	*93.8*	*0.48*

Notes: Minority cabinets are in bold. Data calculated from the Chamber of Deputies public releases as of August 21, 2020. All data is manually counted from the Romania Parliament's database, available at www.cdep.ro. Information is missing prior to 1996. [a] Starting 2005, bills are given two registration numbers from the Chamber of Deputies. We count those that also received a registration number from the Chamber's Permanent Bureau.

PM Năstase chaired two politically stable minority cabinets and achieved two major international successes—Romania was invited to join NATO, and the government opened and ended technical negotiations for EU membership. According to data from the World Bank, at the end of his mandate, the country had GDP growth of 10.4 percent, a figure unmatched before or since. In terms of major promises kept, this could have been considered a successful administration. However, it was also riddled with corruption, an issue that became central to the opposition's campaign. The PSD and its allies narrowly won legislative elections, but Adrian Năstase's bid for the presidency was defeated. As discussed before, President-elect Traian Băsescu used his prerogative to nominate the PM to shape a friendly coalition cabinet that excluded the PSD. Ten years later, PM Năstase was sentenced to four years in jail for corruption.

According to official records from the Chamber of Deputies, there were 7,330 government-proposed bills between 1996 and 2020 (see Table 5.2).[5] Of these, 6,861 passed (93.6 percent). By contrast, parliament initiated 9,231 bills and only approved 1,783 (or 19.3 percent) for the same period. This shows that the executive is the main driver behind legislation in Romania. Of all the government bills presented, minority cabinets proposed 4,233 (or 57.7 percent); 3,973 (or 57.9 percent) of all approved government bills were proposed by minority cabinets. Given that minority cabinets have been in office 53 percent of the period under observation (5,670/10,668 days), this means that their performance in passing legislation is comparable to that of non-minority cabinets. Taken individually, some minority cabinets were more successful in terms of both relative cabinet duration—the share of the maximum possible term that the government is in power—and in passing legislation (Năstase II, Ponta I, Popescu Tăriceanu III). These cabinets had formal, detailed agreements between government coalition parties and support parties. The UDMR was the main partner in both, whether inside or outside the cabinet.

Conclusion

Minority cabinets were initially associated with unpredictable, unique, or crisis situations. The first years of democracy in Central and Eastern Europe appeared to validate such claims, considering the high incidence of minority cabinets throughout the post-communist space. However, this chapter comes in support of more recent scholarship that minority cabinets are neither situational nor do they necessarily perform poorly.

---

[5] All information related to the legislative process is retrieved from the Romanian Parliament's digital archive located at www.cdep.ro. This archive is missing reliable data from the period before 1996. All data related to the legislative process has been manually coded and counted. Data has been collected as of August 21, 2020.

In the case of Romania, they are the result of strategic elite behavior that goes beyond the analysis of parties as unitary actors to include individual rational choices. The preference for minority cabinet formation is mostly the result of party system features, such as the existence of dominant parties, polarizing electoral competition and the strategic calculations of small parties, and institutional features, such as presidential activism and the prevalence of the informal institutions of corruption and clientelism. Individual choices are mostly reflected in frequent party switching and the prioritization of personal gain over the interests of the party as a whole. This creates favorable conditions for minority cabinet formation because payoffs for individuals do not require cabinet office. I find that gaining proximity to ministerial portfolios is at times sufficient to satisfy the needs of individuals dependent on state resources. This opens up new questions on the role of informal institutions, such as corruption and clientelism, in minority government formation and termination.

In the case of Romania, office and vote goals, much more than policy goals, motivate the making and breaking of fragile coalitions. Nevertheless, empirical evidence shows that ethno-regional parties are more influenced by policy goals than mainstream parties in supporting minority cabinets. Also of importance, the Romanian case shows that minority cabinets are no different than majority cabinets in terms of legislative success. Under the conditions of a substantive agreement that signals long-term commitment to shared governance, cabinet duration and performance may improve, even in an environment marked by high volatility.

References

Aisen, Ari, and Francisco José Veiga. 2013. "How Does Political Instability Affect Economic Growth?" *European Journal of Political Economy* 29 (C): 151–167.

Alexiadou, Despina. 2013. "In Search of Successful Reform: The Politics of Opposition and Consensus in OECD Parliamentary Democracies." *West European Politics* 36 (4): 704–725.

Anghel, Veronica. 2017. "Alliance Building Strategies in Post-Communist Romania (1990–2016): Bonding through Dependence." *Südosteuropa: Journal of Politics and Society* 57 (3): 3–16.

Anghel, Veronica. 2018. "'Why Can't We Be Friends?' The Coalition Potential of Presidents in Semi-presidential Republics—Insights from Romania." *East European Politics and Societies* 32 (1): 101–118.

Anghel, Veronica. 2019. "The Institutionalisation of Parties and Coalitions in Romania: An Unfulfilled Process?" In *Institutionalisation of Political Parties: Comparative Cases*, ed. Robert Harmel and Lars Svåsand, London: Rowman and Littlefield, pp. 193–212.

Anghel, Veronica, and Maria Thürk. 2019. "Under the Influence: Pay-Offs of Legislative Support Parties under Minority Governments." *Government and Opposition* 56 (1): 121–140.

Arter, David. 2016. "Neglected and Unloved: Does the Hinge Party Deserve That?" *Scandinavian Political Studies* 39 (4): 411–434.
Artés, Joaquín. 2013. "Do Spanish Politicians Keep Their Promises?" *Party Politic*, 19 (1): 143–158.
Artés, Joaquín, and Ignacio Jurado. 2015. "Fiscal Deficits and Type of Government: A Study of Spanish Local Elections." In *The Political Economy of Governance: Institutions, Political Performance and Elections*, ed. Norman Schofield and Gonzalo Caballero. Switzerland: Springer,pp. 363–376.
Bergman, Torbjörn. 1993. "Formation Rules and Minority Governments." *European Journal of Political Research* 23 (1): 55–66.
Bergman, Torbjörn, Gabriella Ilonszki, and Wolfgang C. Müller, eds. 2019. *Coalition Governance in Central Eastern Europe*. Oxford: Oxford University Press.
Bucur, Cristina. 2017. "Cabinet Ministers under Competing Pressures: Presidents, Prime Ministers, and Political Parties in Semi-presidential Systems." *Comparative European Politics* 15: 180–203.
Cheibub, José Antonio, Shane Martin, and Bjørn Erik Rasch. 2019. "Investiture Rules and Formation of Minority Governments in European Parliamentary Democracies." *Party Politics* 27 (2): 351–362.
Chiru, Mihail. 2015. "Early Marriages Last Longer: Pre-Electoral Coalitions and Government Survival in Europe." *Government and Opposition* 50 (2): 165–188.
Chiva, Cristina. 2015. "Strong Investiture Rules and Minority Governments in Romania." In *Parliaments and Government Formation: Unpacking Investiture Rules*, ed. Bjørn Erik Rasch, Shane Martin, and José Antonio Cheibub. Oxford: Oxford University Press.pp. 198–213.
Coman, Emanuel. 2015. "Electoral Reforms in Romania: From Need for Party System Consolidation to Need for Increased Quality of Representation." *Südosteuropa: Journal of Politics and Society* 63 (1): 75–94.
Doyle, David, and Robert Elgie. 2016. "Maximizing the Reliability of Cross-National Measures of Presidential Power." *British Journal of Political Science* 46 (4): 731–741.
Enyedi, Zsolt, and Fernando Casal Bértoa. 2018. "Institutionalization and De-Institutionalization in Post-Communist Party Systems." *East European Politics and Societies* 32 (3): 422–450.
Fazekas, Mihaly, and Istvan J. Tóth. 2016. "From Corruption to State Capture: A New Analytical Framework with Empirical Applications from Hungary." *Political Research Quarterly* 69 (2): 320–334.
Field, Bonnie. 2016. *Why Minority Governments Work: Multilevel Territorial Politics in Spain*. London: Palgrave Macmillan.
Gherghina, Sergiu, and Mihail Chiru. 2018. "Romania: An Ambivalent Parliamentary Opposition." In *Opposition Parties in European Legislatures: Conflict or Consensus?*, ed. Elisabetta De Giorgi and Gabriella Iloszky. New York: Routledge. pp. 200–212.
Gherghina, Sergiu, and Sergiu Mişcoiu. 2013. "The Failure of Cohabitation: Explaining the 2007 and 2012 Institutional Crises in Romania." *East European Politics and Societies* 27 (4): 668–684.
Gianetti, Daniela, and Kenneth Benoit. 2009. *Intra-Party Politics and Coalition Governments*. New York: Routledge.
Grzymala-Busse, Anna, and Pauline Jones Luong. 2002. "Reconceptualizing the State: Lessons from Post-Communism." *Politics and Society* 30 (4): 529–554.
Klein, Elad. 2016. "Electoral Rules and Party Switching: How Legislators Prioritize Their Goals." *Legislative Studies Quarterly* 41 (3): 715–738.

Köker, Philipp. 2017. *Presidential Activism and Veto Power in Central and Eastern Europe*. London: Palgrave Macmillan.

Krauss, Svenja. 2018. "Stability through Control? The Influence of Coalition Agreements on the Stability of Coalition Cabinets." *West European Politics* 41 (6): 1282–1304.

Krauss, Svenja, and Maria Thürk. 2021. "Stability of Minority Governments and the Role of Support Agreements." *West European Politics*, 45(4): 767–792

Laver, Michael, and Norman Schofield. 1998. *Multiparty Government: The Politics of Coalition in Europe*. Oxford: Oxford University Press.

Ledeneva, Alena. 2006. *How Russia Really Works: The Informal Practices That Shaped Post-Soviet Politics and Business*. New York: Cornell University Press.

Lijphart, Arend. 1999. *Patterns of Democracy: Government Forms and Performance in Thirty-Six Countries*. New Haven: Yale University Press.

National Anti-Corruption Agency. 2019. "Activity Report." Last Accessed March 30, 2021. https://www.pna.ro/comunicat.xhtml?id=9737

Pambuccian, Varujan. June 21, 2017. Cited on Ziare.com. Available at https://ziare.com/varujan-pambuccian/minoritati/varujan-pambuccian-dupa-ce-minoritatile-au-decis-soarta-motiunii-nici-eu-nu-stiu-ce-am-votat-1470579

Ponta, Victor. October 27, 2010. Cited on Hotnews. Available at http://www.hotnews.ro/stiri-politic-7979737-ponta-crede-fost-tradat-cel-putin-zece-parlamentari-puterii-spus-vor-vota-motiunea-acesti-ticalosi-fara-jena-mai-obtinut-victorie-impotriva-romaniei.htm

Popescu Tăriceanu, Călin. September 16, 2019. Cited on Mediafax. Available at https://www.mediafax.ro/politic/calin-popescu-tariceanu-viorica-dancila-evita-venirea-in-parlament-teodor-melescanu-si-a-primit-argintii-sefia-senatului–18401600

Raunio, Tapio, and Thomas Sedelius. 2020. "Informal Avenues of Influence." In *Semi-Presidential Policy-Making in Europe*, ed. Tapio Raunio and Thomas Sedelius, London: Palgrave Macmillan, pp. 93–126.

Ristei, Mihaiela. 2010. "The Politics of Corruption: Political Will and the Rule of Law in Post-Communist Romania." *Journal of Communist Studies and Transition Politics* 26 (3): 341–362.

Romanian Constitutional Court. Decision of February 24, 2020. Last Accessed March 30, 2021 - https://www.ccr.ro/comunicat-de-presa-24-februarie–2020/

Saalfeld, Thomas. 2008. "Institutions, Chance and Choices: The Dynamics of Cabinet Survival in the Parliamentary Democracies of Western Europe (1945–99)." In *Cabinets and Coalition Bargaining: The Democratic Life Cycle in Western Europe*, ed. Wolfgang C. Müller, Kaare Strøm, and Torbjörn Bergman. Oxford: Oxford University Press, pp. 327–368.

Samuels, David and Matthew Shugart. 2010. *Presidents, Parties and Prime Ministers: How the Separation of Power Affects Party Organization and Behavior*. New York: Cambridge University Press.

Schlesinger, Joseph. 1966. *Ambition and Politics: Political Careers in the United States*. Chicago: Rand McNally and Co.

Shugart, Matthew. 2005. "Semi-presidential Systems: Dual Executive and Mixed Authority Patterns." *French Politics* 3: 323–351.

Soare, Sorina, and Sergiu Gherghina. 2017. "From TV to Parliament: The Successful Birth and Progressive Death of a Personal Party: The Case of the People's Party Dan Diaconescu." *Politologicky Casopis* 24 (2): 201–220.

Ştefan, Laurentiu. 2019. "Romania: Presidential Politics and Coalition Bargaining." In *Coalition Governance in Central Eastern Europe*, ed. Torbjörn Bergman, Gabriella Ilonszki, and Wolfgang C. Müller. Oxford: Oxford University Press, pp. 389–434.

Strøm, Kaare. 1990. *Minority Government and Majority Rule*. Cambridge: Cambridge University Press.

Volintiru, Clara. 2015. "The Exploitative Function of Party Patronage: Does it Serve the Party's Interest?" *East European Politics* 31 (1): 39–55.

6
Minority Governments in Spain
Government Strengthening Institutions in a Multilevel State

Bonnie N. Field

Spain is one of the parliamentary democracies with the highest share of minority governments (Field 2016: 9). Since re-democratization in 1977 until 2020, eleven of its fifteen governments (73 percent) governed in minority. This increases to 80 percent between 1990 and 2020. Nearly all of the minority governments have been single party. Yet, in early 2020, a minority coalition formed for the first time since re-democratization.

Spain is interesting for the study of minority government for other reasons. After founding democratic elections in 1977, the political actors wrote and approved a new constitution, shaped many of the regime's political institutions through legislation and took the first steps toward state decentralization *with a minority government in power*. The country is also fascinating because of its territorial politics, including the relevance of regionally based parties[1] and a strong center–periphery cleavage. And, finally, Spain combines parliamentary, executive, and electoral institutions that concentrate power—what Lijphart (1999) calls the executives–parties dimension—with a strongly decentralized state that disperses power across the territory. Perhaps counter-intuitively, this has often facilitated effective minority governments (Field 2016).

This chapter argues that contextual factors during Spain's transition to democracy in the 1970s and historical legacies from Spain's first experience with democracy in the 1930s encouraged single-party minority governments in the early years of the new regime. At the outset of democracy, political actors also established institutions and practices to make single-party minority governments a viable governing formula when minority situations subsequently arose. The formation, functioning, and performance of minority governments in Spain are also intertwined with the relevance and nature of regional parties and the decentralized state. Minority governments have often formed with the support or acquiescence

---

[1] Regionally based parties present candidates for public office in a limited number of territorial constituencies, yet for offices at multiple state levels. For brevity, I use the term regional party going forward.

Bonnie N. Field, *Minority Governments in Spain*. In: *Minority Governments in Comparative Perspective*. Edited by Bonnie N. Field and Shane Martin, Oxford University Press. © Bonnie N. Field (2022).
DOI: 10.1093/oso/9780192871657.003.0006

of regional parties who have little interest in governing Spain, yet want to receive policy concessions, further state decentralization, and political support to govern their regions. Finally, this chapter examines why Spain's minority governments have often performed as well as their majority counterparts, at least up until 2015 when the party system changed. It highlights three factors: political institutions, the government's partisan bargaining position, and the reconcilability of party goals. The same variables help explain why Spain's more recent minority governments have not worked as well.

The Spanish political system

Spain has a parliamentary regime with a constitutional monarch as its head of state. Parliament is bicameral. The Congress of Deputies is significantly stronger than the upper chamber Senate. Most importantly, only the Congress of Deputies votes to invest the prime minister, and only it can remove the government in a constructive vote of no confidence.

After a long period of authoritarian rule (1939–77), Spain returned to democracy and held elections in 1977. Since 1977, there have been distinct party systems. In the early years of democracy (1977–82), there was multiparty competition among four significant national parties along with several small regional and national parties. This was also a period of single-party minority governments of the Union of the Democratic Center (UCD) (see Table 6.1). From 1982 to 1989, Spain had majority governments of the center-left Socialist Party (PSOE), while the national right and center-right were divided and weak. From 1989 until 2011, the PSOE and the conservative Popular Party (PP) dominated party competition at the national level. Minority governments were common during this period, though the PP governed in majority twice (2000–04 and 2011–15). Beginning in 2015, the party system changed dramatically (Gray 2020). Three new parties entered the national parliament, the leftist Podemos (We Can) and the center-right Ciudadanos (Citizens) in 2015, and later, in 2019, the radical right Vox. In the post-2015 period, so far, forming governments has been more difficult and (at least) two governments have been short-lived. They have all been minority governments. Regional parties are still important players in the minority governance game. However, unlike in the past, their support is not sufficient to allow one of the larger parties to govern.

Of the fifteen general elections between 1977 and 2020, eleven produced minority situations—that is, no party won an absolute majority of the seats in the Congress of Deputies. All led to minority governments, except in 2016 and November 2019 when the failure of parliament to form a government led to new elections. Minority governments also formed in 1981 (Calvo-Sotelo I) and 2018 (Sánchez I) without elections. The former occurred because of PM Súarez's

Table 6.1 Types of government, Spain, 1977–2020

Prime Minister	Start date	End date	Government party (parties)	Coalition	Minority	Formal or substantive[a]	Formal support parties	Other Support Parties
Suárez I	05-07-1977	01-03-1979	UCD	No	Yes	Substantive		
Suárez II	06-04-1979	29-01-1981	UCD	No	Yes	Substantive		CD, PAR, UPN, PSA
Calvo-Sotelo I	27-02-1981	28-10-1982	UCD	No	Yes	Substantive		CD, CiU
González I	03-12-1982	22-06-1986	PSOE	No	No	—		
González II	26-07-1986	29-10-1989	PSOE	No	No	—		
González III	07-12-1989	06-06-1993	PSOE	No	Yes[b]	Formal	CC	
González IV	14-07-1993	03-03-1996	PSOE	No	Yes	Formal	CiU, PNV	
Aznar I	06-05-1996	12-03-2000	PP	No	Yes	Formal	CiU, PNV, CC	
Aznar II	28-04-2000	14-03-2004	PP	No	No	—		
Rodríguez Zapatero I	18-04-2004	09-03-2008	PSOE	No	Yes	Substantive	CC	ERC, IU, BNG, CHA
Rodríguez Zapatero II	14-04-2008	20-11-2011	PSOE	No	Yes	Substantive		
Rajoy I	22-12-2011	20-12-2015	PP	No	No	—		

Continued

Table 6.1 Continued

Prime Minister	Start date	End date	Government party (parties)	Coalition	Minority	Formal or substantive[a]	Formal support parties	Other Support Parties
Rajoy II	04-11-2016	02-06-2018	PP	No	Yes	Substantive	Cs, CC	UPN, Foro[c]
Sánchez I	06-06-2018	28-04-2019	PSOE	No	Yes	Substantive		Podemos, PNV, NC, CPV
Sánchez II	13-01-2020	–	PSOE+UP	Yes	Yes	Substantive	PNV, BNG, NC, TE, CPV	MP[d]
			Minority Governments	1977–2020	73%			
			Minority Governments	1990–2020	80%			

Notes: Start date: Publication of ministerial appointments in the official state bulletin (BOE). End date: Date of election or formal resignation/dismissal. Formal support parties: (1) Formal agreement to support investiture of the prospective PM, and (2) yes vote on investiture of PM candidate. Does not necessarily commit the parties to ongoing support. Other support parties: (1) Yes vote on investiture of PM candidate, and (2) expressed willingness in investiture proceedings to work with a government led by the PM candidate. Simply voting to facilitate the government's formation is not sufficient.

[a] At start of government.
[b] MPs of HB did not participate in parliamentary activity, which gave the government a relative majority.
[c] The abstention of some members of the PSOE was essential for investiture.
[d] The abstention vote of ERC MPs was essential for investiture. ERC and PSOE also signed an agreement.

Party key: BNG (Galician Nationalist Block); Cs (Citizens); CC (Canary Coalition); CD (Democratic Coalition, alliance led by the Popular Alliance/AP); CHA (Aragonese Union); CiU (Convergence and Union); CPV (Commitment for the Valencian Country); ERC (Catalan Republican Left); Foro (Asturias Forum); IU (United Left); MP (More Country); NC (New Canaries); Podemos (We Can); PAR (Aragonese Regionalist Party); PNV (Basque Nationalist Party); PP (Popular Party, formerly AP); PSA (Socialist Party of Andalusia); PSOE (Spanish Socialist Workers' Party/Socialist Party); TE (Teruel Exists); UCD (Union of the Democratic Center); UP (Unidas Podemos/United We Can, alliance between Podemos and IU); UPN (Union of the Navarre People).

resignation and the latter due to a successful vote of no confidence against the Rajoy government. Spain's minority governments (11 in total, or 73 percent) were single-party (10), until 2020 when Spain formed its first minority coalition.

The Spanish constitution requires a formal investiture vote in the Congress of Deputies prior to the government taking office. It is therefore an ex ante positive investiture procedure. After a round of parliamentary consultations, led by the president of the Congress of Deputies, and meetings with the head of state, a candidate is asked to submit their program for debate in the Congress of Deputies. There are several important aspects of the investiture procedure. First, the Congress of Deputies votes to invest the candidate for the prime ministership only, not the entire government. In practice, the PM typically announces the government ministers after the investiture vote. Second, the candidate needs the affirmative support of an absolute majority of the MPs in the Congress of Deputies in a first vote. If that threshold is not met, a simple majority of more yes than no votes is sufficient in a second vote.

Table 6.1 summarizes the types of governments in Spain between 1977 and 2020.

Why minority governments form

This section makes two primary arguments about why minority governments form in Spain when minority situations arise. The first is that contextual factors during Spain's transition to democracy in the 1970s and historical legacies from Spain's first experience with democracy in the 1930s favored single-party minority governments, over multiparty coalitions, in the early years of democracy. The institutions and practices established in this period were designed to make single-party minority governments a viable governing arrangement, which facilitated their emergence and subsequent functioning. The second is that minority governments often form because of the nature and goals of regional parties in Spain, which are not typically interested in governing at the national level.

Political context, institutional design and minority governments

The first elections in June 1977 produced a minority situation that led to a minority government of the UCD. UCD minority governments governed for the first five years of democracy. Therefore, it is instructive to look carefully at this period. When the government first formed, the democratic constitution (effective in December 1978) had yet to be written, and the investiture rules discussed previously did not exist and would not regulate government formation until 1979. In fact, Spain had yet to establish a parliamentary regime (Capo Giol 1983).

The government was not responsible to parliament until the approval of a law regulating the relationship between parliament and the government in November 1977.

Spain used a proportional representation electoral system for the Congress of Deputies, purposely designed to distort proportionality and limit fragmentation (e.g. the UCD won 34 percent of the national vote, yet 47 percent of the seats). But, it did not lead to a majority outcome in 1977. The party system was comprised of two dominant parties (UCD and PSOE), flanked on the right and left by two smaller parties (Popular Alliance (AP) and the Spanish Communist Party (PCE), respectively), and a variety of regional and smaller parties. In this context, King Juan Carlos[2] selected the leader of the largest party—Adolfo Suárez, as prime minister and asked him to form a government. Suárez was the sitting and last head of government of the authoritarian regime (having been selected by the monarch in 1976). Suárez was instrumental in moving the regime toward democracy in negotiation with and under pressure from the democratic opposition (Gunther 1992; Threlfall 2008). Of course, the absence of an investiture vote or dependence on parliamentary confidence did not preclude Suárez's UCD from offering cabinet portfolios to another party, but it had no particular need or incentive to do so.[3]

Here the context of the negotiated transition to democracy is important. Negotiations between reformists within the Franco regime, under Suárez's leadership, and the opposition, including the left (Socialists and Communists) and Catalan and Basque nationalists, had been occurring since 1976. Yet, the transition was far from finished with the elections. Spain still needed a democratic constitution, and the territorial organization of the state, a major issue in Spain, had yet to be decided. A government coalition of a subset of parties would certainly have made Suárez's expressed intent to continue broad-based negotiations trickier. Governing alone with a large plurality of the seats, the UCD would be able to build and shift alliances more easily.

The partisan environment was also not conducive to formal coalitions. A coalition with the more right-wing AP[4] would have tainted the UCD. Prominent politicians from the Franco regime founded AP, including seven former ministers. The UCD also contained many officials from the former regime, including Suárez, yet the party also attracted individuals from the centrist democratic opposition to the authoritarian regime and successfully appealed to voters as a centrist, pro-democracy party. AP struggled to be accepted as a democratic party. A coalition of the UCD with leftist and/or regional nationalist parties was near inconceivable given the historical divisions.

---

[2] Designated by Franco, King Juan Carlos became head of state in 1975. He became a pro-democratization actor after Franco's death.

[3] In practice, the UCD was an electoral alliance of multiple nascent political parties/formations. It would become a political party in 1978.

[4] AP was renamed the Popular Party (PP) in 1989. PP is today Spain's major conservative party.

Additionally, many of Spain's political leaders and institution designers were very cognizant of the political instability that existed during Spain's first experience with democracy in the 1930s, the Second Republic, a coup against which led to the Spanish civil war and the Franco dictatorship. The common government format during the Second Republic was coalition government. Seventeen governments existed between the approval of the Second Republic's constitution in December 1931 and the outbreak of the civil war in July 1936 (Vintró Castells 2007: 240). Somewhat akin to the "historical narrative that links minority governments to the downfall of the Weimar Republic" in Germany (Ganghof and Stecker 2015: 80), coalitions during Spain's Second Republic were associated with political instability.

In this context, Spain's politicians designed the regime's political institutions. Core goals were to limit political fragmentation and foster government stability. Spain institutionalized an electoral system that favored the largest parties. Though it did not punish smaller parties with geographically concentrated support, it disadvantaged smaller parties whose support is thinly distribution across Spain's territory. It adopted institutions to strengthen political parties and party leaders in parliament, fortify the executive vis-à-vis parliament, including strong government agenda setting powers, and empower the prime minister. The structure of the party system and the fact that the UCD was governing in minority greatly influenced the design of the investiture and confidence procedures. As Capo Giol shows (1983: 61–68), it was the UCD's initiative that led to investiture rules that would allow minority governments to form easily in a second vote, and there was no alternative proposal from the PSOE. With this, the constituent parliament intended for a single-party government to be able to form without alliances with smaller parties. The censure and confidence institutions they designed would also help a minority government survive. The constructive motion of no confidence requires absolute majority support to bring down the government and simultaneously elect a new PM. In contrast, the confidence vote, called by the PM, only requires a simple majority for the government to survive. In sum, for the two main parties, "it was essential to permit a minority government, hinder parliamentary accountability, avoid government collapse" (Capo Giol 1983: 66).[5] When similar electoral returns produced a minority situation in 1979, the UCD again governed in minority, as it did after Suárez's resignation in 1981.[6]

What the Spanish case shows is that the type of government (minority), political institutions, and party system characteristics interacted in the initial days of democracy. A body of scholarship purports that investiture rules or lack thereof encourage minority governments. For example, Bergman (1993) shows

---

[5] My translation.
[6] Suárez's resignation was not due to a lack of parliamentary allies. It was due to internal divisions in the UCD, and possibly related to threats to the democratic regime.

that negative parliamentarism is associated with minority governments, compared to parliamentary democracies that require a positive investiture vote. In contrast, Cheibub, Martin, and Rasch (2021) find no difference. Instead, within positive parliamentarism, they find that an absolute majority requirement for investiture reduces the likelihood of minority governments compared to lower thresholds. The lack of an investiture vote requirement in 1977 may have facilitated the formation of a single-party minority government, though other contextual factors also worked against a multiparty coalition. However, it was not simply a low threshold for investiture in 1979 that led, again, to a minority government. Rather, the existence of a minority government while institutions were being designed led to a low threshold for investiture. In fact, parliament elected Suárez with an absolute majority in a single vote. Nonetheless, the institutionalization of these rules made it easier for minority governments to form in a second vote, if necessary, given Spain's party system.

To my knowledge, there is no comparative research on the effects of having an investiture vote only on the PM.[7] In the Spanish case, it is difficult to ascertain if it affects the type of government formed. As in 1977, the UCD was the largest party in 1979. While the constitution required an investiture vote, the candidate refused to participate in a parliamentary debate. With the support of the president of the Congress of Deputies, he simply delivered a speech outlining the prospective government's goals, after which the MPs voted and then party leaders explained their votes. While the candidate declared his intention to form a UCD government, as Jordi Pujol (leader of the Catalan nationalist Convergence and Union-CiU) noted, he did so without revealing who would be in the government (Congreso de los Diputados 1979: 98). Investiture debates later institutionalized. But, the practice of announcing government ministers only after the election of the PM persisted.

In sum, political actors in a particular political context (including a minority government in office) created a minority-government-friendly set of institutions. This is in line with a body of literature that examines group and institutional interests in constitution-making processes (Elster 1995). These institutions and practices facilitated the subsequent emergence and functioning of minority governments.

Regional parties and party goals

Parties' office, policy, and vote goals also help explain why minority governments often form in Spain. Yet, it is not because policy-seeking parties can influence policy from strong standing committee in parliament (Strøm 1990). Committees

---

[7] See Rasch et al. (2015) for a discussion of the cross-national variation with regard to what is voted on in investiture votes.

in the Spanish parliament are quite weak (Maurer 2008). It is because regional parties, particularly nationalist ones, in Spain are typically not office seeking at the national level. However, they are office seeking in their regions (Field 2016). Because of the decentralization of the state, which began in 1980, and the creation of seventeen regional governments, parties are engaged in multilevel bargaining over government formation and support, and parties exchange support across state levels, often for mutual benefit (Capo Giol 2003; Reniu 2011; Field 2014, 2016). Thus, the Spanish model of minority governments, for many years, was a large plurality party that governed with the more or less formal support of regional parties.

The most important regional parties represent Catalan and Basque nationalism. In terms of national parliamentary representation, until 2015, center-right Catalan (PDC, later CiU)[8] and Basque (Basque Nationalist Party-PNV) nationalist parties were the largest. They were also ideologically located between the two main national parties in left–right terms, the PSOE and UCD, and later PSOE and AP/PP. Beginning in the mid-1990s, the center-right Canary Coalition (CC) was also relevant, and, after 2008, leftist regional parties. Minority governments have typically formed with the support or acquiescence of regional parties in exchange for policy concessions, state decentralization, and political support to govern their regions.

In the early years of democracy, one of the primary subjects of contention was the form of the Spanish state and political decentralization. The regional parties, particularly those that represented distinct national identities, were staunch advocates of regional autonomy, yet held few seats in parliament. In the investiture session in 1979, CiU party leader Jordi Pujol referred to the party's support for the minority government in the prior parliament—citing a "willingness to help with what we called the governability of Spain; that is to say, we understood that … it was necessary that Spain was governed effectively. That should be understood not necessarily as a desire to participate in the government. … Our parties generally tend not to feel attracted to governing responsibilities" (Congreso de los Diputados 1979: 95). Nonetheless, they were eager to govern at the regional level once elections began to occur in 1980. Similarly Marcos Vizcaya Retana, PNV leader, noted in the 1981 investiture debate that as "a nationalist political group," PNV is not a "power alternative in the State," referring to Spain (Congreso de los Diputados 1981: 9180).

Once the constitution was in effect, regions began to hold elections and form regional governments. The first elections occurred in the Basque Country and Catalonia in 1980, Galicia in 1981, Andalusia in 1982, followed by the rest of the

---

[8] In 2015, CiU, a two-party federation, broke up. One of the component parties, CDC (Democratic Convergence of Catalonia), dissolved in 2016, and a new political party formed from many of its prior leaders and base, Catalan Democratic European Party (PDeCAT). The latter ran candidates in the electoral alliance Together for Catalonia (JxCat).

regions in 1983. These elections confirmed (and in some cases boosted) the support for regional parties, and gave them a strong foothold at the regional level. Some were capable of governing alone or leading regional governments (initially CiU and PNV, and later other parties). This opened up the possibility of political actors exchanging political support across state levels to form and sustain governments. For example, in the early years of democracy, CiU and UCD exchanged support to sustain their respective minority government in Catalonia and Spain. In sum, when minority situations re-emerged beginning in 1989, large plurality national parties could make deals with regional parties that represented distinct national identities. These parties did not join the national government, nor were they interested in doing so.

Minority government formation after 2015

Political institutions and regional parties also influenced the formation of minority governments after the party system changed in 2015. However, the party system and incentives changed dramatically. The 2015 elections resulted in four significant national parties, with the rise of Podemos (20 percent of the seats) and Citizens (11 percent), alongside the previously dominant national parties, PSOE (26 percent) and PP (35 percent). Subsequently, in 2019, the radical right Vox entered parliament with 10 percent of the seats. The support or abstention of regional parties alone was not enough to form a single-party minority government. Additionally, the previously moderate Catalan nationalists moved toward secessionism and openly pushed for independence from Spain (Barrio and Field 2018).

This made forming and sustaining governments more difficult. The 2015 elections failed to yield a government, which led to new elections in 2016. Single-party minority governments formed in 2016 and 2018, the latter after a successful vote of no confidence against the Rajoy (PP) government that simultaneously elected Pedro Sánchez PM. To make sense of why (single-party) minority governments formed, it is important to account for the long-standing practice of minority governments as well as the fluidity and ferocity of party competition. In 2015, party competition was particularly fierce between the PSOE and Podemos, with election results creating the possibility of Podemos overtaking the PSOE in terms of votes and becoming the largest party on the left. The electoral distance between the PP and Cs was greater in 2015, but Cs began to snip at the PP's heels in polls beginning in 2017. Cs made a strategic choice to move rightward to compete with the PP for leadership on the right. This partisan context worked against formal multiparty coalitions.

Thus, parliament was again unable to form a government in April 2019, and new elections occurred in November 2019. After the November election, PSOE agreed to form a minority coalition with its leftwing rival Podemos, allied with the United Left under the label United We Can (*Unidas Podemos*/UP). Yet, it took new elections and a clear victory of the PSOE over Unidas Podemos. It still needed the acquiescence of regional parties.

Minority governments in office

This section briefly examines the types of minority government in Spain, and highlights aspects of how minority governments govern that are not commonly discussed in the existing literature, related to alliance building, office concessions, and multilevel exchanges.[9]

Existing research distinguishes between minority governments that operate with the support of a majority in parliament due to formal government-support party agreements, and those that do not. Strøm (1990) refers to the former as formal minority governments and to the latter as substantive minority governments. Spain has had both, though substantive minority governments (eight) outnumber formal minority governments (three). Even when formal minority governments existed in the 1990s, the agreements upon which they relied were not comprehensive and they co-existed with the possibility of opposition from support parties (Field 2016: 98–111). The five most recent minority governments have been substantive minority governments. There has been no trend toward contract parliamentarism, as found in Sweden and New Zealand (Bale and Bergman 2006). Contract parliamentarism refers to highly institutionalized relationships between minority governments and support parties that in practice approximate majority governments.

In contrast, Spain illustrates the ambiguity of the support party concept and the difficulty of determining whether there is a formal support agreement between the government and a particular parliamentary party. Table 6.1 distinguishes between formal support parties and other support parties. As operationalized here, formal support parties are those that have a formal investiture agreement with the party of the prospective PM, and vote favorably in the investiture vote. In Spain, parties often make clear that ongoing support is contingent on the decisions the government makes along the way. Thus, parties (and governments) use the terms *pacto de investidura* (investiture pact) and *pacto de legislatura* (legislature or parliamentary term pact) very carefully. The "other support party" category refers to parties that do not have a formal support agreement with the government, yet they vote yes in the investiture vote and therein express a willingness to work with a government led by the PM candidate.

---

[9] Also, see Field (2013; Field 2016: 91–122).

However, there is still a lower level of (potential) support, which does not rise, in my view, to support party status. This is when a party abstains to facilitate the formation of a minority government. For example, the Rajoy II government in 2016 only formed because part of the PSOE parliamentary group abstained (and only after the removal of the PSOE's leader and a severe intraparty division). But, the PSOE as a party had no commitment to the government. Also, in 2020, both the secessionist Catalan Republican Left (ERC) and the Basque secessionist Bildu abstained in the second round investiture of Pedro Sánchez (PSOE), which was necessary for him to gain office. To attain the abstention, ERC and PSOE signed a (short) formal agreement to create a roundtable of the government of Spain and the government of Catalonia to "resolve the political conflict," related to the push for independence in Catalonia.[10] Nonetheless, it was and is clear that that ERC's support is far from assured.

Also, (potential) governing parties enter formal agreements with support parties even during substantive minority governments. They are substantive minority governments because the parties that make the agreements do not jointly have enough MPs to bring the government to a majority in parliament. Notably, in the case of the most recent minority coalition, the PSOE and a variety of support parties signed formal agreements. They were not signed by the junior coalition partner *Unidas Podemos*. Therefore, the distinction between formal and substantive minority government masks a lot of variation.

The Spanish case also generates additional insights into alliance building under minority governments. Strøm (1990) linked the type of minority government, formal or substantive, with the greater and lesser consistency of legislative coalitions, respectively. However, in Spain, legislative coalitions have at times been consistent even under substantive minority governments. This is because the government repeatedly negotiated support with the same set of parties, not because of a formal agreement (Field 2016: 91–122). However, at other times, substantive minority governments strategically shifted allies to attain policy outcomes closer to its preferences (Field 2009). Holding constant the party system, both substantive and formal minority governments that formed in the 1990s and early 2000s performed equally well (Field 2016).

As discussed previously, regional parties are often allies of minority governments and therefore essential for building majorities. However, a regional party's willingness to ally interacts with its own need for political support at the regional level. A study of the Rodríguez Zapatero governments (2004–11), when various legislative coalitions were possible, shows that the governing status of a regional party at the regional level—whether it was governing or not, and, if so, in which type of cabinet—is associated with its propensity to ally with the government in parliamentary votes (Field 2014). Regional parties that are governing in their

[10] *El País*. 2020. "Este es el texto íntegro del acuerdo alcanzado entre el PSOE y ERC," January 3.

respective regions, and particularly those governing in minority, were more likely to ally with the governing party in the Spanish parliament. This also means that regional governing circumstances ease or complicate building alliances.

This leads to a final observation about how Spain's minority governments govern. The literature on minority governments tends to focus on policy concessions, whether particularistic (e.g. pork) or programmatic. This is because, presumably, either the governing party (parties) or opposition parties have forgone giving or taking cabinet posts, that is, office concessions. Of course, support parties in Spain attain policy related concessions (Field 2016: 161–167), including the deepening of regional autonomy (Aguilera de Prat 2001; Heller 2002), regionalized investments, and compromise or logroll on socio-economic and other policies (Artés and Bustos 2008).

However, office concessions can also be important in the context of minority governments, and they have been under-researched. In Spain's multilevel state, national minority governments frequently provide the votes necessary for regional parties to govern at the regional level (Falcó-Gimeno and Verge 2013; Field 2016: 175–191). Additionally, regional parties have attained posts on state regulatory boards (Field 2016: 165), though they have not received subcabinet posts in the core executive.

Minority government performance

Judging by recent years, minority governments in Spain have not worked very well.[11] The second Popular Party government of PM Rajoy (2016) lasted only 575 days. The first Socialist government of PM Sánchez, formed after the censure motion against the Rajoy government in 2018, lasted 326 days. For each, it is a relative duration—the share of the maximum time the government could potentially be in office—of 0.42. Both governments struggled to carry out their political agendas and approve budgets, which contributed to Sánchez calling early elections in 2019. The Rajoy II government only presented twenty-three bills (compared to 163 in his first, majority government), seventeen of which passed (74 percent). Even worse, the Sánchez I government passed only one of its twenty-six bills (see Table 6.2).

It has not always been like this. Table 6.2 presents some standard indicators of government performance. It presents averages for majority and minority governments for different periods and categorizations. The first set of averages uses the government statuses listed in Table 6.2 for 1977–2019 (from the beginning of the democratic period) and 1982 to 2019, which is the period after democratic

---

[11] This analysis draws on Field (2016, 2021).

Table 6.2 Government performance indicators, Spain, 1977–2020

Parliamentary legislature	Prime Minister	Government bills presented (N)	Government bills approved (N)	Government bills approved (%)	Relative duration of government (ratio)	Government status
Constituent (1977–79)	Suárez I	173	104	60.1	0.42	Minority
I (1979–82)[a]	Suárez II[b]	212	180	84.9	0.45	Minority
	Calvo-Sotelo I	120	44	36.7	0.77	Minority
II (1982–86)	González I	209	187	89.5	0.87	Majority
III (1986–89)	González II	125	108	86.4	0.82	Majority
IV (1989–1993)	González III	137	109	79.6	0.88	Minority[c]
V (1993–96)	González IV	130	112	86.2	0.66	Minority
VI (1996–2000)	Aznar I	192	172	89.6	0.99	Minority
VII (2000–4)	Aznar II	175	173	98.9	0.98	Majority
VIII (2004–8)	Rodríguez Zapatero I	152	140	92.1	0.98	Minority
IX (2008–11)	Rodríguez Zapatero II	147	121	82.3	0.90	Minority
X (2011–15)	Rajoy I	163	160	98.2	1.00	Majority
XI (2016)	Failed government formation					Caretaker
XII (2016–19)[d]	Rajoy II[b]	23	17	73.9	0.42	Minority
	Sánchez I	26	1	3.8	0.42	Minority
XIII (2019)	Failed government formation					Caretaker

Continued

Table 6.2 Continued

Parliamentary legislature	Prime Minister	Government bills presented (N)	Government bills approved (N)	Government bills approved (%)	Relative duration of government (ratio)	Government status
XIV (2019–)	Sánchez II	-	-	-	-	Minority
With González III as Minority						
	Minority (1977–2019)	1312	1000	76.2	0.69	
	Majority (1977–2019)	672	628	93.5	0.92	
	Minority (1982–2019)	807	672	83.3	0.75	
	Majority (1982–2019)	672	628	93.5	0.92	
With González III as Majority	xsX					
	Minority (1982–2019)[e]	670	563	84.0	0.73	
	Majority (1982–2019)[e]	809	737	91.1	0.91	
	Minority (1982–2015)[e]	621	545	87.8	0.88	
	Majority (1982–2015)[e]	809	737	91.1	0.91	

Notes: [a] In the I Legislature (1979–82), there were 332 government bills, 224 of which passed (67.5%). [b] Approved at any time during the sitting parliament, even if after the end of the government.
[c] In practice, a majority government.
[d] In the XII Legislature (2016–19), there were 49 government bills, 18 of which passed (36.7%).
[e] González III counted as a majority government.
Sources: Field (2016: 80); Congress of Deputies Initiatives Database.

consolidation and the establishment of Spain's most significant political institutions.[12] The second set of averages treats the González III government as a majority government because radical Basque MPs of Herri Batasuna did not take their seats in parliament, which left the government with a *de facto* majority. It provides averages for 1982 to 2015, before the most recent change of the party system, and 1982 to 2019.

My previous research, examining the 1982–2011 period, showed that minority governments were as effective as majority ones (Field 2016).[13] Minority and majority governments presented and passed their bills at similarly high levels, and the governments lasted. They also tended to fulfill their election pledges (Artés 2013). This conclusion does not change when we include the Rajoy I (2011–15) majority government. Counting the González III government as a majority government, minority governments (1982–2015) passed 88 percent of their legislation and lasted 88 percent of their possible maximum length. Majority governments (1982–2015) passed 91 percent of their legislation and lasted 91 percent of their maximum possible length. Majority governments, however, pass a greater number of bills. Yet, using these standard indicators, the performance of majority governments increases compared to minority ones when we include data from 2015 to 2019.

To help explain why minority governments between 1982 and 2015 worked better than those between 2016 and 2020, I highlight three factors: political institutions, the government's partisan bargaining position, and the reconcilability of party goals (Field 2016). First, political institutions in Spain favor governments, which helps minority ones in particular. Governments have advantages when it comes to putting items on the agenda and blocking those items that it does not want. To mention a few consequential powers, the government can block bills that alter the existing general budget, that is, they increase government spending or decrease its receipts. The same is true of amendments to bills. Both limit what parliament can do. Governments can also issue executive decree laws. While parliament must subsequently approve them, they are law when issued. Governments can also carry over budgets into a new fiscal year, if their budget bill does not pass.

Rarely does parliament take a single vote on an entire piece of legislation; rather, votes are normally on articles and amendments, with no final vote required, except in the case of what are called Organic Laws. Roll call votes are rare. Once there is a quorum, most legislation can be approved with more yes than no votes. This means that if MPs are absent (above quorum) or abstain, it lowers the threshold for approval. In certain circumstances, parliamentary committees can pass laws, bypassing a more visible plenary debate. This opaque environment can help the

---

[12] However, the first elections to regional parliaments were not completed until 1983.
[13] This study treats the González III government as a majority government.

government negotiate policy deals when parties are concerned about the electoral costs of being associated with new policies.

Spain's governments are more insulated from votes of no confidence due to its constructive nature, as we discussed previously. The prime minister also, with some restrictions, controls the timing of elections within the maximum four-year span. This means he can use the threat of elections as a bargaining chip as long as opposition parties worry about their performance or the possible alternative government.

The effective minority governments also had strong bargaining positions because the governing party (always only one) controlled a large number of seats. Additionally, when the PSOE governed, it occupied a central policy position in parliament on the two main axes of party competition—the left–right and territorial. This is important because a large, centrally-located party is in a better position to control policy (Schofield 2007), and get what it wants by shifting allies. In Spain, they can negotiate with parties on the left or right, or with more centralist or pro-periphery parties. Or, governing parties (including the PP) encountered potential support parties in parliament that needed political reinforcement to be able to govern at the regional level in Catalonia, the Basque Country, the Canary Islands, and elsewhere. At times, the governing party was the core party in parliament *and* encountered favorable regional governing circumstances.

The objectives of the parties were reconcilable because the government (of the Socialist Party or Popular Party) was able to ally with moderate regional parties. Those parties had little to no interest in governing Spain. But, they were willing to exchange their support for concessions on public policies, regional investment, decentralization, and/or political support at the regional level.

These three factors also help us understand why the Rajoy II and Sánchez I minority governments did not work as well. With respect to the governments' partisan bargaining positions, the change of party system in 2015 produced minority governments that had fewer seats of their own in the Congress of Deputies—Rajoy's Popular Party held 39 percent of the seats and Sánchez's Socialists held 24 percent, compared with between 45 percent and 48 percent for the previous minority governments.

The Popular Party under Rajoy II did not occupy the central position in parliament on either of the two main axes of party competition. Calculated using data from the Chapel Hill Expert Survey of Party Positioning (Polk et al. 2017), on left–right ideological issues, the PP MPs under Rajoy II were more to the right than the median MP. On center–periphery territorial issues, the PP MPs were more centralist than the median MP. The Socialist Party during the Sánchez I government only occupied the median position on the territorial dimension.

These governments also did not face favorable governing dynamics in the regions of Spain. Prior minority governments were able to govern in part because they relied on the parliamentary support of regional parties that also needed political support to govern (or govern more easily) in their regions. After 2015, the circumstances were quite different and regional parties' support alone was insufficient to govern effectively solely based on multilevel deals.

Reconciling party goals also became more complicated. Polarization surrounding the political status of Catalonia and the Catalan nationalist parties' move to secessionism made getting and governing with their support far more difficult. Moderate Catalan nationalist parties had previously been essential supports for minority governments. Nonetheless, other regional parties, particularly the Basque Nationalist Party (PNV), continued to provide support for minority governments. Minority governments also had to govern with support from the new challenger parties, Podemos or Citizens, who were strong electoral competitors with an interest in displacing the dominant parties from power.

Spain's relevant formal institutions did not change. However, the Sánchez I government—formed in 2018 with the successful constructive vote of no confidence against PM Rajoy's government—and its allies never gained control of the parliament's governing board, which has agenda setting power. Instead, there was a right-wing majority of the Popular Party and Citizens, which had gained control of the board after the 2016 elections. This allowed the political right to stymie the Sánchez government's parliamentary agenda.

It is too soon to fully assess the (2020–) minority coalition of PSOE (120 seats) and UP (35 seats), which falls twenty-one seats short of an absolute majority. While the government still has institutional tools that help it govern, the partisan bargaining circumstances and reconciling party goals remain challenging, given the complex parliamentary arithmetic and political polarization, particularly on territorial issues. Nonetheless, at the time of writing, it has been in office for two and a half years, with a state budget that can get it through at least 2022. The government has presented 110 bills, forty-eight of which have become law thus far, and none of which have been rejected. This masks the complexity of alliance building in parliament, however. In one extreme example, the government's labor reform bill passed in the Congress of Deputies in February 2022 only because one of the opposition's MPs voted incorrectly, after two other MPs defied their party's agreement to support the government's bill.[14]

Conclusion

Spain illustrates that the Scandinavian model of minority government is one of many. In contrast to their unitary states and strong parliaments, Spain has a decentralized state and a strong government. Yet, minority governments have often emerged and worked well precisely because a strong government can engage in

---

[14] *Associated Press*. 2022. "Spain passes landmark labor reform, unlocking EU billions," February 3.

multilevel exchanges with regional parties that are policy seeking at the national level and office seeking at the regional level. Political decentralization creates incentives for regional parties to cooperate with minority governments. While certainly easier with moderate regional and national parties, the incentives are visible even today, in the context of high polarization on center–periphery issues, with the precarious cooperation of some Catalan and Basque secessionist parties with the PSOE–UP minority coalition.

Spain also exemplifies the benefits of studying minority governments in newly democratic environments and at the outset of democracy. It shows that the type of government, party system, and political institutions interacted in the initial days of democracy. Institution designers pushed for institutions that would help make minority governments work, in light of the existing party system. This was, in part, because there was a minority government in place and they were concerned about political stability. Historical legacies of political instability and coalition government during the Second Republic in the 1930s amplified those concerns.

The Spanish model of minority governments was that a large national party governed alone and with the external support, primarily, of regional parties. It was a successful one for many years. While it is difficult to disentangle, it is very likely that the success of the model fed back into government formation decisions, making it more likely that decision makers would opt for it. With the poorer performance of recent minority governments, the preference for minority governments could wane if majority coalitions of national parties are an option.

References

Aguilera de Prat, Cesáreo R. 2001. "Convergència i Unió ante los pactos de gobernabilidad de 1993 y 1996." *Sistema* 165: 99–129.

Artés, Joaquín. 2013. "Do Spanish Politicians Keep Their Promises?" *Party Politics* 19 (1): 143–158.

Artés, Joaquín, and Antonio Bustos. 2008. "Electoral Promises and Minority Governments: An Empirical Study." *European Journal of Political Research* 47 (3): 307–333.

Bale, Tim, and Torbjörn Bergman. 2006. "Captives No Longer, but Servants Still? Contract Parliamentarism and the New Minority Governance in Sweden and New Zealand." *Government and Opposition* 41 (3): 422–449.

Barrio, Astrid, and Bonnie N. Field. 2018. "The Push for Independence in Catalonia." *Nature Human Behaviour* 2: 713–715.

Bergman, Torbjörn. 1993. "Formation Rules and Minority Governments." *European Journal of Political Research* 23 (1): 55–66.

Capo Giol, Jordi. 1983. *La Institucionalización de las Cortes Generales*. Barcelona: Publicaciones i Edicions de la Universitat de Barcelona.

Capo Giol, Jordi. 2003. "The Spanish Parliament in a Triangular Relationship, 1982–2000." *The Journal of Legislative Studies* 9 (2): 107–129.

Cheibub, José Antonio, Shane Martin, and Bjørn Erik Rasch. 2021. "Investiture Rules and Formation of Minority Governments in European Parliamentary Democracies." *Party Politics* 27 (2): 351–362.
Congreso de los Diputados. 1979. *Diario de Sesiones del Congreso de los Diputados*. Madrid.
Congreso de los Diputados. 1981. *Diario de Sesiones del Congreso de los Diputados*. Madrid.
Elster, Jon. 1995. "Forces and Mechanisms in the Constitution-Making Process." *Duke Law Journal* 45: 364–396.
Falcó-Gimeno, Albert, and Tània Verge. 2013. "Coalition Trading in Spain: Explaining State-wide Parties' Government Formation Strategies at the Regional Level." *Regional & Federal Studies* 23 (4): 387–405.
Field, Bonnie N. 2009. "Minority Government and Legislative Politics in a Multilevel State: Spain under Zapatero." *South European Society and Politics* 14 (4): 417–434.
Field, Bonnie N. 2013. "Governing Spain in Tough Times and in Minority: The Limits of Shifting Alliances." In *Politics and Society in Contemporary Spain: From Zapatero to Rajoy*, ed. Bonnie N. Field and Alfonso Botti, 61–80. New York: Palgrave.
Field, Bonnie N. 2014. "Minority Parliamentary Government and Multilevel Politics: Spain's System of Mutual Back Scratching." *Comparative Politics* 46 (3): 293–312.
Field, Bonnie N. 2016. *Why Minority Governments Work: Multilevel Territorial Politics in Spain*. New York: Palgrave Macmillan.
Field, Bonnie N. 2021. "Spain: Single-Party Majority and Minority Governments." In *Coalition Governance in Western Europe*, ed. Torbjörn Bergman, Hanna Bäck, and Johan Hellström, 544–573. Oxford: Oxford University Press.
Ganghof, Steffen, and Christian Stecker. 2015. "Investiture Rules in Germany: Stacking the Deck against Minority Governments." In *Parliaments and Government Formation: Unpacking Investiture Rules*, ed. Bjørn Erik Rasch, Shane Martin, and José Antonio Cheibub, 67–85. Oxford: Oxford University Press.
Gray, Caroline. 2020. *Territorial Politics and the Party System in Spain: Continuity and Change since the Financial Crisis*. London: Routledge.
Gunther, Richard. 1992. "Spain: The Very Model of the Modern Elite Settlement." In *Elites and Democratic Consolidation in Latin America and Southern Europe*, ed. John Higley and Richard Gunther, 38–80. Cambridge: Cambridge University Press.
Heller, William B. 2002. "Regional Parties and National Politics in Europe: Spain's Estado de las Autonomías, 1993 to 2000." *Comparative Political Studies* 35 (6): 657–685.
Lijphart, Arend. 1999. *Patterns of Democracy: Government Forms and Performance in Thirty-Six Countries*. New Haven: Yale University Press.
Maurer, Lynn M. 2008. "The Power of Committees in the Spanish Congress of Deputies." In *Democracy and Institutional Development: Spain in Comparative Theoretical Perspective*, ed. Bonnie N. Field and Kerstin Hamann, 90–109. New York: Palgrave Macmillan.
Polk, Jonathan, Jan Rovny, Ryan Bakker, et al. 2017. "Explaining the Salience of Anti-elitism and Reducing Political Corruption for Political Parties in Europe with the 2014 Chapel Hill Expert Survey data." *Research & Politics* 4 (1): 1–9.
Rasch, Bjørn Erik, Shane Martin, and José Antonio Cheibub, eds. 2015. *Parliaments and Government Formation: Unpacking Investiture Rules*. Oxford: Oxford University Press.

Reniu, Josep M. 2011. "'Spain is Different': Explaining Minority Governments by Diverging Party Goals." In *Puzzles of Government Formation: Coalition Theory and Deviant Cases*, ed. Rudy B. Andeweg, Lieven De Winter, and Patrick Dumont, 112–128. London: Routledge.

Schofield, Norman 2007. "Political Equilibria with Electoral Uncertainty." *Social Choice and Welfare* 28 (3): 461–490.

Strøm, Kaare. 1990. *Minority Government and Majority Rule*. Cambridge: Cambridge University Press.

Threlfall, Monica. 2008. "Reassessing the Role of Civil Society Organizations in the Transition to Democracy in Spain." *Democratization* 15 (5): 930–951.

Vintró Castells, Joan. 2007. *La investidura parlamentaria del Gobierno: perspectiva comparada y Constitución española*. Madrid: Congreso de los Diputados.

7
Minority Governments in Sweden
Majority Cabinets in Disguise

Hanna Bäck and Johan Hellström

Sweden stands out in a comparative perspective by virtue of having been ruled by minority cabinets for over 70 percent of the post-war period. The title of the Swedish chapter in one of the most important volumes on parliamentary government formation is tellingly, "Sweden: When Minority Cabinets are the Rule and Majority Coalitions are the Exception" (Bergman 2000). Only Denmark has a higher frequency of minority cabinets during the post-war period when analyzing Western European cabinets (Bergman et al 2021). Since the 1990s, only one out of the ten cabinets that have formed controlled a majority of seats in the parliament.

Several features of the Swedish institutional and political setting account for this high occurrence of minority cabinets—the historically strong emphasis on near-unidimensional political conflict along the left–right economic dimension, the historically dominant position of the Social Democrats, and a negative parliamentary system. Most governments formed during the post-war period have been single-party Social Democrat cabinets, supported by one or more parties in parliament, but there have also been cases of minority coalitions during this period (Bäck and Bergman 2016; Lindahl et al. 2020).

Sweden is a prime example of what has been called "contract parliamentarism," where minority governments have almost "institutionalized" relationships with their support parties that means that they resemble majority cabinets (Bale and Bergman 2006: 422). This kind of support party arrangement, which to our knowledge is relatively uncommon in Western Europe, has often meant that the government has an explicit written contract with one or more parties that remain outside cabinet, publicly committing the partners to a policy agreement. In some Swedish governments, the support parties have even appointed non-cabinet officials in the government (Bale and Bergman 2006; Persson 2016).

Minority governments in Sweden can also be characterized as performing well, at least if we look at the government bills that pass through parliament, how long cabinets last, and their electoral support—no systematic differences can be found when comparing minority and majority cabinets using such indicators.

The Swedish political system

The Swedish parliament, the *Riksdag*, dates back to 1435. However, the foundation of the current parliamentary system was not introduced until the Instrument of Government of 1809, and it would take until 1917 for the King to lose most of his political powers. The Swedish constitution was gradually revised, and in the 1970s major constitutional changes were adopted. Before 1971, the Riksdag was bicameral, with a directly elected lower chamber, and an indirectly elected upper chamber (see e.g. Lindahl et al. 2020).

For much of the post-war period, Sweden had a stable party system with five parliamentary parties. However, since the 1990s the Swedish multiparty system has consisted of seven parties: the socialist Left party (V), the Social Democrats (S), the Greens (MP), the Liberals (L), the agrarian Centre Party (C), the conservative Moderate Party (M), and the Christian Democrats (KD). From 2010, a right-wing populist party, the Sweden Democrats (SD), has also been represented in the Riksdag. The Social Democrats and the Moderates have been the two largest parties in the Riksdag during the past decades, dominating Swedish politics. However, fragmentation has increased over time, and the most significant change has been the increased seat share of the right-wing populist Sweden Democrats, becoming the third largest parliamentary party.

The entry of the Sweden Democrats into the Riksdag also says something about the importance of new conflict dimensions in Swedish politics. For long, scholars have viewed Swedish politics as unidimensional, with party conflict structured along the left–right policy dimension (see e.g. Aylott 2016). As in other countries, political conflict concerning sociocultural values have become more important in recent years, but this conflict has partly been "absorbed" by the left-right dimension. Nonetheless, some evidence suggests the Swedish party system has gradually shifted towards a two-dimensional system, with a growing importance of immigration and integration issues, and a broader, but related, sociocultural dimension of conflict (see e.g. Hellström and Lindahl 2021; Lindvall et al. 2017: 75).

Regarding the rules surrounding government formation, a parliamentary system of government was codified in the constitution with the adoption of a new Instrument of Government in 1975. Before 1975, the King himself acted as an *informateur*, consulting with all party leaders to find a government that would be most likely to have parliamentary approval. In 1975 the monarch's role in cabinet formation was transferred to the Speaker of Parliament (see e.g. Bäck and Bergman 2016; Lindahl et al. 2020).

The new Instrument of Government in 1975 also introduced the investiture vote—formally the vote for the candidate for Prime Minister (PM). In Sweden, the investiture vote is negatively formulated, in that unless half of all MPs

Table 7.1 Types of government, Sweden, 1945–2020

Prime minister	Start date	End date	Government parties	Coalition cabinet	Minority cabinet	Formal/ substantive	Support parties
Hansson	31–07–45	06–10–46	S	No	Yes	Substantive	
Erlander I	11–10–46	19–09–48	S	No	Yes	Substantive	
Erlander II	19–09–48	01–10–51	S	No	Yes	Substantive	
Erlander III	01–10–51	21–09–52	S + C	Yes	No		
Erlander IV	21–09–52	26–09–56	S + C	Yes	No		
Erlander V	26–09–56	26–10–57	S + C	Yes	No		
Erlander VI	31–10–57	01–06–58	S	No	Yes	Substantive	
Erlander VII	01–06–58	18–09–60	S	No	Yes	Substantive	
Erlander VIII	18–09–60	20–09–64	S	No	Yes	Substantive	
Erlander IX	20–09–64	15–09–68	S	No	Yes	Substantive	
Erlander X	15–09–68	14–10–69	S	No	No		
Palme I	14–10–69	20–09–70	S	No	No		
Palme II	20–09–70	16–09–73	S	No	Yes	Substantive	V
Palme III	16–09–73	19–09–76	S	No	Yes	Substantive	V
Fälldin I	07–10–76	05–10–78	C + L + M	Yes	No		
Ullsten	13–10–78	16–09–79	L	No	Yes	Substantive	S + C

Continued

Table 7.1 Continued

Prime minister	Start date	End date	Government parties	Coalition cabinet	Minority cabinet	Formal/ substantive	Support parties
Fälldin II	11–10–79	08–05–81	C + L + M	Yes	No	Substantive	M
Fälldin III	19–05–81	19–09–82	C + L	Yes	Yes	Substantive	V
Palme IV	07–10–82	15–09–85	S	No	Yes	Substantive	V
Palme V	15–09–85	01–03–86	S	No	Yes	Substantive	V
Carlsson I	12–03–86	18–09–88	S	No	Yes	Substantive	V
Carlsson II	18–09–88	15–09–91	S	No	Yes	Substantive	V
Bildt	03–10–91	18–09–94	C + L + M + KD	Yes	Yes	Formal	V/C*
Carlsson III	06–10–94	21–03–96	S	No	Yes	Formal	C
Persson I	21–03–96	20–09–98	S	No	Yes	Formal	V + G
Persson II	20–09–98	15–09–02	S	No	Yes	Formal	V + G
Persson III	15–09–02	17–09–06	S	No	Yes	Formal	V + G
Reinfeldt I	05–10–06	19–09–10	C + L + M + KD	Yes	No	Substantive	
Reinfeldt II	19–09–10	14–09–14	C+L+M+KD	Yes	Yes	Substantive	
Löfven I	03–10–14	09–09–18	S + G	Yes	Yes	Formal	V
Löfven II	21–01–19	28–06–21	S + G	Yes	Yes	Formal	(V) + C + L

Share of minority governments, 1945–2020: 74%
Share of minority governments, 1990–2020: 90%

Notes: Bäck and Bergman 2016; updated by the authors. S=Social Democrats, C=Centre Party, L=Liberal Party, M=Moderates, KD=Christian Democrats, G=Greens, V=Left Party.

* In 1994, the Left Party was a support party and from 1995, Centre Party was a support party.

vote against the PM candidate (i.e. at least 175 MPs), the candidate is elected.[1] Thus, the Swedish 'negative' parliamentary system differs from the system used in most other European countries in that a government must only be tolerated by the Parliament, and does not need to have the support of a majority of its members in order for a government to form when a proposal for a PM has been put forward by the Speaker of Parliament (see e.g. Bergman 1993a; 1995).

In Table 7.1, we describe the governments that have formed during the post-war period. Here, we illustrate the fact that Swedish cabinets have to a large extent been minority single-party governments. In the early and mid-1950s, the Social Democrats governed with the Centre party (Agrarian party) under the lead of PM Tage Erlander. However, since the 1960s, as bloc politics became an increasingly important future, cabinets have come from one of two political "blocs": either from the left to center-left bloc and a center-right to right bloc. More precisely, either the Social Democrats have governed by themselves with the support of one or more of the "socialist" parties (Greens or Left party), or the "non-socialist" parties (Centre party, Liberals, Christian Democrats, Moderates) have coalesced. As we discuss below, from 2010 when the Swedish Democrats entered the Parliament, the party has, at least until recently, been relatively isolated from policy influence and excluded from coalition formation.

Why minority governments form

As mentioned, Sweden has been governed by minority cabinets for long periods since the 1950s. Previous comparative research shows clearly that Sweden, along with some other countries, like Denmark and Spain, is exceptional in this respect, with almost three-quarters of the cabinets being minority governments, whereas many other Western European countries, such as Austria, Belgium, and Germany, have had almost no minority cabinets during the post-war period (Bergman et al 2021). Why is this the case? As we discuss below, it is due to several reasons: the Social Democratic Party's dominant position until the 1970s; the strong committee system; and the situation whereby a new government only needs to be tolerated by the Parliament and does not need to have the support of a majority of its members.

Before 1971 the tendency for minority governments could largely be explained by the fact that the Social Democrats controlled a majority of the legislators in the upper chamber, but usually only a minority in the lower chamber (with one exception after the 1968 election). As legislation needed separate majorities in both chambers, this effectively removed the possibility for a non-socialist government to govern, giving the Social Democrats a clearly dominant position

---

[1] For a short historical overview concerning the reasons why negatively formulated investiture was chosen see Bergman (1993b).

and allowing them to form single-party minority governments (Bergman 2000: 199–201; Hellström and Lindahl 2021: 591).

To explain the large number of minority governments in Sweden, and in particular after the abolition of the second chamber in the early 1970s, we can also draw on Strøm's (1990) work. Strøm argues that in systems where oppositional influence is high, due to the institutional setting giving committees a large degree of influence, minority governments are more likely to form, since parties may view it as unnecessary to be in office when they can influence policy from outside cabinet. Also, as argued by Bergman (2000), internal structures in the Swedish *Riksdag*, such as the system of Standing committees, all authorized to take legislative initiative, provide opportunities for the opposition to exercise influence over policy, thereby reducing the incentives for policy-seeking parties to participate in cabinet. Parties represented in the *Riksdag* but not in the government are thus not necessarily without influence over policy-making, which is likely to have facilitated the formation of minority cabinets (Bäck and Bergman 2016).

Another explanation focuses on the idea that "investiture requirements hinder the formation of minority governments ... because it requires a prospective government to pass a formal vote in the legislature before it can take office" (Martin and Stevenson 2001: 36). Bergman (1995) suggests that the regularity of minority governments in Sweden can be explained by the fact that the Swedish constitution prescribes a *negative* parliamentary system. In this type of system, a proposal for a new government only needs the implicit support of a majority, which may make it easier for parties to acquire the support of other parties without including them in cabinet. Comparative studies have also shown that investiture rules influence the likelihood of minority governments in Europe (e.g. Cheibub et al. 2019; Martin and Stevenson 2001; Mitchell and Nyblade 2008), as well as in parliamentary democracies in general (Thürk et al. 2020). Hence, this institutional feature most likely contributes to the frequent occurrence of minority cabinets in Sweden.

As argued by Strøm (1990), as well as Crombez (1996), a large and centrally located party has good opportunities to be able to form minority governments and reach agreements with other parties without inviting them to the government, at least when there is a dominant dimension of party conflict. As described above, in a comparative perspective, Sweden has historically had an unusually strict left–right alignment in party competition, which implies that a political party holding the median position on this dimension is likely to have a dominant position in coalition bargaining when governments form. Thus, a favorable ideological position of the Social Democrats, in combination with being the largest party, has also been suggested to partly explain the historical record of frequent minority governments in Sweden (Bergman 2000; Hellström and Lindahl 2021).

The increased fragmentation of the party system, the growing representation of the right-wing populist party, the Sweden Democrats, and the potentially growing polarization of immigration issues, has however made government formation in Sweden more complicated (see e.g. Lindvall et al. 2017; Teorell et al. 2020). Some scholars suggest that when a higher number of parties are involved in coalition bargaining, and when there is an increased in ideological differences between the parties, the uncertainty over acceptable offers will increase, and thereby cause bargaining delay (e.g. Martin and Vanberg 2003; Golder 2010). Scholars have also suggested that the type of cabinets that form will be affected by the polarization of the party system, and the presence of "extremist" parties—for example, minority governments may be more likely to form when polarization in parliament is increasing (see e.g. Strøm 1990).

Since Sweden has long been characterized by minority government rule, partly attributable to the institutional setting of the Riksdag, it is not likely that we will see an increased frequency of minority cabinets. However, what we did see after the 2018 election, when the Sweden Democrats increased their share of the seats (to 18 percent), was that the duration of the government formation process increased substantially. Unlike the situations of more recent government formations, neither of the traditional blocs was clearly larger than the other. The formation process following the 2018 election took 134 days, a record for the longest in Swedish history, as most governments have formed immediately or in less than three weeks after the election.

It was clear after the 2018 election that none of the parties were initially prepared to budge from their pre-election promises. The non-socialist parties (also called the Alliance parties) had promised to form a center-right government,[2] and—of great importance for the Centre Party and the Liberal party—this government should form without support from the right-wing populist Sweden Democrats—a commitment both parties had made to the voters. In addition, the Social Democrats stated that they were not going to accept a government formed by the smaller of the two blocs (Teorell et al. 2020; Hellström and Lindahl 2021). Eventually, the Social Democrats formed a minority government with the Green party, supported by the Left party, and two of the Alliance parties, the Centre Party, and the Liberals, but this was only possible after months of negotiations.

The government formation process that followed the 2018 election was the first in Swedish political history where a PM candidate lost an investiture vote, and where several attempts to form a government were needed. Previously, all investiture votes had been successful. The first Prime Minister designate to be tried and to fail to pass the investiture vote was the leader of the Moderate party, Ulf Kristersson, in 2018, with 154 votes in favor (M, SD, and KD) and 195 votes against (S, C, V, L, MP); the leader of the Social Democratic party and former Prime Minister, Stefan Löfven was the subject of the second unsuccessful investiture vote a

---

[2] More specifically, the non-socialist parties aimed for the same constellation of parties that ruled in a coalition cabinet between 2006 and 2014.

few weeks later. It was only in the third investiture vote, held in January 2019 that Stefan Löfven could again be sworn in as Prime Minister.

Minority governments in office

Important to our understanding of how minority governments govern once in office is how they form alliances in parliament. This often means that we should consider so-called support party arrangements that government parties make with (a number of) opposition parties in order to pass an investiture vote and subsequently passing legislation.

In Sweden, minority governments before the 1990s relied on short-term, policy specific, ad hoc agreements with one or a few opposition parties. In the 1990s, this changed as support party arrangements became more formalized.

Many minority cabinets, including Swedish, often have informal and formal support arrangements with parties outside the government. In this respect, as argued by Strøm (1985: 742; 1990) some minority governments "may be majority governments in disguise" or "formal minority governments." That is, minority cabinets that have support negotiated before its formation, as well as that "support is an explicit, comprehensive, and more than short-term commitment to the policies as well as the survival of the government." Bale and Bergman (2006: 422) further develop Strøm's (1985; 1990) classification and suggest that some political systems are characterized by "contract parliamentarism," where minority governments have relationships with their support parties that are "so institutionalized that they come close to being majority governments."

Hence, here we are dealing with something more than minority cabinets being supported by one or more parties to enter government. Explicit support by some of the opposition parties is not uncommon, for example, Sweden has, as we return to below, a long tradition of the Left Party enabling Social Democratic single-party governments. What Bale and Bergman (2006: 422) suggest, in particular with some recent cabinets in Sweden and New Zealand, is that we here find minority cabinets which have an explicit *written* and detailed contract with one or more parties that remain outside cabinet, publicly committing the partners "beyond a specific deal or temporary commitment" but that also includes a sort of joint governance. That is, support arrangements that involve extensive cooperation between a minority government and one or more support parties.

Table 7.1 includes information on support party arrangements in Sweden. Of the sixteen minority governments that formed between 1970 and 2020, the first eight formed because one or more parties preferred to allow them to form instead of using the option to join forces with the other opposition parties to block their formation. The available government alternatives appeared to be a less attractive option. Such relationships do not include a formal contractual agreement. This was also the case when the Left Party declared that it preferred Social Democratic cabinets over center-right ones. In contrast, in 1995 the Social Democrats made an explicit agreement with the Centre Party that secured the state budget. And later, several Social Democratic cabinets have signed comprehensive contracts with the Left Party and the Greens. With a broader definition of a support party, also considering when a party mainly supports the government by not voting against it in an investiture vote[3], there are only two occasions during the post-war period when the minority cabinets have not had an explicit support party. This occurred when Sweden had its first right-wing populist party—New Democracy—in parliament in 1991–94, and again when the second right-wing populist party, the Sweden Democrats, entered parliament in 2010 (Bäck and Bergman 2016; Hellström and Lindahl 2021).

To some extent, these two populist right parties effectively removed the need for support parties, since at least some bills would gain support from a parliamentary majority if the populist party voted in favor. Thus, although both parties were treated as "pariahs" by the mainstream parties and excluded from the usual negotiations between the minority governments and the opposition, they could influence policy by voting or threatening to vote for or against certain bills. The populist party New Democracy was, and, more recently, the Sweden Democrats is, in some sense a "hinge party", not belonging to either of the two equally strong political blocs. Thus, they have the potential to be decisive for many legislative votes. However, they have not, at least not directly, been able to decisively influence their most salient policy—immigration policy, since the mainstream parties have reached agreements across the blocs on such policy issues. For example, the centre-right (Alliance) government reached an agreement on immigration policy with the Green Party in 2011 with the explicit purpose of excluding the Sweden Democrats from influence. Later in 2015, a new agreement on immigration policy was made between the centre-left government and most of the opposition parties in response to the refugee crisis, again excluding the Sweden Democrats (Hellström and Lindahl 2021).

Let us look in more in depth at the various support party arrangements that have been used in Sweden. According to Persson (2016), during most of the post-war period of single-party rule, before 1980, support party coalitions were more of an ad hoc nature, and the dominant Social Democratic party could rely on support in parliament, mainly from the Left party, but sometimes relying on ad hoc support from one of the center-right parties, who were at that point not acting as a cohesive bloc. During this time, the Social Democrats were able to undertake important reforms, without any formal support party arrangement. However, as described by

---

[3] As argued by Bergman (1995: 29), a "support party" can broadly be defined as a party which by its behavior directly contributes to the existence of a minority government, whether this behavior is to vote in favor or abstain to vote in favor of a government.

Persson (2016), this situation changed somewhat in the 1980s and 1990s, when the Social Democrats could not rely on the Left Party as a completely loyal supporter. This was especially evident during the economic crisis of the 1990s, when the government proposed a crisis program which was rejected by the Left Party and led to a breakdown of the government (Persson 2016).

Subsequently, when the Social Democrats regained power in the mid-1990s, they relied on the Left Party as a support party for a brief period, but then during the recession, they instead sought support from the Centre Party to implement a crisis program including large-scale budget cuts. This cooperation was not based on a formal contract, but did entail cooperation on economic, fiscal, and defense policies. This cooperation also entailed some political appointments in government by the Centre Party, who were appointed as advisors in, for example, the Ministry of Finance. As described by Persson (2016: 641), this "practice—giving positions within the Government Offices to a support party—was an innovation in Swedish politics," and it had the goal of improving policy coordination within the support party coalition (see also Bale and Bergman 2006).

After losing a large share of votes in the 1998 election, the Social Democrats turned to the Left Party and the Greens for support. Even though they did not make a formal contract, the three parties agreed to cooperate in a few policy areas, for example in employment and environmental policy. According to Persson (2016), the parties also formed a "coordination group," including top representatives from the Greens, the Left Party, and the Social Democrats (see also Bale and Bergman 2006). However, after the 2002 election, the support parties sought further influence in a wider range of policy areas, and the Greens also expressed that they wanted ministerial posts, and to become part of the cabinet (Persson 2016). This led to a more formal arrangement between the Social Democrat government and its support parties. The policy agreement drafted was very long and detailed, and covered a range of policy areas, clearly resembling a coalition agreement that would be set up by parties cooperating in a formal coalition government, and it also included the setting up of a coordination office in the finance ministry including all parties in the support coalition (Bäck and Bergman 2016; Persson 2016).

As described, the situation after the 2018 election was especially complicated for the parties and, eventually, after lengthy negotiations, led to a minority government coalition between the Social Democrats and the Greens, formed with the support of the Centre Party and the Liberals. These parties negotiated a detailed and comprehensive agreement, which meant a large number of policy concessions from the Social Democrats, to gain the support of the two center-right parties. The policies covered included a deregulation of the housing market, tax deductions on household services, and employer-friendly reforms. The agreement also included cooperation on the budget between the four parties, excluding the Left Party, which was needed for the government to control a Riksdag majority. In the same way as the previous support party arrangements with the Greens and the Left, the agreement included the appointment of support party officials in government. However, only one of the parties—the Liberals—chose to appoint these officials, with the task of monitoring compliance with the agreement (Hellström and Lindahl 2021).

The events after the 2014 election are worth a special mention here since they illustrate the strong tendency in Swedish politics to sustain minority government rule, in a different way than the support party arrangements described above. A few weeks after the election, the Social Democrat Stefan Löfven formed a minority coalition with the Green party, supported by the Left Party—a support party coalition that did not control a majority of seats. This minority cabinet almost became the shortest-lived cabinet in post-war Swedish history, when the Sweden Democrats voted in favor of the 2014 fall budget prepared by the Alliance parties, which passed instead of the government's budget (Hellström and Lindahl 2021).

This led Prime Minister Löfven to immediately announce that an "extra" election would be held. However, this early election, which would have been exceptional considering that no early elections had been held since 1958, was avoided after an agreement was reached by the government parties and the Alliance parties in December of 2014. The core of this agreement, dubbed the December agreement, was that the bloc that emerged as the largest in parliament after an election would be allowed to form a government and to have its budget pass (Bäck and Hellström 2015: 272). In practice, this meant that the smaller opposition bloc would not present a joint budget proposal, ensuring that the minority government could pass and govern on their own budget, simultaneously minimizing the influence of the Sweden Democrats. While the agreement was supposed to last the entire parliamentary term, and did so in reality, it formally died less than a year later, after the Christian Democrats' members voted against continuing to adhere to the agreement at a party conference (Hellström and Lindahl 2021).

Minority government performance

As described by Field (2016: 18), there are several ways that we can look at minority government performance, and "the most common indicators used to measure government performance are legislative success, fiscal performance, cabinet duration and termination, electoral success, and regime survival." In this section we will analyze several of these indicators in the Swedish setting, comparing minority and majority governments. We discuss if, and in such cases to what extent, Swedish minority governments differ from majority cabinets when it comes to: "legislative effectiveness," cabinet duration, fulfillment of cabinet parties' election pledges, fiscal performance, electoral performance, and public approval of the government.

By examining these indicators, we believe that we can give a good description of minority governments' relative performance compared to majority governments.

Let us start by looking at "legislative success," or "legislative effectiveness" (e.g. Cheibub et al. 2004; Field 2016). The legislative effectiveness of Swedish governments has been analyzed in previous research, showing that proposals made by the Riksdag's powerful standing committees rarely fail in parliament (Lindvall et al. 2020). In Table 7.2, we present the number of bills approved by the various governments, confirming the conclusion that Swedish governments, even the ones controlling only a minority of seats, are clearly able to pass their bills. However, it should be noted that Swedish governments typically do not propose legislation unless there is agreement in the Standing committee, suggesting that this is poor indicator of performance in the Swedish context (also see Loxbo and Sjölin 2017).[4]

Nevertheless, looking at the share of government bills that receive parliamentary approval in Table 7.2, we can see that there is no real difference between recent majority and minority cabinets.[5] There are, however, important differences when it comes to bills voted down by Parliament between the two types of cabinets. For minority governments, a rejection of a bill means that the whole bill, or parts of the bill, was simply rejected. In contrast, for the majority cabinet all the bills were voted down for technical reasons. More precisely, because the cabinet or the standing committee had detected ambiguities in the bill which needed correction.

Another related potential indicator of performance is how long governments survive (Field 2016). In Sweden, it is rare for a government to resign before the next regular election, and as described by Hellström and Lindahl (2021), the last time a Swedish government resigned and was replaced prematurely was in 1981 (Fälldin II).[6] From 1945 until 2018, only five out of thirty cabinets have ended prematurely (excluding non-technical terminations, such as deaths of PMs,). In a comparative perspective, this makes Sweden the country with the fewest number of discretionary terminations in Western Europe, even though it is also one of the countries with the largest share of minority cabinets (Hellström and Lindahl 2021).

An important reason why Sweden has had so few early cabinet terminations relates to how the rules of dissolution and early elections are regulated in the Swedish Constitution, which, compared to those of other West European countries, significantly reduce the incentive for incumbents to call for early elections. The Swedish Instrument of Government states that early elections do not

---

[4] In Table 7.2 we only show the number of government bills presented and approved by the parliament for the last two decades as this information is easily accessible. Regardless, it is very plausible to assume that the proportion of approved bills before the 2000s are also at the same high levels.

[5] In the Table 7.2, a rejection of a bill by parliament does not necessarily mean that the whole bill is voted down but could rather mean that parts of a bill were rejected.

[6] The Carlsson government also resigned in 1990, but as there were no viable government alternative, Carlsson was reinvested as PM shortly thereafter.

Table 7.2 Swedish governments' performance, 1945–2020

Prime minister	# of bills presented	# of government bills approved	% of government bills approved–	Relative duration of cabinet	Electoral losses (% votes)	Trust in government (average %)
Hansson	—	—	—	0.38	—	—
Erlander I	—	—	—	1.00	−1.3	—
Erlander II	—	—	—	0.76	—	—
Erlander III	—	—	—	1.00	−2.6	—
Erlander IV	—	—	—	1.00	5.0	—
Erlander V	—	—	—	0.28	—	—
Erlander VI	—	—	—	0.20	2.3	—
Erlander VII	—	—	—	1.00	1.0	—
Erlander VIII	—	—	—	1.00	−0.6	—
Erlander IX	—	—	—	1.00	5.2	—
Erlander X	—	—	—	0.54	—	—
Palme I	—	—	—	1.00	−6.1	—
Palme II	—	—	—	1.00	—	—
Palme III	—	—	—	1.00	−0.9	—
Fälldin I	—	—	—	0.68	—	—

Continued

Table 7.2 Continued

Prime minister	# of bills presented	# of government bills approved	% of government bills approved	Relative duration of cabinet	Electoral losses (% votes)	Trust in government (average %)
Ullsten	—	—	—	1.00	−0.5	—
Fälldin II	—	—	—	0.53	—	—
Fälldin III	—	—	—	1.00	−7.3	—
Palme IV	—	—	—	1.00	−0.9	—
Palme V	—	—	—	0.15	—	51
Carlsson I	—	—	—	1.00	−1.5	45
Carlsson II	—	—	—	1.00	−5.5	21
Bildt	—	—	—	1.00	−5.2	33
Carlsson III	—	—	—	0.37	—	34
Persson I	—	—	—	1.00	−8.9	22
Persson II	—	—	—	1.00	+3.5	31
Persson III	577	570	98.8	1.00	−4.9	27
Reinfeldt I	651	643	98.7	1.00	+1.2	39
Reinfeldt II	601	592	98.5	1.00	−10.0	44
Löfven I	643	634	98.6	1.00	−5.2	32
Löfven II	388	380	97.9	0.69	—	35

Notes: Minority governments are marked in grey. For the Löfven II cabinet the reported data covers the entire period in office (i.e. up to June 2021). Data on trust in government based on the SOM surveys (Arkhede and Oscarsson 2016; Martinsson and Andersson 2020). Average share of people who had high or fairly high trust in the government during the years that the government was in office is reported.

commence a new term of office. This implies that a government formed after an early election only serves the remaining term of office, and the incentive for the PM to announce an early election therefore decreases over time.

Looking at the little variation there is over time when it comes to cabinet duration in Sweden (see Table 7.2), we can also see that minority governments do not seem to perform any worse than majority governments in terms of how long they survive. Of the five cabinets that have not terminated because of a regular election or some technical reason, there are three cases of inter-party conflict within the government, one early election, and one case of coalition enlargement (Hellström and Lindahl 2021). Three of these five cabinets controlled a majority of seats in the Riksdag (Erlander V, Fälldin I and II), whereas two were minority governments without formal support parties (Erlander II and VI).

The performance of minority governments has been a topic of debate in Swedish politics, and several scholars have attempted to evaluate their performance in various ways. For example, Lindvall and colleagues (2017; 2020), analyze the policies adopted in Sweden, focusing on the correspondence between the electoral promises parties make during campaigns and the policies they implement when they are in government. Given that a large-scale comparative study of electoral pledges found that minority coalition governments are least successful in terms of pledge fulfillment (Thomson et al. 2017), the expectation would be that similar patterns would be found in the Swedish case.

However, as shown by Naurin (2014), governing parties in Sweden have typically managed to do most of the things they promised during election campaigns. For example, the Social Democrats kept more than 80 percent of the promises they made between 1994 and 2002, and the Alliance majority coalition that governed between 2006 and 2010 had a similarly high level of pledge fulfillment. As described by Lindvall et al. (2020), the minority Alliance coalition that formed in 2010 performed equally well in terms of pledge fulfillment (78 percent pledge fulfillment rate). Hence, in terms of policies adopted, Swedish minority governments have performed relatively well.

Other scholars have suggested that we should look at the fiscal performance of minority governments, as they may be expected to perform worse in fiscal terms since these governments have to bargain with, and may be "blackmailed" by, opposition parties, which may lead to higher budgetary costs. On this topic the comparative literature has produced varying results, with some early studies showing that minority governments have higher budget deficits, and some more recent studies showing that minority cabinets are not associated with poor fiscal performance (see e.g. Edin and Ohlsson 1991; Falcó-Gimeno and Jurado 2011). In a recent extensive study of the OECD countries over fifty years, Potrafke (2019) shows that minority governments do not have higher fiscal deficits and public expenditure than majority governments. He shows that minority cabinets with more formalized support party arrangements, referring to the Swedish case of "contract parliamentarism," do not increase public expenditure more than majority cabinets.

Another potential indicator of performance is related to the electoral arena, and how governing parties fare in the polls (e.g. Strøm 1990). A number of comparative studies have shown that governing is costly, and that incumbent parties tend to lose electoral support (e.g. Stevenson 2002; Walther and Hellström 2019). In a recent comparative study, Hjermitslev (2020) finds, analyzing electoral data from twenty parliamentary systems (1961–2015), that minority status is associated with lower costs for all parties in government, but especially for the Prime Minister's party.

Looking at Swedish cabinets, there is no clear evidence that minority cabinets perform worse electorally than majority governments (see Table 7.2), but this comparison is somewhat difficult to make because there are so many minority cabinets. It is also not obvious what we should expect theoretically. The fact that minority cabinets have to seek support for their policies from the opposition gives them an opportunity to avoid blame for potential policy failures, as suggested in the literature on clarity of responsibility, where parties in some types of governments are less likely to be held accountable since voters have difficulties assigning blame (e.g. Strøm 1990; Powell and Whitten 1993).

If we instead look at trust in government as an indicator of performance, using data from large-scale representative surveys with Swedish citizens between 1986 and 2019 (e.g. Arkhede and Oscarsson 2016; Martinsson and Andersson 2020), we again do not find any systematic differences between minority and majority governments. A particular problem with this comparison is that there has only been one majority government during the period of study that offers data on trust in the government—the Alliance coalition government that was in office between 2006 and 2010. All other cabinets were minority governments. Trust in government instead seems to co-vary with other factors. For example, the Swedish cabinets associated with the lowest levels of trust are the Carlsson II and Persson I governments that were in office when Sweden faced severe economic difficulties.

Conclusion

As described in this chapter, Sweden stands out in a comparative perspective by having been ruled by minority cabinets for over 70 percent of the post-war period. We suggest that the dominance of the left–right economic dimension, the historically dominant position of the Social Democrats, and a negative parliamentary system most likely explain why minority cabinets are so common in Sweden. Sweden is also unusual in the sense that minority governments in office have, during the past decades, cooperated with their support parties in an institutionalized manner, publicly committing to their support parties through detailed written agreements, and in some cases even allowing support parties to appoint non-cabinet officials to the government and to make budget proposals. Our conclusion is also that Swedish minority governments have performed well—they are highly successful in passing their bills, they seldom terminate early, and they do not perform any worse electorally than other parties. In addition, there are no signs that minority governments are associated with lower public trust, or with poor economic performance.

The institutional setting surrounding government formation suggests that we will continue to see minority governments forming in the Swedish case in the future, even though the dominance of the left-right dimension and the Social Democratic party has waned. Whether Swedish minority governments will continue to perform well is, however, difficult to predict. The rise of the populist radical right party, the Sweden Democrats, which has been treated as a pariah by the mainstream parties, has complicated coalition bargaining. This is also an important reason why it took much longer than usual to form a government after the 2018 election (see e.g. Bäck and Hellström 2018; Teorell et al. 2020). These party system changes may also result in more instability, where we see more government crises occurring, even in a favorable institutional setting like the Swedish one, where early elections do not commence a new term of office.

References

Arkhede, Sofia, and Henrik Oscarsson. 2016. *Svenska demokratitrender*. Gothenburg: The SOM Institute.
Aylott, Nicholas. 2016. "The Party System." In *The Oxford Handbook of Swedish Politics*, ed. Jon Pierre. Oxford: Oxford University Press, 152–168.
Bäck, Hanna, and Torbjörn Bergman. 2016. "The Parties in Government Formation." In *The Oxford Handbook of Swedish Politics*, ed. Jon Pierre. Oxford: Oxford University Press, 206–226.
Bäck, Hanna, and Johan Hellström. 2015. "Efter valet 2014: Regeringsbildningen och det inställda extra valet." *Statsvetenskaplig tidskrift*, 117 (2): 261–278.
Bäck, Hanna, and Johan Hellström. 2018." Kris i regeringsfrågan?" In *Demokratins framtid*, ed. Katarina Barrling and Sören Holmberg. Stockholm: Riksdagen, 269–298.
Bale, Tim, and Torbjörn Bergman. 2006. "Captives No Longer, but Servants Still? Contract Parliamentarism and the New Minority Governance in Sweden and New Zealand." *Government and Opposition* 41 (3): 422–449.
Bergman, Torbjörn. 1993a. "Formation Rules and Minority Governments." *European Journal of Political Research* 23 (1): 55–66.
Bergman, Torbjörn. 1993b. "Constitutional Design and Government Formation: The Expected Consequences of Negative Parliamentarism." *Scandinavian Political Studies* 16 (4): 285–304.
Bergman, Torbjörn. 1995. *Constitutional Rules and Party Goals in Coalition Formation: An Analysis of Winning Minority Governments in Sweden*. Ph.D. thesis, Department of Political Science, Umeå University.

Bergman, Torbjörn. 2000. "When Minority Cabinets Are the Rule and Majority Coalitions the Exception." In *Coalition Governments in Western Europe*, ed. Wolfgang C. Müller, and Kaare Strøm. Oxford: Oxford University Press, 192–230.

Bergman, Torbjörn, Hanna Bäck, and Johan Hellström. 2020. "Coalition Governance Patterns Across Western Europe" In *Coalition Governance in Western Europe*, edited by Torbjörn Bergman, Hanna Bäck, and Johan Hellström. Oxford: Oxford University Press, 680–726.

Cheibub, José Antonio, Shane Martin, and Bjørn Erik Rasch. 2019. "Investiture Rules and Formation of Minority Governments in European Parliamentary Democracies." *Party Politics* 27 (2): 351–362.

Cheibub, José Antonio, Adam Przeworski, and Sebastian M. Saiegh. 2004. "Government Coalitions and Legislative Success under Presidentialism and Parliamentarism." *British Journal of Political Science* 34 (4): 565–587.

Crombez, Christophe. 1996. "Minority Governments, Minimal Winning Coalitions and Surplus Majorities in Parliamentary Systems." *European Journal of Political Research* 29 (1): 1–29.

Edin Per-Anders, and Henry Ohlsson. 1991. "Political Determinants of budget Deficits: Coalition Effects versus Minority Effects." *European Economic Review* 35 (8): 1597–1603.

Falcó-Gimeno, Albert, and Ignacio Jurado. 2011. "Minority Governments and Budget Deficits: The Role of the Opposition." *European Journal of Political Economy* 27 (3): 554–565.

Field, Bonnie N. 2016. *Why Minority Governments Work: Multilevel Territorial Politics in Spain*. New York: Palgrave Macmillan.

Golder, Sona N. 2010. "Bargaining Delays in the Government Formation Process." *Comparative Political Studies* 43 (1): 3–32.

Hellström, Johan, and Jonas Lindahl. 2021. "Sweden—The Rise and Fall of Bloc Politics." In *Coalition Governance in Western Europe*, ed. Torbjörn Bergman, Hanna Bäck, and Johan Hellström. Oxford: Oxford University Press, 574–610.

Hjermitslev, Ida B. 2020. "The Electoral Cost of Coalition Participation: Can Anyone Escape?" *Party Politics* 26 (4): 510–520.

Iyengar, Shanto, Yptach Lelkes, Matthew Levendusky, Neil Malhotra, and Shaun J. Westwood. 2019. "The Origins and Consequences of Affective Polarization in the United States." *Annual Review of Political Science* 22: 129–146.

Lindahl, Jonas, Hellström, Johan, and Bäck, Hanna. 2020. "Minority Government as the Norm." In *Coalition Government as a Reflection of a Nation's Politics and Society: A Comparative Study of Parliamentary Parties and Cabinets in 12 Countries*, ed. Matt Evans. London: Routledge, 127–146.

Lindvall, Johannes, Hanna Bäck, Carl Dahlström, Elin Naurin, and Jan Teorell. 2017. *Samverkan och strid i den parlamentariska demokratin*. Stockholm: SNS Förlag.

Lindvall, Johannes, Hanna Bäck, Carl Dahlström, Elin Naurin, and Jan Teorell. 2020. "Swedish Parliamentary Democracy at 100." *Parliamentary Affairs* 73: 477–502.

Loxbo, Karl, and Mats Sjölin. 2017. "Parliamentary Opposition on the Wane? The Case of Sweden, 1970–2014." *Government and Opposition* 52 (4): 587–613.

Martin, Lanny W., and Randolph T. Stevenson. 2001. "Government Formation in Parliamentary Democracies." *American Journal of Political Science* 45: 33–50.

Martin, Lanny W., and Georg Vanberg. 2003. "Wasting Time? The Impact of Ideology and Size on Delay in Coalition Formation." *British Journal of Political Science* 33 (2): 323–332.

Martinsson, Johan, and Ulrika Andersson. 2020. "Svenska trender 1986-2020." Gothenburg: The SOM Institute. https://www.gu.se/sites/default/files/2020-04/6.%20Svenska%20Trender%20%281986-2019%29.pdf (Retrieved October 8 2020).

Mitchell, Paul, and Ben Nyblade. 2008. "Government Formation and Cabinet Type." In *Cabinets and Coalition Bargaining: The Democratic Life Cycle in Western Europe*, ed. Kaare Strøm, Wolfgang C. Müller, and Torbjörn Bergman. Oxford: Oxford University Press, 201-236.

Naurin, Elin. 2014. "Is a Promise a Promise? Election Pledge Fulfilment in Comparative Perspective Using Sweden as an Example." *West European Politics* 37 (5): 1046-1064.

Persson, Thomas. 2016. "Policy Coordination under Minority and Majority Rule." In *The Oxford Handbook of Swedish Politics*, ed. Jon Pierre. Oxford: Oxford University Press, 634-649.

Potrafke, Niklas. 2019. "Fiscal Performance of Minority Governments: New Empirical Evidence For OECD Countries." Party Politics 27 (3), 501-514.

Powell G. Bingham, and Guy D. Whitten. 1993. "A Cross-national Analysis of Economic Voting: Taking Account of the Political Context." *American Journal of Political Science* 37 (2): 391-414.

Stevenson, Randolph T. 2002. "The Cost of Ruling, Cabinet Duration, and the Median-gap Model." *Public Choice* 113 (1-2): 157-178.

Strøm, Kaare 1985. "Party goals and government performance in parliamentary democracies". *American Political Science Review* 79 (3): 738-754.

Strøm, Kaare. 1990. *Minority Government and Majority Rule*. Cambridge: Cambridge University Press.

Teorell, Jan, Hanna Bäck, Johan Hellström, and Johannes Lindvall. 2020. *134 dagar: Om regeringsbildningen efter valet 2018*. Stockholm: Makadam förlag.

Thürk, Maria, Johan Hellström, and Holger Döring. 2020. "Institutional Constraints on Cabinet Formation: Veto Points and Party System Dynamics." *European Journal of Political Research* 60 (2): 295-316.

Thomson, R., Royed, T., Naurin, E., Artés, J., Costello, R., Ennser-Jedenastik, L., Ferguson, M., Kostadinova, P., Moury, C., Pétry, F. and Praprotnik, K. 2017. "The Fulfillment of Parties' Election Pledges: A Comparative Study on the Impact of Power Sharing." *American Journal of Political Science*, 61 (3): 527-542.

Walther, Daniel, and Johan Hellström. 2019. "The Verdict in the Polls: How Government Stability Is Affected by Popular Support." *West European Politics* 42 (3): 593-617.

PART III
WHERE MINORITY GOVERNMENTS ARE COMMON

8
Minority Governments in Canada
Stability through Voting Alliances

Jean-François Godbout and Christopher Cochrane

The Canadian obsession with single-party government is deeply puzzling. Between 1945 and 2020, the country experienced ten minority governments. In each of these cases, the government refused to enter into a formal or informal coalition agreement with the opposition parties, relying instead on temporary working majorities to pass legislation in the House of Commons. This risky approach to governing is normally associated with higher levels of legislative instability (Russell 2008). Yet Canada seems to defy this assumption. The country has always been governed by relatively stable governments, even when no party controlled a majority of seats in the legislature. Although the average length of majority parliaments has been close to 1,400 days between 1945 and 2020, minority governments have lasted around 500 days, which corresponds roughly to what Strøm (1990) and Saalfeld (2008) find in other comparable cases of single-party minority cabinets around the world.

What, then, makes the Canadian case so unique? This chapter attempts to answer this question by looking at the performance of minority governments in this country. Although our analysis confirms that hung parliaments have a shorter lifespan and are somewhat less productive, these differences are surprisingly small, especially if we consider the fact that minority governments have always been controlled by a single party in the House of Commons.[1] The aim of this chapter is thus to understand how minority governments form and govern, but also to explain why Canadian parties are so averse to coalition bargaining. We argue that the answer to this puzzle lies in Canada's federal structure and plurality electoral rule, which tends to promote the regional fragmentation of the party system (Johnston 2017). For single-party minority governments, the presence of smaller regional parties implies that short-term voting alliances can be negotiated on a wider range of issues. This strategy has proven effective for the most part, since it allowed the last four Liberal (2004, 2019) and Conservative (2006, 2008) minority

---

[1] A hung parliament is a situation where no single party holds a majority of seats in the House of Commons.

Jean-François Godbout and Christopher Cochrane, *Minority Governments in Canada*. In: *Minority Governments in Comparative Perspective*. Edited by Bonnie N. Field and Shane Martin, Oxford University Press. © Jean-François Godbout and Christopher Cochrane (2022). DOI: 10.1093/oso/9780192871657.003.0008

governments to remain in office for up to two years on average, without having to share any cabinet seats with the opposition.[2]

The Canadian political system

This chapter begins by explaining the general structure of Canada's political institutions and party system, with an emphasis on the rules of government formation.

General description of the political system

Canada is a federation and a constitutional monarchy with a Westminster style parliamentary system. As a former colony of the British Empire and a member of the Commonwealth of nations, the country's head of state today remains Queen Elisabeth II. However, in her absence, the executive power is vested in the hands of a governor general who represents the monarchy in Canada. Although the governor general has a great deal of formal constitutional powers, the convention of responsible government limits her influence in the political process. The governor general's role is symbolic, as the real executive power lies in the hands of the cabinet, whose members sit in parliament and are appointed by the prime minister.

Parliament in Canada is divided into two chambers, the elected House of Commons and the appointed Senate, which have basically the same legislative powers, except that finance bills must originate from the elected Lower House. The Canadian population elects 338 members to the House of Commons every four years with a plurality electoral voting system. Each member represents a geographically delimited constituency based on population size. Parliament's upper chamber, the Senate, is a federal assembly representing four distinct regional divisions of the country: the Maritimes, Quebec, Ontario, and Western Canada. The upper chamber is composed of 105 senators who serve until the age of 75. When vacancies occur, new senators are appointed by the governor general, but following the recommendation of the prime minister.

Canada is a parliamentary democracy because the cabinet must govern with the consent of parliament. The convention of responsible government and the British constitutional model stipulate that the crown will only appoint and heed the advice of a prime minister who has the support of a majority of members of the House of Commons. Thus, the monarchy still plays an important role in government

---

[2] Note that an additional Liberal minority government was elected in September 2021. However, since this parliament is ongoing, it is not included in the analysis presented below.

formation, since the governor general has the power to appoint or fire a prime minister. The only guiding principle here is that cabinet retains the confidence of the popularly elected lower house. Therefore, the role of the upper chamber in the Canadian legislative process is marginal; it lacks legitimacy because it is not a popularly elected chamber and it does not participate in the process of government formation.

Party system

Originally composed of two parties, the Liberal (center-left) and the Conservative (center-right), the Canadian party system has experienced several major transformations over the years, which have been characterized by an increase in the number of parties and a change in the issues that divide them. All of the post-war elections have seen an alternance between single-party Conservative and Liberal governments, but the majority/minority status of their respective caucus is explained by the strength of this multiparty system, which has been historically fueled by regional conflicts in the federation.

Canada's two party-system was permanently transformed in the 1920s, a decade which saw the emergence of several new regional agrarian parties in parliament. These minor parties—like the Progressives or United Farmers—have benefited over the years from the single member plurality electoral system because their supporters were concentrated geographically in the western part of the country. In addition to the Liberal and Conservative parties, Canada also has a third smaller party competing at the national level. Created in 1961, the New Democratic Party (NDP) emerged from an alliance between a left-leaning western agrarian party and labor unions. It is the combination of seats won by both the NDP and other regional parties that explain the formation of all six minority governments elected between 1945 and 1993. Note that the control of these minority governments was evenly divided between the Conservatives (1957, 1962, 1979) and Liberals (1963, 1965, 1972).

A more recent transformation of the party system at the end of the twentieth century explains the election of the last four minority governments in Canada between 1993 and 2020. This period saw the emergence of two new strong regional parties—one with support among populists in the west (Reform) and one found exclusively in Quebec, with support among nationalists (Bloc Québécois). Both of these parties were created from a split within the Conservative coalition in the late 1980s, which led to the realignment of voters on the right. As long as the traditional supporters of the Conservative Party remained divided, the plurality voting system created an advantage for the Liberals, who managed to win enough seats to form three successive majority governments in 1993, 1997, and 2000. This lasted until the remainder of the Conservative Party merged with the

Reform Party (now called the Canadian Alliance) to create a new united party on the right in 2003. By coordinating their supporters toward a single party, this rebranded Conservative Party was successful enough to force three consecutive minority governments in 2004, 2006, and 2008. Although the Liberals were capable of holding on to power in 2004, the Conservatives won the next two elections, but still had to contend with three opposition parties in the House (Liberals, Bloc Québécois, and NDP). Canada has had three more elections between 2011 and 2020: two resulted in majority governments (Conservative in 2011 and Liberal in 2015), while the 2019 one led to another minority government (Liberal).

The continuous presence of the Bloc in parliament after the consolidation of the right explains why minority governments have become more frequent over the last twenty years. The Bloc has significantly weakened the electoral strength of the Liberal and Conservative parties in Quebec. Because of its population size and its tendency to vote as a coordinated block, this province was historically instrumental in promoting strong majorities in the House by almost always electing a large delegation of MPs on the government side (Johnson 2017). Deprived of this advantage, both major parties now face a greater challenge in finding the necessary seats to reach majority status, particularly when the Bloc does well in Quebec.

Overview of the government formation rules

For the casual observer, the process of government investiture in Canada appears to follow two simple rules. First, whichever party wins the most seats in the House after an election is expected to form the next government. This outcome is fairly easy to predict when a single party holds a majority. But this is also what happens when no party holds a majority: in all ten cases of hung parliaments between 1945 and 2020, the party that won the most seats also formed the government. The second rule of government formation is that the party who finishes first should govern alone, even without a majority. In other words, there will be no formal coalitions or even a confidence and supply agreement between parties during a hung parliament in Canada. This is the outcome observed for all twelve minority governments between 1921 and 2020.

Of course, from a constitutional standpoint, both of these conventions are wrong. There is nothing in the written or unwritten Constitution of Canada that stipulates that a party winning the most seats is expected to form a government after an election. Rather, Westminster constitutional conventions dictate that the governor general will appoint as prime minister the party leader who has the highest likelihood of having the confidence of a majority of members in the House. Thus, an incumbent prime minister can always decide to hold on to power, even if one or more of the opposition parties win more seats after an election.[3] Under this scenario, the governor general would not intervene. Unlike the UK and New Zealand, Canada does not have an official cabinet manual, so the only guiding principle here is that the PM maintains the confidence of the new House.

Although Canada, like other Westminster style parliamentary systems, does not have a formal investiture rule to approve the government, it does have an indirect vote to confirm confidence in the prime minister and the cabinet at the start of each parliament. This first vote of confidence occurs following the reading of the speech from the throne (i.e. the Queen's Speech), which represents the government's official program for the upcoming session of parliament. This is a confidence type investiture vote that is both *reactive* and *closed*; a simple majority of the lower house must either approve or reject the government (Rasch, Martin, and Cheibub 2015). Usually, the confidence vote is a pure formality when the government controls a majority, but it is much more important when parliament is hung. In this case, an incumbent prime minister might lose the confidence of the House at the beginning of a new term. Under this scenario, the governor general would then consult the leaders of the opposition to see if another party has the necessary support to form a new government; if no one else can, she will dissolve parliament.[4] The replacement of a sitting prime minister by the governor general used to occur more frequently in Canada's colonial days when party unity was much weaker, however, no government ever lost a vote of confidence following the reading of a speech from the throne since Confederation.[5]

Following Cheibub, Martin, and Rasch (2021), we can thus summarize the dimensions of parliamentary investiture in Canada as follows. First, the timing of the vote is ex post, meaning that it occurs after the government is formed by the head of state. Second, the right to nominate the prime minister is officially the prerogative of the crown, who must remain neutral by appointing whomever has the highest likelihood of winning the confidence of the lower house. Third, the target of the first vote of investiture is the government's policy platform (or the throne speech). Fourth, in order to govern, the cabinet must always maintain the confidence of the lower house by having the support of a simple majority of MPs.

---

[3] The results of the 1925 federal election confirm that a party in second place (the Liberals won 100 seats) can remain in office even if the official opposition wins more seats (the Conservative won 115 seats). In this case, the Liberals held on to power because they were able to convince the governor general that their government had the support of a third party (the Progressives with 22 seats).

[4] A governor general could also refuse the request to dissolve parliament after a vote of confidence. This will most likely occur shortly after an election. In 1926, the governor general Lord Byng refused a request to dissolve parliament ten months after the 1925 election when Prime Minister Makenzie-King lost a vote of confidence in the House.

[5] It does still happen from time to time in provincial elections, but never in federal elections. The two most recent cases were in British Columbia (2017) and New Brunswick (2018). In these two cases, the incumbent Premier refused to resign following the election of a hung parliament; both were later defeated when the opposition parties adopted an amendment to the throne speech.

Overview of the types of government since 1945

Table 8.1 confirms that ten out of the twenty-four elections between 1945 and 2020 (42 percent) resulted in hung parliaments. Only two of these elections have produced "real popular" majorities with the government winning more than 50 percent of the vote (the Conservatives in 1958 and 1984). The rest of these majorities have been artificial, resulting from the unequal transfer of votes to seats, a consequence of the plurality voting system. The smallest majority was obtained with just under 39 percent of the popular vote in 1997, whereas the largest minority government was supported by 41 percent of the electorate in 1964. Control of these minority governments is evenly split between Conservatives (five) and Liberals (five). On the other hand, majority governments have almost exclusively been associated with Liberal victories: ten of the fourteen cases. Between 1990 and 2020, Canada experienced four minority governments (40 percent). Once again, their control was split evenly between the Liberal (2004, 2019) and Conservative (2006, 2008) parties.

As we saw earlier, Canada is an interesting case because all of its minority parliaments have been "substantive minority governments" controlled by a single party, with no formal or informal coalition agreements with the opposition (Strøm 1990). For many Canadians, minority governments are seen as a temporary "half-way house," that will eventually transition towards a majority. Although new minority governments are somewhat more likely to subsequently transform into majorities (1957, 1965, 2008), there are as many exceptions (1974, 1979, 2019). Still, as we will see below, the preference for single-party government has many advantages, but also greatly reduces the average length of hung parliaments in Canada.

Why minority governments form

In this section, we consider why single-party minority governments are the norm in Canada. The main explanation is linked to the structure of the party system, which facilitates the formation of ad hoc voting coalitions and renders this type of arrangement relatively effective when compared to other forms of agreements between parties.

Government formation and institutions

Government formation rules in Canada follow a negative form of parliamentarism (Bergman 1993). Although recent work by Keslo (2015) and Cheibub, Martin, and Rasch (2021) claim that the Queen's speech process in Westminster can be interpreted as a positive form of parliamentarism, we fail to see how this matters for

Table 8.1 Types of government, Canada, 1945–2020

Prime minister	Start date	End date	Government party	Coalition	Minority	Formal or substantive	Support parties
Mackenzie King	06-09-1945	30-04-1949	Liberal	No	No	—	—
St-Laurent	15-09-1949	13-06-1953	Liberal	No	No	—	—
St-Laurent	12-11-1953	12-04-1957	Liberal	No	No	—	—
Diefenbaker	**14-10-1957**	**01-02-1958**	**Conservative**	**No**	**Yes**	**Substantive**	—
Diefenbaker	12-05-1958	19-04-1962	Conservative	No	No	—	—
Diefenbaker	**27-08-1962**	**06-02-1963**	**Conservative**	**No**	**Yes**	**Substantive**	—
Pearson	**16-05-1963**	**08-09-1965**	**Liberal**	**No**	**Yes**	**Substantive**	—
Pearson	**18-01-1966**	**23-04-1968**	**Liberal**	**No**	**Yes**	**Substantive**	—
Trudeau P.	12-09-1968	01-09-1972	Liberal	No	No	—	—
Trudeau P.	**04-01-1973**	**09-05-1974**	**Liberal**	**No**	**Yes**	**Substantive**	—
Trudeau P.	30-09-1974	26-03-1979	Liberal	No	No	—	—
Clark	**09-10-1979**	**12-12-1979**	**Conservative**	**No**	**Yes**	**Substantive**	—
Trudeau P.	14-04-1980	09-07-1984	Liberal	No	No	—	—
Mulroney	05-11-1984	01-10-1988	Conservative	No	No	—	—
Mulroney	12-12-1988	08-09-1993	Conservative	No	No	—	—
Chrétien	17-01-1994	27-04-1997	Liberal	No	No	—	—
Chrétien	22-09-1997	22-10-2000	Liberal	No	No	—	—
Chrétien	29-01-2001	23-05-2004	Liberal	No	No	—	—
Martin	**04-10-2004**	**29-11-2005**	**Liberal**	**No**	**Yes**	**Substantive**	—
Harper	**03-04-2006**	**07-09-2008**	**Conservative**	**No**	**Yes**	**Substantive**	—
Harper	**18-11-2008**	**26-03-2011**	**Conservative**	**No**	**Yes**	**Substantive**	—
Harper	02-06-2011	02-08-2015	Conservative	No	No	—	—
Trudeau J.	03-12-2015	11-09-2019	Liberal	No	No	—	—
Trudeau J.	**05-12-2019**	**15-08-2021**	**Liberal**	**No**	**Yes**	**Substantive**	—

Notes: Bold lines represent minority governments.
Share of minority governments 1945–2020: 42%.
Share of minority governments 1990–2020: 40%.

the formation of minority governments in the Canadian context. We agree that this process operates just like a formal investiture vote. However, we do not find empirical evidence that it promotes the formation of coalition governments in Canada, as the presence of positive parliamentarism would imply.

Several facts seem to confirm our interpretation. First, Canada has only experienced one formal coalition in its history. This was done to create an all-party wartime cabinet between the Conservatives and the Liberals during World War I. There are several other examples of coalition agreements in the country, but all of these are found at the subnational level.[6] At the federal level, no successful coalition agreement of any kind has been adopted after World War I, although a coalition of three opposition parties came close to replacing the incumbent Conservative minority government following the 2008 election. This coalition agreement was negotiated shortly after parliament first convened. At the time, the Liberals, NDP, and the Bloc Québécois were highly critical of the Conservative's response to the 2008 economic crisis and agreed to form an alliance to replace the incumbent government: the Liberals and NDP would enter cabinet with shared portfolios and collective ministerial responsibility, whereas the Bloc would agree to support this coalition for a period of two years in the House. The opposition needed a vote of confidence to move ahead with this plan, but the Conservatives were able to postpone the vote indefinitely by proroguing parliament. This interlude lasted just long enough for the coalition to unravel. Following intense internal divisions on the merit of forming an alliance with a nationalist party, the Liberals selected a new leader who refused to pursue the matter further once parliament reconvened in January of 2009.

This brief overview confirms that Canadian parties prefer to form single-party governments, even when they do not control a majority of the seats in the House. Not only are Canadian parties reluctant to negotiate coalition alliances with shared ministerial responsibility, they are also refusing to engage in the less stringent requirements of confidence and supply agreements. What explains this aversion? After all, hung parliaments occur frequently in Canada and parties are aware of the existence of coalition agreements, which have been negotiated elsewhere, either at the provincial level or in other Westminster style parliamentary systems.

This atypical situation is most likely explained by the flawed perception that single-party minority governments should be the default mode for governing in the federal parliament. Of course, there are important advantages associated with

---

[6] For instance, confidence and supply agreements were negotiated at the provincial level after the 1985 Ontario and 2017 British Columbia elections. In both of these cases, a smaller opposition party agreed to support the minority government for a period of two years in exchange for legislative concessions. Formal coalition agreements with shared ministerial portfolios have also occurred in the provinces, the most famous example being the 1999 coalition agreement between the incumbent NDP government and the opposing Liberals in Saskatchewan, which saw a transfer of three cabinet seats in exchange for legislative support.

controlling the cabinet exclusively. Canada has a strong executive, even compared to other Westminster style parliaments; party discipline is high, and the government can take full advantage of the bureaucracy and the state apparatus to win the support of a large number of voters at election time. This would be much more difficult to achieve under a coalition agreement, which tends to dilute government accountability and reduces the potential benefits of credit claiming (Cheibub and Przeworski 1999). The fact that six of the nine incumbent single-party minority governments between 1945 and 2020 won re-election in the next term seems to confirm this advantage.

There is also probably some level of path dependency in the approach of government formation. Ad hoc voting coalitions have been the norm since 1921, and they have so far served minority governments well. The three most recent confidence and supply agreements negotiated at the provincial level in Canada all entailed a contract of two years, but the ad hoc solution gets a single party very close to this timeframe; the average length of minority governments in the post-war era is around one and a half years, closer to two years after 2000. Once again, with ad hoc voting coalitions, there are fewer strings attached, especially if the parties do not have to share cabinet seats. So, for these reasons, it seems likely that the single-party minority government approach will remain the norm for quite some time in Canada (Deptner 2014).[7]

Government formation and the party system

Aside from traditions and the advantages of exclusively controlling the executive, the structure of the party system probably contributes the most to explain why Canadian parties prefer single-party minority governments. With a strong party in the center (the Liberals), a weaker party on the left, and strong regional parties, it is much easier for minority governments to rely on ad hoc voting coalitions to remain in power. Indeed, a majority can always be built on at least two types of issues: the left–right ideological continuum and a central–periphery regional dimension.

The presence of a minor party on the left, the NDP, and a strong party in the center, the Liberals, also seem to defy the logic of coalition formation. If we follow the argument of Crombez (1996), we should expect a larger centrist party like the Liberals to be less inclined to form coalition governments during hung parliaments, since it can benefit from the support of the parties on either side of its flanks. So far, the empirical evidence confirms this pattern for the Liberals. However, the theory fails to explain why Conservative single-party governments are

---

[7] The potential effect of the fixed Election Date Act adopted in 2007 is worth mentioning. This law stipulates that elections should be held on the first Tuesday of the fourth calendar years of a parliament. However, there is nothing in the law that prevents a prime minister from calling an election before this date, as the 2008 election shows.

also the norm in Canada. According to Crombez (1996), the more extreme party on the right should be able to govern only if it has coalition partners and shares ministerial portfolios. But this ignores the potential support that can be achieved by pandering to regional parties, both in the west and in Quebec.

The three main national parties in Canada have historically been office-seeking. Although the country has so far been exclusively governed by the Liberals and the Conservatives, the left leaning NDP saw its best electoral performance in 2011, when it achieved the status of official opposition in parliament for the first time. Regional parties are different. The most important of these emerged from two provinces only: Alberta (Reform, Social Credit) and Quebec (Bloc, Crédit social). The Bloc Québécois is the only party officially looking to stay out of government, because it is a nationalist party promoting the independence of Quebec. The other regional parties may have claimed at some point or another that their official goal was to form the next government, but this would have been very difficult, given the limited scope of their electoral appeal.

It makes sense to assume that the three main parties, as well as the regional ones (except the Bloc), would be willing to participate in a governing coalition. The NDP has probably the most to gain in such a scenario, since it competes nationally but has historically been penalized by the plurality voting system. The situation is somewhat different for regional parties. Unlike the NDP, these smaller parties can only hope to form the government if they broaden their electoral appeal. Therefore, holding the balance of power during a hung parliament is often perceived as a more realistic goal (Russell 2008). Under this scenario, smaller parties can obtain concessions from the government in exchange for their support, without having to risk the electoral consequences of a more formal coalition agreement.

To be sure, we still find evidence that opposition parties will sometimes attack one another for voting with the government during hung parliaments. Deptner (2014) claims that the CCF paid a price for collaborating with the Conservatives in the 1958 minority government. More recently, a campaign strategy used by the Conservatives in the 2006 election was to accuse the NDP of having kept the Liberals in power in the previous parliament by advertising the number of times they had voted with the government. Nevertheless, we lack empirical evidence to confirm that these claims have an impact on election results.

Minority governments in office

In this section, we show that minority governments in Canada are supported by shifting ad hoc voting coalitions between two or more parties in the House of Commons. These agreements are usually explained by ideological proximity, but also by regionalism and electoral incentives.

Minority government types and majority building in parliament

As we saw earlier, Canadian parties do not enter into multiparty governing arrangements during hung parliaments, implying that the governments have always been supported by ad hoc voting coalitions. This type of minority government leaves the executive with the highest possible degree of freedom in the legislature (Field 2016; Strøm 1990). Since all of the voting agreements are negotiated in private before a vote is taken, we cannot talk of "partnership" or even "one-time arrangement" between the parties, which makes Canada an unusual case (see Kent 2009).

How do these voting coalitions work? The substantive nature of minority governments in Canada (Strøm 1990) implies that no parties rely on comprehensive support agreements to maintain a stable majority coalition. Rather, the government strategy is to find common grounds with enough opposition parties to build a working majority before a vote is taken. These voting alliances can be negotiated with the same opposition party over the course of a single parliamentary term, or they can be negotiated between different opposition parties, depending on the issues at stake during the vote. An opposition party may declare that it will support the government in a series of recorded divisions, usually in exchange for some legislative concession, but these deals are usually rare and never last more than a few votes. The important thing to remember here is that, in the absence of stable coalition partners, minority governments can lose the confidence of the House at almost any given moment.

One of the primary factors explaining who enters these voting coalitions is the size of the caucuses in the House. A minority government that can build a majority with each of the opposition parties is in a better position than one who has to rely exclusively on one partner or a combination of two or more partners to pass legislation. In the 1960s, the Liberals had enough seats to form a close working relationship with the NDP during the minority governments of Lester Pearson, but the government could have chosen to build an ad hoc coalition with either one of the two remaining opposition parties, since it was only a few seats short of a majority (i.e. the Conservatives and the Social Credit in that case). In fact, Gervais (2011: 190) confirmed that the Social Credit, not the NDP, was the party most likely to support the Liberals during confidence votes in that term. A different scenario unfolded after the 2004 election, when the NDP fell one seat short of providing the minority Liberal government of Paul Martin with enough seats to reach a majority. For a time, the government had to rely either on the Conservatives or the Bloc Québécois to govern, until one Conservative MP crossed over to the government side in 2005, thus transforming the NDP-Liberal voting coalition into a workable majority.

Of course, opposition parties may not always agree with what the government is doing when parliament is hung. A minority government can usually expect at least some level of collaboration with opposition parties immediately following an election. For a time, common policy preferences are likely to be found among the different party platforms. Sometimes, opposition parties even declare publicly that they are willing to support the government on specific promises made during a campaign (Deptner 2014: 189). Still, legislative compromises are usually the norm and must be negotiated between parties, either to make the budget more appealing, or to drop or modify controversial bills. A government that chooses to ignore the opposition parties must tread carefully in the first few months after the election of a hung parliament, since a loss of confidence in the House can potentially lead to the formation of a new cabinet, instead of an early election, as we saw in the 2008 prorogation controversy.

Opposition parties also have at their disposal different procedural tools to oppose the government during hung parliaments. Aside from openly voting against the government, opposition parties can also abstain *en masse*, or they can send only a handful of MPs to vote against a government bill, so as to make sure that the cabinet is not defeated in the House. This strategy is especially convenient if one or more opposition parties have publicly declared that they will stop supporting the government in the legislature; it allows a party to take a stance against the government, while in effect avoiding an early election.

On the other hand, a minority government can also use procedural tools to remain in office. As we saw, it can prorogue parliament to avoid a confidence vote. It can also choose simply to ignore the confidence convention during certain votes. For example, the minority Liberal government of Pierre Trudeau in 1972 decided that "not all non-confidence votes would be treated as non-confidence votes," following the practice of earlier parliaments, when government defeats were more frequent (Deptner 2014: 241). Given that there is no cabinet manual in Canada, the interpretation of the confidence convention is rather wide. If parliament loses an important vote (such as on the budget or a major bill), the prime minister can attempt to remain in power by demonstrating rapidly that it retains the confidence of the House. This extra time can be used to shore up the ranks of the government side by convincing one or two opposition MPs to cross the floor, as in the case of the defection of a Conservative MP after the Liberals lost a supply vote in 2005, which gave them enough seats to win a more explicit vote of confidence a few days later.

Voting alliances

Canada is an interesting case because small regional parties usually have enough seats to give the government a majority when parliament is hung. Indeed, in eight of the ten post-war minority governments elected before 2020, at least three different opposition parties held the balance of power, so it has always been relatively easy to find partners to produce winning voting coalitions in the House (the exceptions being in 1958 and 1974). But on what basis do these coalitions form?

Using bargaining theories of cabinet formation to account for the dynamics of party voting coalitions in the 2004, 2006 and 2008 minority governments, Godbout and Høyland (2011) found that the formation of vote-by-vote alliances in Canada is best explained by the ideological proximity of parties. Parties that are near each other on the left–right dimension are more likely to vote together in the legislature (Axelrod 1970; Laver and Shepsle 1996). This common ground is easier to find when the Liberals are in power. Located near the center, the Liberals can form an alliance with the NDP on the left or the Conservatives on the right. However, shared preferences can also be found on another policy dimension related to regional conflicts, where parties like the Bloc Québécois or Social Credit occupy the most extreme positions. In this case, Conservatives are usually the ones closer to these parties, followed by the Liberals and the NDP. Thus, most minority governments in Canada are resilient because they can always build a winning voting coalition by compromising with parties on either side of these dimensions.

There are of course natural partners in these voting alliances, such as the more progressive NDP-Liberal coalition, or the more decentralized Bloc-Conservative partnership. Who ends up supporting the governing party is ultimately explained by the types of issues under consideration. For example, in the four most recent minority governments, the Bloc Québécois publicly declared that it would support all legislation that would benefit the interests of the province of Quebec in the federal parliament. Similarly, during the 1970s, the NDP lent its support to the Liberal minority government, whenever more progressive legislation was introduced to promote benefits for the unemployed, veterans, and families (Deptner 2014: 243).

But these types of proximal voting alliances do not explain everything. Godbout and Høyland (2011) also confirmed that every single opposition party, at one point or another, ended up supporting the government in the House between 2004 and 2011. A similar pattern was also observed in earlier terms: Liberal governments often had to rely on the Social Credit party to stay in power during Pearson's first minority government, while the Conservatives of Diefenbaker were also frequently supported by the left leaning CCF between 1957 and 1958 (Deptner 2014).

These ends-against-the-middle coalitions are much easier to understand when we consider electoral incentives. Opposition parties may want to support the government not for ideological reasons, but simply to avoid an early election, because they are unpopular, in the process of selecting a new leader, or because their finances are in disarray. Under these conditions, preventing an election is a matter of political survival. Godbout and Høyland (2011) have shown that there is indeed an electoral calculus made in the decision to support or oppose the government in this situation; the less popular an opposition party is, the more likely it is to vote with the government to avoid an early election.

Minority government performance

In this section, we take a closer look at the legislative performance of minority governments in Canada. Because hung parliaments have so far operated under single-party governments in this country, we should expect them to be less effective than their majority counterparts. Though our analysis confirms this trend, we still find that they perform relatively well when we focus on legislative accountability.

There is a rich literature in Canada arguing about the effectiveness of minority governments. Scholars like Russell (2008) and Migneault (2010) claim that they are very effective, while others argue the opposite (e.g. Conley 2011; Deptner 2014). The different conclusions reached by these authors can be explained by the indicators used in their study of performance. If, for instance, one looks at the length of parliamentary sessions (see Table 8.1), then the evidence clearly indicates that minority governments have a shorter lifespan. Furthermore, Table 8.2 confirms that minority governments are also less efficient since they tend to introduce and adopt fewer bills on average: 79 bills introduced and 51 adopted during minority governments, compared to 204 bills introduced and 167 adopted under majority governments, which represent success rates of 62 and 81 percent, respectively.

These measures, however, are somewhat misleading because legislative terms have different lengths in Canada, especially when parliament is hung. Table 8.2 confirms this by looking at several different indicators of performance, such as the relative duration ratio of governments after 1945. These data demonstrate that minority governments last on average 33 percent of the maximum allotted time when parliament is hung, compared to 79 percent when the government has a majority. If we weight the number of bills by the inverse of the duration ratio so that all parliaments have the same maximum length, we still find that minority governments have an overall lower success rate than their majority counterpart. These results are comparable to what Saalfeld (2008: 232) observed in Western Europe during the post-war era, with an average maximum duration of 31 percent in Canada versus 47 percent in Europe for single-party minority cabinets, and 79 percent versus 80 percent for single-party majority cabinets (see also Field 2016: 20).

That being said, minority governments in Canada are probably much more successful at weakening the influence of the executive in the legislature. The absence of any formal coalition and the ad hoc nature of voting alliances gives opposition parties, and even some independent MPs, a lot more leverage when it comes

Table 8.2 Legislative record and duration, Canada, 1945–2020

Prime minister	Government bills presented (N)	Government bills approved (N)	Government party bills approved (ratio)	Relative duration of government (ratio)
Mackenzie King	244	234	0.96	0.73
St-Laurent	251	240	0.96	0.75
St-Laurent	184	179	0.97	0.68
Diefenbaker	**30**	**27**	**0.90**	**0.06**
Diefenbaker	215	203	0.94	0.79
Diefenbaker	**33**	**17**	**0.52**	**0.07**
Pearson	**106**	**93**	**0.88**	**0.46**
Pearson	**112**	**105**	**0.94**	**0.45**
Trudeau P.	204	157	0.77	0.79
Trudeau P.	**89**	**57**	**0.64**	**0.27**
Trudeau P.	276	176	0.64	0.90
Clark	**28**	**6**	**0.21**	**0.04**
Trudeau P.	228	178	0.78	0.85
Mulroney	285	233	0.82	0.78
Mulroney	234	200	0.86	0.95
Chrétien	216	152	0.70	0.66
Chrétien	132	97	0.74	0.62
Chrétien	156	96	0.62	0.66
Martin	**82**	**46**	**0.56**	**0.23**
Harper	**125**	**65**	**0.52**	**0.65**
Harper	**128**	**59**	**0.46**	**0.59**
Harper	138	105	0.76	0.93
Trudeau J.	102	83	0.81	0.94
Trudeau J.	**56**	**31**	**0.55**	**0.43**
Average:				
Minority	79	51	.62	.33
Majority	205	167	.81	.79

Notes: Bold lines represent minority governments. A fixed four-year parliamentary term was adopted in the 38th Parliament (Martin). We include all of the information from the last minority government of Justin Trudeau which ended on August 15, 2021.

to controlling the agenda and shaping legislation. This is especially true when considering non-government public bills. Under normal circumstances, these bills have a very small chance of being adopted in parliament, especially if they are sponsored by opposition party members. However, when parliament is hung, the balance is reversed: not only are public bills sponsored by opposition party members more likely to be adopted, the government's own bills are also more likely to be amended in committees and on the floor of the House (Thomas 2007).

Another way to look at the performance of minority governments in Canada is to consider executive oversight. A hung parliament implies that the government does not control a majority of seats in the standing committees of the House. Since committees have the power to amend bills, call witnesses, review estimates, or challenge government appointments, they can greatly affect a government's legislative program. In fact, Stephen Harper sought and obtained the dissolution of parliament in 2008 precisely for these reasons by claiming that the numerous committee hearings requested by the opposition were rendering the House of Commons "dysfunctional."

Ultimately though, the debates surrounding the question of the performance of minority governments in Canada rest on several normative assumptions. Hung parliaments are often seen as "good" for the country because they have promoted the adoption of major progressive legislations in the 1960s, such as Canada's pension plan or universal healthcare, through a voting alliance between the Liberals and the NDP. The same can be said about more regionally focused programs, such as to give Quebec a greater role in the international organization UNESCO, following a pledge made by the Conservatives in 2006 to win the support of the Bloc Québécois in the House. Hung parliaments are also more likely to be seen as a better outcome for people who did not vote for the party in government, especially supporters of smaller parties such as the NDP or the Bloc Québécois (see Dufresne and Nevitte 2014).

There is, however, one study that attempts to measure more objectively the consequences of minority government in Canada by looking at the relationship between public opinion data and government annual expenditures from 1958 to 2009 to estimate the trade-off between legislative responsiveness and effectiveness (Pickup and Hobolt 2015). The authors find that minority governments tend to adopt fewer bills but become more responsive to public opinion as their popularity declines. The reverse is also true: majority governments tend to adopt more bills, but become less responsive, as their popularity increases. These last findings suggest that there can be a consensual approach to governing when parliament is hung in Canada, but only if the party in power is unpopular. When popularity increases, it reverts back to a majoritarian model of democracy.

Conclusion

The important number of minority governments in Canada during the post-war era can be explained by the election of strong regional parties, whose presence results from the combination of a plurality voting system with a regionally/ethnically diverse population. The executive dominance and majoritarian structure of its parliamentary system should normally lead us to expect at least some level of ex ante control mechanisms over government formation. However, the opposite is true: opposition parties in Canada are never involved in the selection of cabinet members, and this is perhaps the most troubling aspect of this case.

Canadian parties have never managed to build a successful governing coalition during a hung parliament (the 2008 Liberal-NDP-Bloc alliance came close), and the latest Liberal minority government of Justin Trudeau elected in September 2021 has once again confirmed this trend. The absence of formal agreements between parties implies that minority governments have to rely on ad hoc voting alliances to build majorities in the House. The composition of these coalitions varies somewhat over the course of a legislative term. Some are explained by the ideological proximity of parties, while others are linked to regional conflicts in the federation. Another factor that aids an understanding of who will support the government when parliament is hung relates to elections: opposition parties are more likely to abstain from voting, or even to openly support the government despite strong ideological differences, when they are unpopular, or when they suffer from organizational problems. Finally, in terms of performance, we saw that hung parliaments in Canada have a shorter lifespan and are always less productive than their majority counterparts. However, we also saw that they provide more opportunities for opposition party members to influence the legislative process.

Overall then, Canada represents an interesting case for testing existing theories of minority government formation, duration, and efficacy. Its obsession with single-party government and the absence of formal coalition agreements are deeply puzzling, especially if we consider the fact that slightly over 40 percent of parliaments have been without a majority between 1945 and 2020. So far, the reasons put forward to explain this anomaly, such as political culture or federalism, remain unconvincing, since the country has already experienced several governing coalitions at the subnational level.

The most recent episode of party system change in 2003, which saw the creation of a unified Conservative party on the right, but also confirmed the resilience of the Bloc Québécois, has created the perfect conditions for electing minority governments in Canada. Five of the last seven elections (2004, 2008, 2019, 2021) have produced hung parliaments; both majority governments (2011, 2015) were formed when the Bloc won less than 3 percent of the seats in the House. As long as state rights and the protection of the French language remain salient issues in Canadian politics, the likelihood of seeing a strong protest party representing Quebec in the federal parliament will be high. Therefore, to increase their chances of securing a majority in the House, the three main national parties will have to win more seats in this province. Unfortunately, this can only happen if they appeal to nationalist voters in Quebec, which could further exacerbate national unity in the rest of Canada.

References

Axelrod, Robert M. 1970. *The Conflict of Interest: A Theory of Divergent Goals with Applications to Politics*. Chicago: Markham.

Bergman, Torbjörn. 1993. "Formation Rules and Minority Governments." *European Journal of Political Research* 23 (1): 55–66.

Cheibub, José Antonio, and Przeworski, Adam. 1999. "Democracy, Elections, and Accountability for Economic Outcomes." In *Democracy, Accountability, and Representation*, ed. Adam Przeworski, Susan C. Stokes, and Bernard Manin, 222–250. Cambridge: Cambridge University Press.

Cheibub, José Antonio, Shane Martin, and Bjørn Erik Rasch. 2021. "Investiture Rules and Formation of Minority Governments in European Parliamentary Democracies." *Party Politics* 27 (2): 351–362.

Conley, Richard S. 2011. "Legislative Activity in the Canadian House of Commons: Does Majority or Minority Government Matter?" *American Review of Canadian Studies* 41 (4): 422–437.

Crombez, Christophe. 1996. "Minority Governments, Minimal Winning Coalitions and Surplus Majorities in Parliamentary Systems." *European Journal of Political Research* 29 (1): 1–29.

Deptner, Wolfgang. 2014. *The Effectiveness and Legitimacy of Federal Minority Government in Canada since 1945*. Doctoral Thesis. Okanagan: University of British Columbia.

Dufresne, Yannick, and Neil Nevitte. 2014. "Why do Publics Support Minority Governments? Three Tests." *Parliamentary Affairs* 67 (4): 825–840.

Field, Bonnie. 2016. *Why Minority Governments Work: Multilevel Territorial Politics in Spain*. New York: Palgrave Macmillan.

Gervais, Marc. 2011. *Minority Governments in Canada: A Study of Legislative Politics*. Doctoral Thesis. School of Political Studies. University of Ottawa.

Godbout, Jean-François, and Bjørn Høyland. 2011. "Coalition Voting and Minority Governments in Canada." *Commonwealth & Comparative Politics* 49 (4): 457–485.

Johnston, Richard. 2017. *The Canadian Party System: An Analytic History*. Vancouver: UBC Press.

Kelso, Alexandra. 2015. "Parliament and Government Formation in the United Kingdom: A Hidden Vote of Investiture?" In *Parliaments and Government Formation: Unpacking Investiture Rules*, ed. Bjørn Erik Rasch, Shane Martin, and José Antonio Cheibub, 29–48. Oxford: Oxford University Press.

Kent, Tom. 2009. "When Minority Government Worked: The Pearson Legacy." *Policy Options* 30 (9): 26–30.

Laver, Michael, and Kenneth A. Shepsle. 1996. *Making and Breaking Governments: Cabinets and Legislatures in Parliamentary Democracies*. Cambridge: Cambridge University Press.

Migneault, Pier-Luc. 2010. *Les gouvernements minoritaires au Canada et au Québec: Historique, contexte électoral et efficacité législative*. Montréal: Presses de l'Université du Québec.

Pickup, Mark, and Sara B. Hobolt. 2015. "The Conditionality of the Trade-off between Government Responsiveness and Effectiveness: The Impact of Minority Status and Polls in the Canadian House of Commons." *Electoral Studies* 40: 517–530.

Rasch, Bjørn Erik, Shane Martin, and José Antonio Cheibub, eds. 2015. *Parliaments and Government Formation: Unpacking Investiture Rules*. Oxford: Oxford University Press.

Russell, Peter H. 2008. *Two Cheers for Minority Government: The Evolution of Canadian Parliamentary Governments*. Toronto: Emond Montgomery Publications Limited.

Saalfeld, Thomas. 2008. "Institutions, Chance, and Choices: The Dynamics of Cabinet Survival." In *Cabinets and Coalition Bargaining: The Democratic Life Cycle in Western Europe*, ed. Kaare Strøm, Wolfgang C. Müller, and Torbjörn Bergman, 327–368. Oxford: Oxford University Press.

Strøm, Kaare. 1990. *Minority Government and Majority Rule*. Cambridge: Cambridge University Press.

Thomas, Paul E. J. 2007. "Measuring the Effectiveness of a Minority Parliament." *Canadian Parliamentary Review* 30 (1): 22–31.

9
Minority Governments in France
A Mix of Presidential and Parliamentary Logics

Olivier Rozenberg

Since a new Constitution implemented a semi-presidential system in 1958/1962, minority governments have not been numerous in France.[1] Indeed, from 2002 to 2022, the main party of the majority has benefited from an absolute majority alone, confirming that France belongs to the majority category during a period when the UK experienced coalitions and minority governments. Two types of minority government can be distinguished in the French case. The first one is classical and consists in a dominant but minoritarian party governing alone for a full term—with no support party. It took place from 1988 to 1993 with three successive prime ministers. After the parliamentary elections of June 2022, an unprecedented situation emerged in France - with a minority government supported by only 250 MPs out of 577 (43 %), far less than in 1988. The division of the opposition to it between three groups (left, right and radical right) contributed to its survival. The second type is more original and involves a newly elected president forming a new government that is not backed by the Assembly, in the shadow of upcoming parliamentary elections. These one-month governments were formed on five occasions (1981, 1988, 2002, 2012, 2017).

Although rare, minority governments are interesting to analyze given the very nature of semi-presidentialism under the 5th Republic (1958–). Indeed, as we will demonstrate, the duality of the types of minority governments reveals the hybrid nature of semi-presidentialism, at least as it operates in the French case. On the one hand, the existence of one-month minority governments strikingly illustrates the domination of presidents over French politics. On the other hand, the functioning of the "regular" minority governments from 1988 to 1993 reflected a full parliamentary logic where law-making supposes patient bargaining in parliament. Analysis of the cases of French minority governments confirms many of the results established by the comparative literature: the capacity of minority governments to form is dependent on the institutional rules relative to the shaping and ending

---

[1] There have been many minority cabinets under the Third Republic (1875–1940), especially during the 1910–14 and 1924–26 periods, and a few ones under the Fourth Republic (1946–1958) in 1956–57 (Döring and Manow 2018). Semi-presidentialism is understood as a regime where the head of State is directly elected while the parliament can pass a no-confidence vote against the government.

Olivier Rozenberg, *Minority Governments in France*. In: *Minority Governments in Comparative Perspective*. Edited by Bonnie N. Field and Shane Martin, Oxford University Press. © Olivier Rozenberg (2022). DOI: 10.1093/oso/9780192871657.003.0009

of governments (Rasch, Martin, and Cheibub 2015), their existence also results from a mix of policy, vote, and office considerations from political actors (Strøm 1990) and procedural arrangements that strengthen governments also help minority ones to govern and last (Field 2016). In addition, the tale of the Rocard 2 cabinet (1988–91) indicates that the political skills in the subtle management of parliamentary bargains are also essential to the adoption of an ambitious legislative agenda. In practice, the passing of bills under minority governments requires both deliberation and negotiation—persuasion and particularism (pork)—and often a difficulty to distinguish one from the other.

The next section of this chapter presents the French semi-presidential regime. The second details the circumstances of the creation of minority governments in France since 1981. The third provides an explanation for their duration during the full 1988–93 term. An assessment of the performances of these special governments is provided in the fourth part, before a final section concluding.

The French political system

The French political system is characterized by the weakness of the French Parliament—made up of a lower house, the National Assembly, and an upper house, the Senate[2]—although there have been attempts to reassess its role more positively (Kerrouche 2006; Brouard, Costa, and Kerrouche 2013; Costa 2014). It is clear that an important shift occurred in 1958, when a new Constitution was adopted. Previously, under the 4th Republic, France was characterized by a traditional parliamentary regime where unstable parliamentary majorities regularly broke governments. In 1958, De Gaulle conditioned his come-back on a new constitutional settlement that was far less favorable to parliament. Constitutionally, the legislative branch faces two types of disadvantage. First, the President of the Republic holds important powers which do not require the countersignature of the Prime Minister. Since 1962, the president is elected not by parliament, but directly by the people and, most importantly, parliament can neither dismiss nor oversee him. This constitutes a major source of disequilibrium because the National Assembly (but not the Senate) can be easily dissolved by the president. Second, there is still a government which is headed by a prime minister and which can be censured by the Assembly (but not the Senate), but many constitutional provisions are designed to protect the government's stability and agenda to the detriment of the parliament. Those rules are numerous and cover many aspects of political life: Government formation and resignation (Nguyen-Duy 2015), the oversight of the government (Rozenberg and Surel 2018), and, last but not least, the legislative procedure (Brouard 2011).

---

[2] Bicameralism is unbalanced in France: the National Assembly has the last word in case of disagreement and the Senate has no role in expressing confidence in the government. Yet, the Senate is both active and influential in the law-making procedure.

Table 9.1 Minority governments in France, 1958-2021

Prime Minister	Start date	End date	Government party	Coalition
Mauroy 1	21-05-1981	22-06-1981	Socialists, radicals	Yes
Rocard 1	10-05-1988	28-06-1988	Socialists	No
Rocard 2	28-06-1988	15-05-1991	Socialists	No
Cresson	15-05-1991	02-04-1992	Socialists	No
Bérégovoy	02-04-1992	29-03-1993	Socialists	No
Raffarin 1	06-05-2002	17-06-2002	Gaullists, center-right	Yes
Ayrault 1	15-05-2012	21-06-2012	Socialists, radicals, greens	Yes
Philippe 1	15-05-2017	21-06-2017	Macron's party, Center	Yes

Note: All these governments are substantive minority governments, not formal ones, with no support parties (see introduction to this volume).

In addition to these numerous constitutional limitations, a political limitation was added in 1962 with the election of a pro-president majority in the Assembly following a tense dissolution. Ever since, presidents have usually had at their disposal a rather solid majority in the Assembly, which strictly follows the voting instructions of the Government (Sauger 2009; Lecomte and Rozenberg 2021). Many elements contribute to maintaining such discipline: the choice of the voters, the threat of dissolution, the effect of the two-round majority electoral system and the over shadowing of the presidential election over political life. Exceptions to this have been the three periods of divided governments (*cohabitation*) in 1986-88, 1993-95, and the longest one in 1997-2002 (Baumgartner et al. 2014). As a result of the opposition between the Assembly majority and the president, the prime minister was *de facto* imposed on the president and held most of the power. However, two reforms undertaken in the early 2000s have made such a situation less likely: the alignment of the presidential term with the legislative one (five years), and the decision to vote for the president before the Assembly—the parliamentary majority consequently owing its victory to the president (Dupoirier and Sauger 2010).

Regarding government formation, it is the sole responsibility of the president to choose a prime minister, though he should of course anticipate a possible non-confidence vote in the future. Once selected, the constitution stipulates that the prime minister should propose a list of ministers to the president. In practice, except for the rare periods of divided governments, the president is powerful enough to effectively select most of the ministers. Once the president and the PM have jointly signed the decree of nomination of the ministers, the government exists. Investiture votes are not required but, should a parliamentary majority exist, the vote is typically organized in the Assembly a few days after.

Table 9.1 gives background information on the minority governments that have been shaped in France in recent decades and that are analyzed further in the rest of the chapter.

Why minority governments form in France

The absence of a compulsory investiture vote in parliament is a major reason for the existence of minority governments in France: a presidential decree is sufficient to shape a new government. Therefore, governments that are not backed by a parliamentary majority can exist. But this absence is not the only explanation for the existence of minority cabinets. It is essential, here, to distinguish between the two types of minority governments mentioned in the introduction.

Regarding the "regular" type of minority governments that France experienced between 1988 and 1993, the procedural details of the non-confidence vote also matters. For a government to be forced to resign in France, an absolute majority is needed. Negative votes only are counted, those who abstain or who do not participate being de facto counted among the government supporters. This provision was crucial during the 1988–93 term, at least at the beginning when the main right-wing opposition needed the extreme left to shape an absolute majority. The Communist party announced early they will not vote to remove the socialist government. Several reasons justified this choice: the fear of a dissolution, the refusal to vote with the right (for cultural and/or electoral reason), the legacy of the previous coalition period (1981–84), and the influence of coalitions within local governments. They once changed their mind in 1991 when a major tax reform was proposed which seriously threatened the existence of the government: five votes were missing for the censure to pass (see section on Pork).

Beyond rules, we know minority governments are also the result of strategic choices (Strøm 1990). Strategies result from both the rules of the political game and what political actors want to secure: agreeable political positions, agreeable electoral results, or agreeable policies. Two possibilities were open in 1988 to shape a majority government, either a coalition of the socialists with their right (i.e. with a center-right party or one of its components) or with their left (i.e. with the Communists). Regarding the left option, it seems that the refusal came from the Communists. They were said to refuse the pro-market agenda that had been adopted by the Socialists since 1983. From a more vote-seeking standpoint, they also stated that their past coalition with the Socialists, as minority partners, from 1981 to 1984, was consequential to their electoral fall. Declining to govern with them again was therefore a way to appear as an alternative in the eyes of the left-wing voters at the next election. In addition, from an office-seeking perspective, the Communist leaders had, at that time, local governments to take care of: they headed a number of cities and districts throughout the country and therefore were able to secure paid political positions for some of their members.

Regarding the centrist option, a coalition with them could have been possible from a policy perspective. The Socialists had indeed set aside their Marxist credo and put their emphasis on issues dear to the center right: European unification and state devolution. Convergent testimonies indicate that, after the reelection of the Socialist Mitterrand as President in May 1988, they secretly met with the majority and asked the President not to dissolve the right-wing Assembly, where they were numerous (Jaffré 2020). The Socialists unanimously rejected that condition as they expected a logical victory in the anticipated parliamentary elections. As a result, the centrists were pushed to ally with their usual coalition partners for parliamentary elections: the neo-Gaullist right.[3] They lost seats and logically refused to ally with the left, despite the nomination of a few isolated personalities as ministers. As a minority form of government was new at that time, they could also expect a failure of the Socialists would lead to new elections: a good reason not to ally with them.

The Socialists initially did not anticipate that they would perform moderately during the parliamentary elections of June 1988. Therefore the formation of a minority government cannot be considered to be the result of an anticipated strategy. Yet, they accepted this unprecedented configuration based mainly on vote- and policy- seeking considerations. The vote-seeking considerations were, as noted, that they would bring about a dissolution of the parliament in the hope of future gains.[4] There were policy-seeking considerations as they may have feared being unable to implement their agenda with a balance of power in which the centrist parliamentary group was too numerous. It is doubtful that they acted as office-seekers as the government was open to many non-political figures and isolated centrist ones. As famously said by President Mitterrand: "I want the Centrists but one by one and nude" (Huchon 2017). Table 9.2 offers a summary of the rationales of the main actors.

The situation is different for the "irregular" type of minority government in France, that is, those that last approximately one month between the presidential election and the parliamentary election. On five occasions thus far during the 5th Republic, a candidate from the parliamentary opposition has won the presidential election (be they incumbent as in 1988 and 2002, or not). The day after, the prime minister has tendered his or her resignation, which seems logical from

---

[3] Two types of coalition are possible during parliamentary elections. At the first round, the components of the right-wing family may agree in advance to present only one candidate. Should this not transpire, at the second round, the less successful candidate within the right will systematically call her voters to support the remaining right-wing candidate.

[4] They also wanted not to give the power to the centrists to break the government at any time in the future—which can also be understood as a safe electoral strategy.

Table 9.2 The rationales of three political forces when a minority government was shaped in 1988, France

	Vote-seeking	Policy-seeking	Office-seeking
Socialists (main group)	Gain during coming parliamentary elections	Fear to be unable to implement their agendas with Centrists	-
Communists (pivot)	Negative assessment of the past coalition/Hope to win from being in the opposition	Critical of the Socialist *aggiornamento*	Offices already enjoyed within local governments
Centrists (pivot)	Bipolar logic of the parliamentary elections/Bet on anticipated elections	-	Isolated leaders

a democratic standpoint as this prime minister has just been defeated during the Presidential elections—personally (1988, 2002) or his party family (1981, 2012, 2017). The president was therefore in a position to name a new prime minister and typically select someone from his political camp. Constitutionally, as noted above, the new government is not required to be invested. Moreover, parliamentary elections are to be organized within one month—as a result of a dissolution (1981 and 1988), or an agreement between political forces to schedule the presidential race first (2002), or the regular electoral calendar (2012, 2017).[5] The National Assembly is in recess at this time as most of its members are campaigning to be reelected. It cannot therefore meet to pass a non-confidence vote against the newly shaped minority government.

Politically, the choice of a minority government by the president is made possible by the legitimacy provided by his "fresh" direct election. Based on the (presidential) election outcome, the minority government is also in charge of framing the next (parliamentary) elections, through sending positive signals to voters. For the prime minister, winning the parliamentary election is a question of career life or death. If successful, he/she will be logically re-nominated by the president at the head of a majoritarian government. In case of failure, he/she will have to resign to avoid a non-confidence vote. Therefore, contrary to the regular types of minority government, these ones are transitory only.

---

[5] The constitution does not require that parliamentary elections take place one month after the presidential election. Yet, it is de facto the case: (a) if the president decides to dissolve the National Assembly once elected; (b) since 2002, given the choice made at that time to hold the presidential election first and the similarity of the duration of the presidential and parliamentary terms.

Why minority governments lasted

In this section, we develop an explanation for how a minority government survives in office in France. By definition, we set aside the cases that exist just for one month. After the 1988 parliamentary elections, many observers doubted that the Rocard Government would last. The team was supported by 47 percent of the MPs only and by just one party group.[6] The Senate was dominated by the right. Apart from the socialists, the government did not enjoy the regular support of a given group in the Assembly. The Communists said they would not vote for the censure with the right but did not make any commitment regarding ordinary bills. Likewise, the centrist group indicated that it was open to support some texts but not on a systematic basis. Neither formal nor secret agreements were passed with the governing socialists. And yet, it worked. The minority governments were not forced to resign after a non-confidence vote (they won all of them) and even passed, as we will see, an ambitious legislative agenda. The change of prime ministers during the terms with the nomination of Cresson in 1991 and then Beregovoy in 1992 did not result from tension in parliament but from the preferences of President Mitterrand. The duration of the three governments—Rocard 2 (2 years and 11 months), Cresson (11 months), and Bérégovoy (1 year)—are close to what can be observed during other parliamentary terms under the 5th Republic: 1 year and 8 months (the one-month type excluded).

How can we account for this duration? To us, the successive governments' ability to survive and even push through an ambitious legislative agenda, despite falling sixteen seats short of an absolute majority, can be attributed to three factors: one is institutional (in this case constitutional), a second is political (related to the structure of the opposition), and the third is managerial, pertaining to the management of relations with elected officials, especially those from swing groups. While success resulted from the combination of these three factors, there is an apparent order to the explanation: institutions enabled the government's existence and survival, the political situation led to the emergence of two accommodating partners—the centrists and the communists—and the managerial skills of the Prime Minister and his teams facilitated the situation.

Support from rationalized parliamentarianism

The notion of "rationalized parliamentarianism" refers to a reformist movement initiated by European legal scholars in the inter-war period with a view to strengthening the governing capacity of liberal democracies at a time where they were challenged (Huber 1996; Pinon 2003). It consists in bounding the parliament's

---

[6] With the support of a satellite marginal party, the Leftwing Radicals.

sovereignty by all legal means, be it from the law-making or oversight side. The 1958 French Constitution accumulates many of the institutional arrangements developed in that perspective: a lack of parliamentary investiture, the requirement for a negative majority in non-confidence votes, blocked votes imposed by the government, and the setting of the agenda being in the hands of the prime minister (up to 2008). The diversity of these tools certainly helped minority governments to last—in France as elsewhere (Field 2016). In addition to the way non-confidence votes are counted, a specific arrangement was particularly helpful: the prospect of passing legislation without an Assembly vote, enshrined in Article 49, paragraph 3, of the Constitution, which was extensively used (Huber 1996).[7]

When the government activated this provision, the law was deemed to have been adopted by the Assembly for the reading in progress unless the government was censured. It therefore forced MPs to determine whether they opposed a bill to the point of wanting the government to fall and risk the fallout of an institutional crisis, such as dissolution. The Article 49.3 provision, which had been used thirty-seven times in thirty years from 1958 to 1988, was used thirty-nine times during the 1988–93 term for twenty bills. The first use of the procedure in December 1988 underscored the government's propensity to use available tools not so much to prevent the rejection of a bill, but rather to guard against unwanted amendments. Indeed, the centrist group sought to cash in on its support for the bill that established an agency for audio-visual regulation by securing the appointment of one of its members to the future board in exchange—but this was rebuffed by the Prime Minister (Favier and Martin-Rolland 1996: 111). Figure 9.1 presents the number of cases for which the procedure was activated. Article 49.3 can be used for different readings in the National Assembly of the same bill. As we see, the opposition tabled a motion of no-confidence in less than one-fifth of the cases. This can be explained by the fact that the procedure is rather costly in terms of backbench mobilization: as only negative votes are counted, opposition leaders should ensure all their troops come to Paris, which is all the more difficult when a failure of the motion is likely.

Article 49.3 was used every year for the budget, except for the 1989 budget, as well as for landmark and polarizing measures. The use of Article 49.3 "worked for everyone" (Chevalier et al. 2017: 366). It allowed prime ministers to deliver on their pet measures. It provided an opportunity for the right to express democratic outrage, for example in the context of a motion of censure tabled in December 1990 that specifically addressed violations of Parliamentary rights. Finally, it prevented the centrists and Communists from having to abstain or support a project

---

[7] Article 49.3 is sometimes mentioned as the guillotine in the literature which is a source of confusion as the notion of guillotine usually designs a procedure which allows to limit floor time and therefore to fight against filibustering.

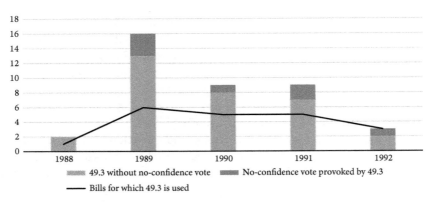

Fig. 9.1 The use of Article 49.3 in France (1988–1992)

since, precisely, the procedure replacing the vote on a text with a vote on a possible and infrequent no-confidence motion.

An accommodating stereo majority

The term "stereo majority" is an expression from Rocard's parliamentary advisor, the legal scholar Guy Carcassonne (Chevalier et al. 2017: 366). It conveys that the government could find supportive partners on the left, among the Communists, or on the right, among the centrists. This situation was particularly beneficial for the majority to the extent that it reduced the leverage of either one of the two partners: the possibility of reaching agreement with a third party helped limit one-upmanship in bilateral negotiations. As Jean-Jacques Hyest—a centrist MP at the time—described the negotiations led by Michel Rocard's parliamentary counsel: "Carcassonne was devilishly clever, playing the PCF and the UDC[8] [Centrist] off one another; if we weren't budging, he would go to them, and vice versa" (Favier and Martin Rolland 1996: 143). Alliances were therefore conditional and fluid. A case in point was the 1989 budget vote, over which alliances shifted depending on the topic: on education, the Communists abstained and the centrists opposed; on housing, the situation was reversed. While the government had to prevent a coalition of its opponents, the abstention of any number of them sufficed to ensure a relative majority.

While the duality of swing groups strengthened the government's ability to legislate, their accommodating approach was just as important, if not more. Most parliamentarians did not want to bring down the government. The prospect of going back to the voters rarely appealed to incumbent MPs, especially after the

---

[8] Union of the Center, a small centrist parliamentary party group.

very close elections of 1988. It frightened both ommunists in decline and centrists who had been rather successful in the 1988 legislative elections. Moreover, specific reasons led the two swing groups to periodically support government bills. Some communist parliamentarians embraced the socialists and their bills, since they had shared power from 1981 to 1984. Moreover, the USSR's economic reforms and social policies (Mikhail Gorbachev launched *perestroika* in 1985), and the fall of the Berlin Wall, profoundly shook the Communist party, and left it unsure of its strategy. Participation in a coalition government, considered an electoral disaster, was rejected in 1984. But many PCF leaders did not see this as a reason for head-on opposition. A certain level of cooperation with the socialists made sense given that many communist MPs had been elected thanks to the reciprocal withdrawal strategy between left-wing candidates in the second round of the legislative elections.

The centrists' position was more complex. Some centrist figures joined the government, such as the Minister of Labor Jean-Pierre Soisson. Having been elected as an MP for the first time in 1968, and having served as a minister for Valery Giscard d'Estaing (1974–81), he maintained strong relationships within the centrist group, and personally and discreetly conducted certain negotiations—including ones outside of his ministerial portfolio (Favier and Martin-Rolland 1996: 145; Flauraud 2016). The Rocard Government also took advantage of the divisions among centrists. A small parliamentary party group (the UDC), which branched off from the main center-right party (the UDF), formed at the beginning of the legislature under the presidency of Pierre Mehaignerie. This independence, which received the blessing of Gaullists who were keen on remaining the primary opposition group, attested to a willingness "to oppose differently," to use the terms of its president. It can also be understood as a bet on the future, given Prime Minister Rocard's presidential ambitions.

The capacity of the government to be supported by either the communists or the center-right challenges the comparative literature on government formation. Thürk, Hellström, and Holger (2021) demonstrates that within political systems characterized by a low number of veto points, such as the French one,[9] a greater polarization of the party system leads to more frequent minority governments. In part, this accounts for what happened in France: The divergences between the center-right, the socialists, and the communists made it impossible to shape a majority government. But France in 1988 was not *that* polarized: the proximity of views between center-right and socialists on many topics (Europe, state governance, ...) and between communists and socialists on other issues (welfare, ...) enabled minority governments to pass laws. Within a more deeply polarized party system, the capacity of the Rocard 2 cabinet to act would have been more limited.

---

[9] Given the lack of a compulsory investiture vote as well as the unbalanced bicameralism, the lack of real veto legislative power for the head of state and the total lack of veto rights of the opposition.

Pork in parliamentary negotiations

Finally, a third factor is that the minority governments of the 1988–93 period were able to survive in office and push through an ambitious legislative agenda thanks to them developing good relations with various MPs from the opposition benches. This notion of "good relations" refers to the relations of confidence established between the governmental teams and some pivotal MPs thanks to a subtle mix of seduction, log-rolling, and particularism (pork). We will distinguish here between the resources available to the governments, and their instruments of action.

First, the resources were linked to the organization and quality of the governmental team, in particular their knowledge of the parliamentary world. Carcassonne played a key role in conducting negotiations under Rocard (1988–91). He had the full confidence of the Prime Minister—which was not the case for most of the ministers selected by Mitterrand. He centralized parliamentary negotiations without monopolizing them, especially negotiations with the president of the centrist group, Pierre Mehaignerie, and with the communist group's leader Andre Lajoinie (Favier and Martin-Rolland 1996: 152). This delegation was a source of credibility. It also enabled cross-sector negotiations and agreements that ministers would have been less likely to pursue given the duties of their administration. In addition to Rocard's confidence, Carcassonne had many assets: he was not a politician; he combined the authority of a law professor with practical knowledge of the Parliament acquired on the benches of the socialist group at the end of the 1970s; he was deemed trustworthy. He also enjoyed debates, was nonpartisan, and actually had charm.

A second asset was the extensive knowledge of Parliament and its members of the Prime Minister's team. This was attributable to the team's advisers, to Rocard's ministerial experience during Mitterrand's first term (1981–85), and to the key role played by Rocardian MPs within the majority. These relationships allowed him to accurately anticipate how officials would behave, to identify possible majorities, and to know when to take risks and when to play it safe. Two examples are worth mentioning here. In the summer of 1990, Carcassonne warned Rocard that he was unlikely to get a majority on a bill on campaign financing that proposed political amnesty (Andrieu 2020). The review was postponed for a few months and the law then passed. On the eve of passing the tax reform of November 1990, he announced to the Prime Minister that the censure vote was three to four MPs short of the number required to pass—it was ultimately short of five (Chevalier et al. 2017: 371).

Given its resources, the government implemented a two-pronged strategy that consisted of accepting some amendments sought by the centrists and/or communists and, on the other hand, of granting special benefits to some MPs. These two tactics played out on a continuum. For example, an amendment that benefited a district could also be seen as a personal benefit for the incumbent MP, particularly in view of upcoming elections. The Prime Minister was therefore willing to pay for the adoption of their bills by accepting amendments. This constraint was anticipated during the early drafting of bills. A secrete note from Carcassonne to the Prime Minister on a constitutional amendment—that was eventually abandoned—and statements that the latter later made attest to this state of mind:

> Two conditions must absolutely be met to ensure that things go smoothly. The first one is that the whole operation must be entrusted to one person and one person only. The second one is that this person must have some leeway to negotiate and possibly compromise. All we need to do is determine how far we would be willing to go, knowing that the bill was crafted in such a way as to leave room for a discussion and should not result in any painful sacrifice.[10]

> We were reasonably attentive to the MPs' demands. We sometimes expedited the resolution of their legitimate requests, but it applied to all, without exception. Grants and equipment were distributed, and some gestures were made to the communist deputies, but was all peanuts.[11] There was never a quid pro quo—a grant in exchange for a vote—because I couldn't count on securing the vote of an MP and a fortiori of a group until I could convince them that the bill aligned with the general interest. At the time I know that people said "Carcassonne makes it rain", but that's a bit simplistic. ... It was all about greasing the wheels, a bit like when the president of the Republic offers a Sèvres vase to a foreign visitor (Favier and Martin-Roland 1996: 146).

These "small gifts" were sometimes for districts—Minister Soisson mentioned the extension of an airport runway or a hospital (Favier and Martin-Roland 1996: 145)—and sometimes involved issues relevant for the whole group. Thus, for the vote on the first law of the term which dealt with amnesty, the communists included in the bill the names of ten Renault labor union members convicted of property damage. Later, their newspaper *L'Humanité* received a grant after a fire destroyed its printing house.

The recruitment of centrist and communist MPs ultimately resulted more from give-and-take than horse-trading. We know for instance that Carcassonne facilitated an audience with the Pope for a pious centrist MP (Duhamel 2014). The idea was not so much to offer access to the Holy Father in exchange for a vote, but rather to create the conditions conducive to support in the future—in this case, an abstention on the censure motion tabled during a censure vote over a fiscal reform

---

[10] February 15, 1990, confidential memorandum from Carcassonne to the Prime Minister on expanding the remit of the Constitutional Council, French National Archives 920622/1. Let us note in passing that the person meant to direct the operations is probably its author.

[11] In English in the original version.

Table 9.3 The rationales of two pivotal political forces to occasionally support government bills, 1988–1993, France

	Vote-seeking	Policy-seeking	Office-seeking
Communists (pivot)	Fear of anticipated elections/Pork	Amendments passed	-
Centrists (pivot)	Fear of anticipated elections/Pork... taking the risk of electoral sanctions	Amendments passed	Bet on a victory of Rocard at the next presidential election

in November 1990. The example illustrates the Rocard team's ingenuity in identifying pathways to unblock a bill. This was also the case for the party and campaign finance law adopted in the aftermath of huge scandals involving the socialist party. Carcassonne suggested excluding the MPs involved from the amnesty, which made the text more palatable to the centrists (Andrieu 2020). Finally, strong parliamentary relations also meant knowing how to respond promptly to an opponent's shots. Thus, on the 1991 fiscal reform, Carcassonne got UDF MP Emile Koehl to announce to the French news agency that he would not censure the government, in order to thwart a false proxy vote strategy attempted by the UDF's group leader (Favier and Martin-Roland 1996: 545).

Table 9.3 offers a synthesis of the explanations developed throughout this section on the duration of the 1988–93 minority governments. The communists and the centrists decided to abstain on numerous occasions in the course of the legislative procedure, and not to vote no-confidence jointly with the right, for a mix of strategic reasons. From an electoral standpoint, both wanted to avoid a dissolution and hoped to gain from local subsidies. Yet, the centrists ran an electoral risk as their voters traditionally belong to the right. Nevertheless, they made this choice as there were other outcomes of this strategy: modifying the content of bills (for communists as well) and, possibly, participating in a future governing coalition in case of a future victory by the rather popular Rocard.

Outcomes of the French minority governments: Policies vs. public opinion

Assessment of the performance of "irregular" minority governments is necessarily limited given their short existence. Bills cannot be passed during that period, as the National Assembly is in recess. However, the government can table bills and these are discussed in the Senate—which is still open. The legislative procedure therefore offers an opportunity for the government to advertise its platform, a few weeks before parliamentary elections. Though temporary, the government still has access to all the state facilities, including the police and the army. So far, there has been no major crisis, such as a terrorist attack, during the one-month existence of these governments, but it could happen in the future. In that case, the legitimacy of a government, fully decided by the president but not backed by a majority in parliament, could be questioned. In 2017 for instance, the Philippe 1 cabinet was composed of members of a newly created party, the president's party, which had no parliamentary group at all in either assembly.

Doubts about the legitimacy of this kind of minority government could also be raised if a radical candidate were to win the presidential election. In such a case, the success of the president's party would appear less secure in the forthcoming parliamentary elections than for moderate parties, for diverse reasons. As a result, the shaping of a minority government campaigning for the President's party would be controversial. This would constitute a threat for the functioning of the regime as the home affairs minister is in charge of organizing elections.

Regarding the performances of the minority governments of 1988–93, a major contrast between the policy achievements and the electoral outputs can be seen. Many experts estimate that they achieved noticeable policy outputs, especially the Rocard governments (Bergounioux and Fulla 2020). A major tax reform was painfully implemented. Minimal subsidies were provided to any residents in the country. Peace was restored in New Caledonia. The participation of France in the first gulf war was largely supported by political forces. The statutes of major public utilities evolved to prepare for future privatization. The legal code for civil, private, and family affairs was modernized. The fight against tobacco and alcohol made huge progress. The regulation of politics, and especially the financing of political campaigns, started from scratch. A huge number of decisions from the European communities were implemented in order to prepare for the 1993 single market. The records show that fewer laws were adopted during that period but this was an official aim of Rocard's team—with the view that executive tools could be more efficient than legal ones. Moreover, the literature has established that governments sometimes legislate heavily to hide their incapacity (Tsebelis 2004).

The governments also faced very few failures. They abandoned plans to open referral to the Constitutional Council to ordinary citizens—that was passed in 2008. But this failure was due to opposition by the Senate, which has veto powers for constitutional amendments. The lock would have been similar with a majority government. The three subsequent socialist prime ministers were also inactive on pension reform. Their right-wing successor was to take significant decisions on that issue just after his nomination. But again, the minority base can hardly be made responsible for this non-decision. The fear of losing public support and the tensions between the President and Rocard are more likely to be the explanations.

In contrast, in terms of public and electoral support the episode can be assessed negatively. The socialists were supported during the first half of the term with a "rally to the flag" effect during the Iraq war and the positive personal image of Rocard. But they rapidly suffered from the *usure* of Mitterrand (who had been President since 1981) and from a series of corruption scandals. The end of the term was catastrophic for the left: the socialists experienced their highest electoral defeat ever (at that time) at the 1993 parliamentary elections; the last Prime Minister, Bérégovoy, committed suicide a few days after leaving office; and Rocard never became President contrary to the expectations of many.

To a major extent, this dramatic ending was not dictated by the minority status of the governments. Yet, it contributed to the negative mood for two reasons. First, as said, the three governments made unprecedented use of the Article 49.3 procedure. Surveys have since established how the perception of something unfair in the legislative procedure can be costly in terms of popular support (Becher and Brouard 2022). Second, everything seems to indicate that the closed-door bargains between the socialists and their pivotal partners were negatively perceived by public opinion. In a majoritarian country such as France, where the tension between right and left had reached a peak during the 1988 presidential campaign, the fact that trans-party compromises could be bargained was not positively perceived by many observers and voters. The centrists were accused of "losing their soul" by the Gaullist right. A proportion of the left's supporters saw their deals with the government as proof of the socialists' supposed lack of ideological purity (Grunberg 2020).

Political science is certainly unsuited to saying who is pure or not. Yet, comparing the law-making procedure between parliamentary terms suggests that public opinion was unfair on one point: parliament has been treated rather well during that period (see also Rozenberg 2020). In 1990, the Government circulated a provisional legislative agenda to the parliament for the first time. The emergency procedure was used slightly less than during the previous terms (30 percent of the bills versus 35 percent in 1981–86[12]). The practice was implemented to consult and inform the leaders of the opposition, especially during the Iraq war. Each group was given the right annually to propose an inquiry committee. Committee hearings were made public. The Article 49.3 procedure itself was used with some care vis-à-vis the Parliament. Whereas prime ministers may decide at any time to use it during the legislative procedure, including at the very beginning, Rocard and his followers usually activated it at the end, once the bills had been discussed and amended. In other words, it did not serve as an anti-filibustering tool—contrary to other episodes during the 5th Republic (Foucault Godbout 2014). The relation with the right-wing Senate was also soothed. In the unequal bicameral French system, the final word was given to the National Assembly in 41 percent of the cases in 1981–86 versus only 31 percent in 1988–93.

---

[12] Source for this section: yearly statistical record of the National Assembly. The 1981–86 term is relevant for the comparison as the socialists had an absolute majority at that time.

The way the parliament has been treated by the government certainly derives, in part, from the minority status of the governments. Prime ministers had to pass ad hoc deals with their left or their right, which constituted a strong incentive for keeping good relations with parliamentary leaders and backbenchers. Again, these good relations were sought by offering new venues for oversight or allowing speaking time in law-making rather than merely buying votes.

Conclusion

In conclusion, minority governments in France, although rare, are an interesting case to analyze given the hybrid nature of the regime. France is half-presidential: temporary minority governments are potentially formed the day after the presidential election with no consideration for the state of the forces in parliament. But France is half-parliamentary as well: the durable minority governments that have existed have employed subtle case-by-case bargains in order to pass laws. Small groups in a pivotal position obtained a disproportional influence in comparison to their absolute strength. For five years, the details of the legislative provisions were not dictated by a ministerial office but were a matter of deliberation or negotiations in parliament. The episode was also beneficial to the whole parliament, encouraging a need for the executive power to adopt a more cooperative attitude.

The "regular" types of minority governments are generally in line with the comparative literature on this issue: (a lack of) rules matter greatly for their success and these governments are the result of a complex mix of motivations comprised of electoral, career, and policy considerations. The French case provides two further points that have received less attention. First, the day-to-day passing of bills under minority governments depended on long-term cooperative relations with pivotal actors. These strategies seem to be as important as ad hoc log-rolls relative to a given piece of legislation. Second, contrary to conventional views, we observe that a limited polarization of the party system is essential to secure ad hoc agreements when passing legislation under minority governments. Should a populist and/or radical force be present in parliament, it would be more difficult to pass an ambitious legislative agenda.

A number of general observations can be developed from these episodes. First, as already demonstrated by Huber (1996), tools of rationalized parliamentarism are not necessarily detrimental to parliamentary democracy. Article 49.3 is useful not only in order to help the government deliver policies but also to force MPs to position themselves vis-à-vis the government. And the procedure does not come without costs for the government with the risk of being censured by parliament and rejected by public opinion. Second, anecdotal evidence related to negotiations over bills show both that pork is only one option among others to obtain support and that there is a continuum between vote-buying, give-and-take relations, and in-depth discussions related to the general merits of the project. Although, from an analytical standpoint, deliberation and negotiations constitute two distinct modalities of cooperation (Eslter 2000), in real politics there is a large gray zone. Third and last, the tale of the minority governments in France provides a striking example of the gap between the ways the parliament plays, sometimes secretly, and the way legislative politics is perceived by the public. Arguably, such a gap is especially marked in a country like France that is characterized by a majoritarian political culture: closed-door deals are not familiar to the public and, for that reason, are negatively viewed. Yet, it also says something deeper given the unpopularity of most legislatures in the world (Inter-Parliamentary Union 2012): what is perceived of what happens inside their walls appears to be structurally biased. This constitutes a huge challenge for legislatures in their communication but also, like it or not, for parliamentary scholars.

References

Andrieu, Claire. 2020. "Le financement des activités politiques, entre contrôle et amnistie." In *Michel Rocard Premier ministre*, ed. Alain Bergounioux and Mathieu Fulla. Paris: Presses de Sciences Po, pp. 201–213.

Baumgartner, Franck R., Sylvain Brouard, Emiliano Grossman, Sébastien G. Lazardeux, and Jonathan Moody. 2014. "Divided Government, Legislative Productivity, and Policy Change in the USA and France." *Governance* 27 (3): 423–447.

Becher, Michael and Sylvain Brouard. 2022. "Executive Accountability Beyond Outcomes: Experimental Evidence on Public Evaluations of Powerful Prime Ministers." *American Journal of Political Science* 66 (1): 106– 122.

Bergounioux, Alain and Mathieu Fulla, eds. 2020. *Michel Rocard Premier ministre*. Paris: Presses de Sciences Po.

Brouard, Sylvain. 2011. "The role of French Governements in Legislative Agenda Setting." In *The role of Governments in Legislative Agenda Setting*, ed. Bjorn E. Rasch and George Tsebelis, London: Routledge, pp. 240–253.

Brouard, Sylvain, Olivier Costa, and Eric Kerrouche. 2013. "The 'New' French Parliament: Changes and Continuities." In *Developments in French Politics 5*, ed. Alistair Cole, Sophie Meunier, and Vincent Tiberj. Basingstoke: Palgrave, pp. 35–52.

Chevalier, Jean-Jacques, Guy Carcassonne, Olivier Duhamel, and Julie Benetti. 2017. *History of the 5th Republic*. 16th ed. Paris: Dalloz.

Costa, Olivier, ed. 2014. *Parliamentary Representation in France*. London: Routledge.

Döring, Herbert, and Philip Manow. 2018. *Parliaments and Governments Database (ParlGov): Information on Parties, Elections and Cabinets in Modern Democracies*. Development Version.

Duhamel, Olivier. 2014. "Conclusions: quatre leçons de lui." Conference *Hommage à Guy Carcassonne* at the Conseil constitutionnel.

Dupoirier, Elisabeth and Nicolas Sauger. 2010. "Four Rounds in a Row: The Impact of Presidential Election Outcomes on Legislative Elections in France." *French Politics* 8 (1): 21–41.

Elster, Jon. 2000. "Arguing and Bargaining in Two Constituent Assemblies." *Journal of Constitutional Law* 2 (2): 345–421.
Favier, Pierre and Michel Martin-Rolland. 1996. *La Décennie Mitterrand. Vol. 3.* Paris: Seuil.
Field, Bonnie N. 2016. *Why Minority Governments Work: Multilevel Territorial Politics in Spain.* London: Palgrave.
Flauraud, Vincent. 2016. "'You have Decided to Govern Differently. We Have Decided to Oppose Differently.' The Parliamentary Group Union du center (UDC) under the Rocard Government (1988–1991)." *Histoire@Politique* 1 (28): 108–125.
Foucault, Martial, and Jean-François Godbout. 2014. "Restrictive Legislative Procedures and Coalition Support in France." *E-prints Centre d'étude européenne.*
Grunberg, Gérard. 2020. "Michel Rocard et le parti socialiste (1988–1991)." In *Michel Rocard Premier ministre*, ed. Alain Bergounioux and Mathieu Fulla. Paris: Presses de Sciences Po, pp. 115–124.
Huber, John. 1996. *Rationalizing Parliament, Legislative Institutions and Party Politics in France.* Cambridge: Cambridge University Press.
Huchon, Jean-Paul. 2017. *C'était Michel Rocard.* Paris: L'Archipel.
Inter-Parliamentary Union. 2012. *The Changing Nature of Parliamentary Representation.* Global parliamentary report.
Jaffré, Jérome. 2020. "Le moment 1988." In *Michel Rocard Premier ministre*, ed. Alain Bergounioux and Mathieu Fulla, Paris: Presses de Sciences Po, pp. 71–88.
Kerrouche, Eric. 2006. "The French Assemblée nationale: The Case of a Weak Legislature?" *The Journal of Legislative Studies* 12 (3–4): 336–365.
Lecomte, Damien, and Olivier Rozenberg. 2021. "A Gently Slopped Leadership: Parliamentary Support for Presidents in France." In *Presidents, Unified Government and Legislative Control*, ed. Jung-hsiang Tsai. London: Palgrave Macmillan, pp. 31–66.
Nguyen-Duy, Iris. 2015. "France: Excluding Parliament from Government Formation." In *Parliaments and Government Formation. Unpacking Investiture Rules*, ed. Bjorn E. Rasch, Shane Martin, and José A. Cheibub, Oxford: Oxford University Press, pp. 292–308.
Pinon, Stéphane. 2003. *Les Réformistes constitutionnels des années trente aux origines de la Ve République.* Paris: LGDJ.
Rasch, Bjorn Erik, Shane Martin, and José Antonio Cheibub, eds. 2015. *Parliaments and Government Formation: Unpacking Investiture Rules.* Oxford/New York: Oxford University Press.
Rozenberg, Olivier. 2020. "Du parler-vrai au Parlement ? Les gouvernements Rocard, l'Assemblée nationale et le Sénat." In *Michel Rocard Premier ministre*, ed. Alain Bergounioux and Mathieu Fulla. Paris: Presses de Sciences Po, pp. 89–113.
Rozenberg, Olivier, and Yves Surel. 2018. "Beyond Weakness: Policy Analysis in the French Parliament." In *Policy Analysis in France*, ed. Charlotte Halpern, Patrick Hassenteufel, and Philippe Zittoun. Bristol: Bristol University Press, pp. 137–154.
Sauger, Nicolas. 2009. "Party Discipline and Coalition Management in the French Parliament." *West European Politics* 32 (2): 310–326.
Strøm, Kaare. 1990. *Minority Government and Majority Rule.* Cambridge: Cambridge University Press.

Thürk, Maria, Johan Hellström, and Holger Döring. 2021. "Institutional Constraints on Cabinet Formation: Veto Points and Party System Dynamics." *European Journal of Political Research* 60 (2): 295–316.
Tsebelis, George. 2004. "Veto Player and Law Production." In *Patterns of Parliamentary Behaviour. Passage of Legislation across Westyern Europe*, ed. Herbert Döring and Marc Hallerberg. Aldershot: Ashgate, pp. 169–200.

10
Ireland

Minority Government with a Majoritarian Twist

Liam Weeks

Ireland has been one of the more active exponents of minority government in Europe (Mitchell 2000, 2001). This might seem something of a puzzle, as the Irish political system leans more towards the Westminster than the consensus form of government, where minority cabinets are usually more prevalent. With few tangible benefits from being in opposition, outsiders looking in might wonder why almost 40 percent of Irish governments have been of a minority disposition. Could it be that parties have such ideological differences that they would rather remain powerless in opposition than share office with each other? While this is partially true in some instances, the primary reason, and a motivating factor to study minority government in Ireland, is the presence of independent parliamentarians. Defined here as a legislator with no ties to, or formal association with, a political party, independents have experienced the fate of the dodo in most democracies, but have maintained a continuous existence in the Irish parliament, even experiencing a resurgence in numbers in recent decades. Their presence both deprives parties of majorities, but also facilitates their forming minority governments. Independents are the main reason why such administrations have prevailed in Ireland, as parties or coalitions close to a majority have looked to independents for external support rather than bring another party into cabinet. It facilitates their acting in a majoritarian manner, as parties can either coerce or cajole some independents into supporting them.

The frequency of minority governments has increased since 1989, comprising 45 percent of administrations, compared to 35 percent in the previous forty-five years. The increasing presence of independents is one contributory factor, while another is the fragmentation of the party system. The traditional two and a half party system has become a multiparty model, with rising support for independents and left-wing parties making it more difficult for parties to find coalition partners. As shown in this chapter, the old shibboleths that persist in a changed landscape makes government formation an ever more protracted process. That was why it took a record 70 days to form a government in 2016, which was the smallest ever minority administration in Ireland, and why it took twice as long (139 days) in 2020.

Liam Weeks, *Ireland*. In: *Minority Governments in Comparative Perspective*. Edited by Bonnie N. Field and Shane Martin, Oxford University Press. © Liam Weeks (2022).
DOI: 10.1093/oso/9780192871657.003.0010

The Irish political system

The Irish legislature, the Oireachtas, comprises two houses, the lower House of Representatives (known as the Dáil), and a Senate, or Seanad. The Dáil currently has 160 seats, with MPs known as TDs (Teachta Dála, meaning messenger of the people), and the Seanad 60 seats. The Irish parliament is traditionally seen as one of the weaker in Europe, a perception also shared by the state's directly elected president, who has no executive power, and is primarily a ceremonial figurehead (Gallagher 2018). Traditionally, Ireland had a two-and-a-half party system, in part a product of a civil conflict in the 1920s (Weeks 2018). The two main parties, Fianna Fáil and Fine Gael, represented opposing sides from the conflict, a division that, while it was the main difference between them, has eroded over time, culminating in their entering coalition government together for the first time in 2020. Until 1989 Fianna Fáil preferred to govern on its own, with Fine Gael's primary option for office being to coalesce with the half party of the system, the center-left Labour Party. Fianna Fáil's forming a coalition government with the liberal Progressive Democrats in 1989 threatened to break the mold of the party system, but the real change came at the 2011 election, when Fianna Fáil lost more than half its support and two-thirds of its seats. Since then the party system has been in a state of considerable upheaval, marked by increased fragmentation, most notably rising support for independents and Sinn Féin, an ethno-nationalist party.

The process of government formation combines a mix of formal and informal rules. The informality takes place in the post-election process prior to the assembly of a new parliament, when parties meet (sometimes also with independents) to discuss the nature of their participation in a potential government. No constitutional recognition is given to formatuers or informateurs, and even where electoral deadlock arises, the president stays out of the process. A formal vote of investiture to elect a *Taoiseach* (prime minister) takes place when parliament first meets following an election. To be elected Taoiseach, a nominee must secure more votes "for" than "against."

Deputies are free to nominate and second any member, but the convention is that parties nominate their respective leaders, unless an agreement has already been made to support another party. An outgoing Taoiseach is usually the first nominee, but if re-election is not forthcoming, he is obliged to resign. If no one is elected, the outgoing Taoiseach retains the post in a caretaker capacity, about which the constitution says very little. Parliament can then continue to meet until it elects a new Taoiseach, or the outgoing incumbent can request the president to dissolve the Dáil. For example, when the Dáil met on March 10, 2016 following a general election two weeks previously, four party leaders were formally nominated to be Taoiseach. All four, including the outgoing Taoiseach, Fine Gael's Enda Kenny, failed to be elected, following which Kenny tendered his resignation to the President, while remaining on as Taoiseach. Further votes took place in the Dáil

Table 10.1 Types of government, Ireland, 1945–2020

Prime minister	Start date	End date	Government party	Coalition	Minority	If minority, formal or substantive	Support parties
De Valera VI	09-06-1944	04-02-1948	Fianna Fáil	No	No		
Costello I	18-02-1948	30-05-1951	Fine Gael–Labour–National League–Clann na Talmhan–Clann na Poblachta	Yes	Yes	Substantive	
De Valera VII	13-06-1951	18-05-1954	Fianna Fáil	No	Yes	Substantive	
Costello II	02-06-1954	05-03-1957	Fine Gael–Labour–Clann na Talmhan	Yes	No		
De Valera VIII	20-03-1957	23-06-1959	Fianna Fáil	No	No		
Lemass I	23-06-1959	04-10-1961	Fianna Fáil	No	No		
Lemass II	11-10-1961	07-04-1965	Fianna Fáil	No	Yes	Substantive	
Lemass III	21-04-1965	10-11-1966	Fianna Fáil	No	No		
Lynch I	10-11-1966	18-06-1969	Fianna Fáil	No	No		
Lynch II	02-07-1969	28-02-1973	Fianna Fáil	No	No		
Cosgrave I	14-03-1973	16-06-1977	Fine Gael–Labour	Yes	No		
Lynch III	05-07-1977	12-12-1979	Fianna Fáil	No	No		
Haughey I	12-12-1979	11-06-1981	Fianna Fáil	No	No		
FitzGerald I	30-06-1981	18-02-1982	Fine Gael–Labour	Yes	Yes	Substantive	
Haughey II	09-03-1982	24-11-1982	Fianna Fáil	No	Yes	Substantive	Sinn Féin the Workers' Party
FitzGerald II	14-12-1982	20-01-1987	Fine Gael–Labour	Yes	No		
FitzGerald III	20-01-1987	17-02-1987	Fine Gael	No	Yes	Substantive	

Continued

Table 10.1 Continued

Prime minister	Start date	End date	Government party	Coalition	Minority	If minority, formal or substantive	Support parties
Haughey III	10-03-1987	15-06-1989	Fianna Fáil	No	Yes	Substantive	Fine Gael
Haughey IV*	12-07-1989	11-02-1992	Fianna Fáil–Progressive Democrats	Yes	Yes		
Reynolds I*	11-02-1992	25-11-1992	Fianna Fáil–Progressive Democrats	Yes	Yes		
Reynolds II	12-01-1993	17-11-1994	Fianna Fáil–Labour	Yes	No		
Bruton I	15-12-1994	06-06-1997	Fine Gael–Labour	Yes	No		
Ahern I	26-06-1997	17-05-2002	Fianna Fáil–Progressive Democrats	Yes	Yes	Substantive	
Ahern II	06-06-2002	24-05-2007	Fianna Fáil–Progressive Democrats	Yes	No		
Ahern III	14-06-2007	07-05-2008	Fianna Fáil–Progressive Democrats–Greens	Yes	No		
Cowen I	07-05-2008	23-01-2011	Fianna Fáil–Progressive Democrats–Greens	Yes	No		
Cowen II	23-01-2011	25-02-2011	Fianna Fáil	No	Yes	Substantive	
Kenny I	09-03-2011	26-02-2016	Fine Gael–Labour	Yes	No		
Kenny II	07-05-2016	14-06-2017	Fine Gael	Yes	Yes	Substantive	Fianna Fáil
Varadkar I	14-06-2017	08-02-2020	Fine Gael	No	Yes	Substantive	Fianna Fáil
Martin I	27-06-20		Fianna Fáil–Fine Gael–Greens	Yes	No		
Share of minority governments 1945–2020			42%				
Share of minority governments 1990–2020			46%				

Note: *The parties in government had a combined total of 50 percent of Dáil seats. End date refers to the date of the election called by the incumbent Taoiseach, except in the cases of a mid-term change in Taoiseach, when it refers to the date of investiture of a new Taoiseach. In all cases, the outgoing government remains in place until the investiture of a new one. Start date refers to the formal investiture.

on April 6 and April 14, but no candidate was elected. After seventy days following the election, on May 6, Kenny's nomination was approved, by 59 votes to 49 (50 TDs abstained) (O'Malley 2016).

The different types of government in the post-1945 era are detailed in Table 10.1. The year 1989, when Fianna Fáil first entered a coalition, marked a watershed in the Irish party system (Weeks 2018). It might have been thought that this event would result in fewer minority governments, since the primary reason they arose in the past was Fianna Fáil's failure to win a majority. With the party open to sharing power, this meant it could look to other parties to form majority coalitions, rather than being reliant on independents. That this did not materialize was primarily due to the fragmentation of the party system, something that is detailed later in the chapter.

Why minority governments form

The presence of minority governments is due to a combination of institutional factors and party competition. The operation of a particular electoral system contributes to the presence of a type of parliamentarian who makes minority government realizable for parties close to a winning majority. This combined with the structure of the party system often makes minority government the only workable outcome for many of the relevant actors.

Government formation and institutions

Traditional arguments for the presence of minority governments often refer to influence outside of government. This can come in the form of extra-parliamentary organizations such as unions and interest groups, or influence within parliament from the opposition benches (Luebbert 1986). As Mitchell (2001: 189) persuasively argues, none of these points are that applicable to the Irish case. Interest groups, known as "social partners," have affected policy via tripartite agreements involving employers, unions, and government, but the influence of opposition parties on these discussions has been minimal. Likewise, the Irish parliament has traditionally been considered weak, with the committee system lacking the powers to scrutinize government effectively (Gallagher 2018).

One institution, however, that is lacking elsewhere, but contributes to the formation of minority governments in Ireland is the electoral system, the single transferable vote (Mitchell 2001). Its influence comes in the manner by which this highly candidate-centered system facilitates the election of independents (Weeks 2014). Ireland is unusual in that it has always had a presence of independents in the Dáil. As shown in Figure 10.1, the number of these independents has

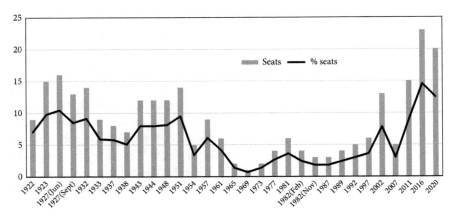

Fig. 10.1 Independent parliamentarians in Ireland, 1922–2020

Note: "Seats" denotes number of seats won by independents per Dáil election; "% seats" denotes the overall proportion. *Source*: Weeks (2017).

fluctuated considerably, but has been steadily increasing since the 1990s, to the point where there are regularly more independents in the Dáil than all other western parliaments combined (Weeks 2011, 2016, 2017).

For many who view them as mavericks, independents defy analysis, but they are a core component of Irish political life, often being the conduit for disaffection within the party system. Some independents are dissidents who have fallen out with their mother party; others comprise politicians unable to find a suitable party for their policies, while others exist purely to act as their constituency's mouthpiece (see Weeks (2009) for a greater discussion of these categories). It is difficult to define independents ideologically, as they vary from one to the other. Many of them are centrists, driven more by people than policy, but what they have in common is that they are entirely independent of parties, with no formal ties or associations. The continuous presence of independents in Irish politics has proven too difficult for parties to ignore, especially those tantalizingly close to a parliamentary majority. Independents are generally easier to buy off than parties, the latter of whom usually demand cabinet seats and policy influence in return for their support. Possibly a consequence of their solitary position, which lessens their bargaining stance, independents are less demanding, and tend to be happy with patronage and pork for their respective constituencies. Table 10.2 details the minority governments that have involved independents and their level of support (Kefford and Weeks 2020). None of the agreements were formal and many were not even substantive as there were no explicit (or at least public) contracts between the parties and independents. Initially this was because governments did not want to be seen to reward independents for their non-aligned status, in case it encouraged more to pursue the independent path, and also because parties preferred

Table 10.2 Governments formed with support of independents, Ireland, 1945–2020

Year(s)	Party or parties involved	Nature of agreement
1948–51	Fine Gael–Labour–National Labour–Clann na Poblachta–Clann na Talmhan	Six independents form informal group to support government. One independent (Dillon) made minister
1951–4	Fianna Fáil	Five independents support government, but no manifest agreement
1961–5	Fianna Fáil	Two independents (Carroll & Sherwin) support government, with occasional support from two independents (Sheridan & Leneghan). No manifest agreement
1981–2	Fine Gael–Labour	One independent (Kemmy) supports government & three other independents abstain, but no agreement
1982	Fianna Fáil	Two independents (Gregory & Blaney) support government in return for patronage agreements
1987–9	Fianna Fáil	One independent (Gregory) abstains, one (Blaney) supports government, but no agreement
1989–92	Fianna Fáil–Progressive Democrats	One independent (Foxe) supports government in return for unpublished patronage agreement
1997–2002	Fianna Fáil–Progressive Democrats	Three independents (Blaney, Fox, Healy-Rae) support government in return for unpublished patronage agreements. Another independent (Gildea) onboard in 1998
2007–11	Fianna Fáil–Progressive Democrats–Greens*	Three independents (Healy-Rae, Lowry, McGrath) support government in return for patronage agreement. McGrath withdraws support in 2008
2016–20	Fine Gael	Independent Alliance (5 TDs) agrees to support government on motions of confidence & finance bills. One becomes minister & three junior ministers. Two other independents (Zappone & Naughten) become ministers. One independent (Lowry) provides external support

Note: * This only became a minority government in the last month of its lifetime.

to call independents' bluff, knowing that the latter feared an early election and a potential loss of their hard-won seat. In more recent decades, independents have been more demanding, extracting formal agreements and patronage deals for their respective constituencies. The benefit of this has been unwavering support for the minority government, as such independents tend to vote with them in parliament almost all the time.

Government formation and the party system

While the party system has in recent decades evolved from a structured and rigid format to one in a near-permanent state of flux, both models have proved conducive to the emergence of minority governments. The dualistic nature of the party system, where until recently neither of the two main components, Fianna Fáil and Fine Gael, contemplated sharing power with each other, meant that if neither of these two (or the coalitions they led) won a majority in parliament, the only feasible option for the party (or parties) with the most seats was to form a minority government with the help of independents. Because independents tend to be moderates occupying the center ground, they can be courted by rival government alternatives, affording them the opportunity to hold the balance of power. Such minority arrangements are also a product of the Westminster distaste for coalitions, which Ireland inherited from previous centuries of British rule. The first formal coalition was not formed until 1948, twenty-six years after the foundation of the state, and the parties involved did not describe it as such, preferring to call it an "inter-party" government. As previously mentioned, it was not until 1989 that Fianna Fáil first entered a coalition, which even then it described as a "temporary little arrangement" (Girvin 1993: 1). Prior to this, the party had formed minority governments with independent support in 1932, 1937, 1943, 1951, 1961, 1981, and 1987. While Fianna Fáil's embracing of coalition in the 1990s might have spelled the end of the influence of independents, the increasing presence of the latter in the Dáil has meant their being included in the government formation process in 1997, 2007, 2016, and 2020.

The formation of minority governments has also been a product of party intransigence, with a number refusing to work with each other. In previous decades this contributed to Fianna Fáil remaining in office, while in more recent years the fragmentation of the party system has made the process of government formation more protracted. Voters have drifted to a number of small left-wing parties, but most particularly, to independents and latterly, Sinn Féin. The rise of this party has had a particular impact, as neither Fianna Fáil nor Fine Gael have, for now, been willing to enter a coalition with Sinn Féin, for reasons related to its historical association with the paramilitary Irish Republican Army. Combined with a number of independents and some far-left parties, the result is the presence of a large non-coalitionable bloc in the Dáil, making the process of government formation more difficult, and minority government more likely. For example, following the 2016 election, Sinn Féin, independents, and the Solidarity party had between them almost 50 seats, nearly one-third of the Dáil's capacity. With Fianna Fáil ruling out coalition with Fine Gael, the only possible outcome was a Fine Gael single-party minority government. The administration that ensued was the smallest ever Irish administration, commanding barely one-third of Dáil seats, but put into power by the abstention of Fianna Fáil in a confidence and supply agreement.

Government formation and parties' office, policy, and vote goals

As the Irish political system is executive-dominated, it is only by being in office that parties can hope to affect policy. What does the considerable presence of minority governments then reveal about parties' goals? Why also are such administrations more likely to rely on independents over parties?

The answer to the first question could be that office is not for everyone, and it is fair to say that not all parties in the Dáil have been purely office-seeking. Since the 1990s, there have been a number of far-left parties not willing to work with the other established parties, including the various guises of the Socialist Party and Socialist Workers' Party. While these groups are not necessarily anathema to being in power, their rejection of coalition with the mainstream parties means they are to all intents and purposes not office-seeking. For the first twenty years of its parliamentary life (it re-entered the Dáil in 1997), Sinn Féin also pursued a similar strategy. For these parties, the primary reason why they appeared to be rejecting office was because of their anti-system ideology. It would have been too much of a compromise to contemplate coalition with the establishment they virulently opposed. It is also likely that a belief prevailed that a betrayal of such a policy would be punished by their supporters, as this is a fate that has befallen the more centrist Labour Party whenever it formed a government with Fine Gael. Martin (2018) calls this "office shyness," with parties placing what he labels a "reservation price" on the potential costs of entering government.

It is not just the smaller, more extreme parties who have not always prioritized office. The stance of Fianna Fáil and Fine Gael in ruling out sharing power with each other and with Sinn Féin for so long suggests that they may not be 100 percent office-seeking. The latter is a more recent development, and stresses the importance of policy goals, with both Fianna Fáil and Fine Gael anathema to some of Sinn Féin's aims and directives. In terms of sharing power with each other, Fine Gael has been more open to such arrangements in government negotiations in 1989, 2016, and 2020, but it was a no-go area for Fianna Fáil until 2020, when it formed a coalition with Fine Gael. In 2016, Fianna Fáil's party leader, fulfilling a pre-election pledge, had rejected an invitation to participate in such an arrangement, preferring to support Fine Gael externally in a confidence and supply arrangement. This historical reluctance within the two parties to work with each other also reflects a fear that it could contribute to the losing of their stranglehold on the Irish political system, allowing others to grow in opposition. Such fears are indicative of the importance of long-term vote goals.

The smaller, moderate parties place greater emphasis on short-term strategies, and for those who are not anti-system like their far-left counterparts, the focus is usually on being in government to demonstrate relevance. There have been so few cases of these parties providing external support because there is not a great deal that can be offered to them in the executive-oriented political system.

Given these considerations of party goals, it explains why independents have a role to play in the government formation process. They permit the existence of minority governments, who do not have to give up valuable seats at the cabinet table, and rarely have to compromise on policy. The governing party can pick off the independents one-by-one, who lack the cohesion to wield blackmail influence over a government akin to an external party. The independents themselves are often not interested in office; given their anti-party position and oppositional nature, which is usually a key factor in their election, participation in government would be anathema to many, not to mention electoral suicide. At the same time, independents' ostracized position on the sidelines makes the temptation to realize some constituency-related policy goals too difficult to overlook if a party attempting to form a minority government comes abegging with pork and patronage aplenty. This is particularly the case for "apostate independents" (Weeks 2009), who, sharing a historical connection with a party, are generally less anti-party and less anti-establishment than other independents. For many of these independents, support status with no firm commitments is the perfect compromise as they can realize some of their policy and other goals without having to be seen to compromise on their independence. This was the case for what were called the Fianna Fáil "gene pool independents" in the 1990s and 2000s, whose constituencies were the beneficiaries of a number of infrastructural projects, including roads, schools, and hospitals. One independent claimed to have received £250 million in government funding for his constituency, while another recalled "I remember there was nothing we asked for that they didn't say was OK" (Weeks 2017: 236–237). One such item the latter independent requested was a bridge in his constituency, which when opened in 2009 was named in his honor. The examples of independents receiving such patronage from minority governments are numerous, with most cases comprising constituency-related expenditure. It should be noted that any such arrangements were often unpublished, with the responsibility (or culpability) for the expenditure difficult to identify, so as to protect the government from accusations of attempting to buy legislative votes.

Minority governments in office

There have been two categories of support provided to minority governments in office—from parties, and from independents—with none involving formal agreements. The three instances of a support party since 1945 have been Sinn Féin the Workers' Party (SFWP) supporting a minority Fianna Fáil government in 1982, Fine Gael supporting a minority Fianna Fáil government from 1987 to 1989, and Fianna Fáil returning the favor to a Fine Gael minority government from 2016 to 2020. In the first instance, the far-left SFWP said: "our support is unconditional and we have made no deal or pact" (*Dáil Debates*, Vol 333(1), March 9, 1982). Along with two independents, the SFWP kept Fianna Fáil in power for nine months, even though it opposed elements of the government's Finance Bill. After backing Fianna Fáil in a vote of no-confidence in July, the SFWP lost faith in the government when it launched a new economic policy in October that proposed a series of cuts in expenditure to cut a budget deficit and stimulate growth. When a second vote of no confidence was called the following month, the three SFWP TDs voted against the government, which was defeated by two votes, becoming the first administration in the history of the state to lose such a motion, with an election duly called.

The second instance of a support party came just over four years later in 1987, when the outgoing Fine Gael–Labour government was heavily defeated, but Fianna Fáil fell three seats short of a majority. Fine Gael's newly elected leader, Alan Dukes, said that in the national interest he would not oppose Fianna Fáil's proposed reforms (i.e. spending cuts) to the Irish economy. This was not the result of a negotiation between the two parties, nor was any agreement drawn up. It was all on Fine Gael's terms as Dukes announced, without consulting Fianna Fáil, that "I will not oppose the central thrust of its policy. If it is going in the right direction, I do not believe that it should be deviated from its course, or tripped up on macro-economic issues" (*The Irish Times*, September 3, 1987). This statement was the extent of the commitment provided by Fine Gael; there was no sense of it being either a substantive or formal agreement.

The arrangement between the same two parties from 2016 to 2020 was considerably different. After Fianna Fáil had initially rejected overtures from Fine Gael to form a coalition, it ultimately agreed to support the latter outside of government, in a form of abstention on matters of confidence and supply. Although this commitment was perhaps more explicit than that provided by Fine Gael in 1987, it had more of an impact on the minority government's ability to govern. The Fine Gael government of 2016–20 was in a particularly weak position, not just because it owed its existence to Fianna Fáil, but also because it was a long way short of a majority. The government faced an opposition twice its size, with parliament christened the "do-nothing Dáil" by some commentariat as it struggled to get legislation through. In contrast, the Fianna Fáil minority government of 1987 had as many seats as all the other parties combined. So, while governing in the 2016–20 parliament was a tortuous process that required endless negotiation, it was much more expeditious in the 1987–89 parliament. Fianna Fáil took Fine Gael for their word, and ruled accordingly, as if it was a single-party majority government. What is obvious from these three cases is that support parties get little in return for putting minority governments into office, which might explain why there has been only a handful of cases of this phenomenon. From a quid pro quo viewpoint, this also accounts for why governing parties are reluctant to go down this path. If they are going to work with other parties they prefer to bring in coalition partners who can provide more stable support and greater longevity than those outside of office. Of course, many are not willing to share office, and for such parties, independents are easier to work with than support parties. Greater pressure can be placed on independents, whose hold on a seat is often precarious, and parties can appease them with some constituency-specific concessions. This explains why the main forms of support party arrangement in Ireland have been provided not by parties, but by independents. The nature of this relationship between the minority government and independents has varied from simple external parliamentary support to formal agreements that are not far removed from contract parliamentarism. Following on from a model developed by Mitchell (2001), there are four broad types of relationships between independents and these minority governments (Weeks 2017): ad hoc management, in office, vote for investiture, and negotiated deals, each of which are discussed below.

Ad hoc management (1961–65; 1981–82; 1987–89)

Ad hoc management refers to the situation where the parties in a minority government have no formal arrangement with independents, who are instead managed on a case-by-case basis. This tends to involve discussions with independents when their votes are needed in parliament, and their being ignored otherwise. Minority governments adopted this strategy when there were only a handful of independents in parliament, and parties were able to act in a domineering manner over them. This was the case for the 1981–82 Fine Gael–Labour minority coalition, which, two seats short of a majority, acted as if it already had one. With four independents in the Dáil with whom it could have negotiated ad hoc majorities, the government chose generally to ignore them, taking their support for granted. This ultimately proved the coalition's downfall as in January 1982 it became the first (and only) Irish government to have its budget defeated in parliament. Jim Kemmy, one of the independents who brought down the government, recalled "a take it or leave it attitude at the crucial moment. I got the impression that they thought I was only bluffing, that I would back down at the last second and cast my vote with the government as I had done on every key division" (Smith 1985: 68–69).

In government (1948–51; 2016–20)

An "in government"[1] arrangement involves independents having a seat at the cabinet table. There have been two cases of Irish governments including elected independent ministers, which most recently includes the Fine Gael minority government formed in 2016. It had four independents sitting in cabinet (three full ministers and one "super junior"), as well as two external ministers of state. These cases of independents in government were a product of their having a significant presence in parliament, but also where the main governing party lacked a strategic advantage. For example, Fine Gael led both these governments, having suffered its worst electoral showing in 1948, and its worst electoral losses in 2016. By contrast, independents won approximately 40 percent as many seats as the same party in both elections, giving it a presence that could not be ignored. What these two instances also had in common is that they involved some independents working together in an alliance, a group of six in 1948 with their own leader, and an Independent Alliance of five in 2016. By acting akin to a party in negotiations, the independents were able to wield unparalleled influence over the minority governments, hence securing seats in cabinet. Related to the weak strategic positioning of the main governing party was the precarious nature of the administration—the government formed in 1948 had five parties and the 2016–20 cabinet was thirty seats short of a majority. They may have felt little alternative to bringing independents into cabinet, as relying on them from the outside might have severely restricted the shelf life of the minority administrations. Bringing independents into cabinet is one measure to guarantee their vote, as ministers are constitutionally prohibited from voting against their own government.

Vote for investiture (1951–54; 1982; 1989–92)

Under a "vote for investiture" arrangement, independent TDs agree to support the nomination of a Taoiseach and the appointment of his cabinet, but no commitment is given beyond the formation stage. The main difference from the ad hoc style of management is that the initial support of independents is courted by the parties over explicit negotiations. This is more a consequence of independents' tougher negotiating skills—they prefer to exploit their strategic position to the maximum, without compromising their independence (hence not agreeing to a deal beyond the investiture vote). The prime example of this arrangement came in 1982 when an independent, Tony Gregory, held the balance of power after the February election of that year (caused by the failure of the ad hoc strategy pursued

---

[1] There was also an independent minister in the Fianna Fáil–Green coalition from 2009 to 2011, but this case is not included because the individual concerned was not elected an independent, only becoming one following the termination of her party in office.

by the Fine Gael–Labour coalition of 1981–82). The leaders of the two main parties both courted Gregory's support, and he ultimately opted for the package offered by Fianna Fáil's Charlie Haughey, amounting to over £200 million, and which came to be known, rather infamously, as the "the Gregory Deal." The arrangement was read into the parliamentary record, but all Gregory promised in return was to vote for Haughey as Taoiseach, with his support thereafter being decided on an ad hoc issue-by-issue basis. Such a deal might seem unstable from the outside, but it was the most level of support that minority governments could extract from independents. It is worth noting that the reason the administrations falling into this category do not last a full term has not been because of unreliable independents, but because minor parties involved in the arrangements have withdrawn their support.

Negotiated deals (1997–2002; 2007–11)

A negotiated deal involves explicit deals to support parties in power provided they meet particular pledges laid out at the beginning of the government's term, commitments that are often not made public. These deals were to the fore during the tenure of the Fianna Fáil Taoiseach Bertie Ahern, who had seemingly learned from the experience of investiture deals in the 1980s. He did not want to have to worry about independents' support on a daily basis, preferring to lock them into longer-term arrangements. This came at a greater cost for minority governments, as they had to offer more to independents to secure their loyalty, but the rationale was that this would allow them to govern in a majoritarian fashion. For example, in the first such arrangement in 1997, Ahern negotiated individual deals with three independents, all of whom had a history of connection with his party. This was not a coincidence, and it helped to further stabilize the arrangement. In return for their support in parliament, Ahern was able to deliver on promises of considerable expenditure in the independents' respective constituencies. This largesse was not the limit of their influence, as the independents met together with the chief whip on a weekly basis, and a senior civil servant was assigned to deal with their queries. Ahern was happy to maintain this arrangement because the independents delivered on their promise to support him in the Dáil. In total, two of the independents voted against the government on just three out of over 400 motions, while another two provided 100 percent support, with the government lasting a full term.

Minority government performance

Since Strøm (1990) challenged the negative image of minority governments, a number of studies have shown that they need not be the weak, unstable, ineffective administrations many would have us believe. In spite of this, that image of minority governments persists in Ireland, primarily because most of them rely on independents for external support. In this section, this hypothesis is put to the test to consider the performance of minority governments in more systematic detail. The first measure, as detailed in Table 10.3, is legislative output. First of all, minority governments produce less legislation (on average 86 bills per cabinet) than their

Table 10.3 Legislative record and duration, Ireland, 1945–2020

Taoiseach (prime minister)	Minority	Number of government bills presented	Number of government bills approved	Percent of government bills approved	Relative duration of government
De Valera VI	No	128	124	96.9	0.73
Costello I	Yes	112	100	89.3	0.67
De Valera VII	Yes	99	97	98.0	0.60
Costello II	No	116	105	90.5	0.57
De Valera VIII	No	78	78	100.0	0.92
Lemass I	No	116	115	99.1	0.92
Lemass II	Yes	135	127	94.1	0.70
Lemass III	No	44	41	93.2	0.32
Lynch I	No	83	76	91.6	0.76
Lynch II	No	124	114	91.9	0.73
Cosgrave I	No	177	165	93.2	0.86
Lynch III	No	82	82	100.0	0.47
Haughey I	No	60	57	95.0	0.59
FitzGerald I	Yes	29	26	89.7	0.12
Haughey II	Yes	22	16	72.7	0.15
FitzGerald II	No	148	123	83.1	0.85
Haughey III	Yes	87	85	97.7	0.47
Haughey IV	Yes	78	76	97.4	0.52
Reynolds I	Yes	26	25	96.2	0.31
Reynolds II	No	76	76	100.0	0.38
Bruton I	No	103	98	95.1	0.82
Ahern I	Yes	217	212	97.7	0.98
Ahern II	No	213	205	96.2	0.99
Ahern III	No	23	21	95.5	0.20
Cowen I	No	138	125	90.6	0.71
Kenny I	No	296	292	98.6	0.99
Kenny II	Yes	18	16	88.9	0.23
Varadkar I	Yes	129	124	96.1	0.72
Martin I	No	32	31	96.9	N/A

Note: Number of government bills presented denotes the combined number of (a) bills enacted into legislation and (b) bills lapsed in a government's tenure.

majority counterparts (118 bills on average), which is not surprising since minority governments are shorter in duration. Controlling for length of time in office, minority governments are actually more productive, introducing on average just over thirty-six bills per annum, compared to almost thirty-four for majority governments. Overall, majority governments are slightly better at getting their bills enacted into legislation, though both types of government have high rates, in excess of 90 percent. It is a rare occasion that Irish governments are defeated in parliament on any motion, let alone on their own legislation. Using roll-call data from an eighty-year period, the twelve minority governments that formed between 1937 and 2007 were defeated seventeen times in total in the Dáil (with very few of these defeats on legislative matters), with nine opposition motions passed (Hansen 2009, 2010). Under the eighteen majority administrations in the same time period, just nine government motions were defeated and one opposition passed.

In terms of government duration, majority governments last considerably longer, three years and six months in total, compared to two years and four months for minority governments. This does not necessarily imply greater instability, however, as there are a number of caveats. First, some governments are shorter due to mid-term changes in the governing party's leadership. This was the case for Fianna Fáil in 1961, 1979, 1992, and 2008, and for Fine Gael in 2017. The governments of the outgoing Taoisigh did not necessarily end early, with their lifespan being the product of intra-party politics and the measurements employed here. Second, as Mitchell (2001: 150) discusses, in a system where the prime minister has the power of dissolution it is unlikely that a government will serve a full term, as the strategic interests of the governing party will be to the fore. Some elections are called before the government has served its full term for reasons of blatant electoral advantage. Éamon de Valera called snap elections barely a year into the lifetime of a minority government on three separate occasions (1933, 1938, and 1944). Controlling for the maximum lifespan of governments, including those formed mid-term, minority cabinets see out just half of their legislatively allowed term, with an equivalent figure of 0.7 for majority ones. One of the factors behind the shorter duration of minority governments concerns the nature of the relationship they have with independents. Treating the four different categories of such support status, those where the governments negotiated ad hoc support with independents and relied on alternative majorities lasted the shortest period of time, at almost exactly two years. In contrast, those with more formal arrangements (involving independents in cabinet and/or contracts with each) lasted almost twice as long. This indicates a significant institutional dimension to the stability of minority governments involving independents—the more formal the relationship between them, the longer the government lasts.

The final dimension to consider is electoral performance, where, perhaps surprisingly, minority governments fare considerably better than their majority counterparts. If performance is defined as electoral support, minority governments do better. The mean change in the government party's vote in the eight minority administrations between 1948 and 2020 in Ireland was a loss of 1.8 percentage points. Comparing the electoral record of the eleven majority administrations over the same time frame (excluding 2011[2]), they lost an average of 9 percentage points at their outgoing election (Kefford and Weeks 2020). There is no obvious reason why minority governments do better; it could be that expectations are lower for the parties involved. Another reason could be that minority governments ensue when parties don't fare as well as expected, and that majority governments are the outcome of a good election for parties. Parties' fortunes fluctuate, and this observed difference could be a case of a regression to the mean, where parties in majority governments regress after one good election, and parties in minority governments have an improved performance after a poor election.

Conclusion

Minority governments are a common feature of the Irish political landscape, but they do not occur for the typical reasons. Such governments in Ireland are unusual in that they tend to control more parliamentary seats than the opposition parties—they are, in effect, majoritarian. This outcome is the product of an exceptional presence of independent parliamentarians, who play a role both in the formation and maintenance of these administrations. The relationship between independents and minority governments is a product of both institutional factors and party competition and strategies. In particular, the single transferable vote electoral system gives independents a presence in the legislature that cannot be ignored, while the dynamics of the party system mean that independents are an invaluable means of resolving seemingly intransigent government formation outcomes.

While minority governments involving parties attract criticism from those who claim their lacking a majority makes them undemocratic and unaccountable, such reproachment is even greater when governments have looked to the support of independents in Ireland. Many are the criticisms of arrangements involving independents for being secretive, prioritizing constituency over national interests, lacking accountability, and contributing to instability. This taps into the general concept of good governance, and is something that could be the subject of future research. In a previous study, Weeks (2017: 276–285) found that recent periods of

---

[2] The outgoing government in 2011 had held a majority up until its last month in office when the Green Party withdrew from the coalition. Considering the governing parties lost 27 percentage points between them, whichever category this government falls into clearly has an impact on the results (an approximate three percentage point swing either way); the averages stated do not include the 2011 result.

minority government rule reliant on independents had little effect on Worldwide Governance Indicators produced by the World Bank, but this is a relationship that could be explored in greater detail.

It would be unfair to place all the blame for the perceived failings of minority government on independents, as the parties and the party system also have a role to play in their proliferation in Ireland. Where once it was the stubbornness, if not bravado, of a dominant Fianna Fáil, that allowed the party to form minority cabinets but rule in a majoritarian disposition, now it is the unravelling of the party system that perpetuates minority government. Although the players and the nature of the competition between them are changing, some cling to the old rules, making it more difficult to play the game of government formation. This combined with the increased costs of governing might increase the likelihood of parties being less willing to enter government. This was particularly noticeable after the 2016 and 2020 general elections, when some parties were almost queuing up not to be in office. Such scenarios in Ireland, as elsewhere, make minority rule an inevitable feature of the political landscape, and one that is unlikely to change unless parties are more willing to adapt to an ever-changing environment.

References

Farrell, Brian. 1990. "Forming the government." In *How Ireland Voted 1989*, ed. Michael Gallagher and Richard Sinnott, 179–191. University College Galway: Centre for the Study of Irish Elections:.

Gallagher, Michael. 2011. "Ireland's Earthquake Election: Analysis of the Results." In *How Ireland Voted 2011. The Full Story of Ireland's Earthquake Election*, ed. Michael Gallagher and Michael Marsh, 139–171. London: Palgrave.

Gallagher, Michael. 2016. "The Results Analysed. The Aftershocks Continue." In *How Ireland Voted 2016. The Election that Nobody Won*, ed. Michael Gallagher and Michael Marsh, 125–158. London: Palgrave.

Gallagher, Michael. 2018. "The Oireachtas: President and Parliament." In *Politics in the Republic of Ireland*, ed. Michael Gallagher and John Coakley, 164–190. London: Routledge.

Girvin, Brian. 1993. "The Road to the Election." In *How Ireland Voted 1992*, ed. Michael Gallagher and Michael Laver, 1–20. Dublin: PSAI Press.

Hansen, Martin E. 2009. "The Positions of Irish Parliamentary Parties 1937–2006." *Irish Political Studies* 24 (1): 29–44.

Hansen, Martin E. 2010. "The Parliamentary Behaviour of Minor Parties and Independents in Dáil Éireann." *Irish Political Studies* 25 (4): 643–660.

Kefford, Glenn, and Liam Weeks. 2020. "Minority Party Government and Independent MPs: A Comparative Analysis of Australia and Ireland." *Parliamentary Affairs* 73 (1): 89–107.

Luebbert, Gregory M. 1986. *Comparative Democracy: Policymaking and Governing Coalitions in Europe and Israel*. New York: Columbia University Press.

Martin, Shane. 2018. "Bargaining in Legislatures, Portfolio Allocation, and the Electoral Costs of Governing." *West European Politics* 41 (5): 1166–1190.

Mitchell, Paul. 2000. "Ireland: From Single-party to Coalition Rule." In *Coalition Governments in Western Europe*, ed. Wolfgang C. Muller and Kaare Strom, 126–157. Oxford: Oxford University Press.

Mitchell, Paul. 2001. "Divided Government in Ireland." In *Divided Government in Comparative Perspective*, ed. Robert Elgie, 182–208. Oxford: Oxford University Press.

O'Malley, Eoin. 2016. "70 Days: Government Formation in 2016." In *How Ireland Voted 2016. The Election that Nobody Won*, ed. Michael Gallagher and Michael Marsh, 255–276. London: Palgrave.

Smith, Raymond. 1985. *Garret. The Enigma*. Dublin: Aherlow.

Strøm, Kaare. 1990. *Minority Government and Majority Rule*. Cambridge: Cambridge University Press.

Weeks, Liam. 2009. "We Don't Like (to) Party. A Typology of Independents in Irish Political Life, 1922–2007." *Irish Political Studies* 24 (1): 1–27.

Weeks, Liam. 2011. "Rage against the Machine: Who Is the Independent Voter?" *Irish Political Studies* 26 (1): 19–43.

Weeks, Liam. 2014. "Crashing the Party. Does STV Help Independents?" *Party Politics* 20 (4): 604–616.

Weeks, Liam. 2016. "Why are there Independents in Ireland?" *Government and Opposition* 51 (4): 580–604.

Weeks, Liam. 2017. *Independents in Irish Party Democracy*. Manchester: Manchester University Press.

Weeks, Liam. 2018. "Parties and the Party System." In *Politics in the Republic of Ireland*, ed. Michael Gallagher and John Coakley, 111–136. London: Routledge.

11
Minority Governments in Italy
From Structural Stability to Political Change

Daniela Giannetti

In his path-breaking contribution, Strøm (1990) proposed a theory of minority governments' formation that became a benchmark for subsequent research. Until then, minority governments were seen as deviations from the baseline prediction of rational choice office-seeking models of coalition formation. Starting from policy-seeking assumptions, Strøm provided an explanation of the rationality of minority government based on the cost–benefit calculus of political actors evaluating whether or not to enter government. In short, minority governments were more likely to form when the policy benefits of entering a government were low and the electoral costs were high. This theoretical argument was first tested on a wide sample of Western European countries, then in two critical cases studies covering Norway and Italy. As in the period studied (1948–87) the incidence of minority governments was remarkably high (around 40 percent), Strøm (1990: 132) concluded that "beyond its value in the pairing with Norway, the experience of Italy is singularly relevant to any effort to understand minority governments". In the early 1990s Italian democracy underwent radical changes in its electoral rules as well as in its party system. Thereafter Italy experienced a dramatic shift in the frequency of minority governments, as they account for 17.4 percent of the cabinets that formed in the period 1992–2021.[1] The aim of this chapter is to revisit Strøm's analysis thirty years later, building on the research engendered by his seminal study. I will argue that in the period 1948–92 the high frequency of minority governments can be explained by a stable structure of the policy space centered on the presence of a core party, while their reduced incidence in the subsequent phase is due to the disappearance of such a stable structure. Turning to minority governments' performance, the Italian case provides evidence for the conjecture that they do not differ substantially from majority cabinets in terms of duration and legislative effectiveness.

---

[1] This statistic is based on governments that do not have a majority in the lower chamber of the Italian parliament.

Daniela Giannetti, *Minority Governments in Italy*. In: *Minority Governments in Comparative Perspective*. Edited by Bonnie N. Field and Shane Martin, Oxford University Press. © Daniela Giannetti (2022).
DOI: 10.1093/oso/9780192871657.003.0011

The Italian political system

As established in the 1948 Constitution, Italy is a parliamentary democracy where governments must win an ex post formal vote of investiture in both the lower and upper houses of a bicameral parliament and can be dismissed by losing a vote of no confidence in either house. The voting rule is a simple majority in both chambers.[2] The formal investiture rules as stipulated in the Italian Constitution qualifies Italy as a clear case of positive parliamentarism (Articles 93 and 94).[3] Both the Chamber of Deputies and the Senate are elected on a popular basis and have exactly the same prerogatives in the law-making process (symmetric bicameralism). Although the constitutional framework established at the end of World War II remains substantially unchanged, scholars distinguish two phases—called respectively the First and Second Republics—to indicate the rupture marked by those changes in the electoral rules and the party system that occurred in the early 1990s. Throughout the phase known as First Republic (1948–92), an open-list proportional representation (PR) system with large electoral constituencies underpinned a party system centered upon the Christian Democratic Party (DC) with "bilateral" opposition parties on the left (the Communist Party, PCI) and on the right (the post-fascist MSI) (Sartori 1976).

In the early 1990s such a political landscape was dramatically reshaped as a consequence of a change in the identity of the relevant players and the emergence of a north–south/institutional policy dimension composed of a demand for federal reforms, partially overlapping the issue of corruption, championed by a regionalist party, the Northern League (NL). Eventually the Italian party system collapsed after a wave of judicial prosecutions against the political elites (Cotta and Verzichelli 2007). In 1993 Italy adopted a mixed-member majoritarian (MMM) electoral system where 75 percent of seats were filled by plurality in single-member districts (SMD) and the remaining seats were allocated to closed party lists by PR in twenty-six constituencies for the Chamber and eighteen for the Senate. In the watershed elections of 1994, the DC was decimated as a brand new political party founded by Silvio Berlusconi (FI/Go Italy) led a center-right coalition to a decisive victory. From 1994 onwards, the Italian party system was characterized by a bipolar pattern of party competition. The right-wing bloc included FI, the post-fascist National Alliance (AN), the NL, and the most conservative former DC segments. The left-wing bloc involved the former Communist Party, relabeled the

---

[2] The rule for computing the votes was different in the two chambers: in the Chamber of Deputies abstentions were equivalent to "absentees", neither helping nor hindering the final decision; in the Senate, abstentions were equivalent to voting "no" (Russo 2015). These rules have been modified in 2017 making the Senate vote similar to that of the chamber.

[3] In particular, Article 94 states that "The Government must have the confidence of both Houses. Each House grants or withdraws its confidence through a reasoned motion and which is voted on by roll-call. Within ten days of its formation the Government shall come before the Houses to obtain their confidence."

Democratic Party of the Left or PDS (then Left Democrats or DS), and the most progressive heirs of the DC (the Italian Popular Party or PPI, then the Daisy), with the occasional participation of extreme left parties. Three elections (1994, 1996, and 2001) were held under the MMM system outlined above. In the late 2000s two large parties were created from mergers between the main center-left (Democratic Party, PD) and center-right political groups (People of Freedom, PDL). In 2005 a new electoral law introducing a closed-list PR with a seat bonus for the coalition (or party list) winning a plurality of votes was approved by the center-right government. This electoral system was applied three times (2006, 2008, and 2013). The 2013 elections marked a turning point in Italian politics, witnessing the emergence of a new policy dimension tapping pro- and anti-EU attitudes as well as the successful entry of the Five Star Movement (M5S), a populist party which gained one-fourth of the popular vote (Giannetti, Pedrazzani, and Pinto 2016). Despite a further change in the electoral rules, the 2018 elections confirmed the growing electoral success of the M5S which became the largest party with 33 percent of the vote.

From 1948 to 2021 Italy experienced sixty-three governments, most of which have been short-lived.[4] Despite the nominal turnover of cabinets, the DC was part of every government, single-party or more typically within a coalition from 1948 to 1992. Based on the partisan configuration of the Chamber only, surplus coalitions were the most frequent type accounting for 45 percent of the cabinets formed between 1948 and 1993, followed by minority governments (42.5 percent) and minimal winning coalitions (MWC) (12.5 percent). Minority cabinets were mostly single-party governments (65 percent) or, alternatively, DC-dominated multiparty minority coalitions (35 percent) (See Appendix Table 11.1A).

From 1992 to 2021—when single-party governments never formed—two cabinets lacked a majority in both chambers, three cabinets lacked a majority in the Chamber but not in the Senate, while seven governments lacked a majority in the Senate but not in the Chamber (see Table 11.1). I underline the previous distinctions in light of the "dual responsibility" (Diermeier, Eraslan, and Merlo 2007) of the Senate and Chamber in appointing and dismissing governments, which makes Italy unique in this respect. Strictly speaking, according to the categorization adopted in this volume, all these cabinets should be classified as minority governments. However, in what follows I will restrict my attention to parliamentary support in the lower house for two reasons. First, the Chamber is commonly regarded as the privileged arena for bargaining over government formation. Second, focusing on the lower chamber allows us to compare Italy meaningfully with the other democracies examined in this volume.[5] Governments lacking a

---

[4] About the way governments are counted see Chapter 1 in this volume.

[5] Percentages are calculated over the total number of governments in the Second Republic (23) starting from the Amato I government (see Table 11.1).

Table 11.1 Types of government, Italy, 1992–2021

Legislature	Cabinet	Election date	Date in	Date out	Government parties	Coalition	Cabinet type	Government strength (%, Senate in parenthesis)	Seats in parliament (Senate in parenthesis)	If minority, formal or substantive	Support parties	Duration (days)	Duration (%)
XI	Amato I	06-04-1992	28-06-1992	22-04-1993	DC (206)—PSI (92)—PLI (17)—PSDI (16)	Yes	Minimal winning	52.5 (52.6)	630 (325)			298	16.33
	Ciampi		29-04-1993	13-01-1994	DC (206)—PSI (92)—PLI (17)—PSDI (16)	Yes	Minimal winning	52.5 (52.6)	630 (325)		PDS (abs)	259	16.96
XII	Berlusconi I	28-03-1994	11-05-1994	22-12-1994	LN (117)—AN (109)—FI (99)—CCD (29)—UDC (4)	Yes	Surplus majority (min)	56.8 (46.9)	630 (326)			225	12.33

Continued

Table 11.1 Continued

Legislature	Cabinet	Election date	Date in	Date out	Government parties	Coalition	Cabinet type	Government strength (%, Senate in parenthesis)	Seats in parliament (Senate in parenthesis)	If minority, formal or substantive	Support parties	Duration (days)	Duration (%)
	Dini		17-01-1995	30-12-1995	Technical government				630 (325)			347	21.69
XIII	Prodi I	21-04-1996	18-05-1996	09-10-1998	DS (172)—PPI (67)—DINI-RI (26)—FdV (14)	Yes	Minority (min)	44.3 (48)	630 (325)	Formal	PRC (for)	874	47.89
	D'Alema I	21-10-1998		18-12-1999	DS (169)—PPI (67)—UDR (26)—DINI-RI (23)—PdCI (21)—FdV (15)—SDI (9)	Yes	Surplus majority (sur)	52.4 (55.1)	630 (325)			423	44.48

D'Alema II	21-12-1999	17-04-2000	DS (165)—PPI (59)—UDR (20)—DINI-RI (6)—PdCI (21)—FdV (15)	Yes	Minority (sur)	45.4 (53.7)	630 (324)	Formal	SVP (for)—Other	118	22.35
Amato II	25-04-2000	31-05-2001	DS (165)—PPI (58)—UDR (20)—DINI-RI (6)—PdCI (21)—FdV (15)—SDI (8)	Yes	Minority (sur)	46.5 (54)	630 (324)			401	97.80
XIV											
Berlusconi II	13-05-2001	11-06-2001	20-04-2005	FI (194)—AN (99)—CCD+CDU (40)—LN (30)	Yes	Surplus majority (mwc)	57.6 (53.6)	630 (323)		NPSI (for)—PRI (for)	1409	77.21

Continued

Table 11.1 Continued

Legislature	Cabinet	Election date	Date in	Date out	Government parties	Coalition	Cabinet type	Government strength (%, Senate in parenthesis)	Seats in parliament (Senate in parenthesis)	If minority, formal or substantive	Support parties	Duration (days)	Duration (%)
	Berlusconi III		23-04-2005	02-05-2006	FI (194)—AN (99)—CCD+CDU (40)—LN (30)—NPSI (3)—PRI (1)	Yes	Surplus majority (sur)	58.1 (54.1)	630 (320)			374	89.90
XV	Prodi II	10-04-2006	17-05-2006	16-05-2007	DS (226)—PRC (41)—RnP (18)—IdV (17)—PdCI (16)—FdV (15)—UDEUR (10)	Yes	Surplus majority (min)	54.4 (45.7)	630 (322)		SVP (for)—Other	364	19.95

									SVP (for)—Other	253	17.32
	Prodi III	16-05-2007	24-01-2008	PD (205)—PRC (41)—SD (21)—R (18)—IdV (17)—PdCI (16)—FdV (15)—UDEUR (10)	Yes	Surplus majority (min)	54.4 (44.7)	630 (322)			
XVI	Berlusconi IV	08-05-2008	30-07-2010	PdL (276)—LN (60)	Yes	Minimal winning (mwc)	53.3 (53.40)	630 (322)		MpA (for)—Other	813	44.55
	Berlusconi V	30-07-2010	15-11-2010	FI (240)—LN (59)—FLI (33)	Yes	Minimal winning (mwc)	52.7 (53.1)	630 (322)		MpA (for)—Other	108	10.67
	Berlusconi VI	15-11-2010	23-03-2011	FI (240)—LN (59)	Yes	Minority (min)	47.5 (49.8)	630 (321)	Formal		128	14.16
	Berlusconi VII	23-03-2011	12-11-2011	FI (227)—LN (59)—IR (29)	Yes	Minimal winning (mwc)	50 (52)	630 (321)			234	30.15

Continued

Table 11.1 Continued

Legislature	Cabinet	Election date	Date in	Date out	Government parties	Coalition	Cabinet type	Government strength (%, Senate in parenthesis)	Seats in parliament (Senate in parenthesis)	If minority, formal or substantive	Support parties	Duration (days)	Duration (%)
	Monti		16-11-2011	21-12-2012	Technical government				630 (322)			401	73.99
XVII	Letta I	25-02-2013	27-04-2013	15-11-2013	PD (297)—PdL (98)—SC (39)—UDC (8)	Yes	Surplus majority (sur)	70.2 (69.9)	630 (319)		CD (for)—SVP (for)—Other	202	11.07
	Letta II		18-11-2013	14-02-2014	PD (297)—SC (39)—NCD (29)—UDC (8)	Yes	Surplus majority (min)	59.2 (48.9)	630 (321)		CD (for)—SVP (for)—Other	88	5.42
	Renzi		22-02-2014	07-12-2016	PD (297)—SC (39)—NCD (29)—UDC (8)	Yes	Surplus majority (min)	59.5 (46.6)	630 (320)		CD (for)—SVP (for)—Other	1019	66.38

	Gentiloni	12-12-2016	24-03-2018	PD (297)—NCD (29)—UDC (8)	Yes	Surplus majority (min)	53 (43.9)	630 (321)	CD (for)—SVP (for)—Other	467	90.50
XVIII	Conte I	04-03-2018	01-06-2018	M5S (227)—LN (124)	Yes	Minimal winning (mwc)	55.7 (52.2)	630 (320)	PLI (for)—Other	476	26.08
	Conte II	05-09-2019	13-02-2021	M5S (227)—PD (112)—LeU (14)	Yes	Surplus majority (mwc)	56 (53.3)	630 (321)	CD—SVP—Other	509	27.89

Minimal winning coalitions %* 26.1
Minority governments % 17.4
Surplus majority coalitions % 47.8
Caretaker governments % 8.7

Notes: 1992 is used as a starting point because of the change of the party system in Italy and the analytical focus of this chapter. *Percentages refer to the Chamber of Deputies. Using the counting rules outlined in Chapter 1 of this volume, the share of minority governments would increase to 48 percent between 1992 and 2021. The latter statistic counts a government as being in a minority (50 percent+1) of the seats in each chamber, given that the government is responsible to both in Italy. For comparative purposes, the share of minority governments for the period 1990–2020 analyzed in the collective volume is 44 percent.

majority in the Chamber account for 17.4 percent of the cabinets that formed in the period 1992–2021.[6] An explanatory account of the occurrence (or lack thereof) of minority governments will be provided in the following section.

Government formation and institutions

In what follows I will argue that the formation of minority governments in the Italian First Republic was the outcome of a structurally stable configuration of the policy space centered upon the presence of a core party. In a specular way, the structural instability of the policy space explains the sharp decrease of minority governments in the subsequent period. Given a change in structural spatial conditions, the occasional formation of minority governments in the Second Republic can be accounted for by looking at institutional features, sometimes combined with intra-party politics effects.

Within the literature on coalition formation Italy has been regarded as a particularly troubling case as minority governments and surplus coalitions predominated over minimal winning coalitions (MWC). This was at odds with the basic prediction of pure office-seeking models. Starting from policy-seeking assumptions, Strøm proposed a theory of minority government formation based on the benefits of governing, seen in terms of the *policy influence differential* between government and opposition, and the costs of incumbency, seen in terms of anticipated electoral losses for governing parties. Strøm (1990: 151) expected minorities to govern with "intermediate frequency" in Italy, since both electoral costs and policy benefits were low. Indeed, Italy's governing parties suffered smaller electoral losses, on average, than governing parties in many other democracies as elections were not competitive (Strøm 1990: 124, 181–182). On the other hand, a strong committee system allowed the opposition to extract significant policy concessions.

Strøm's analysis paved the way to several attempts to incorporate minority cabinets into a general policy-based spatial account of government formation. The first generation of policy driven uni-dimensional models of coalition formation predicted a comparative advantage for the core party, as it can control policy and govern alone (De Swaan 1973). On one dimension, the core always exists and coincides with the party that controls the median legislator. A one-dimensional representation of Italian politics prior to 1992—the DC occupied the median position from 1945 to 1987—was presented by Laver and Schofield (1990). They defined post-World War II Italy as a classic example of a party system of

---

[6] Using the counting rule proposed in Chapter 1 of this volume, the share of minority governments would increase to 48 percent. The latter statistic counts a government as being in a minority in Italy if it does not have a majority (50%+1 of seats) in each chamber, given that the government is responsible to both.

"bipolar opposition." In such a polarized system DC-dominated minority governments were policy "viable" as it was impossible for opposition parties on the right and on the left of the policy spectrum to agree on a policy package preferred by more legislators than the policy package of the government.[7]

Subsequent theoretical work on coalition formation assumes that a multidimensional account of the policy space is better able to explain the complexity of multiparty systems (Schofield 1987; Laver and Shepsle 1996; Benoit and Laver 2006). Institution-free two-dimensional models predict that a party will control policy and will govern if it occupies the *core*, a policy position that cannot be overturned given the configuration of actors' sizes and positions (e.g. Schofield 1993, 1995).[8] Such models predict that large parties whose policy positions are located in the core of the policy space may form minority governments. Following Schofield (1993), I have shown in previous work that the configuration of parties' sizes and policy positions qualifies the DC as a core party on two dimensions from 1946 through 1992 (Giannetti and Sened 2004) (Figure 11.1).[9] This is consistent with the fact that the DC always governed, forming single-party or coalition governments. The transition to the Second Republic can be interpreted in terms of the disappearance of a core party (Figure 11.2).

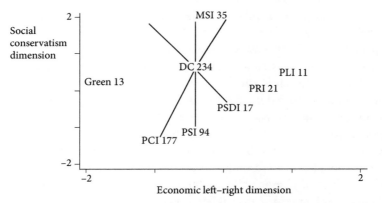

Fig. 11.1 Party policy positions and seats, 1987 showing a non-empty core, Italy (Intersection of median lines at the DC position)
Source: Giannetti and Sened 2004. Based on Manifesto data set 1987.

---

[7] Despite the relative frequency of minority government, Laver and Schofield (1990) categorized Italy as a multipolar fragmented system where surplus majority coalitions predominate.
[8] In a two-dimensional space, a core party (i.e. a party that occupies the median positions on two dimensions) exists only in very special circumstances.
[9] Curini and Pinto (2013) located the disappearance of the core slightly earlier. This is mainly due to the use of different data to estimate parties' policy positions.

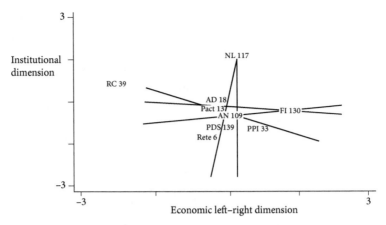

Fig. 11.2 Party policy positions and seats, 1996 showing an empty core, Italy

Source: Giannetti and Sened 2004. Based on Manifesto data set 1994.

The April 1992 parliamentary elections marked a profound shift in spatial conditions in Italy, as the DC's support dipped below 30 percent.[10] The emergence of a new institutional policy dimension associated with the electoral success of the NL determined the destruction of this structure and opened up a new era in coalition politics. Indeed, the most remarkable feature of the Second Republic resulted in alternating coalitions that were different both in terms of partisan composition and policy goals (Zucchini 2011). An empty core also explains why minority governments rarely occurred in post-1992 Italy. As summarized by Crombez (1996) minority governments are a sign of the strength and central location of a party in the policy space and are less likely in the absence of such a party.

To understand the occasional formation of minority governments after 1992, the focus should shift to institutional conditions (i.e. electoral rules) combined with the effects of internal party politics. Between 1993 and 2005 the MMM electoral system generated two different party systems at the electoral and the legislative level (Giannetti and Laver 2001). While parties formed pre-electoral coalitions in order to contest single-member districts, in the post-electoral stage legislative politics rewarded parties that broke away from pre-electoral cartels and bargained as smaller units over government formation. With the exception of the Prodi I executive, which is the only post-electoral minority government in the Second Republic, the minority cabinets that formed in this period of time can mainly be seen as an outcome of intra-party dynamics in the inter-electoral stage.

---

[10] In the 1992 national elections the Northern League became the second largest party after the DC in Northern Italy with about 20 percent of the vote.

The Prodi I government (1996–98) was a "formal" minority government as it relied on an *ex ante* agreement among center-left parties that had run the election under the pre-electoral coalition labeled as "Ulivo" and the extreme left Communist Refoundation party (PRC) having no cabinet posts.[11] The coalition controlled 285 seats in the Chamber and needed the support of PRC (35) to reach a majority. The Prodi I government lasted two years and was defeated in a confidence vote requested by the government as the PRC refused to approve the annual budget bill. The Prodi I government was replaced by a center-left surplus coalition led by D'Alema after the PRC split into two factions, one of which was willing to enter the government *(Partito dei Comunisti Italiani (PdCI)*. The formation of the following two inter-electoral governments—the D'Alema II (1999–2000) and the Amato II (2000–01)—that lacked a majority in the Chamber was also a consequence of fissions and fusions of party factions at the legislative level.

In 2005 a new electoral system was adopted with the purpose of stabilizing pre-electoral coalitions in the post-electoral stage by assigning a seat bonus to the pre-electoral coalition winning a plurality of seats. Notwithstanding this, legislative politics kept exhibiting a remarkable fluidity (Ceron 2016). Internal party dynamics underpins the formation of the Berlusconi VI (2010–11), an inter-electoral government lacking a majority in both chambers that formed after the defection of a legislative faction. Between 2009 and 2010 a war of attrition and succession had developed within the PDL. Gianfranco Fini—speaker of the Chamber of Deputies—openly challenged the Berlusconi leadership demanding more intra-party democracy and simultaneously building his own organized minority faction. In July 2010 a new parliamentary party—Future and Freedom for Italy (Fli)— was created. Initially Fli claimed to be the "third leg" of the center-right governing majority. Later in December 2010 Fli withdrew its support from the government in a failed attempt to remove Berlusconi's from power. Having lost its parliamentary majority, the Berlusconi government tried to replace the Fli switchers. In December 2010 the government survived a no-confidence motion with a narrow margin. In January 2011 the governing coalition was able to gain the support of approximately thirty MPs coming from opposition parties and from Fli. A new parliamentary party *(Iniziativa Responsabile)* formed but it was divided into subgroups with a lot of switchers moving in and out. The Berlusconi VII government lasted until November 2011 when it was replaced by a caretaker government led by Mario Monti.

The electoral rules that have been in place from 1993 onwards also exacerbated the partisan incongruence between the Chamber and the Senate. The literature has mainly focused on the symmetry dimension of Italian bicameralism, by looking at the constitutional powers of the two chambers. The presence of formal investiture

---

[11] The PRC was born in 1991 as a splinter of the old PCI after the latter was dissolved changing its name into PDS (Partito Democratico della Sinistra).

rules attracted scholarly attention as they were supposed to discourage minority government formation (Bergman 1993). This conjecture was at odds with the high incidence of minority governments. A more detailed examination of the specific design of investiture rules (Cheibub, Martin, and Rasch 2015) led scholars to conclude that the presence of a simple majority threshold (i.e. weak investiture rules) might have facilitated minority government formation in Italy (Russo 2015; Cheibub, Martin and Rasch 2019). Less attention has been paid to the congruence dimension, that is, the extent to which the partisan composition of the two chambers differs (Tsebelis 2002). This feature became prominent especially from 2005 onwards, when different rules to elect the two houses of Parliament produced a different distribution of party seats.[12] As a consequence, a number of governments lacked a majority of seats in the Senate (see Table 11.1). Although important in many respects, these rather "mechanical" effects of electoral laws should not be mistaken for a deeper structural explanation of the occurrence of minority governments.[13]

In this section I have argued that to account for the variance in the incidence of minority governments the greatest explanatory weight should be given to structural spatial conditions. To assess the extent to which my main argument about minority governments' formation in Italy reconciles with Strøm's analysis, it is useful to consider the most recent research conducted by Strøm himself (Strøm and McClean 2016). Testing several hypotheses that have been put forward in the literature about minority governments' formation on a wide sample of countries in the period 1945–2012, the authors that stated "One of the strongest and most consistent results in these models concerns the bargaining power of the largest party ... the stronger this party is, the more likely a minority cabinet." The Italian case provides evidence for this conclusion.

Minority governments in office

The focus of this section is how Italian minority governments managed to build legislative coalitions to pass legislation. As any coalition government has to rely on governance mechanisms at both the executive and legislative level, minority governments face a special challenge to sustain a legislative coalition with parties not represented in the cabinet. Strøm (1990) noted that for minority governments

---

[12] According to the electoral reform of 2005, the seat bonus was assigned in different ways for the two houses. For the Chamber, the prize went to the coalition (or party list) winning on the entire national territory, while for the Senate it was assigned at the regional level, to meet the constitutional requirement (Art. 54) that the Senate must be elected on a regional basis (Chiaramonte and Di Virgilio 2006).

[13] The link between bicameral incongruence and cabinet types has not yet been explored in the literature. Comparative research conducted by Giannetti, Pedrazzani, and Pinto (2020) focuses on bargaining delays.

this task begins well before government formation. He distinguished among governments that rely on *ex ante* agreements with at least one support party that does not take cabinet positions (*formal* minority governments) and governments that do not rely on such explicit, comprehensive support agreements and consequently face the challenge of building *ad hoc* legislative coalitions to pass legislation (*substantive* minority governments). According to Strøm, most of the Italian minority governments in the period 1948–87 lacked a pre-committed legislative majority, with very few exceptions.[14] However, while most support agreements were not explicitly negotiated prior to government formation, Italian minority governments rarely sought to build legislative coalitions on a purely *ad hoc* basis.

The vote on the investiture motion provides some indication of the size of the legislative coalitions supporting minority governments (see Table 11.1). Most of the minority governments that formed in the First Republic could rely on a vote in favor of outside parties or on their abstention. Until 2017 the standing orders of the Chamber counted abstentions as favorable votes while in the Senate they were counted as negative votes.[15] In the phase known as *centrismo* (1948–63) the DC obtained the support of right-wing parties and the more centrist PRI. In the phase known as *center-left* (1968–76) support to DC-dominated minority governments was provided by the Socialist and other left-wing parties. The Andreotti III government—labeled as the government of *non sfiducia* (lack of no confidence)—obtained the abstention of the Communist Party for the first time. In the national election of 1976 the PCI had come close to the DC in terms of electoral support, gaining 34.4 percent of the vote while the DC obtained 38.5 percent. The Andreotti III government represents the culmination of a strategy of inclusion of the Communist Party into national institutions that was defined as an "historic compromise" by politicians and intellectuals.[16] This period is also known as the *national solidarity* phase (1976–79) where the DC minority governments were able to gain the support of all the Italian parties, the PCI included. In the Second Republic the Prodi I government that formed in 1996 could rely on the external support of the extreme left Communist Refoundation (PRC). For other minority governments that formed afterwards, external support came from regionalist parties such as the centrist *Sud Tiroler Volkspartei* (VP) or legislative factions formed in the inter-electoral period.

As Strøm (1990: 178) noted, Italian minority governments relied on a combination of office benefits and policy concessions to build legislative coalitions.

---

[14] Other scholars have pointed out the absence of *ex ante* explicit agreements among coalition partners identifying two exceptions at the beginning of the *center-left* phase in the 1960s and the *national solidarity* phase in the 1970s (Verzichelli and Cotta 2000).
[15] In the Senate, parties or MPs who did not want to explicitly support the government while enabling its formation left the house before the vote took place.
[16] This strategy was tragically interrupted by the kidnapping and murder of his main inspiration—the DC leader Aldo Moro—by the terrorist group Red Brigade in 1978.

Excluding by definition ministerial posts, office benefits mostly had to do with parliamentary offices assigned to members of the opposition such as *rapporteur* or chairman of important committees and, last but not least, through the allocation of "megaseats" (Carroll, Cox, and Pachón 2006) such as the Chairmanship of the Chamber of Deputies which was assigned to PCI leaders from 1976 onwards. Turning to policy benefits, the literature agrees that a consensual pattern of policy making predominated in the First Republic (Cotta 1994). As highlighted by Strøm (1990), the most important institutional mechanism underpinning such a consensual pattern of policy making was undoubtedly the committee system. Since about 70 percent of the legislation was processed in committees through the so called *decentralized procedure*, three out of four laws passed with the approval of the opposition parties, including the PCI (Di Palma 1977; Capano and Giuliani 2001).

A huge literature examining the elements of continuity and change in the executive-legislative relations from the First to the Second Republic investigated the persistence of such a consensual pattern of policy making (Cotta 1994; Cotta and Marangoni 2015). Research shows a constant decrease of the laws passed in committees, from 80 percent in the V Legislature (1968–72) to 60 percent in the X Legislature (1987–92) to less than 2 percent in the XVI legislature (Kreppel 2009; Pedrazzani 2017). These data provide some evidence that the relevance of committees as privileged arena of parliamentary bargaining between government and opposition has declined over time. While some scholars have argued that consensualism simply shifted from committees to the floor as, between 1996 and 2006, laws were approved with an average consensus of 90 percent (Giuliani 2008), others examining final votes on bills over a longer period of time (1987–2013) show that, although the percentage of final votes in favor of bills initiated by the government remains high on average (85 percent), from 1994 onwards voting behavior on government legislation increasingly reflects the divide between government and opposition (Pedrazzani and Zucchini 2013).

Turning to *ex post* governance mechanisms, the literature has shown that in the First Republic external or mixed mechanisms such as "majority summits" involving party leaders proved to be crucial arenas in coordinating actions and managing conflict (Criscitiello 1993). Marangoni and Vercesi (2015) examined in great detail the coalition governance mechanisms in the Second Republic. The Prodi I cabinet tended to rely on internal conflict management arenas in a similar way to other majority cabinets while the D'Alema I–II and the Amato II cabinets employed purely external arenas more extensively. What can be inferred from this analysis is that the crucial difference is not between majority and minority cabinets but between post-electoral and inter-electoral governments. The lack of a direct electoral connection made less autonomous and more party-dependent those executives that formed out of a compromise reached in parliament in the inter-electoral period.

Minority government performance

Examining the performance of Italian minority governments, Strøm (1990) considered three indicators: duration, electoral success, and legislative success. Electoral success provides little information about Italian minority governments performance before 1992 because of the dominant position of the DC in Italian politics. Over the years, the Christian Democrats gradually lost votes (dropping from 48.5 percent in 1948 to 29.7 percent in 1992) and seats in parliament but government formation was hardly ever affected by the relative election results (Mattila and Raunio 2004). Strøm (1990) ranked Italy relatively high in terms of "negative responsiveness." Focusing on DC allies, he noted that they tended to fare better at the polls when in opposition rather than in government, explaining their decision to enter government mostly on the basis of a trade-off between office benefits and electoral costs. In the Second Republic—where minority governments rarely occur—Italy scores first among Western European countries in terms of overall electoral volatility (Chiaramonte and Emanuele 2017), which Strøm (1990) categorized as one of the main dimensions of electoral decisiveness. The fissiparous nature of the party system—where new parties appear and old parties become extinct—makes it difficult to compare governments in terms of their electoral success (Emanuele and Chiaramonte 2018).

Turning to government duration, it is well known that Italy has the most short-lived governments of any parliamentary democracy in Western Europe (Curini and Pinto 2017). Data reported in Table 11.1 show that the average duration of minority governments in the First Republic was about seven months while MWC and surplus coalitions tended to last longer (13 and 16 months respectively).[17] These data are consistent with the results provided by Strøm and McClean (2016) who found robust evidence that structural attributes of governments affect the risk of government termination. However, they noted that while single-party majority governments and MWC outlast all others, some minority governments manage to stay in power for relatively long periods of time. This is the case of the Prodi I minority government that ranks third among the more long-lasting governments in the history of Italian democracy (874 days).[18]

Laver and Shepsle (1988) made a clear distinction between empirical accounts of duration and theoretical accounts of stability, which should be seen as robustness to perturbations of key parameters generating an equilibrium cabinet. Despite the fact that the formation of minority cabinets has been interpreted as an equilibrium solution given certain spatial and/or institutional conditions, to date there

---

[17] Laver and Schofield (1990) and Strøm (1990) reported similar data about minority governments' duration, although they found that the average duration of MWC was longer than that of surplus coalitions.
[18] The longer lasting cabinets are the Berlusconi II government (1,409 days) and the Craxi government (1,307 days).

is no comprehensive theoretical model addressing the issue of their stability as defined by Laver and Shepsle. This may help to explain why empirical accounts offer at best mixed evidence. According to the interpretation of minority governments' formation presented in the section "Government formation and institutions" above, the existence of a core party explains *policy stability* across cabinet types including minority ones but does not explain governments' survival. Mershon (1996) was the first one to address the "perplexing pattern" of ephemeral governments and permanent incumbents that was typical of pre-1992 Italy. She explained the co-existence of policy stability and short-lived governments on the basis of the spatial and institutional conditions that curbed the costs of making and breaking coalitions. The party occupying the core of the policy space, that is the DC, faced a relatively low risk of not regaining office and dictating policy. A wide array of institutional conditions lowered the costs of breaking coalitions and also encouraged parties to adopt strategies aimed at reducing those costs further, such as portfolio inflation.

It is also well known that Italian governments have traditionally been considered significantly weak in their agenda-setting power and in their capacity to control legislative dynamics (Döring 2001). Executives' control on legislative activity has undoubtedly been strengthened in the past twenty years. However, scholarship emphasizes that this has happened by avoiding the ordinary legislative procedure to rely on "extraordinary" tools such as urgency decrees and delegated legislation, combined with a frequent use of the confidence vote requested by the government most often on "omnibus bills" (*maxi-emendamenti*) (Cotta and Marangoni 2015; Cotta and Verzichelli 2016). As most of the available data are collected by legislature and not by government, the information they provide does not allow us to make a proper comparison between legislative performance of majority and minority governments; only some general trends can be identified. The first one is the continuous declining trend in the average monthly production of laws from 41.1 during Legislature I (1948–53) to approximately 18.3 per month on average during Legislature X (1987–92). These data have been interpreted as evidence of the decline of the DC led coalition's ability to manage the policy process effectively (Kreppel 2009). A parallel trend is a constant increase in the use of urgency decrees to ensure the governments' proposal are passed.[19] The use of urgency decrees became widespread starting from Legislature VI (1972–76) reaching a maximum of twenty-four law decrees per month in Legislature XII (1987–92), despite their conversion rate dropping significantly

---

[19] Article 77 of the Italian Constitution allows the Government to initiate decree laws in cases of "extraordinary necessity or urgency." Such decrees take effect immediately, but are valid for just sixty days unless they have been converted (adopted) by the parliament.

Table 11.2 Legislative activity, Italy, 1996–2018

	Legislature XIII	Legislature XIV	Legislature XV	Legislature XVI	Legislature XVII
Approved laws	906	687	112	384	339
Government initiative	697	539	99	292	263
Parliament initiative	170	137	13	80	71
Other	39	11	0	12	5
Type: ratification	286	231	41	142	136
Type: conversion of law-decrees	174	200	32	104	82
Type: budget	33	29	9	25	26
Type: other	413	227	30	113	95
Monthly approval average rate	14.93	11.93	4.96	6.79	6.15

Source: Author's elaboration of parliamentary data provided by the Chamber of Deputies.

(Kreppel 2009; Cotta and Marangoni 2015).[20] Together with the decline of the decentralized procedure as a primary method of adopting legislation, these trends confirm what already noted by Strøm (1990: 185), that is, that "legislative effectiveness has varied more over time than between cabinet types in aggregate" (Table 11.2).

The trends described above consolidated further after 1992, but they became open to a different interpretation. Legislative activity continued to shrink as the average monthly legislative production fell from 14.93 in the Legislature XIII (1996–2001) to the 6.15 in Legislature XVII (2013–18). The same declining trend concerns the use of law-decrees (Cotta and Marangoni 2015). However, this reduction in the volume of legislation may be taken as evidence of a strengthening of the agenda-setting power of Italian executives. Anticipating the possibility of alternation, governments have been encouraged to concentrate their activity on a limited number of relevant initiatives rather than engaging in a proliferation of bills. The reduced use of law-decrees is by no means a sign that this tool is less important as governments choose to focus on a limited number of priorities, forcing parliament to approve them quickly and often combining them with a confidence vote.

---

[20] Following the decision of the Constitutional Court in 1996 prohibiting the re-issuing of law decrees, the effectiveness of the emergency decrees as an alternative legislative tool to the ordinary procedure started to decrease as well as their conversion rate.

Data about governments' legislative "success"—measured as the percentage of the approved bills over the total initiatives initiated by the cabinet in their first eighteen months of activity—are available only for four post-electoral governments (Marangoni 2009). These cabinets include the Prodi I (minority in both Chambers), the Berlusconi II (surplus majority in the Chamber, MWC in the Senate), the Prodi II (surplus majority in the Chamber, minority in the Senate), and the Berlusconi IV (MWC in both Chambers) governments. The percentage of government bills approved ranges from 41.6 percent (Prodi I) to 67.3 percent (Berlusconi II) to 33.8 percent (Prodi II) to 71.3 percent (Berlusconi IV).[21] Obviously, such limited information does not allow us to draw any general conclusion about the effects of a government's size on its performance. However, it has been suggested that a greater capacity to implement a government's agenda—keeping institutional rules constant—appears to be related to a lack of cohesion of center-left coalitions in comparison to the more cohesive center-right coalitions rather than their respective size. Data about coalitions' ideological range provide evidence supporting this interpretation (Curini and Pinto 2017).

Conclusion

Changes in electoral rules and party system that occurred in the early 1990s make Italy a "quasi-experimental" setting where patterns of government formation can be analyzed while keeping constant the basic constitutional framework. In this chapter I have attempted to answer the question whether or not, thirty years after Strøm's pathbreaking contribution, Italy is still a relevant case for studying minority governments. The relatively high frequency of minority governments in post-war Italy was explained by Strøm mainly on the basis of the opportunities offered to opposition parties to influence policy, especially by means of a strong committee system. The analysis carried out in this chapter shows that, despite no change in the formal rules, committees have ceased to work as a privileged setting for negotiation over policy among governing and opposition parties but have increasingly become a bargaining arena for the members of governing coalitions. This implies that institutional variables *per se* do not explain minority government incidence. On the other hand, notwithstanding a sharp increase in electoral volatility and the occurrence of alternating governments, minority governments have become less likely. What the Italian case highlights is that spatial conditions (i.e. the presence or absence of a centrally located large party) constitute the

---

[21] Marangoni (2009) also examined the rate of programmatic activity reflected in the legislative initiatives of the four executives—that is, the number of bills implementing the policy goals underlined in pre-electoral coalition agreements—as a percentage of the total bills presented to parliament, showing that it ran from 19 percent for the Prodi I government to over 48 percent for the Berlusconi IV government. Again, these data appear to reflect a change over time rather than across cabinet types.

most important explanatory factor of the occurrence (or lack thereof) of minority governments. Turning to performance, the Italian case shows that minority cabinets do not differ substantially from their majoritarian counterpart in terms of duration and legislative effectiveness. The analysis conducted in this chapter leaves room for future research. The issue of the stability of minority governments from an equilibrium perspective and the effects of intra-party politics on governments' survival appear to me the most important issues to be addressed in a systematic way in forthcoming work.

References

Benoit, Kenneth, and Michael Laver. 2006. *Party Policy in Modern Democracies*. London: Routledge.

Bergman, Torbjörn. 1993. "Formation Rules and Minority Governments." *European Journal of Political Research* 23: 55–66.

Capano, Giliberto, and Marco Giuliani. 2001. "Governing Without Surviving? An Italian Paradox: Law-Making in Italy, 1987–2001." *The Journal of Legislative Studies* 7 (4): 13–36.

Carroll, Royce, Gary W. Cox, and Mónica Pachón. 2006. "How Parties Create Electoral Democracy, Chapter 2." *Legislative Studies Quarterly* 31 (2): 153–174.

Ceron, Andrea. 2016. "Inter-factional Conflicts and Government Formation." *Party Politics* 22 (6): 797–808.

Chiaramonte, Alessandro and Aldo Di Virgilio, A. (2006). "Da una riforma elettorale all'altra: partiti, coalizioni e processi di apprendimento", *Rivista Italiana di Scienza Politica*, 36 (3): 363–392.

Chiaramonte, Alessandro, and Vincenzo Emanuele. 2017. "Party System Volatility, Regeneration and De-institutionalization in Western Europe (1945–2015)." *Party Politics* 23 (4): 376–388.

Cheibub, Jose Antonio, Shane Martin, and Bjorn Erik Rasch. 2019. "Investiture Rules and Formation of Minority Governments in European Parliamentary Democracies." *Party Politics* 27 (2): 351–362.

Cotta, Maurizio. 1994. "The Rise and Fall of the 'Centrality' of the Italian Parliament: Transformations of the Executive–Legislative Subsystem After the Second World War." in *Parliaments in the Modern World: Changing Institutions*, ed. Samuel C. Patterson and Gary W. Copeland. Ann Arbor: University of Michigan Press, 59–84.

Cotta, Maurizio, and Francesco Marangoni. 2015. *Il governo*. Bologna: Il Mulino.

Cotta, Maurizio, and Luca Verzichelli. 2007. *Political Institutions in Italy*. Oxford: Oxford University Press.

Cotta, Maurizio, and Luca Verzichelli. 2016. *Il sistema politico italiano*. Bologna, Il Mulino.

Crisciitiello, Annarita. 1993. "Majority Summits: Decision-making Inside the Cabinet and Out: Italy 1970–1990." *West European Politics* 16 (4): 581–594.

Crombez, Christophe. 1996. "Minority Governments, Minimal Winning Coalitions and Surplus Majorities in Parliamentary Systems." *European Journal of Political Research* 29 (1): 1–29.

Curini, Luigi, and Luca Pinto. 2013. "Government Formation under the Shadow of a Core Party: The Case of the First Italian Republic." *Party Politics* 19 (3): 502–522.

Curini, Luigi, and Luca Pinto. 2017. *L'arte di fare (e disfare) i governi*. Milano: Egea.

De Swaan, Abram. 1973. *Coalition Theories and Cabinet Formation*. Amsterdam: Elsevier.

Di Palma, Giuseppe. 1977. *Surviving Without Governing*. Berkeley: University of California Press.

Diermeier, Daniel, Hulya Eraslan, and Antonio Merlo. 2007. "Bicameralism and Government Formation." *Quarterly Journal of Political Science* 2 (3): 227–252.

Döring, Herbert. 2001. "Parliamentary Agenda Control and Legislative Outcomes in Western Europe." *Legislative Studies Quarterly* 26 (1): 145–165.

Emanuele, Vincenzo, and Alessandro Chiaramonte. 2018. "A Growing Impact of New Parties: Myth or Reality? Party System Innovation in Western Europe after 1945." *Party Politics* 24 (5): 1–36.

Giannetti, Daniela, and Michael Laver. 2001. "Party System Dynamics and the Making and Breaking of Italian Governments." *Electoral Studies* 20 (4): 529–553.

Giannetti, Daniela, Andrea Pedrazzani, and Luca Pinto. 2016. "Party System Change in Italy: Politicising the EU and the Rise of Eccentric Parties." *South European Society and Politics* 22 (1): 21–42.

Giannetti, Daniela, Andrea Pedrazzani, and Luca Pinto. 2020. "Bicameralism and Government Formation: Does Bicameral Incongruence Affect Bargaining Delays?" *European Political Science Review* 12 (4): 469–484.

Giannetti, Daniela, and Itai Sened. 2004. "Party Competition and Coalition Formation, Italy 1994–96." *Journal of Theoretical Politics* 16 (4): 483–515.

Giuliani, Marco. 2008. "Patterns of Consensual Law-making in the Italian Parliament." *South European Society and Politics* 13 (1): 61–85.

Kreppel, Amie. 2009. "Executive-Legislative Relations and Legislative Agenda Setting in Italy: From Leggine to Decreti and Deleghe." *Bulletin of Italian Politics* 1 (2): 183–209.

Laver, Michael, and Norman Schofield. 1990. *Multiparty Government: The Politics of Coalition in Europe*. Oxford: Oxford University Press.

Laver, Michael, and Kenneth A. Shepsle. 1996. *Making and Breaking Governments: Cabinets and Legislatures in Parliamentary Democracies*. Cambridge: Cambridge University Press.

Laver, Michael, and Kenneth A. Shepsle. 1998. "Events, Equilibria and Government Survival." *American Political Science Review* 42 (1): 28–54.

Marangoni, Francesco. 2009. "The Legislative Activity of the Government in Figures: The Prodi I, Berlusconi II, Prodi II and Berlusconi IV Executives Compared." *Bulletin of Italian Politics* 1 (2): 321–331.

Marangoni, Francesco, and Michelangelo Vercesi. 2015. "The Government and Its Hard Decisions: How Conflict Is Managed within the Coalition" in *The Challenge of Coalition Government: The Italian Case*, ed. Nicolò Conti and Francesco Marangoni. London: Routledge, 17–35.

Mattila, Mikko, and Tapio Raunio. 2004. "Does Winning Pay? Electoral Success and Government Formation in 15 West European Countries." *European Journal of Political Research* 43 (2): 263–285.

Mershon, Carol. 1996. "The Costs of Coalition: Coalition Theories and Italian Governments." *American Political Science Review* 90 (3): 534-554.
Pedrazzani, Andrea. 2017. *Fare le leggi nella Seconda Repubblica*. Milano: Egea.
Pedrazzani, Andrea, and Francesco Zucchini. 2013. "Horses and Hippos: Why Italian Government Bills Change in the Legislative Arena, 1987-2006." *European Journal of Political Research* 52 (5): 687-714.
Rasch, Bjørn Erik, Shane Martin and José Antonio Cheibub (eds). 2015. *Parliaments and Government Formation, Unpacking the Investiture Rules,* Oxford: Oxford University Press.
Russo, Federico. 2015. "Government Formation in Italy: The challenge of Bicameral Investiture." In *Parliaments and Government Formation, Unpacking the Investiture Rules,* ed. B.J. Rasch, S. Martin, and J.A. Cheibub. Oxford: Oxford University Press, 136-152.
Sartori, Giovanni. 1976. *Parties and Party Systems*. New York: Cambridge University Press.
Schofield, Norman. 1987. "Stability of Coalition Governments in Western Europe: 1945-1986." *The European Journal of Political Economy* 3 (4): 555-591.
Schofield, Norman. 1993. "Political Competition and Multiparty Coalition Governments." *European Journal of Political Research* 23 (1): 1-33.
Schofield, Norman. 1995. "Coalition Politics. A Formal Model and Empirical Analysis." *Journal of Theoretical Politics* 7 (3): 245-281.
Strøm, Kaare. 1990. *Minority Government and Majority Rule*. Cambridge: Cambridge University Press.
Strøm, Kaare, and Charles T. McClean. 2016. "Minority governments revisited." presented at the ECPR Joint Session of Workshops.
Strøm, Kaare, Wolfgang C. Müller, and Torbjörn Bergman (eds). 2008. *Cabinets and Coalition Bargaining: The Democratic Life Cycle in Western Europe*. Oxford: Oxford University Press.
Tsebelis, George. 2002. *Veto Players: How Institutions Work*. Princeton: Princeton University Press.
Verzichelli, Luca, and Maurizio Cotta. 2000. "Italy: From "Constrained" Coalitions to Alternative Governments?" in *Coalition Governments in Western Europe*, ed. Wolfgang C. Müller and Kaare Strøm (eds). Oxford: Oxford University Press, 433-497.
Zucchini, Francesco. 2011. "Government Alternation and Legislative Agenda Setting." *European Journal of Political Research* 50 (6): 749-774.

Appendix

Table 11.1A Government Types in Italy, 1948–1992

Legis-lature	Cabinet	Election date	Date in	Date out	Government parties	Coalition	Cabinet type	Government strenght (%, Senate in parenthesis)	Seats in parliament (Senate in parenthesis)	If minority, formal or substantive	Support parties	Support Duration (days)	Duration (%)
I	De Gasperi V	18-04-1948	23-05-1948	12-01-1950	DC (305)—PSDI (33)—PLI (19)—PRI (9)	Yes	Surplus majority	63.8 (52.8)	574 (343)			599	32.82
	De Gasperi VI		27-01-1950	16-07-1951	DC (305)—PSDI (33)—PRI (9)	Yes	Surplus Majority	60.5 (55.7)	574 (336)			535	43.64
	De Gasperi VII		26-07-1951	29-06-1953	DC (305)—PRI (9)	Yes	Surplus Majority	54.7 (47)	574 (336)			704	100
II	De Gasperi VIII	07-06-1953	16-07-1953	28-07-1953	DC (263)	No	Minority	44.6 (45.9)	590 (242)	Substantive		12	0.66
	Pella		17-08-1953	05-01-1954	DC (263)	No	Minority	44.6 (45.9)	590 (242)	Formal	PNM (for)—PSDI (abs)	141	7.78
	Fanfani I		18-01-1954	30-01-1954	DC (263)	No	Minority	44.6 (45.9)	590 (242)	Formal	PRI (for)	12	0.72

MINORITY GOVERNMENTS IN ITALY 233

Scelba		10-02-1954	22-06-1955	DC (263)—PSDI (19)—PLI (13)	Yes	Minimal winning	50 (48.8)	590 (242)		PRI (for)	497	29.94
Segni I		05-07-1955	19-05-1957	DC (263)—PSDI (19)—PLI (13)	Yes	Minimal winning	50 (48.6)	590 (243)		PRI (for)	671	57.70
Zoli		19-05-1957	19-06-1958	DC (263)	No	Minority	44.6 (45.5)	590 (242)	Formal	PNM (for)—MSI (for)	396	80.49
Fanfani II	25-05-1958	01-07-1958	26-01-1959	DC (273)—PSDI (22)	Yes	Minimal winning	49.5 (50.2)	596 (253)			209	11.45
Segni II		15-02-1959	24-02-1960	DC (273)	No	Minority	45.8 (47.8)	596 (253)	Formal	PLI (for)	374	23.14
Tambroni		25-03-1960	19-07-1960	DC (273)	No	Minority	45.8 (48.6)	596 (249)	Formal	MSI (for)	116	9.34
Fanfani III		26-07-1960	02-02-1962	DC (273)	No	Minority	45.8 (48.6)	596 (249)	Formal	PSDI (for)—PRI (for)—PLI (for)—PNM (abs)—PSI (abs)	556	49.38

Continued

Table 11.1A *Continued*

Legis- lature	Cabinet	Election date	Date in	Date out	Government parties	Coalition	Cabinet type	Government strenght (%, Senate in paren- thesis)	Seats in parliament (Senate in parenthe- sis)	If minority, formal or substan- tive	Support par- ties	Dura- tion (days)	Dura- tion (%)
	Fanfani IV		21- 02- 1962	17- 05- 1963	DC (273)— PSDI (22)— PRI (6)	Yes	Minimal winning	50.5 (50.8)	596 (248)		PSI (for)	450	78.95
IV	Leone I	28-04- 1963	21- 06- 1963	05- 11- 1963	DC (260)	No	Minority	41.3 (41.3)	630 (320)	Formal	PSDI (abs)— PRI (abs)— PSI (abs)— PNM (abs)	137	7.51
	Moro I*		04- 12- 1963	05- 06- 1968	DC (260)— PSI (87)— PSDI (33)— PRI (6)	Yes	Surplus majority	61.3 (60.6)	630 (320)			1645	97.45

MINORITY GOVERNMENTS IN ITALY 235

V	Leone II	19-05-1968	24-06-1968	19-11-1968	DC (266)	No	Minority	42.2 (42.5)	630 (322)		PRI (abs)—PSDI (abs)—PSI (abs)	148	8.11
	Rumor I		12-12-1968	05-07-1969	DC (266)—PSU (91)—PRI (9)	Yes	Surplus majority	58.1 (57.5)	630 (322)			205	12.22
	Rumor II		05-08-1969	07-02-1970	DC (266)	No	Minority	42.2 (42.5)	630 (322)	Formal	PSI (for)—PSU (for)—PRI (abs)	186	12.64
	Rumor III		27-03-1970	06-07-1970	DC (266)—PSI (62)—PSDI (29)—PRI (9)	Yes	Surplus majority	58.1 (57.6)	630 (321)			101	7.85
	Colombo		06-08-1970	01-02-1972	DC (266)—PSI (62)—PSDI (29)—PRI (9)	Yes	Surplus majority	58.1 (57.6)	630 (321)			544	45.91
	Andreotti I		17-02-1972	26-02-1972	DC (266)	No	Minority	42.2 (42.1)	630 (321)	Substantive		9	1.40

Continued

Table 11.1A *Continued*

Legis-lature	Cabinet	Election date	Date in	Date out	Government parties	Coalition	Cabinet type	Government strenght (%, Senate in parenthesis)	Seats in parliament (Senate in parenthesis)	If minority, formal or substantive	Support parties	Duration (days)	Duration (%)
VI	Andreotti II	07-05-1972	26-06-1972	12-06-1973	DC (266)—PSDI (29)—PLI (20)—PRI (15)	Yes	Minimal winning	50 (49.4)	630 (322)			351	19.23
	Rumor IV		07-07-1973	02-03-1974	DC (266)—PSI (61)—PSDI (29)—PRI (15)	Yes	Surplus majority	58.9 (58.7)	630 (322)			238	16.15
	Rumor V		14-03-1974	03-10-1974	DC (266)—PSI (61)—PSDI (29)	Yes	Surplus majority	56.5 (57.1)	630 (322)		PRI (for)	203	16.42
	Moro II		23-11-1974	07-01-1976	DC (266)—PRI (15)	Yes	Minority	44.6 (43.8)	630 (322)	Formal	PSI (for)—PSDI (for)	410	39.69
	Moro III		12-02-1976	30-04-1976	DC (266)	No	Minority	42.2 (42.2)	630 (322)	Formal	PSDI (for)—PSI (abs)—PRI (abs)	78	12.52

MINORITY GOVERNMENTS IN ITALY 237

VII	Andreotti III	20-06-1976	29-07-1976	29-01-1979	DC (262)	No	Minority	41.6 (42.2)	630 (322)	Formal	PCI (abs)	914	50.08
											PSI (abs)		
											PSDI (abs)		
											PRI (abs)		
											PLI (abs)		
	Andreotti IV**		20-03-1979	31-03-1979	DC (262)—PSDI (15)—PRI (14)	Yes	Minority	46.2 (47.5)	630 (322)	Substantive		11	1.21
VIII	Cossiga I	03-06-1979	05-08-1979	19-03-1980	DC (262)—PSDI (20)—PLI (9)	Yes	Minority	46.2 (46.6)	630 (322)	Substantive	PSI (abs)	227	12.44
											PRI (abs)		
	Cossiga II		04-04-1980	27-09-1980	DC (262)—PSI (62)—PRI (16)	Yes	Surplus majority	54 (55.6)	630 (322)			176	11.01
	Forlani		18-10-1980	26-05-1981	DC (262)—PSI (62)—PSDI (20)—PRI (16)	Yes	Surplus majority	57.1 (58.7)	630 (322)		PLI (abs)	220	15.47

Continued

Table 11.1A *Continued*

Legislature	Cabinet	Election date	Date in	Date out	Government parties	Coalition	Cabinet type	Government strenght (%, Senate in parenthesis)	Seats in parliament (Senate in parenthesis)	If minority, formal or substantive	Support parties	Duration (days)	Duration (%)
	Spadolini		28-06-1981	13-11-1982	DC (262)—PSI (62)—PSDI (20)—PRI (16)—PLI (9)	Yes	Surplus majority	58.6 (59.3)	630 (322)			503	41.85
	Fanfani V		10-12-1982	29-04-1983	DC (262)—PSI (62)—PSDI (20)—PLI (9)	Yes	Surplus majority	56 (56.5)	630 (322)			140	20.03
IX	Craxi	26-06-1983	04-08-1983	03-03-1987	DC (225)—PSI (73)—PRI (29)—PSDI (23)—PLI (16)	Yes	Surplus majority	58.1 (57.8)	630 (322)			1307	71.62
	Fanfani VI	17-04-1987	28-04-1987	DC (225)	No	Minority	35.7 (37.3)	630 (324)	Substantive		11	2.12

X	Goria	14-06-1987	29-07-1987	11-03-1988	DC (234)—PSI (94)—PRI (21)—PSDI (17)—PLI (11)	Yes	Surplus majority	59.8 (59)	630 (324)	226	12.38
	De Mita		13-04-1988	19-05-1989	DC (234)—PSI (94)—PRI (21)—PSDI (17)—PLI (11)	Yes	Surplus majority	59.8 (59.1)	630 (323)	401	25.08
	Andreotti V		23-07-1989	29-03-1991	DC (234)—PSI (94)—PRI (21)—PSDI (17)—PLI (11)	Yes	Surplus majority	59.8 (59.3)	630 (322)	614	51.25

Continued

Table 11.1A *Continued*

Legis- lature	Cabinet	Election date	Date in	Date out	Government parties	Coalition	Cabinet type	Government strenght (%, Senate in parenthesis)	Seats in parliament (Senate in parenthesis)	If minority, formal or substantive	Support par- ties	Dura- tion (days)	Dura- tion (%)
	Andreotti VI		12- 04- 1991	24- 04- 1992	DC (234)— PSI (94)— PSDI (17)— PLI (11)	Yes	Surplus majority	56.5 (55.9)	630 (322)			378	64.73

Minimal winning coalitions %***   12.5
Minority governments %   42.5
Surplus majority coalitions %   45

Notes: See also notes on Table 11.1. * According to conventional Italian numbering this cabinet is divided into Moro I, Moro II, and Moro III. ** According to conventional Italian numbering this cabinet is divided into Andreotti III, IV, and V. New cabinets are defined for (i) any change in the partisan composition of the government (ii) any change in the identity of the prime minister; (iii) any general election, (iv) any change in cabinet status. For post-electoral governments, the duration (%) is computed as the ratio between the number of days of government in office and the duration of the entire mandate. For inter-electoral governments, the duration is computed as the ratio between the number of days the government holds office and the time left at the end of the mandate. Support parties are defined as those parties not having cabinet posts voting in favor or abstaining.
*** Percentages refer to the Chamber of Deputies. Using the counting rules outlined in the Chapter 1 of this volume, the share of minority governments would increase to 55 percent between 1948 and 1992. The latter statistic counts a government as being in a minority if it does not have a majority (50 percent+1) of the seats in each chamber, given that the government is responsible to both in Italy.

12
Minority Governments in Poland

Governing after a Crisis with Ad Hoc Majorities

Radoslaw Zubek

This chapter examines why minority cabinets formed in Poland, how they governed, and with what success. The analysis focuses on the period of more than twenty years since the new constitution was adopted in 1997. Between October 1997 and the time of writing, five out of fifteen (33 percent) governments between 1997 and 2020 had a minority status, and such governments remained in office for more than one fifth of the time (see Table 12.1). Minority cabinets were particularly frequent between 1997 and 2007. During that time, five out of nine cabinets governed without having a majority in parliament, and did so for more than one third of the time.

To anticipate, I find that most Polish minority cabinets started life in the wake of major political crises when majority coalitions broke down and governments slipped into minority status. Many of such minority cabinets had a weak position in policy terms, leaving them vulnerable to alternative legislative majorities in parliament. I further find that a complex interplay of electoral, office, and policy motivations discouraged the formation of stable support arrangements, and minority cabinets typically governed by building ad hoc legislative coalitions. Finally, I show that Polish minority cabinets have had a mixed record in terms of legislative performance, with supported minority cabinets and unsupported cabinets formed by disciplined core parties demonstrating high effectiveness.

The Polish political system

Poland has a parliamentary political system with a directly elected president, a system that has been classified conventionally as semi-presidential (see e.g. Elgie and Moestrup 2008). It has a bicameral parliament, consisting of the *Sejm* and the *Senat*. The *Sejm* has 460 members who are elected every four years according to a proportional electoral system. The *Senat* is elected concurrently with the *Sejm*. Since 2011, senators have been elected from 100 single-member districts. The Polish president is elected every five years in a popular vote. While the president has important formal powers in the process of government formation and

Table 12.1 Governments in Poland, 1997–2020

Cabinet	Start date†	Cabinet parties	Status	Minority type	Support	Duration
1997–2001						
Buzek I	31-10-1997	AWS, UW	Majority	—	—	0.66
Buzek II	08-06-2000	AWS	Minority	Unsupported	—	0.95
2001–2005						
Miller I	19-10-2001	SLD, UP, PSL	Majority	—	—	0.34
Miller II	03-03-2003	SLD, UP	Minority	Unsupported	—	0.44
Belka I	02-05-2004	SLD, UP	Minority	Unsupported	—	0.94
2005–2007						
Marcinkiewicz I	31-10-2005	PiS	Minority	Supported††	SO, LPR	0.12
Marcinkiewicz II	05-05-2006	PiS, LPR, SO	Majority	—	—	0.05
Kaczyński I	14-07-2006	PiS, LPR, SO	Majority	—	—	0.33
Kaczyński II	13-08-2007	PiS	Minority	Unsupported	—	0.09
2007–2011						
Tusk I	16-11-2007	PO, PSL	Majority	—	—	0.97
2011–2015						
Tusk II	18-11-2011	PO, PSL	Majority	—	—	0.70
Kopacz	22-09-2014	PO, PSL	Majority	—	—	0.92
2015–2019						
Szydło	16-11-2015	PiS	Majority	—	—	0.50
Morawiecki I	11-12-2017	PiS	Majority	—	—	0.95
2019–present						
Morawiecki II‡	15-11-2019	PiS	Majority	—	—	na
Share of Minority Governments in 1997–2020: 33%‡‡						

† The start date is (a) the date of appointment by the president following the previous cabinet resignation, or (b) the date of a ministerial reshuffle which modifies the governing coalition. Following resignation, a cabinet continues in office until the president appoints a new cabinet.
†† Since February 2006. ‡The cabinet in office at the time of writing on 30 December 2020.
‡‡ Two Polish cabinets had a minority status between the first fully democratic elections in October 1991 and October 1997. The share of minority governments for 1991–2020 is 35 percent.

Source: Author's own compilation, except for the relative duration values until 2014 which are taken from Antoszewski and Kozierska (2019).

termination, Polish incumbents have only rarely played a significant role in this area. The presidency is furnished with extensive appointment powers and the right to veto legislation. Presidential veto can be overridden by the *Sejm* with a three-fifths majority. Polish presidents are expected to stand above party politics, but all incumbents since 1997 have had links to one of the major political parties. The non-concurrency of parliamentary and presidential elections has from time to time given rise to periods of cohabitation, during which the president came from a different party than the majority of the members of parliament.

Since 1997, the Polish party system has been characterized by a strong bipolarity, but the nature of the main cleavage has changed over time. Between 1997 and 2005, political competition was dominated by the SLD party on the left and AWS, and later PO and PiS, on the right. The left–right split was largely non-ideological and reflected a deep regime divide between a sizeable communist successor party and a more fragmented coalition of post-dissident forces (Grzymala-Busse 2001). This divide was rooted in the history of confrontation between the communist party and the Solidarity movement (see Grabowska 2005). This structure of party competition ended abruptly with the 2005 elections (Markowski 2006). The dramatic collapse of support for the SLD party following a series of unprecedented corruption scandals paved the way for a progressive polarization of the political arena between the liberal Civic Platform (PO) and the conservative Law and Justice party (PiS). Since 2005, these two parties have dominated Polish politics, competing along more ideological lines.

Poland has a positive investiture procedure (see Zubek 2015 for details). Under the constitution the formal cabinet formation process is activated after new elections are held, and also during the legislative term in three situations: when the cabinet loses a vote of confidence; when the *Sejm* passes a no-confidence vote; or when the prime minister resigns from office. In all such cases, any new government that forms must survive an explicit investiture vote in the *Sejm*. In this vote, the new cabinet must secure a majority of votes in favor of its formation over the sum of votes against and abstentions, in the presence of at least half of all members.[1] The Polish positive investiture comes with an important nuance. Once a government has been invested, changes in the party composition of the government do not require the formal consent of the *Sejm* as long as the prime minister remains in office. This aspect of the Polish investiture rules allows cabinets to shift between majority and minority status without having to face an explicit investiture vote in parliament. Finally, once invested, Polish cabinets are hard to remove during the legislative term: an early cabinet termination can happen only if the *Sejm* passes a

---

[1] This majority requirement is lowered in the third round of the cabinet formation process to a simple majority of votes in favor of the government over the votes against, in the presence of at least half of all members, with abstentions being disregarded. See Zubek 2015 for details.

constructive no-confidence vote, two-thirds of all MPs support early elections, or the government loses a confidence vote it has called.

Two further elements of the Polish institutional framework hold particular relevance for minority cabinet governance and performance. First, legislative committees in the *Sejm* are furnished with extensive procedural privileges, including the powers to merge, split, and rewrite bills, to control their timetable, and to be consulted at various stages of the legislative process (see Zubek 2021). This procedural context facilitates policy bargaining not only within the executive coalition, but also between the government and opposition parties, especially under minority cabinets. Second, the Polish executive exercises a significant level of control over the legislative agenda through the speakership of the *Sejm* (Zubek 2011; Nalepa 2016). Since 1997, the speaker—who has invariably been a senior member of the prime minister's party—has had the power to set the *Sejm*'s agenda. While non-cabinet parties can submit proposals to the agenda, if the speaker rejects such proposals, a floor vote to confirm this decision can be delayed for several months. This ability to gate-keep proposals has been a powerful tool that Polish governing parties have increasingly used to fashion their legislative accomplishments (Nalepa 2016).

Why minority governments form

In studying the question of minority government formation, I focus on a combination of party political and institutional factors. Regarding the former I examine the patterns of winning coalitions and in particular the existence of a core party. As argued by Schofield (1993, 1996) and Schofield and Sened (2006), if a party occupies a core position in parliament, it is able to govern alone. In the absence of a core party, minority coalitions can also be formed by parties that border the cycle set if supported by one or more of the weaker players (Schofield 1993). I further consider the balance of policy and office motivations in shaping the behavior of parties. Much research has argued that where parties are motivated more by policy than by office considerations, minority governments are more likely to form (Strøm 1990; Bassi 2017). Regarding institutions, I examine the investiture vote procedure and its impact on minority government formation. As argued by Bergman (1993) "negative" investiture provisions can help minority governments to form (see also Cheibub, Martin, and Rasch 2019).

Using these theoretical lenses, I proceed by analyzing the formation of each of the five minority governments that formed in Poland between 1997 and 2020 (see Table 12.1). To anticipate, I find that since 1997 minority governments have formed in Poland both in situations when a core party was present and in those when it was absent. While governing as a minority cabinet may have been a rational choice for core parties, non-core parties found themselves leading a minority government typically after a major political crisis ended the life of the immediately preceding majority coalition. This left such minority governments in a relatively weak position, vulnerable to alternative legislative majorities in parliament. I further find that a complex interplay of electoral, office, and policy motivations was responsible for leading some parties to stay in opposition and others to desire government office. Finally, I show that the acquisition of minority status by some cabinets has been facilitated by the constitutional provisions that allow for cabinet reshuffles to take place without a need for an explicit investiture. This said, positive investiture rules that are activated after new elections, or when the prime minister resigns, have not proved to be an insuperable barrier against minority cabinet formation.

The shift to minority under PM Buzek

In the 1997 election, no party won an overall majority. Figure 12.1(a) shows the policy positions of all parties on the economic and social policy dimensions using data from Savage (2014).[2] The pattern of winning coalitions is represented by median lines that divide the policy space so that coalition majorities lie on either side of the line (Schofield 1996).[3] There was no core party and at least in policy terms multiple winning coalitions were possible. The largest party, AWS, expected to form a government with ROP, but the latter's disappointing result forced it to revise its plans. A strong non-ideological divide between the AWS party and the post-communist parties prevented a coalition with PSL. The AWS–UW majority coalition that eventually formed was a second-best choice for AWS given the relatively large differences in policy positions (cf. Jednaka 2004: 182–197).

Besides substantial inter-party policy differences, the AWS–UW coalition suffered from a further handicap: AWS's internal fractiousness. AWS was an electoral coalition of the Solidarity trade union and several small parties, and soon after the 1997 elections, its parliamentary party started to lose MPs. By autumn 1998, its size had declined from 201 to 186. This changed the pattern of winning coalitions in parliament, as the AWS–PSL–ROP coalition was no longer possible. See Figure 12.1(b). Moreover, a group of around twenty AWS MPs began openly opposing cabinet proposals, in particular those made by UW ministers (Zubek 2001; Zakrzewski 2015: 220–232). This lack of discipline inside AWS undermined the viability of the AWS–UW coalition.

In the mid 2000s, when AWS took hostile, if minor, steps against UW over a local government issue, the UW leaders took a serious look at the balance of

---

[2] This and the other figures are produced based on graphical outputs from the Cybersenate software.
[3] With 460 seats, a majority is 231. The political heart of a parliament is marked with dashed lines. In this spatial analysis and those that follow below, I assume that independent MPs and small MP groups whose positions cannot be estimated vote to retain the status quo.

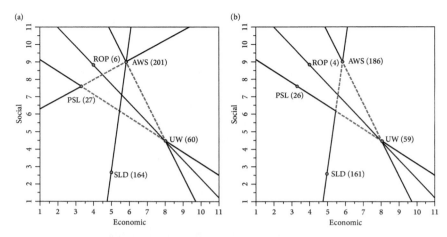

Fig. 12.1 Winning coalitions in the 1997–2001 parliament, Poland

benefits from the coalition. Policy payoffs were low and uncertain given that a small but decisive group within AWS opposed UW's proposals. Moreover, since early 1999, the government's popularity had started to decline rapidly because of major blunders in the implementation of important healthcare and educational reforms. The fast-declining popularity of the coalition cabinet threatened UW's electoral prospects in 2001 and its future access to office. Given this balance of payoffs, the UW party decided to cut its losses and to join the opposition, offering its support to the AWS party on a case-by-case basis. This move left the AWS-led minority cabinet in a relatively weak position: AWS's position in parliament was not at the core and it had to seek support for its proposals in a setting where alternative majorities could form that excluded AWS.

The acquisition of minority status by the Buzek cabinets can be said to have been facilitated by constitutional provisions regarding investiture. As explained in the previous section, the Polish constitution allows cabinet reshuffles to take place with no need for an explicit investiture vote as long as the prime minister continues in office. The prime minister submits requests for the dismissal and appointment of ministers directly to the president who has to accept them. This is exactly what happened in this case. When UW ministers resigned, Prime Minister Buzek asked the president to dismiss them and to appoint AWS nominees. There was no need to seek the formal consent of parliament.

The shift to minority under PM Miller

No party won an overall majority in the 2001 elections, though the SLD–UP electoral coalition came close by winning 216 out of 460 seats. Figure 12.2(a) shows the

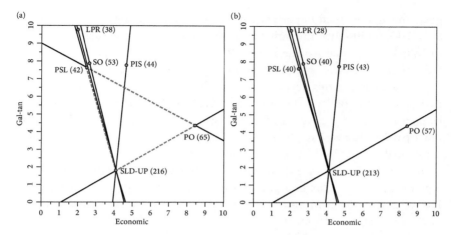

Fig. 12.2 Winning coalitions in the 2001–2005 parliament, Poland

positions of parties on the economic and libertarian-traditional (galtan) dimensions using data from the Chapel Hill survey (Bakker et al. 2015).[4] The pattern of winning coalitions is shown using median lines. In parallel to the situation in 1997, there was no core party and multiple coalitions were viable. The non-ideological divide between post-communist and post-dissident parties prevented the formation of a coalition of SLD–UP and the Civic Platform (PO) (Jednaka 2004: 197–200). A minority coalition of PO and PSL, supported by SO, PiS, and LPR, was also out of bounds. The government that actually formed was a majority coalition of SLD–UP and PSL, and was dominated by two post-communist successor parties.

The PSL party was divided on whether to form a coalition with SLD–UP (Michalak and Winclawska 2006). To enter cabinet, the party had to make important policy concessions which could prove costly at a time when it had to fend off a strong competition for rural votes from Samoobrona (SO), a new populist protest party. The final stages of EU accession negotiations in 2001–02 created further tensions for PSL which championed the interests of Polish farmers. In effect, the PSL party was often split on important votes in parliament. These internal tensions came to a head in early 2003 when the president (a former SLD member) vetoed a PSL-championed eco-fuel bill and, in retaliation, PSL voted to reject a flagship UP initiative introducing a new road toll system. In March 2003, Prime Minister Miller decided to dismiss PSL ministers from cabinet and to carry on as a minority cabinet.

The March 2003 crisis provided a trigger for the coalition to break down, but other reasons may have prompted Miller to try his luck at leading a minority

[4] The position of SLD–UP is calculated as a seat-weighted mean of the position of each party.

government. One such important consideration was a gradual strengthening of SLD–UP's position within parliament. This was due to numerous splits within the other parties that won seats in 2001. By early 2003, there were thirty-nine independent MPs and small splinter groups, making up 8 percent of all MPs. A key consequence of this development was that SLD–UP came to occupy a core party position in policy terms (see Figure 12.2(b)). From a policy perspective, it could now effectively govern by forming issue-by-issue legislative coalitions with other parties. By ejecting PSL from the coalition, Miller was thus able to achieve substantial gains in both policy and office terms.

In the same fashion as with the Buzek II cabinet, the constitutional provisions regarding investiture can be argued to have facilitated the formation of the Miller II government. Prime Minister Miller simply asked the president to dismiss PSL ministers and the government continued as a minority cabinet. There was no need to seek the formal consent of parliament.[5]

From Miller to Belka minority cabinets

The Miller minority cabinet, while occupying a strong position in parliament, was shaken by a series of corruption scandals in 2003 and 2004. The most serious—the Rywin affair—implicated the prime minister and his closest collaborators. Moreover, an internal rift opened up within SLD over an ambitious fiscal adjustment plan championed by the economics minister (Zubek 2008). Miller's political standing weakened, but despite increasing pressure to resign, he refused to step down. It was only when a group of thirty-five MPs left SLD and set up a new party, SdPL, that Miller agreed to tender his resignation. The prime minister's departure activated a formal cabinet formation process and according to the constitutional framework a new prime minister and the government had to be confirmed through an explicit vote of investiture in the lower chamber.

Despite its reduced size, SLD–UP continued to occupy a pivotal role in parliament and there was no viable government that could form without its participation (Rydlewski 2006). None of the opposition parties were willing to enter a coalition with SLD–UP, not least because the cost of sharing government with parties tainted by corruption was considerable. There were two feasible options: a renewed SLD–UP minority cabinet or early elections. The positions of the breakaway SdPL party and of the numerous unaffiliated MPs were critical in this regard. Initially, SdPL pressed for new elections and the Belka cabinet lost its first investiture vote in May 2004. But only a few weeks later SdPL achieved a poor result in the

---

[5] But note that a few months later, in June 2003, PM Miller voluntarily requested a confidence vote which he won—see Zubek (2015: 174). This further confirms that SLD held a core position in that parliament.

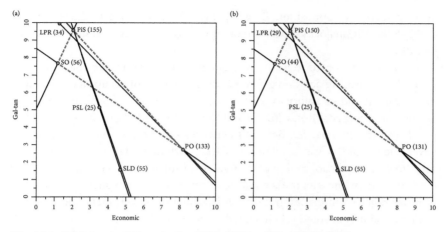

Fig. 12.3 Winning coalitions in the 2005–2007 parliament, Poland

European elections and changed its mind. Helped by numerous unaffiliated MPs who preferred to keep their seats, the Belka government won an absolute majority in June 2004.

Minority cabinet formation after the 2005 elections

The 2005 elections marked the eclipse of the non-ideological cleavage between post-communist and post-dissident parties. Electoral support for the main successor party, SLD, collapsed in the wake of the Miller-era scandals and the party's splintering in 2004. SLD's strength fell from 201 to only 55 seats. The new parliament came to be dominated by PiS and PO, two parties with a post-dissident lineage. The 2005 elections were also exceptional because they were held almost concurrently with presidential elections. After the SLD candidate withdrew unexpectedly, the presidential contest pitted Donald Tusk, PO leader, against Lech Kaczynski, a senior PiS politician. This paved the way for the polarization of electoral competition around the two competing visions offered by PO and PiS.

Figure 12.3(a) shows the positions of all parties after the 2005 elections in the economic and libertarian-traditional (galtan) dimensions using data from the Chapel Hill survey (Bakker et al. 2015). The pattern of winning coalitions is shown using median lines. In the same way as the situation after the elections of 1997 and 2001, there was no core party and multiple winning coalitions were possible. PiS was the largest party in parliament and, by formateur convention, was asked by the president to lead government formation talks. Having been defeated narrowly in both legislative and presidential elections, PO ruled out forming a coalition with PiS and decided to stay in opposition. This left PiS with two viable coalition options: a PiS–SO–LPR majority coalition or a PiS–SO minority cabinet supported by LPR.

In the end, PiS opted to lead a single-party minority government. This was a somewhat surprising decision given that the party did not occupy a core position in parliament and its ability to govern alone was limited. A key factor militating against forming a coalition with SO and LPR was the strong populist and radical profile of these two parties. Both of the parties showed a willingness to join the government, but PiS was reluctant to coalesce with them. Their votes were necessary, however, as the formation of the new government was taking place after new elections and, in line with the constitutional framework, an explicit vote of investiture was required in the lower chamber in which the government had to win an absolute majority of votes. When offered as an alternative to the outgoing SLD–UP government, the PiS-led minority cabinet was clearly preferable for both SO and LPR, and possibly for PSL. After a surprisingly successful election, both SO and LPR also saw an opportunity to trade their votes for senior parliamentary posts, including committee chairs. After LPR and SO publicly pledged their support, PiS put a single-party government to an investiture vote. Four parties supported the motion—PiS, SO, LPR, and PSL—and the Marcinkiewicz I minority cabinet was confirmed in office.

The shift to minority under PM Kaczynski

In the course of 2005–06, the PiS minority government acquired a majority status after SO and LPR had taken seats in cabinet when the minority formula became unsustainable (see the next section for details). In July 2006, Marcinkiewicz was also replaced by Kaczynski as prime minister. Only minimal changes had occurred in the parliamentary strength of individual parties since the 2005 elections. Figure 12.3(b) shows the pattern of winning coalitions in mid 2007. The PiS–SO–LPR governing coalition combined left-wing economic policies with a conservative social policy stance. No party occupied a core position in parliament.

While fairly cohesive in pure policy terms, the PiS–SO–LPR coalition under Kaczynski was dogged by fierce infighting. More often than not, the struggle was over office spoils. It was SO in particular that made extensive demands in this area, and PiS retaliated by trying to break up its partner (Zakrzewski 2015). The tensions were so high that the SO leader was briefly expelled from cabinet in the autumn of 2006. What finally broke the government were corruption, graft, and sex scandals that implicated senior SO politicians. The SO leader was dismissed from cabinet in early July 2007, though his party formally remained in the coalition. As the crisis escalated, PiS had three options: terminate the coalition and support early elections, continue as a minority government, or form a new majority coalition. In August 2007, PiS decided to choose the first of these options, SO and LPR ministers were dismissed from government and PiS supported early dissolution.

Why did PiS not decide to govern as a single-party minority cabinet? One key consideration is that PiS's position continued to be weak. In mid 2007, the pattern of winning coalitions in parliament was virtually identical to that at the start of parliament two years earlier (see Figures 12.3(a) and 12.3(b)). Without the support of SO and LPR, a single-party minority cabinet led by PiS was not viable, as it would have been vulnerable to be defeated by a PO–SO coalition supported by PSL and SLD.[6] PiS's ability to form another majority coalition was also limited. A coalition with PO was not possible, as the latter definitely ruled out coalescing with PiS after the presidential election had pitted the two parties against each other. Therefore new elections probably offered the best outcome that PiS could achieve under these circumstances.

Minority governments in office

How did Polish minority cabinets govern while in office? In examining this question, I rely on a standard distinction between unsupported and supported minority governments (Herman and Pope 1973; Strøm 1990). The former govern by forming ad hoc legislative coalitions with opposition parties, while the latter operate based on stable arrangements with one or more support parties that remain outside the cabinet. When discussing Polish experiences with minority support arrangements, I focus on the nature of agreements that existed between cabinet and non-cabinet parties. As shown by Bale and Bergman (2006) and Boston and Bullock (2012), support arrangements may range from implicit understandings of support on important votes, through more robust confidence and supply contracts, to explicit written agreements committing parties to longer-term cooperation. I further consider the motivations that opposition parties may have to support a minority government. As argued by Strøm (1990), these may vary from pure policy-seeking to more instrumental motives.

In what follows, I find that almost all Polish minority cabinets governed by building ad hoc alliances with opposition parties. Opposition parties had both policy and office motivations for offering support, with the exact nature of pay-offs showing considerable variation by party and government. While talks about securing more stable support were normally held after the formation of minority

---

[6] Indeed, in September 2007, PO threatened PiS with such an alternative majority when it submitted no-confidence motions against *all* ministers in the cabinet. It is likely that this attempt would have been successful, had Kaczynski not used a constitutional trick by dismissing and then re-appointing his ministers.

cabinets, they were rarely successful. Unwilling to share responsibility, and often wary of openly supporting governments tainted by corruption scandals lest they be punished by association, non-cabinet parties preferred to offer support only on a case-by-case basis, and with minimum commitment. Only one Polish minority cabinet concluded a formal public support agreement. However, this arrangement proved to be short-lived, not least because it was viewed by the support parties as a mere stepping stone to a formal executive coalition.

Governing with ad hoc coalitions

Four of the five minority cabinets that have formed since 1997 governed by relying on ad hoc legislative coalitions. In the several weeks following the breakdown of the AWS–UW majority coalition, AWS and its prime minister held talks with various opposition parties, including its former partner UW, to test the water for the viability of securing stable support for the government agenda. UW and PSL signaled they would be willing to offer support but only on specific initiatives, while SLD showed less interest in supporting the government (Zakrzewski 2015: 226). In the end, no formal arrangements were concluded, and the Buzek II cabinet had to seek support for its initiatives case by case. In a similar fashion, when the Miller cabinet lost its majority, SLD–UP held informal talks with PSL and other parties to secure firmer backing for its agenda, but opposition parties were largely non-committal on future support (Zakrzewski 2015: 235). In the final stages of its life, the Miller II cabinet moved to establish a more structured alliance with a new opposition group, FKP, but this attempt was cut short by Miller's resignation. The Belka I cabinet relied on the support of SLD's splinter group, SdPL, but this arrangement was not formalized. Finally, after the PiS–LPR–SO coalition had terminated, the Kaczynski minority government did not seek stable support arrangements in the knowledge that new elections were imminent.

This pattern of minority cabinet governance is confirmed by data on legislative voting. Table 12.2 shows the numbers of final passage votes on which parties other than the prime minister's party supported government bills under the Buzek, Miller, Belka, and Kaczynski governments.[7] These figures demonstrate two things. First, the level of voting support from opposition parties increased after governments lost their majority status. SLD voted for almost 90 percent of bills proposed by the AWS minority cabinets up from just above 70 percent under the AWS–UW majority government. Similar increases can also be observed for PO under the Miller and Kaczynski minority governments. Second, with a partial exception of

---

[7] A final vote is defined as the vote at the end of the third reading. A single vote could be taken on a package of two or more government bills. A party supports a bill if the majority of its MPs vote for the bill.

Table 12.2 Party support on government bill votes, Poland

Non-PM party	Supported (number)	Supported (percent)	Total votes
Buzek I (Majority)			
UW	218	98.6	221
PSL	176	79.6	221
ROP	165	76.7	215
SLD	161	72.9	221
Buzek II (Minority)			
UW	229	96.2	238
SLD	211	88.7	238
PSL	206	86.6	238
ROP	166	86.5	192
Miller I (Majority)			
PSL	238	97.9	243
PO	179	73.7	243
SO	176	72.4	243
PiS	145	59.7	243
LPR	92	37.9	243
Miller II (Minority)			
PO	245	89.1	275
PSL	243	88.4	275
SO	233	84.7	275
PiS	214	77.8	275
LPR	152	55.3	275
Belka I (Minority)			
PSL	211	92.5	228
PO	202	88.6	228
SO	200	87.7	228
PiS	194	85.1	228
LPR	158	69.3	228
Kaczynski I (Majority)			
SO	170	100.0	170
LPR	169	99.4	170
PSL	154	90.6	170
SLD	141	82.9	170
PO	140	82.4	170
Kaczynski II (Minority)			
PSL	22	100.0	22
SO	21	95.5	22
SLD	21	95.5	22
PO	21	95.5	22
LPR	20	90.9	22

Source: Author's own calculations based on raw data obtained from *www.sejm.gov.pl*.

the UW party, the level of support for government bills by former coalition partners declined markedly after governments acquired minority status. This was the case when PSL was forced out of government, and also when PiS ejected SO and LPR.

There is evidence that non-cabinet parties were motivated by policy payoffs when supporting proposals by minority governments. Many of the government bills proposed by the AWS minority government were ones which the UW party was in charge of developing when it was in government, and after UW had moved into opposition, AWS showed a willingness to offer further policy concessions during the parliamentary law-making process (Sobolewska-Myslik and Kasprowicz 2012). In a similar vein, the SLD–UP minority government adjusted the shape of its proposals to secure support from PSL and other opposition parties (Simlat 2012). Many of the bills proposed by the Kaczynski cabinet also resonated with the policy priorities of oppositon parties (Forys 2012). Strong committees, and in particular the less transparent but very influential system of sectoral sub-committees, facilitated policy bargaining among government and opposition parties. Office motivations were equally important, especially under the Buzek and Miller minority governments. The UW party traded its votes for the 2001 budget bill for the AWS's agreement to support the UW leader's appointment as the central bank governor (Jednaka 2004: 262). The SLD–UP government notoriously wooed opposition MPs with office payoffs, ranging from positions in state-owned enterprises, through parliamentary posts, to administrative posts at local level (Paradowska 2003).

Governing with external support

During 1997–2020, the Marcinkiewicz I cabinet was the only Polish government which governed with formal external support. In the initial months of this cabinet's life, the PiS party hoped to leverage its central position on the economic dimension by changing alliances depending on whether it wanted to move policy left or right (Dudek 2016: 598). But this plan turned out to be fraught with difficulties. First, the PiS party's hand was weak: the median position on the traditional-libertarian dimension belonged to PSL, and there existed winning coalitions that excluded PiS (see Figure 12.3(a)). Moreover, SO and LPR—two populist, office-seeking parties that supported the cabinet on the investiture—repeatedly raised the price for their legislative support. Both demanded seats on boards of state-owned enterprises and jobs for party activists in public agencies. At the same time, neither party had any qualms about entering into issue-specific alliances with other non-cabinet parties. Meanwhile, the largest opposition party, PO, was set on undermining the PiS party, and showed little interest in wining policy payoffs (Dudek 2016: 599).

Table 12.3 Party support on government bill votes, Marcinkiewicz I & II, Poland

Non-PM party	Supported (number)	Supported (percent)	Total votes
Marcinkiewicz I (Minority)			
SO	75	100.0	75
LPR	75	100.0	75
PSL	71	94.7	75
SLD	69	92.0	75
PO	67	89.3	75
Marcinkiewicz II (Majority)			
SO	29	100.0	29
LPR	29	100.0	29
PSL	28	96.6	29
PO	27	93.1	29
SLD	26	89.7	29

Source: Author's own calculations based on raw data obtained from *www.sejm.gov.pl*.

It was thus not long before PiS had to change its strategy. It proposed to conclude a "stabilization pact" with SO and LPR, and the final agreement was signed in February 2006 at a press conference with its contents being made public. The contract was intended to last for one year during which SO and LPR committed to support specific government bills and not to support other parties' bills or attempts to make changes in the cabinet or parliamentary leadership. The support agreement further envisaged opportunities for PiS and its support parties to collaborate on joint legislative proposals. In the end, this external support arrangement proved to be unsustainable, as it soon became clear that SO and LPR would not be satisfied unless they were offered seats in cabinet. As early as in April 2006, the pact was superseded by a formal coalition agreement between PiS, SO, and LPR.

Table 12.3 presents the numbers of final passage votes on which parties other than the PM's party supported government bills under the Marcinkiewicz minority and majority governments. The data make it possible to compare the patterns of legislative coalitions during the time when the PiS minority cabinet had external support from SO and LPR and the time when SO and LPR participated in the executive coalition. Two patterns are evident. First, SO and LPR voted with PiS on all final passage votes on government bills, and this pattern can be seen in both periods. This suggests that SO and LPR operated "as if" they were already in cabinet during the time when they provided external support to the PiS cabinet. Second, other opposition parties supported government bills on 90–95 percent of all final votes, and this pattern has not changed between the two periods. This suggests that cabinet proposals attracted support from beyond SO and LPR, especially in the early stages of the majority coalition.

Minority government performance

In this final section, I analyze the performance of Polish minority cabinets, with a special focus on legislative success. There is much consensus in comparative government research that, if political and institutional conditions are right, cabinets with a minority status can perform as well as majority governments (Strøm 1990; Artés 2011; Field 2016; Klüver and Zubek 2018; Potrafke 2019). Existing work has linked the ability of minority cabinets to be effective in policy terms to the presence of a core party (Schofield 1996). If no core party is present, multiple winning coalitions are possible, and there is a risk of policy cycling. For a minority cabinet to be effective in these circumstances, it must be formed by parties bordering the cycle set, with the support of one or more weaker parties (Schofield 1993, 1996; Schofield and Sened 2006). Even strong, centrally located parties may struggle when heading a minority cabinet if opposition parties prioritize non-policy payoffs (see e.g. Ganghof and Bräuninger 2006).

Poland has had three types of minority cabinets since 1997: (a) unsupported cabinets formed by a core party, (b) cabinets formed by non-core parties with external support, and (c) unsupported cabinets formed by non-core parties. Existing theories would expect cabinets in the first and second group to outperform those in the third group and also to perform on a level comparable with that shown by majority governments. Are these expectations borne out by the Polish case? To check this, I analyze the patterns of rolls and defeats on final passage votes.[8] Rolls are defined as votes on which the majority of the PM's party votes against a bill but the bill passes; defeats are defined as votes on which the majority of the PM's party votes in support of a bill, but the bill is rejected (see Jenkins and Monroe 2016). Numerous rolls and defeats signal the legislative weakness of the party leading a minority government. Conversely, a low number of rolls and defeats as a proportion of all votes can be viewed as being indicative of strong legislative performance.

Table 12.4 presents the patterns of rolls and defeats for the PM's party for all Polish cabinets between 1997 and 2011. The first thing to note is that PM parties, leading both majority and minority governments, are very rarely rolled or defeated on final passage votes. Over the ten cabinets during the fourteen years between 1997 and 2011, the PM's party was rolled only on seventeen (0.6 percent) and defeated on twenty-seven (0.9 percent) final passage votes. This indicates a high level of overall legislative performance similar to that found in other parliamentary democracies (cf. Cox and McCubbins 2011). What most likely lies behind this successful record are extensive agenda control powers exercised by the speaker of the lower chamber, an office invariably held by a senior leader of the PM's party. As discussed earlier in this chapter, a key prerogative in this area is the ability by

---

[8] See also the patterns of bill approval reported in the Appendix.

Table 12.4 Rolls and defeats on final passage votes, Poland

Cabinet	Status Votes	Rolls	Percent	Defeats	Percent	Combined	Percent
1997–2001							
Buzek I	Majority 359	5	1.4	6	1.7	11	3.1
Buzek II	Minority 335	6	1.8	5	1.5	11	3.3
2001–2005							
Miller I	Majority 294	0	0.0	1	0.3	1	0.3
Miller II	Minority 310	0	0.0	1	0.3	1	0.3
Belka I	Minority 310	3	1.0	9	2.9	12	3.9
2005–2007							
Marcinkiewicz I	Minority 86	0	0.0	0	0.0	0	0.0
Marcinkiewicz II	Majority 38	0	0.0	0	0.0	0	0.0
Kaczynski I	Majority 236	0	0.0	2	0.9	2	0.9
Kaczynski II	Minority 32	0	0.0	1	3.1	1	3.1
2007–2011							
Tusk I	Majority 965	3	0.3	2	0.2	5	0.5

Source: Author's own calculations based on raw data obtained from *www.sejm.gov.pl*.

the speaker to delay motions to place bills on the agenda for several months, and PM parties in Poland have increasingly resorted to the strategic use of this power to shape their legislative accomplishment (Nalepa 2016).

These data also show some variation in the rate of rolls and defeats across cabinets. Two patterns are especially interesting for present purposes. First, while majority governments outperform minority cabinets overall by a small margin, in particular by having a slightly lower defeat rate, some minority governments perform on a par with those having a majority status. The minority cabinet under PM Miller has exactly the same record as the preceding majority government under the same prime minister. Similarly, Marcinkiewicz's majority cabinet performed as well as his immediately preceding minority cabinet. Second, there is some evidence that minority cabinets formed by a core party and those formed by non-core parties with external support perform better than unsupported cabinets formed by non-core parties. This is especially visible when one compares the legislative record of Miller I and Marcinkiewicz I with the performance of the Buzek II and Kaczynski II cabinets. This said, the Belka I cabinet does not conform to this pattern: although formed by a core party, it was rolled and defeated relatively frequently. One reasonable explanation is that this government presided over an unprecedented decomposition of the SLD party which undermined its ability to legislate effectively (Rydlewski 2006).[9]

---

[9] In spring 2005, even PM Belka left SLD to join another party while continuing as prime minister.

Conclusion

The Polish case holds at least four interesting lessons for research on the formation, governance, and performance of minority governments. First, minority cabinets were often formed by non-core parties and without stable external support. Such cabinets typically emerged in the wake of a major political crisis that broke the life of the immediately preceding majority government. Thus, at least in the Polish case, minority governments were not always a rational bargaining solution. Second, the acquisition of minority status by Polish cabinets can be said to have been facilitated by constitutional provisions that allow cabinet reshuffles to occur without an explicit investiture vote. This said, positive investiture rules that were activated after new elections, or when the prime minister resigned, did not prove to be a significant obstacle to minority cabinet formation. Third, Polish parties had both office- and policy-related motives to support minority governments. The exact balance of the different types of payoffs varied by issue, party, and cabinet. This chapter also confirms that office payoffs beyond cabinet seats can act as an important inducement for parties to support a minority government. In the Polish case, this was particularly true of new populist and radical parties that sought office spoils as a means to reward supporters and expand their party networks. Finally, though minority and majority governments demonstrated comparable legislative performance, cabinets formed by non-core parties without external support were rolled and defeated more often. At the same time, being positioned at the core did not guarantee high performance by the PM's party if it was internally divided and lacked discipline.

References

Antoszewski, Andrzej, and Joanna Kozierska. 2019. "Poland: Weak Coalitions and Small Party Suicide in Government." In *Coalition Governance in Central and Eastern Europe*, ed. Torbjörn Bergman, Gabriella Ilonszki, and Wolfgang C. Müller. Oxford: Oxford University Press, pp. 344–387.

Artés, Joaquín. 2011. "Do Spanish Politicians Keep their Promises?" *Party Politics* 19 (1): 143–158.

Bakker, Ryan, Liesbet Hooghe, Seth Jolly, Gary Marks, Jonathan Polk, Jan Rovny, Marco Steenbergen, and Milada Anna Vachudova. 2015. "1999–2014 Chapel Hill Expert Survey Trend File." Version 1.13 Available on chesdata.eu. Chapel Hill, NC: University of North Carolina, Chapel Hill.

Bale, Tim, and Torbjorn Bergman. 2006. "Captives No Longer, but Servants Still? Contract Parliamentarism and the New Minority Governance in Sweden and New Zealand." *Government and Opposition* 41 (3): 422–449.

Bassi, Anna. 2017. "Policy Preferences in Coalition Formation and the Stability of Minority and Surplus Governments." *The Journal of Politics* 79 (1): 250–268.

Bergman, Torbjörn. 1993. "Formation Rules and Minority Governments." *European Journal of Political Research* 23 (1): 55–66.

Boston, Jonathan, and David Bullock. 2012. "Multi-Party Governance: Managing the Unity-Distinctiveness Dilemma in Executive Coalitions." *Party Politics* 18 (3): 349–368.
Cheibub, José Antonio, Shane Martin, and Bjørn Erik Rasch. 2019. "Investiture Rules and Formation of Minority Governments in European Parliamentary Democracies." *Party Politics* 27 (2): 351–362.
Cox, Gary W., and Mathew D. McCubbins. 2011. "Managing Plenary Time: The U.S. Congress in Comparative Context." In *The Oxford Handbook of the American Congress*, ed. Frances E. Lee and Eric Schickler. Oxford: Oxford University Press, pp. 451–472.
Dudek, Antoni. 2016. *Historia polityczna Polski 1989-2015*. Warszawa: Znak.
Elgie, Robert, and Sophie Moestrup, eds. 2008. *Semi-presidentialism in Central and Eastern Europe*. Manchester: Manchester University Press.
Field, Bonnie N. 2016. *Why Minority Governments Work*. London: Palgrave Macmillan.
Forys, Grzegorz. 2012. "Wielokierunkowa opozycja parlamentarna w okresie rzadow Kazimierza Marcinkiewicza i Jaroslawa Kaczynskiego (2005–2007)." In *Opozycja Parlamentarna w Polsce w latach 1997–2010*, ed. K. Labedz. Krakow: Wydawnictwo Naukowe Uniwersytetu Pedagogicznego, pp. 130–163.
Ganghof, Steffen, and Thomas Bräuninger. 2006. "Government Status and Legislative Behaviour: Partisan Veto Players in Australia, Denmark, Finland and Germany." *Party Politics* 12 (4): 521–539.
Grabowska, Miroslawa. 2005. *Podzial postkomunistyczny: Spoleczne podstawy polityki w Polsce po 1989 roku*. Warsaw: Wydawnictwo Naukowe Scholar.
Grzymala-Busse, Anna. 2001. "Coalition Formation and the Regime Divide in New Democracies: East Central Europe." *Comparative Politics* 34 (1): 85–104.
Herman, Valentine, and John Pope. 1973. "Minority Governments in Western Democracies." *British Journal of Political Science* 3 (2): 191–212.
Jednaka, Wiesawa. 2004. *Gabinety koalicyjne w III RP*. Wroclaw: Wydawnictwo Uniwersytetu Wroclawskiego.
Jenkins, Jeffery A., and Nathan W. Monroe. 2016. "On Measuring Legislative Agenda-Setting Power." *American Journal of Political Science* 60 (1): 158–164.
Klüver, Heike, and Radoslaw Zubek. 2018. "Minority Governments and Legislative Reliability: Evidence from Denmark and Sweden." *Party Politics* 24 (6): 719–730.
Markowski, Radoslaw. 2006. "The Polish Elections of 2005: Pure Chaos or Restructuring of the Party System?" *West European Politics* 29 (4): 814–832.
Michalak, B., and M. S. Winclawska. 2006. "Rzad Leszka Millera." In *Rzady koalicyjne w III RP*, ed. M. Chmaj. Olsztyn: Wydawnictwo Uniwersytetu Warminsko-Mazurskiego, pp. 223–255.
Nalepa, Monika. 2016. "Party Institutionalization and Legislative Organization: The Evolution of Agenda Power in the Polish Parliament." *Comparative Politics* 48 (3): 353–373.
Paradowska, J. 2003. "Trzy twarze premiera." *Polityka*, 25–203, 21 June 2003.
Potrafke, Niklas. 2019. "Fiscal performance of minority governments: New empirical evidence for OECD countries." *Party Politics* 27 (3): 501–514.
Rydlewski, Grzegorz. 2006. "Rzad Marka Belki." In *Rzady koalicyjne w III RP*, ed. M. Chmaj. Olsztyn: Wydawnictwo Uniwersytetu Warminsko-Mazurskiego, pp. 257–275.

Savage, Lee Michael. 2014. "Who Gets In? Ideology and Government Membership in Central and Eastern Europe." *Party Politics* 20 (4): 547–562.

Schofield, Norman. 1993. "Political Competition and Multiparty Coalition Governments." *European Journal of Political Research* 23 (1): 1–33.

Schofield, Norman. 1996. "The Heart of a Polity." In *Collective Decision-making: Social Choice and Political Economy*, ed. Norman Schofield. Boston: Kluwer Academic Publishers, pp. 183–220.

Schofield, Norman, and Itai Sened. 2006. *Multiparty Democracy: Elections and Legislative Politics*. Cambridge: Cambridge University Press.

Simlat, Marek. 2012. "Struktura i funkcjonowanie opozycji w IV kadencji Sejmu (2001–2005)." In *Opozycja Parlamentarna w Polsce w latach 1997–2010*, ed. K. Labedz. Krakow: Wydawniwctwo Naukowe Uniwersytetu Pedagogicznego, pp. 82–129.

Sobolewska-Myslik, Katarzyna, and Dominika Kasprowicz. 2012. "Opozycja parlamentarna w III kadencji Sejmu (1997–2001)." In *Opozycja Parlamentarna w Polsce w latach 1997–2010*, ed. K. Labedz. Krakow: Wydawniwctwo Naukowe Uniwersytetu Pedagogicznego, pp. 27–81.

Strøm, Kaare. 1990. *Minority Government and Majority Rule*. Cambridge: Cambridge University Press.

Zakrzewski, Piotr. 2015. *Rzady Mniejszosciowe w III Rzeczpospolitej*. Warszawa: ASPRA-JR.

Zubek, Radoslaw. 2001. "A Core in Check: The Transformation of the Core Executive in Poland." *Journal of European Public Policy* 8 (6): 911–932.

Zubek, Radoslaw. 2008. "Poland: From Pacesetter to Semi-Permanent Outsider?" In *The Euro at Ten: Europeanization, Power and Convergence*, ed. K. Dyson. Oxford: Oxford University Press, pp. 292–306.

Zubek, Radoslaw. 2011. "Negative Agenda Control and Executive–Legislative Relations in East Central Europe, 1997–2008." *The Journal of Legislative Studies* 17 (2): 172–192.

Zubek, Radoslaw. 2015. "Investiture Rules and Minority Governments in Poland." In *Parliaments and Government Formation: Unpacking Investiture Rules*, ed. B. Rasch, S. Martin, and J. Cheibub. Oxford: Oxford University Press, pp. 165–181.

Zubek, Radoslaw. 2021. "Committee Strength in Parliamentary Democracies: A New Index." *European Journal of Political Research* 60 (4): 1018–1031.

Appendix

Table 12.1A Government bills and approval rates, Poland

Cabinet	Bills	Approved[†]	Percent
1997–2001 Parliament			
Buzek I	356	302	84.8
Buzek II	196	143	73.0
2001–2005 Parliament			
Miller I	316	305	96.5
Miller II	273	253	92.7
Belka I	217	176	81.1
2005–2007 Parliament			
Marcinkiewicz I	91	88	96.7
Marcinkiewicz II	42	35	83.3
Kaczynski I	192	143	74.5
Kaczynski II	28	7	25.0
2007–2011 Parliament			
Tusk I	644	623	96.7

[†] calculated based on approval by the end of legislative term.
Source: Author's own calculations based on raw data obtained from www.sejm.gov.pl.

13
Minority Governments in Portugal
Institutions as Solutions to Historical Legacies

Jorge M. Fernandes

Minority governments are one of the most popular governing arrangements in Portugal. Between the inception of democracy in the mid-1970s and 2020, 42 percent of the governments have been minority arrangements. This increases to 50 percent between 1990 and 2020. Minority governments are particularly common on the left. The Portuguese case is of particular interest as it adds to our understanding of how minority governments can be institutional solutions to break gridlocks coming out of historical legacies. In the Portuguese case, institutions were purportedly created to permit the emergence of minority governments as a solution to the impossibility of a coalition between the Socialists and the parties to its left.

This chapter examines minority government formation and functioning in Portugal. Specifically, I discuss how and why minority governments form, paying close attention to the design of rules when the constitution was written. I also examine why different types of minority governments form. While the norm has been for minority governments to govern without formal support, António Costa's government (2015–19) departed from this pattern. Furthermore, I examine how minority governments fare in office compared to their majority counterparts.

In addition to advancing historical legacies as a motivation for minority government formation, the chapter makes several contributions to the understanding of minority governments in Portugal. First, I show that minority governments are as successful as their majority counterparts in passing legislation, and that election pledge fulfillment is similar in minority and majority governments, suggesting that minority governments can be an efficient way to advance policy-making. Second, evidence suggests that minority governments are less stable than their majoritarian counterparts, particularly after the majoritarian turn in Portuguese democracy in the mid-1980s. Finally, a plethora of policy indicators, such as unemployment, gross domestic product growth, public deficit, and social expenses, does not show a systematic difference between the two types of governments. The success of minority governments in delivering good public policy, together with the absence of incentives for change in the policy-seeking

Jorge M. Fernandes, *Minority Governments in Portugal*. In: *Minority Governments in Comparative Perspective*. Edited by Bonnie N. Field and Shane Martin, Oxford University Press. © Jorge M. Fernandes (2022). DOI: 10.1093/oso/9780192871657.003.0013

and outsider nature of some Portuguese parties, creates enduring incentives for the formation of this type of government.

The Portuguese political system

Portugal is a semi-presidential democracy. A directly elected president, whose tenure lasts five years, co-exists with a popularly elected parliament. Presidential powers are weak. The government is only accountable to the parliament, which places Portugal firmly in the president-assembly category (Shugart and Carey 1992). However, the president has the power to dismiss the assembly on the grounds of "institutional peril." This constitutional provision turns the presidential prerogative to dismiss the assembly into a purely political decision, not least because of the vagueness of the phrase "institutional peril."

The *Assembleia da República* is a unicameral assembly whose 230 members are elected every four years under a closed-list proportional representation system. Together with a party-centered organization of the legislature, the electoral system creates weak incentives for personalism. Instead, legislators focus on delivering benefits to party leaders who hold the keys to their reselection and, subsequently, reelection. However, recent research paints a slightly more nuanced vision of the effects of the Portuguese electoral system. According to Fernandes and colleagues (2020), legislators cater to the interests of their districts to satisfy the wishes of candidate selection officials who operate, in most cases, at the district level. Nevertheless, Portugal is the epitome of the party-centered political system (Leston-Bandeira 2009).

The Portuguese party system has been remarkably stable over the years. Since the first free and fair elections in 1975, the same parties have dominated. The Socialist Party (PS), the Social Democrats (PSD), the Communists (PCP), and the Christian Democrats (CDS-PP) have been the primary actors in the legislature. In 1999, the Left Bloc (BE) emerged as a post-material libertarian leftist party, uniting a constellation of small parties. In 2019, three new parties entered parliament for the first time—Liberal Initiative (*Iniciativa Liberal*), Enough (*Chega*), and Free (*Livre*)—a watershed moment in party politics in a country whose consequences remain to be seen. The growth of these parties in the 2022 elections points to their consolidation in the party system.

According to Jalali (2019), the Portuguese party system has two defining traits. First, the pivotal dimension of competition is between the Socialists and the Social Democrats. Since democratization, both parties have dominated control of the executive. The Social Democrats have governed alone with a majority and in coalitions with the Christian Democrats.[1] The Socialists' passages through power have

---

[1] The Social Democrats in Portugal are the main center-right party. The leftist name stems from the context of the Portuguese democratization.

always been in minority governments, except for the single-party majority government under José Sócrates (2005–9), and, recently, the unexpected majority under Costa in 2022.

The second defining trait of the Portuguese party system is the difficulty of cooperation between the Socialists and the parties to their left. The coalescing difficulties between the Socialists and the Communists and the Left Bloc are, by far, the most enduring legacy of the transition to democracy (Pinto 2006). The revolutionary nature of the Portuguese transition left a strong imprint on the party system. During the complicated transition, two strains of parties emerged. On the one hand, anti-system parties (the Left Bloc and the Communists) positioned themselves against European integration, NATO, and capitalism in general. On the other hand, pro-system parties (the Socialists, the Social Democrats, and the Christian Democrats) defended the anchoring of the fledgling Portuguese society in the European project and its associated institutions. This cleavage to this day poses an obstacle to left-wing coalition politics, creating what Freire (2009: 224) dubs a "bias to the right" in the party system.

Over the years, Portugal has experienced both divided and unified government, referring to the partisan make up of parliament compared to the presidency. Although the president's formal powers are weak, the most important weapon has always been their agenda-setting capacity. Indeed, the president can highlight topics and policy issues that are inconvenient for the government. The cohabitation between President Soares and Prime Minister Cavaco Silva in the 1990s is the best example of how a left-wing president can wage guerilla politics on a right-wing government by promoting civil society activities whose goal is to set an alternative agenda (Amorim Neto and Lobo 2009; Fernandes and Magalhães 2016).

The government formation process in Portugal clearly falls into the negative parliamentarism category (Rasch, Cheibub, and Martin 2015). Absent a formal investiture vote, the parliament only has to tolerate the incoming government. There is no constitutional provision that requires the parliament to support the government. If the parliament or the executive choose to trigger a vote of confidence, to force the former to express its position on the latter, and it fails, the government formation process starts over again. The president recovers his *informateur* powers, holds hearings with parties, and invites a new *formateur* to form a government. In the past, only the second Passos Coelho government, in 2015, was voted out of office during the government formation process (see Fernandes 2016).

Table 13.1 shows an overview of Portuguese governments since 1976. There are two interesting patterns worth underlining. First, except for Cavaco Silva's first government and Passos Coelho's short-lived second executive, all minority governments in Portugal have been headed by the Socialist Party. As the next section discusses, political competition dynamics and institutions create strong incentives for the Socialists to resort to minority solutions. Rightist parties, by contrast,

Table 13.1 Types of government, Portugal, 1976–2022

Prime minister	Start date	End date	Government parties	Coalition	Minority	If minority, formal or substantive	Support parties
Soares I	23-07-1976	23-01-1978	PS	No	Yes	Substantive	No
Soares II	23-01-1978	29-08-1978	PS/CDS	Yes	No	–	–
Carneiro	03-01-1980	09-01-1981	PSD/CDS/PPM	Yes	No	–	–
Balsemão I	01-09-1981	04-09-1981	PSD/CDS/PPM	Yes	No	–	–
Balsemão II	04-09-1981	09-07-1983	PSD/CDS/PPM	Yes	No	–	–
Soares III	09-07-1983	06-11-1985	PS/PSD	Yes	No	–	–
Silva I	06-11-1985	17-08-1987	PSD	No	Yes	Substantive	No
Silva II	17-08-1987	31-10-1991	PSD	No	No	–	–
Silva III	31-10-1991	25-10-1995	PSD	No	No	–	–
Guterres I	28-10-1995	25-10-1999	PS	No	Yes	Substantive	No
Guterres II	25-10-1999	06-04-2002	PS	No	Yes	Substantive	No
Barroso	06-04-2002	17-07-2004	PSD/CDS-PP	Yes	No	–	–
Santana Lopes	17-07-2004	12-03-2005	PSD/CDS-PP	Yes	No	–	–
Sócrates I	13-03-2005	26-10-2009	PS	No	No	–	–
Sócrates II	26-10-2009	20-06-2011	PS	No	Yes	Substantive	No
Passos Coelho I	20-06-2011	30-10-2015	PSD/CDS-PP	Yes	No	–	–
Passos Coelho II	30-10-2015	26-11-2015	PSD/CDS-PP	Yes	Yes	Substantive	No
Costa I	26-11-2015	06-10-2019	PS	No	Yes	Formal	BE, PCP, and PEV
Costa II	06-10-2019	28-03-2022	PS	No	Yes	Substantive	No

Notes: Share of minority governments 1976–2022: 42%. Share of minority governments 1990–2022: 50%.

tend to form coalitions. Second, except for Costa's first minority government, all minority governments have been substantive (Strøm 1990), with no supporting parties nor alliances that provide continuous support for the government.

Why minority governments form

This section focuses on the institutional and political incentives that create the conditions for the formation of minority governments in Portugal. It explains the origins of the constellation of rules and informal practices that create strong incentives for minority government formation.[2] Minority governments in Portugal emerge as an institutional solution to a historical legacy of the transition to democracy. Additionally, the absence of an investiture vote, the structure of party competition as a legacy of democratization, and the policy-seeking orientation of the two leftist parties create incentives to form minority governments on the left.

The remote origins of minority governments in Portugal can be traced back to the constitution-making process in 1975, which created incentives for power-sharing and minority governments (Fishman 2011). Institutions are endogenous because they are a result of the preferences and choices of designers (Boix 1999). However, the Portuguese case has an unusual pattern in European democracies because, as Linz and Stepan (1996) argue, the constitution-making environment was fundamentally "nondemocratic." Elected political actors were not allowed to craft rules according to their preferences because they were under exogenous pressure from the Armed Forces (MFA).

On April 25, 1975, voters elected an assembly whose sole goal was to draft the constitution. However, the so-called "revolutionary legitimacy" of the army, derived from its role in overthrowing the authoritarian regime, created what Pinto (2006) calls a dual legitimacy problem. Democratic legitimacy had competing demands from revolutionary legitimacy. In a highly polarized and fragmented society, political parties were forced into signing pacts with the military (*Pactos MFA-Partidos*), detailing several conditions and red lines during the constitution-drafting process that parties needed to abide by in designing the institutions (Rezola 2006).

In the second pact between political parties and the MFA, a moderate subset of the military coalesced with mainstream parties—the Socialists, the Social Democrats, and the Christian Democrats—to create the institutional conditions to sideline the Communists from power and pave the way to pro-capitalism representative democracy (Ferreira 1983; Teles 1998). The Socialists were the only party that could bridge the divide between the extreme left and, at the same time, keep rightist parties from office, not least because the latter were still seen as somewhat

---

[2] On the importance of constitution-making for government formation, see Bucur et al. (2018).

illegitimate in light of the long right-wing dictatorship (Dinas and Northmore-Ball 2020). The absence of an investiture vote emerged as the mechanism to square the circle and permit the Socialist Party to form a minority government with the tacit agreement of mainstream right-wing parties.

Against this backdrop, minority governments emerged as an institutional solution to avoid potential gridlock, polarization, and instability coming out of the revolutionary Portuguese transition to democracy. This governing arrangement has become sticky and prevailing, even after the consolidation of democracy in 1982 and the weakening of the Communist Party.

The formation of minority governments in Portugal is facilitated by negative parliamentarism; that is, the legislature needs only to tolerate the government and does not need to lend its explicit support (Leston-Bandeira and Fernandes 2015). Absent the investiture vote, there are strong incentives for parties not to pursue costly and time-consuming coalition bargaining. Instead, parties controlling a plurality of seats in the legislatures can form a government that does not need the confirmation of the chamber (Bergman 1993).

Unpacking the investiture procedure helps us understand the dynamics behind government formation in Portugal. The president acts as *informateur*. In the days following a general election, the president holds hearings with all the parties that have won seats. According to the Constitution, in light of those hearings and the electoral results, the president invites the leader of the party with the most votes to become the *formateur*. The would-be prime minister chooses a team of ministers and prepares a government program. Symbolically, the legislative debate about the government program (*debate do programa de governo*) is the rite of passage of government formation in Portugal. Over two consecutive days, the government presents its policy guidelines for the years ahead. Absent a formal investiture vote, opposition parties take the opportunity to hold the government accountable, using the legislative debate as a position-taking venue.

At the end of the legislative debate on the government's program, there is an institutional opportunity for the government or the opposition to table a vote of confidence on the government. However, the motion is a political choice. If no political actor tables a confidence motion, the debate terminates, and the government takes office. However, it is not unheard of for political actors to *choose* to table a vote of confidence at the end of the debate on the government's program. Votes of confidence are more common in the government formation process for coalitions in Portugal. The vote serves to signify to voters and to the opposition that the coalition is a cohesive majority in the parliament. In 2002, for example, Durão Barroso's rightist coalition presented a vote of confidence.

Importantly, there have also been votes of confidence on minority governments. Cavaco Silva's first government (1985) and António Guterres's (1999) experienced votes of confidence during the discussion of the government's program, the functional equivalent of the government investiture process. In both cases, the anti-system Communists triggered a motion of confidence. Both governments survived thanks to the abstention of the major opposition party.

The only consequential vote of confidence on a minority government happened in 2015. The incumbent rightist coalition, which had hitherto governed with a majority, won a plurality of votes. After several difficult austerity years, extreme-left parties called for a vote of confidence. The Socialist Party departed from its long-standing tacit agreement with the Social Democrats, which posited that whoever won the election could count on the abstention of the major opposition party in order for them to take office in case of a vote of no confidence. The Socialists coalesced with the Communists and the Left Bloc to defeat the minority right-wing coalition. A few weeks later, the Socialists formed a minority government with the legislative support of the latter. In the next section, we discuss the nature of supporting parties in minority governments in Portugal.

In addition to the institutional design, the party system's competition structure provides further incentives for the formation of minority governments. Unlike most Western European counterparts, the Portuguese party system does not revolve around a primary left–right cleavage. Instead, as a part of the legacy of the democratic transition, the primary cleavage is between pro- and anti-system parties (Jalali 2007). Minority governments keep anti-system parties out of government while delivering some policy benefits that matter to extreme left voters. In what follows, I describe in more detail how parties relate to minority governments in Portugal.

The Socialists, Social Democrats, and Christian Democrats are pro-system parties, whose policy preferences are aligned with some of the structural choices taken in Portugal over the past half a century. Importantly, these three parties share preferences about Portugal's integration in the European Union and the Eurozone, NATO, and a welfare state.

The Communists and the Left Bloc are outsider parties, that is parties that "even when their vote-share would have enabled it—due to their ideology and/or attitude towards mainstream parties—have gone through a period of not being 'coalitionable,' whether of their own volition or that of other parties in the system" (McDonnell and Newell 2011: 445).[3] In addition to legacies from the transition, the difficulty of forming coalitions between outsider parties and the Socialists creates further incentives for the formation of minority governments in Portugal.

Furthermore, the parties (the units of the party system) create incentives for the formation of minority governments. Pro-system parties in Portugal have both

---

[3] In 2015, the Communists and the Left Bloc came close to putting an end to their historical outsider position. Several authors argue that the change occurred—for example, De Giorgi and Cancela (2021). As I have argued elsewhere (Fernandes, Magalhães, and Santana-Pereira 2018), the Costa I government did not fundamentally alter the nature of the Portuguese party system. The 2019 elections, after which the Socialists returned to their canonical minority government format, suggest that the Communists and the Left Bloc remain outsider opposition parties.

office- and policy-seeking motivations. Their historical development and organizational structures create a strong dependence on patronage as an instrument to deliver office-seeking benefits (Jalali et al. 2012). Unlike mainstream parties, the Communists and the Left Bloc are policy-seeking parties only, which adds to their reluctance to coalesce with the Socialists.[4] There are both ideological and strategic explanations of why the two outsider parties in Portugal have policy-seeking goals only. From an ideological perspective, both parties are deeply concerned with what Cunha (2008) dubs "ideological purity." Their political discourse and vote-seeking appeal revolve around the distinction between them and us. Importantly, they create a divide between them—the pro-system parties whose policies are responsible for corruption and frailties in Portuguese society—and us, the anti-system parties whose ideological purity would not stain their reputation with the governing process. If they did, they would become accomplices of the neo-liberal consensus governing the country under Brussels' wing.

There are also strategic considerations that make the Communists and the Left Bloc policy-seeking parties only. Not only do they compete for (partially) the same electorate, they also want to maintain recognition as anti-system parties (Cancela and Magalhães 2020). They are trapped in an equilibrium from which neither has an incentive to defect. If one of them were to defect and coalesce with the Socialists, it would leave space for the other to garner anti-system votes and establish itself as the pivotal party to the Socialists' left.[5] Party leaders of the two anti-system parties tread carefully between the potential tradeoff of going mainstream, having more votes, or remaining entrenched in their anti-system position with admittedly limited electoral growth.

The rationale for minority government formation also hinges on parties' capacity to reap policy benefits without paying the reputational costs associated with office (Strøm 1990). In the Portuguese case, no institutional features facilitate the exchange of benefits between the government and opposition parties in minority contexts. Unlike Strøm's (1990) original proposition, Portugal's committee system and the influence of the opposition in parliament are weak (Fernandes and Riera 2019). In contrast to Strøm's argument, Portugal has a strong executive which concentrates power at the expense of the opposition. In practice, the pivotal moment for opposition parties to obtain gains from trade is the yearly discussion of the state budget. The latter has high political importance, particularly for minority governments whose survival is at stake if they fail to get it approved. Opposition parties

---

[4] This characterization only applies at the national level. For example, the Communists have a robust local presence, controlling several municipalities, particularly in southern Portugal.
[5] The policy-seeking nature of the Left Bloc has been a matter of fierce internal dispute in the party. Over the years, organized groups of militants have left the party after internal attempts to change its orientation and make it more pro-system and office-seeking. For example, in 2014, several famous members left to form a new leftist party whose declared purpose was to dispute the same electoral turf of the Left Bloc, promising voters that they would coalesce with the Socialists.

exchange their support for the budget for policy benefits. Primarily, meetings happen behind closed doors, involving high-ranking members of the government and party leaders.

Taken together, the absence of an investiture vote, the competition structure of the party system as a legacy of democratization, and the policy-seeking orientation of the two leftist parties create a robust constellation of incentives to form minority governments on the left.

Minority governments in office

The existing literature distinguishes between substantive and formal minority governments (Strøm 1990). The former consists of executive arrangements based on flexible alliances and continuous negotiations with opposition parties. By contrast, the latter establish detailed and reliable alliances with opposition parties that function *de facto* as majority governments. Bale and Bergman (2006) dub formal minority governments as contract parliamentarism. This section explores three aspects of minority government in Portugal: the distinction between substantive and formal minority governments, alliances and majority building, and the role of support parties.

Except for António Costa's government (2015-19), all minority governments in the Portuguese democracy have been substantive minority governments whose alliance practices I explore later in this chapter. The coalescing difficulties between left-wing parties identified in the previous section, together with the policy-seeking nature of anti-system parties, create strong incentives for substantive minority governments. Being an outlier, it is worth exploring the motivations behind António Costa's formal minority government. What explains the different nature of Costa's government?

Fernandes, Magalhães, and Santana-Pereira (2018) adduce three reasons why leftist parties opted to form a formal minority government instead of the canonical substantive minority government. First, unlike previous elections that resulted in a Socialist-led substantive minority government, in 2015, the Socialists came in behind the rightist coalition. If they joined a voting coalition in parliament with the Communists and the Left Bloc, the Socialists had the chance to topple the rightist minority coalition. Second, there were strong intra-party incentives in all three leftist parties to take down the right-wing coalition. After four years of austerity, there was a perception that maintaining the status quo and permitting right-wing parties to govern was more costly than creating a *de facto* left-wing coalition to bring about a formal minority government. Third, the Communists and the Left Bloc had specific policy goals that could not be achieved from the opposition. They had to gain access to executive channels. Importantly, those goals were contingent on timing. If rightist parties took office, they would privatize critical sectors of the economy whose importance was vital for the unions. Although entailing reputational risks, the price for being a support party to the Socialists was rather low compared to the potential gains.

Unlike several authors (Lisi 2016; Freire 2021), who heralded the formal minority government as a sea change in Portuguese politics, I think that the arguments above suggest that Costa's minority government did not substantively change the coalition dynamics on the left. Instead, the causes for its formation were contingent on the politics of the moment. Indeed, in 2019, after winning a plurality of the vote, the Socialists decided to go back to their substantive minority government formula that had prevailed since 1976. In November 2021, Costa's former allies coalesced with rightist parties to defeat the State Budget vote, thus confirming the instrumental nature of their 2015 alliance with the Socialists. Costa's second government terminated as the President of the Republic dissolved the legislature and called for early elections in which the Socialists gained their second absolute majority in history, bringing about Costa's third government in March 2022.

Turning to the alliances' practices and the strategies that minority governments use to build majorities, Portugal follows a flexible pattern first identified by Green-Pedersen (2001). Substantive minority governments tend to have strong flexibility in their alliances, not least because there are no tacit agreements for continuing support. In the Portuguese case, alliances are marked by the cleavages discussed above. The Socialist party facilitates flexible alliance practices because the party is in a pivotal position to create alliances to its left and to its right.

The nature of policy issues defines the party(ies) that minority governments approach to obtain support for their policy proposals. There is a clear pattern in alliance formation in Portugal (De Giorgi and Russo 2018). Socialist minority governments tend to coalesce with the right-wing Social Democrats and Christian-Democrats in matters related to foreign policy, taxation, Eurozone matters, European policy in general, and labor politics. The level of policy agreement between the three mainstream parties is much higher than that of the Socialists with the Communists and the Left Bloc. For example, during Costa's formal minority government, where there was, by and large, the highest ever left–right policy polarization in Portuguese democracy, the Left Bloc put forth a policy proposal to revert pro-market changes in labor rules made during the Troika years. Even in the context of a strong formal minority government, the Socialists defied their partners. They coalesced with the Social Democrats and Christian Democrats to maintain the more conservative status quo.

The Socialists ally with the leftist Communists and Left Bloc in matters related to minority rights, post-material policies, and targeted benefits. For example, the Socialists make alliances with the leftist parties to deliver targeted benefits—wage increases and benefits—to public servants who make up an electoral stronghold for the three parties.

Taken together, the evidence suggests that the Socialist Party tends to ally to a much greater degree with the Social Democrats and the Christian Democrats. In their empirical analysis of opposition voting behavior, De Giorgi and Russo (2018) show that, on average, in minority governments, the Social Democrats vote with the Socialists 54.3 percent of the time, and the Christian Democrats align with minority governments on 51 percent of policy proposals. By contrast, the Communists only vote with the minority government 43.4 percent of the time. The Left Bloc votes with the Socialists only 27 percent of the time. Furthermore, from De Giorgi and Russo's (2018) work, a growing pattern of polarization emerges. For example, during Guterres's first government (1995–1999), the Communists displayed a roughly similar pattern of support of policy proposals to the Social Democrats (around 57 percent). More recently, during Sócrates's minority government (2009–2011), the Communists only coalesced with the government in 29 percent of the votes.

Minority government performance

This section examines the performance of minority government. In so doing, I turn to several indicators that gauge whether minority government solutions are less stable and efficient than their majoritarian counterparts. I examine four indicators: bill approval, government duration and survival, pledge fulfillment, and economic and welfare state indicators. Given the popularity of minority governments in Portugal, my expectation is that they perform at least as well as majority governments. Otherwise, parties would have incentives to change the rules of the game to fulfill their office- and policy-seeking goals.

First, I look at bill proposals and the extent to which governments are successful in passing legislation in the *Assembleia da República*. Table 13.2 shows law-making success for all partisan governments in Portugal from 1976 through 2019.[6] Evidence suggests that minority and majority governments are equally successful in law making. On average, both types of governments are unbeaten in 70 percent of their bill initiatives. Such evidence suggests that minority governments are, at least, as effective as majority governments in terms of their legislative success. As mentioned above, the historical development of the Portuguese political system offers parties experience in exchanging benefits and approving legislation, even in minority contexts.

---

[6] The analysis does not include presidential governments, promoted by President Eanes in 1977 and 1978, because they would introduce analytical biases. Presidential governments were political arrangements in which the executive emerged from presidential political power, in most cases against the wishes of parties in the legislature. After the consolidation of democracy, in 1982, with the curbing of presidential powers, there were no more presidential governments.

Table 13.2 Law-making success and duration of Portuguese governments, 1976–2019

Prime minister	Government bills presented (N)	Government bills approved (N)	Government bills approved (ratio)	Relative duration of government (ratio)
Soares I	N/A	N/A	N/A	0.25
Soares II	N/A	N/A	N/A	0.15
Carneiro	6	3	0.50	0.25
Balsemão I	50	31	0.62	0.16
Balsemão II	110	49	0.45	0.46
Soares III	95	58	0.61	0.58
Silva I	56	34	0.61	0.44
Silva II	203	181	0.89	1.05
Silva III	135	118	0.87	1.00
Guterres I	288	228	0.79	1.00
Guterres II	112	81	0.72	0.61
Barroso	132	113	0.86	0.57
Santana Lopes	23	9	0.39	0.16
Sócrates I	297	260	0.88	1.16
Sócrates II	60	38	0.63	0.41
Passos Coelho I	348	322	0.93	1.09
Passos Coelho II	3	0	0.00	0.02
Costa I	203	160	0.79	1.00

Notes: Shading indicates minority government. The table does not show presidential governments in 1977–78. For the Soares I and II, I could not find reliable data on law-making.
Source: Official API of the Portuguese Parliament (https://www.parlamento.pt/Cidadania/Paginas/DadosAbertos.aspx).

Next, I turn to government duration and survival, a key measure of government stability (Saalfeld 2013). In looking at this indicator, it becomes apparent whether minority governments are more unstable and prone to early termination than majority governments. Table 13.2 shows the ratio of government duration. The ratio is calculated by taking the maximum possible duration of the government (measured in days) and dividing it by the number of actual days the government survived in office. Minority governments tend to be more stable than majority ones. While minority governments complete, on average, 78 percent of their mandate, majority governments only completed 65 percent of their mandate from 1976 through 2019.

The evidence that majority governments are more likely to face early termination than minority governments is somewhat puzzling, not least because the former command a majority in the legislature. Existing research shows that, starting in the mid-1980s, the Portuguese political system underwent a rationalization process. Institutions become more majoritarian, more stable, and consolidated (Lobo 2001; Leston-Bandeira 2004). In light of this evidence, I break down the window of observation into two sub-periods: before and after the Portuguese accession to the European Union in 1986. The analysis washes out the potential bias introduced by the highly unstable first decade of democracy.

In breaking down the period of observation, a different picture emerges. From 1986 until 2019, minority governments survived 60 percent of their mandate. By contrast, majority governments, both single-party and coalition, were in office, on average, for 84 percent of their mandate. The separate analysis of a more rationalized institutional period suggests that minority governments face the higher perils of early termination. Furthermore, anecdotally we can see that Portuguese minority governments are more likely to fail in their second term, irrespective of economic conditions. For example, Guterres's second government (1999–2001) terminated early after sustained political gridlock. After six years in power, the Socialist government had come to gridlock at a point where the government could no longer meet the increasingly costly demands of the opposition.

Next, I turn to election pledge fulfillment as an indicator of the government's capacity to deliver on its promises. Existing research suggests that a minority government would face more hurdles in delivering their promises, not least because they have to negotiate with opposition parties. Research on pledge fulfillment in Portugal, between 1995 and 2015, shows that there were no differences between minority and majority governments (Moury and Fernandes 2018). Minority governments fulfilled, on average, 61.1 percent of their pledges while their majoritarian counterparts fulfilled 62.9 percent. The critical difference between minority and majority governments, the authors find, is the possibility to accommodate opposition parties' pledges. In minority governments, opposition parties have much more capacity to fulfill their pledges. Moury and Fernandes (2018) show that mainstream opposition parties fulfill 64.8 percent of their pledges under minority governments and only 19.8 percent under majority governments. Taken together, this evidence suggests that minority governments are more inclusive and accommodate the pledges of both governing parties and opposition, which contributes to higher responsiveness to the median voter.

Finally, I turn to a plethora of governing indicators, including social expenditures, unemployment, gross domestic product (GDP) growth, and deficit, to compare minority and majority governments' policy performance. Evidence on the impact of minority governments on policy performance is mixed. However, there is an emerging consensus in the literature that minority governments are as efficient as majority governments (e.g. Green-Pedersen 2001; Falcó-Gimeno and Jurado 2011; Potrafke 2021). In what follows, I take advantage of the case study nature of this chapter to examine in-depth within-system variation of four indicators of government performance.

Table 13.3 Government performance indicators, Portugal, 1976–2019

Government	Social Expenses	Unemployment	GDP Growth	Public Deficit
Soares I	58.04	19.61	11.15	7.79
Soares II	0.0	0.00	0.00	0.00
Carneiro	2.69	5.96	2.13	0.00
Balsemão I	0.00	0.00	0.00	0.00
Balsemão II	0.15	0.56	3.06	−28.81
Soares III	6.53	8.41	0.57	35.16
Silva I	−1.51	−24.31	10.08	−42.19
Silva II	13.32	−60.85	20.16	−42.22
Silva III	23.67	37.47	5.97	−7.14
Guterres I	8.70	−53.22	15.02	−147.06
Guterres II	16.75	15.38	6.24	58.54
Barroso	1.37	24.64	0.83	32.79
Santana Lopes	3.80	13.25	0.78	−5.17
Sócrates I	6.06	19.89	1.23	27.50
Sócrates II	−4.56	25.50	0.01	100.00
Passos Coelho I	0.12	−3.05	−2.54	−29.03
Passos Coelho II	0.00	0.00	0.00	0.00
Costa I	−10.34	−73.68	7.73	−72.22

Notes: Shading indicates minority government. Entry values represent the cumulative change (in percentage) for each government.
Source: PORDATA (www.pordata.pt).

Table 13.3 shows performance indicators of the Portuguese governments from 1976 through 2019. Each entry shows the percentage increase for each indicator for each government. Looking at social expenditures, the evidence suggests a divide between majority and minority governments. The former have consistently increased social expenditures. At the end of the term of all majority governments, social expenditures had a larger slice of the budget pie. In contrast, minority governments present more internal heterogeneity. Some governments greatly increased social expenditures, for example, the first Soares government (1976–78). At the same time, there are minority governments that cut social expenditures, such as Costa's first minority government (2015–19). The latter offers an interesting example of policy choices. Although Costa benefited from excellent economic conditions, his minority government chose to spend most of its public investment on wage increases to public servants.[7]

Turning to unemployment and GDP growth, the divide between majority and minority governments is less clear. Importantly, our anecdotal evidence suggests

---

[7] Fernandes (2020) decomposes public expenses in European countries in the context of the Eurocrisis, showing that Costa's government severely cut public goods (e.g. health and education) at the expense of targeted benefits (e.g. public servants' wages).

that there is a strong economic cycle effect. Data show governments' performance cuts across the type of government. Existing research on Portuguese economic development shows a golden economic period between the mid-1980s when the country joined the European Union and the early 2000s that coincided with its incorporation in the Eurozone (Reis 2013). Over this period, data suggest that both Cavaco Silva's majority governments and António Guterres's minority governments performed well on both indicators, suggesting an effect of the economic cycle.

Finally, an analysis of the public deficit suggests two conclusions. First, the effect of the economic cycle. From Cavaco Silva's minority government (1985–87) through Guterres's first (1995–99), there is a systematic decrease in the public deficit. Starting in the early 2000s, the patterns become more irregular and subject to contingent conditions. Second, it is worth noticing that the two governments that, by far, contributed the most to curb the public deficit have been minority arrangements. Guterres's (1995–99) first minority government shrank the deficit by −147.06, in no small part thanks to the extremely favorable exogenous and economic conditions. Although firmly anchored in a contract parliamentarism agreement with extreme-left parties, Costa's (2015–19) minority government accomplished the second-highest contraction of the public deficit in the history of Portuguese democracy, mostly because of exogenous pressures from the European Union to conform to Eurozone rules and regulations.

Taken together, evidence gathered here suggests that minority governments perform (at least) as well as majority governments. Importantly, minority governments allow for more inclusive democracy by promoting the fulfillment of the opposition's pledges. In terms of public policy indicators, the most crucial take-home message is that the economic cycle influences how well governments perform in terms of the public deficit or GDP growth, irrespective of the size of their support in the legislature. Ultimately, the success of minority governments in Portugal hollows out any incentives that political parties might have for institutional reform, for example, to create a vote of investiture. Furthermore, the functioning of minority governments permits the continuing success of policy-seeking extreme-left parties. If minority governments failed to produce good policy outcomes, these parties would need to change their profile with uncertain consequences.

Conclusion

Minority governments are a prevailing governing arrangement in Portugal that warrant theoretical and empirical examination. This chapter examines not only the roots of minority governments and the rationale for their formation but also their performance once in office.

There are two primary take-home messages from this chapter. First, minority governments are an institutional solution to historical legacies. The constellation of formal rules and informal practices that lead to the formation of a minority government is a mechanism to break down a potential gridlock that would emerge if minority governments were not a viable governing solution. In the Portuguese case, as Teles (1998) argues, the formation of minority governments emerged in the context of constitution-making to attain two goals. First, to sideline the Communist party and anti-system parties. Furthermore, to permit the Socialist party to govern with no need for the acquiescence of a leftist party. In so doing, the Socialists emerge as the pivotal party (*partido charneira*) in the Portuguese party system, able to build flexible alliances with parties to its left and its right. Of course, the absence of stable support parties or more stable institutional solutions increases transaction costs. Minority governments in Portugal are well known for having continuing rounds of negotiations between the executive and opposition parties.

The second take-home message relates to the performance of minority governments in Portugal. Taken together, the evidence gathered in this chapter suggests that minority governments are as efficient as their majority counterparts. Although less stable and more prone to early termination, minority governments deliver as many pledges and pass as many laws as majority governments. Importantly, in minority contexts, the chapter suggests that opposition parties have more opportunities to fulfill their pledges, without denting the government's pledges. The latter points to the accommodating and inclusive nature of minority governments.

Future research on minority governments in Portugal should focus on intra-party politics and minority government. More specifically, it should focus on potential change within the Left Bloc, and how that could affect relations with a new generation of cadres in the Socialist Party. The hollowing out of the historical legacy of the transition is creating a new cohort of politicians in both the Socialist and the extreme-left parties who do not face the historical constraints to coalesce. Generational replacement in parties' leadership might be a watershed in Portuguese politics. Minority governments might become a less and less popular solution. Instead, formal coalitions might emerge on the left, normalizing partisan competition. An in-depth examination of intra-party politics and party factions can shed light on how party elites view minority governments.

Acknoweldgements

I would like to thank the editors of this volume for their generous and thoughtful comments. Thanks are also due to João Jerónimo for excellent research assistance. Daniel Fernandes and Mafalda Pratas provided ideas and read several drafts. All remaining errors are my own.

References

Amorim Neto, Octavio, and Marina C. Lobo. 2009. "Portugal's Semi-presidentialism (Re) Considered: An Assessment of the President's Role in the Policy Process, 1976-2006." *European Journal of Political Research* 48 (2): 234-255.

Bale, Tim, and Torbjörn Bergman. 2006. "Captives No Longer, but Servants Still? Contract Parliamentarism and the New Minority Governance in Sweden and New Zealand." *Government and Opposition* 41 (3): 422-449.

Bergman, Torbjörn. 1993. "Formation Rules and Minority Governments." *European Journal of Political Research* 23 (1): 55-66.

Boix, Carles. 1999. "Setting the Rules of the Game: The Choice of Electoral Systems in Advanced Democracies." *American Political Science Review* 93 (3): 609-624.

Bucur, Cristina, José A. Cheibub, Shane Martin, and B.E. Rasch. 2018. "Constitutional Making and Legislative Involvement in Government Formation." In *Constituent Assemblies*, ed. Jon Elster, Roberto Gargarella, Vatsal Naresh, and Bjørn Erik Rasch. Cambridge: Cambridge University Press, pp. 186-206.

Cancela, João, and Pedro C. Magalhães. 2020. "As Bases Sociais dos Partidos Portugueses." In *45 Anos de Democracia em Portugal*, ed. Rui Branco and Tiago Fernandes. Lisboa: Assembleia da República, pp. 99-126.

Cunha, Carlos. 2008. "Few but Pure Good Members are Preferred to a Mass Party. The Portuguese Communist Party's Continued Orthodoxy." In *Communist and Post-Communist Parties in Europe*, ed. Uwe Backes and Patrick Moureau. Berlin: Vandenhoeck & Ruprecht, pp. 193-201.

De Giorgi, Elisabetta, and João Cancela. 2021. "The Portuguese Radical Left Parties Supporting Government: From Policy-Takers to Policymakers?" *Government and Opposition* 56 (2): 281-300.

De Giorgi, Elisabetta, and Federico Russo. 2018. "The Unexpected Path of Far Left parties, From Permanent Opposition to Government Support." In *Opposition Parties in European Legislatures: Conflict or Consensus?*, ed. Elisabetta De Giorgi and Gabriella Illonski. London: Routledge, pp. 95-112.

Dinas, Elias, and Knesia Northmore-Ball. 2020. "The Ideological Shadow of Authoritarianism." *Comparative Political Studies* 53 (12): 1957-1991.

Falcó-Gimeno, Alberto, and Ignacio Jurado. 2011. "Minority Governments and Budget Deficits: The Role of the Opposition." *European Journal of Political Economy* 27 (3): 554-565.

Fernandes, Jorge Miguel, 2016. The seeds for party system change? The 2015 Portuguese general election. *West European Politics*, 39 (4), 890-900.

Fernandes, Daniel. 2020. "Between a Fiscal Europe and a Social Europe: The Euro Crisis and National Welfare Policy." Working paper. Florence: European University Institute.

Fernandes, Jorge M., and Pedro C. Magalhães. 2016. "Government Survival in Semi-Presidential Regimes." *European Journal of Political Research* 55 (1): 61-80.

Fernandes, Jorge M., and Pedro C. Magalhães. 2020. "The 2019 Portuguese General Elections." *West European Politics* 43 (4): 1038-1050.

Fernandes, Jorge M., Pedro C. Magalhães, and José Santana-Pereira. 2018. "Portugal's Leftist Government: From Sick Man to Poster Boy?" *South European Society and Politics* 23 (4): 503-524.

Fernandes, Jorge M., Miguel Won, and Bruno Martins. 2020. "Speechmaking and the Selectorate: Persuasion in Nonpreferential Electoral Systems." *Comparative Political Studies* 53 (5): 667-699.

Fernandes, Jorge M., and Pedro Riera. 2019. "Committee Systems in Portugal and Spain." In *The Iberian Legislatures in Comparative Perspective*, ed. Jorge M. Fernandes and Cristina Leston-Bandeira. London: Routledge, pp. 71–88.

Ferreira, José Medeiros. 1983. *Ensaio Histórico sobre a Revolução do 25 de Abril: O Período Pré-constitucional*. Lisboa: INCM.

Fishman, Robert M. 2011. "Democratic Practice after the Revolution: The Case of Portugal and Beyond." *Politics & Society* 39 (2): 233–267.

Freire, André. 2009. "Mudança do Sistema Partidário em Portugal, 1974–2009: O Papel dos Factores Políticos, Sociais e Ideológicos." In *Eleições e Sistemas Eleitorais: Perspectivas Históricas e Políticas*, ed. Manuel Braga Cruz. Porto: Universidade do Porto Edições.

Freire, André. 2017. *Para lá da "Geringonça": O Governo de Esquerdas em Portugal e na Europa*. Lisboa: Contraponto.

Freire, André. 2021. "Left-Wing Government Alliance in Portugal, 2015-2019: A Way of Renewing and Rejuvenating Social Democracy?" *Brazilian Political Science Review* 15 (2): 1–34.

Green-Pedersen, Christian. 2001. "Minority Governments and Party Politics: The Political and Institutional Background to the 'Danish Miracle'." *Journal of Public Policy* 21 (1): 53–70.

Jalali, Carlos. 2007. *Partidos e Democracia em Portugal: 1974–2005: Da Revolução ao Bipartidarismo*. Lisboa: Imprensa de Ciências Sociais.

Jalali, Carlos. 2019. "The Portuguese Party System: Evolution in Continuity?" In *Political Institutions and Democracy in Portugal*, ed. António Costa Pinto and Conceição Pequito Teixeira. London: Palgrave Macmillan, pp. 77–100.

Jalali, Carlos, Patrícia Silva, and Diogo Moreira. 2012. "Party Patronage in Portugal: Treading in Shallow Water." In *Party Patronage and Party Government in European Democracies*, eds. Petr Kopecky, Peter Mair, and Maria Spirova. Oxford: Oxford University Press, pp. 294–315.

Leston-Bandeira, Cristina. 2004. *From Legislation to Legitimation: The Role of the Portuguese Parliament*. London: Routledge.

Leston-Bandeira, Cristina. 2009. "Dissent in a Party-Based Parliament: The Portuguese Case." *Party Politics* 15 (6): 695–713.

Leston-Bandeira, C., and Jorge M. Fernandes. 2015. "Parliamentary Investiture Rules in Portugal's Semi-Presidential Democracy." In *Parliaments and Government Formation: Unpacking Investiture Rules*, ed. Bjørn Erik Rasch, José António Cheibub, and Shane Martin. Oxford: Oxford University Press, pp. 217–232.

Linz, Juan J., and Alfred Stepan. 1996. *Problems of Democratic Transition and Consolidation: Southern Europe, South America, and Post-Communist Europe*. Baltimore: Johns Hopkins University Press.

Lisi, Marco. 2016. "U-turn: the Portuguese Radical Left from Marginality to Government Support." *South European Society and Politics* 21 (4): 541–560.

Lobo, Marina C. 2001. "The Role of Political Parties in Portuguese Democratic Consolidation." *Party Politics* 7 (5): 643–653.

McDonnell, D., and James L. Newell. 2011. "Outsider Parties in Government in Western Europe." *Party Politics* 17 (4): 443–452.

Moury, Catherine, and Jorge M. Fernandes. 2018. "Minority Governments and Pledge Fulfilment: Evidence from Portugal." *Government and Opposition* 53 (2): 335–355.

Pinto, António C. 2006. "Authoritarian Legacies, Transitional Justice and State Crisis in Portugal's Democratization." *Democratization* 13 (2): 173–204.

Potrafke, Niklas. 2021. "Fiscal Performance of Minority Governments: New Empirical Evidence for OECD Countries." *Party Politics* 27 (3): 501–514.

Rasch, Bjørn Erik, Shane Martin, and José António Cheibub (editors). 2015. *Parliaments and Government Formation: Unpacking Investiture Rules*. Oxford: Oxford University Press.

Reis, Ricardo. 2013. *The Portuguese Slump and Crash and the Euro Crisis* (No. w19288). National Bureau of Economic Research.

Rezola, Maria Inácia. 2006. *Os Militares na Revolução de Abril: O Conselho da Revolução e a Transição para a Democracia em Portugal (1974–1976)*. Lisboa: Campo da Comunicação.

Saalfeld, Thomas. 2013. "Economic Performance, Political Institutions and Cabinet Durability in 28 European Parliamentary Democracies, 1945–2011." In *Party Governance and Party Democracy*, ed. Wolfgang C. Müller and Hanne Marte Narud. Springer: New York, pp. 51–80.

Shugart, Matthew S., and John M. Carey. 1992. *Presidents and Assemblies: Constitutional Design and Electoral Dynamics*. Cambridge: Cambridge University Press.

Strøm, Kaare. 1990. *Minority Government and Majority Rule*. Cambridge: Cambridge University Press.

Teles, Miguel G. 1998. "A Segunda Plataforma de Acordo Constitucional entre o Movimento das Forças Armadas e os Partidos Políticos." In *Perspectivas Constitucionais: Nos 20 anos da Constituição de 1976—Vol. III*, ed. Jorge Miranda. Coimbra: Coimbra Editora, pp. 681–770.

PART IV
WHERE MINORITY GOVERNMENTS ARE EXCEPTIONAL

14
Minority Government in Australia
Lesson Learning and Making It Work

Kate Crowley (with Cath Hughes)

Australia has a majoritarian democracy in the Westminster tradition with the two major electoral rivals—Labor and the Coalition[1]—expecting to govern alone and not share power. They will govern in minority in preference to offering cabinet posts to other parties, and it is worth studying their attempts at doing so. At the time of writing, since 1989, there have been twenty-six minority governments at the subnational level, but few at the federal level. At the federal level, they occur where majority government is not delivered at an election, and where the loss of seats for the governing party results in a minority government.

Australia is interesting for the study of minority governments because it shows in particular how a national minority government, the Gillard Labor government (2010–13), drew upon the experience of minority government in the states and territories in order to lock in sufficient supporters to be able to govern in effective majority. Minority governments, led by either Labor or the Coalition, offer independents and/or minor parties policy benefits for their support in attaining or regaining a majority (Griffith 2010). Such supporters provide the minority government with the crucial confidence and supply votes needed to govern. At the federal level, neither Labor nor the Coalition share executive power with other parties. Where cabinet posts have been awarded to supporters at the subnational level, contrary to normal practice (Kalandrakis 2015), the relationship is not described as a coalition.[2]

Australia's most significant federal minority governments were the 1941–43 Curtin government and the 2010–13 Gillard government. There were also three further short-lived minority governments between 1939 and 1941 (Appendix 1), and one in both 2013 and 2018–19 (Table 14.1). Only the Gillard Labor government (2010–13) was a notable success in terms of its longevity, legislative agenda, executive efficiency, and administrative ability, but its achievements were undersold and Labor lost the next election. However, the lessons learned from Australia

---

[1] The "Coalition" refers to the perpetual electoral coalition of the Liberal and National parties.
[2] Discussion of such cabinets at the subnational level is beyond the scope of this chapter.

Kate Crowley (with Cath Hughes), *Minority Government in Australia*. In: *Minority Governments in Comparative Perspective*. Edited by Bonnie N. Field and Shane Martin, Oxford University Press. © Kate Crowley (with Cath Hughes) (2022).
DOI: 10.1093/oso/9780192871657.003.0014

are that whilst federal minority government has been rare, it can form, govern, and deliver, and in the future Australia may indeed embrace power sharing despite its Westminster context.

The Australian political system

Australia is a parliamentary democracy. The British colonized the Australian continent in 1788 without acknowledging prior Indigenous occupation of over 60,000 years. In 1901 the Australian colonies adopted a constitution that established, under British rule, a federal system of government, with a House of Representatives (HoR) where a majority (50 percent+1) is required to form government and legislate, and a Senate elected by proportional representation. Both houses have legislative powers, with HoR elections every three years and simultaneous elections for half of the Senate. The prime minister is the leader of the governing party, elected, as is the deputy prime minister, not by parliament but by the party's members of parliament (MPs). The prime minister appoints the cabinet which is typically drawn from lower house government MPs, but the Queen's representative, the governor general, confirms it, and swears in the government having received evidence of its majority. The government, majority or minority, controls the executive and the workings, committees, and processes of government.

As is the case in Westminster parliaments, an absolute majority (50 percent+1) of MPs (Bergman 1995: 56) is required to retain office in Australia. No rules guide minority government formation; the only principle being that the confidence of the house must be secured (Hazell and Paun 2009: 6) and evidence accepted by the governor general. This evidence can vary, but typically includes "testing the will of the house" with a vote confirming the government's majority support. The government may lose lesser votes without losing office, but if it loses the "testing the will" vote, or confidence and/or supply votes, it will likely resign and the governor general appoint an alternative government or dissolve the house. Confidence votes confirm the government's majority support and supply votes secure its budget. There is no formal investiture process (Hazell and Paun 2009: 12), as occurs elsewhere (Cheibub, Martin, and Rasch 2021); though a minority government will likely, but may not always, test the will of the house.

Australia's two-party system comprises the Australian Labor Party (ALP) and the Coalition. However, the "Coalition" refers to the perpetual coalition, particularly when in government, of the Liberal and National parties. These parties also campaign jointly for office, albeit with differing policy emphasis at times. Nonetheless, they are two distinct political parties with their own separate organizational structures, parliamentary parties and party meetings that they retain when governing in coalition (and we count them as such in both Table 14.1 and Appendix Table 14.1A). Members of both parties sit in cabinet, with cabinet posts determined as part of a written coalition agreement that is renewed after winning government, or after the prime minister changes.

The Greens are the most significant minor party and have supported subnational minority governments, including a conservative government (Crowley 2017) as well as the federal Gillard government. Voting in elections is compulsory. Most Australian parliaments, including the federal parliament, are elected by preferential voting[3] for the lower houses, which decide on government formation, and proportional preferential voting for the upper houses. Preferential voting in single-member districts sees a candidate elected who secures 50 percent+1 of the vote from first preferences, or first preferences plus preferences from eliminated candidates. Independents (typically single-issue MPs, MPs who have defected from parties, or who offer an alternative to the parties) and minor parties are common in upper houses. Their growing presence in lower houses increases the prospect of future minority governments.

As Table 14.1 and Appendix Table 14.1A[4] show, majority governments of either Labor or the Coalition have been the norm in Australia. A minority government forms where the major parties fall short of a majority of seats. This is typically, but not always, at an election. Minority governments have also formed without elections. In 1941, independents supporting a conservative minority government switched allegiance to the Labor opposition, which formed a minority government. In a 2013 Labor Party leadership battle, Kevin Rudd deposed Prime Minister Julia Gillard (who was leading a minority government and had previously deposed him), and briefly led a minority government. And a Coalition government fell into minority prior to the 2019 election after losing a seat to an independent at a by-election (Table 14.1). In each circumstance, stability and efficacy (Bassi 2016) were achieved by governing with full control of the executive, as if in majority, albeit with the backing of independents in each instance, and the Greens as well from 2010–13.

Why minority governments form

Two features are critical to the formation of federal minority government in Australia. First, Australia's Westminster party system is two-party dominant with Labor and the Coalition typically alternating in government. Second, when returned as minority governments, the major parties are resistant to sharing

---

[3] TPP—Two-Party Preferred voting—electors rank candidates in order of preference. Ballots are counted. If no candidate has 50 percent+1 of the vote, an elimination process and preference distribution is triggered. The candidate with the lowest votes is eliminated first. Their votes are distributed to the second preferences on their ballot. Elimination of the lowest ranked candidates continues until a candidate with a vote of 50 percent+1 is identified. The tally of votes before preference distribution is known as the "primary vote."

[4] Appendix 1 shows that federal minority government is not a recent phenomenon in Australia.

Table 14.1 Types of government, Australia, 1987–2020

Parliament[a]	Prime minister[b]	Start date	End date	Government party(s)	Coalition	Minority	If minority, formal/ substantive?[c]	Support parties, if any	Term length (days)[d]
35th	Robert (Bob) Hawke	11-07-1987	24-03-1990	ALP	No	No	—	—	987
36th	Robert (Bob) Hawke	24-03-1990	20-12-1991	ALP	No	No	—	—	636
36th	Paul Keating	20-12-1991	13-03-1993	ALP	No	No	—	—	449
37th	Paul Keating	13-03-1993	11-03-1996	ALP	No	No	—	—	1,094
38th	John Howard	11-03-1996	03-10-1998	LP/NP Coalition	Yes	No	—	—	936
39th	John Howard	03-10-1998	10-11-2001	LP/NP Coalition	Yes	No	—	—	1,134
40th	John Howard	10-11-2001	9-10-2004	LP/NP Coalition	Yes	No	—	—	1,064
41st	John Howard	09-10-2004	03-12-2007	LP/NP Coalition	Yes	No	—	—	1,150
42nd	Kevin Rudd	03-12-2007	24-06-2010	ALP	No	No	—	—	934
42nd	Julia Gillard	24-06-2010	21-08-2010	ALP	No	No	—	—	58
43rd	Julia Gillard	21-08-2010	27-06-2013	ALP	No	Yes	Formal	1 AG + 3 ind.	1,041
43rd	Kevin Rudd	27-06-2013	18-09-2013	ALP	No	Yes	Formal	1 AG + 3 ind.	83
44th	Tony Abbott	18-09-2013	15-09-2015	LP/NP Coalition	Yes	No	—	—	727

44th	Malcolm Turnbull	15-09-2015	02-07-2016	LP/NP Coalition	Yes	No	—	—	291
45th	Malcolm Turnbull	02-07-2016	24-08-2018	LP/NP Coalition	Yes	No	—	—	783
45th	Scott Morrison[e]	24-08-2018	18-05-2019	LP/NP Coalition	Yes	Yes	Substantive	+ 1 ind.	267
46th	Scott Morrison	18-05-2019	11-04-2022	LP/NP Coalition	Yes	No	—	—	
47th	Anthony Albanese	23-05-2022	Current	Labor	No	No	—	—	

Summary statistics (1 January 1990 to 31 December 2020)
Total number of governments 17
Number of minority governments 3
Percentage of minority governments 17.6%

Notes: Shading indicates minority government. Governments formed by the Coalition are counted as coalition governments.
[a] The Australian federal general elections are not fixed term. Constitutionally the House of Representatives can sit for a maximum of three years from the first meeting of the House following a general election.
[b] Prime ministers may change within a parliament period *without* a general election required.
[c] At start of government. See Strøm (1990).
[d] For the purpose of this discussion, days in government are calculated from commencement to conclusion of each PM's respective tenure in that role. It is considered a new government upon the change of PM whether a general election was held or not.
[e] Following a Liberal Party leadership spill, Scott Morrison was elected as new Liberal leader, and was sworn in as PM without going to a general election. Former PM Turnbull resigned from parliament on 31 August 2018, triggering a by-election for his seat, which was won by an independent candidate, seeing the Coalition lose its majority.
[f] Government term in session at time of writing, 10 March 2022.
Source: Australian Parliament House, 2018, Australian House of Representatives Practice (7th Edition), Canberra https://www.aph.gov.au/About_Parliament/House_of_Representatives/Powers_practice_and_procedure
Party key: Australian Greens Party [AG]; Australian Labor Party [ALP]; Country Party [CP]; Liberal Party of Australia [LP]; Liberal Party/Country Party Coalition [LP/CP]; Liberal Party/National Party Coalition [LP/NP]; National Party [NP]; United Australia Party [UAP].

power. Appreciating this, independents and minor parties are primarily policy- (and not office-) seeking.

Minority government formation and the two-party system

In Australia's two-party system, federal government falls to either Labor or the Coalition (Table 14.1; Appendix Table 14.1A). Independents and minor parties feature only at the margins, given preferential voting. For instance, in 2022, 31.7 percent of the federal vote was for independents and minor parties, including 12.2 percent for the Greens, but independents won only twelve seats, and the Greens four seats, in the 151-seat House of Representatives. The major parties gained 35.7 percent (Coalition) and 32.6 percent (ALP) of the vote. However, after preference distribution, their final tally of the Two-Party Preferred (TPP) vote (see footnote 3) was 47.9 percent/58 seats (Coalition) and 52.1 percent/77 seats (ALP).

Given the deep policy divides between the major parties, which is typical of Westminster's adversarial style of politics (Russell 2008: 85), it is not possible to form grand coalitions where the major parties fall short of majority government. As in other Westminster jurisdictions, there is no investiture vote. Instead the practice has been that the leader of the party holding a majority of seats in the lower house is asked to form a government by the governor general (Hazell and Paun 2009 14), though not without complications at times (Griffith 2010). The previous government remains in caretaker mode, but unable to make major decisions without the agreement of the opposition, until the situation is resolved. Indeed the governor general is likely to turn first to the caretaker government and ask it to attempt to assemble a majority, which can only be achieved by approaching independents or minor parties.

With so few federal minority governments, it is clear that the electorate has not yet embraced the concept of a more fragmented party system at the federal level, but there is still scope for independents and minor parties to dent the major party vote and capture the balance of power. At the subnational level, independents have routinely done this, and can be expected to do so in the future given that independents and minor parties are clearly diminishing major party support there as the 2022 federal election result also clearly shows. In this sense, it was unsurprising that the 2010 federal election result mirrored subnational experiences, with independents, including rural independents, and a Greens MP holding the balance of power and supporting the ALP in minority government.

Whether or not more federal minority governments form in the future depends upon whether the two-party vote continues to fragment, and whether the major parties remain resistant to power sharing coalitions with minor parties and independents. Australia is not a multiparty system, but the chances of it becoming one, with more minority governments, and even power sharing governments, are enhanced where major party support declines. Eventually, a balkanized federal party system would see power sharing attempted, potentially even a coalition of Labor and the Greens on the left to match the longstanding Liberal/National Coalition on the right.

Minority government formation and resistance to power sharing

The federal party preference for governing in majority, or as if in majority, means independents and minor parties, other than the National party, are excluded from government. As a consequence, the independents and minor parties are policy-oriented rather than office-seeking, but do seek the balance of power and the leverage this generates in upper houses. As the major party vote fragments, they are increasingly seeking the balance of power in lower houses, to which governments are responsible, as well, looking to trade their support of minority governments for policy gains, or, in some subnational jurisdictions, for cabinet posts. In Australia, the norm is to formalize agreements—a process described as "contract parliamentarianism"—between minority governments and their supporters (Crowley 2003; Bale and Bergman 2006; Griffith 2010), though there are exceptions.

Australia's federal minority governments have been "almost winning" majority governments that require minimal additional support to reach a majority. The incumbent government, or party with the most votes, seeks to establish a majority in parliament (Bassi 2016) with support from independents and/or minor parties. This has not included sharing power or cabinet posts, although such "coalition avoidance" (Reniu 2011) is no longer the practice at the subnational level. The Gillard and Morrison governments confirmed that the federal major parties will not share power,[5] with both having fallen just short of a majority and establishing majority support in return for minimal concessions. Differing arrangements were made with their supporters, with Labor (2010–13) offering more formal agreements and concessions than the Coalition (2018–19).

Incumbent Prime Minister Julia Gillard only just failed to secure a majority of seats in 2010, and formally negotiated support from three independents and the Greens. This delivered carbon pricing and dental healthcare to the Greens, $AUD9.9 billion regional funding to the two rural independents, and promised $AUD100 million hospital funding and anti-poker reform to independent Andrew

---

[5] However, independents and minor parties have entered into executive power-sharing arrangements at the subnational level, at times achieving cabinet positions, although never as recognized coalition members. The Australian practice has therefore been that minority government supporters holding these positions are government ministers with the status of government supporters not coalition partners, so they can openly criticize their cabinet colleagues, the government and its policies (Griffith 2010).

Wilkie (Liddy 2010). She excluded her supporters from government entirely but undertook to canvas the government's agenda with them and to receive their policy suggestions (P&PARG 2013). Following his leadership coup, Kevin Rudd abandoned these arrangements with the government's supporters prior to the 2013 election but confidence and supply remained assured by the independents and Greens.

Following a further leadership coup against the Prime Minister Malcolm Turnbull, the conservative Coalition lost its majority of one at the August 2018 election, and the new Prime Minister Scott Morrison turned to a sympathetic rural independent and secured his support with a promise of AUD$200 million of rural expenditure (Murphy 2018). When parliament resumed after a by-election where the government lost another seat, and government MP Julia Banks also resigned to sit as an independent, the government minimized its chances of losing votes or indeed losing office by cutting parliamentary sittings to just two weeks before the 2019 election (Manning 2018). However, with an election pending, opposition parties rarely waste political capital by bringing down a minority government.

Formation, minor parties, and independents

Thus far, conservative independents have been the most likely to support federal minority governments. A wheat farmer and supermarket businessman supported governments in the 1940s. Rural based independents supported governments between 2010 and 2013. And from 2018 to 2019, the Katter Australia Party, representing conservative rural interests, briefly supported the Coalition minority government. The only minor parties to support minority governments in Australia have been the Nationals at the subnational level where they depart from their Coalition with the Liberals, or the Greens, which have supported government in the Australian Capital Territory (ACT), Tasmania, and at the federal level in 2010. The Australian Democrats in the ACT, and the Katter Australia Party at the federal level have also supported a minority government once each.

Australian experience shows that independents and minor parties proactively develop policies that they can trade for supporting government. Australia's minor parties reflect the country's federal system by differing between jurisdictions and levels of government, so their making of such trades may differ across the country. The federal National party has never left its longstanding coalition with the Liberals to enhance its policy leverage, however the West Australian National party did so in 2008 when supporting a state Liberal minority government. They secured 25 percent of mining royalties for the rural regions, which by 2015 was an investment of $AUD 6.1 billion of royalties in 3,600 projects (DPIRD 2015). They also negotiated cabinet posts as supporters, not coalition partners, and retained the right to criticize the government, as the Greens have done as ministers in Tasmanian and ACT Labor minority government (see also footnote 5).

The decision to support a minority government or not is still a fraught one for independents and minor parties, and is weighed up, as it is in other countries (Reniu 2011: 118), in terms of likely policy gains, against likely electoral consequences and impacts upon the party. Whilst Australia's majoritarian system dissuades independents and minor parties from office seeking, it is apparent from developments at the subnational level that this could change. In the meantime, at the federal level, they continue to seek policy influence in the upper house or on occasion as supporters of minority government. Experience has shown that they receive little in return, with federal minority governments rarely supporting an independent or minor party bill, even though these may offer a useful policy compromise that may break a major party deadlock. At the subnational level, independents and minor parties may at times chair or sit upon review committees in upper houses that influence policy. In Tasmania and the ACT, Green MPs have held cabinet posts and executive roles as supporters of minority governments with mixed impact on their vote at the next election. Greens typically see policy gains at such times as worth any subsequent electoral cost.

Minority governments in office

At the federal level, only the Gillard government offers substantive lessons about governing in minority and making it work in terms of longevity and productivity. Australia's other minority governments were short-lived and less efficacious. The Gillard government offers a promising minority government model based upon contract parliamentarianism (Bale and Bergman 2006) but demonstrates the limitations of excluding supporters from sharing cabinet power.

Minority government types in Australia

Of Australia's forty one federal parliaments between 1939 and 2022, seven included single-party minority governments, with two of these were supported by formal agreements with independents and a minor party (Table 14.1; Appendix Table 14.1A). Once in office, these governments adopted a majoritarian demeanor. In addition to not sharing executive power, they did not welcome any policy or procedural challenges from their supporters beyond what was agreed at formation. Indeed, at times they have strongly resisted such challenges, for instance when independents and the Greens called for refugee policy reform from the 2018–19 Coalition minority government. Such supporters brought down a wartime federal minority government in 1941 over policy differences, but typically are more likely to simply withdraw their support, and to continue offering the government confidence and supply votes until the next election. Such supporters have no interest in harming their chances of re-election by causing political instability.

The Gillard government ran nearly full term, as minority governments routinely do at the subnational level. This government, supported by independents and the Greens, had a clear legislative pathway in the Senate where the Greens held the balance of power. But increasingly strained relations with its supporters reflected similar difficulties at the subnational level and highlighted the need to manage the unity–distinctiveness dilemma (Boston and Bullock 2010) of differing government–supporter expectations. Tasmanian minority governments in the 1990s experienced this when the Greens withdrew their support for policy, offering only confidence and supply support until the next election (Crowley 2003). The Gillard government strained relations with its supporters, championing few of their initiatives, beyond those agreed at the outset, but it also pragmatically withdrew its own bills where these would fail to achieve sufficient support.

In terms of recent minority governments, the Gillard (2010–13) and Morrison (2018–19) governments differed politically, as Labor and Coalition governments, and in terms of formality, with Labor striking written agreements with its supporters and the Coalition negotiating on an ad hoc basis to pass legislation. The Gillard government never lost a vote, whilst the Morrison government failed to prevent asylum-seeker law reform initiated by independents, the Coalition's first loss of such a vote since 1929. The Gillard government was elected as a minority, ran nearly full term, and was legislatively productive, although Labor was not re-elected, whilst the Morrison government formed mid-term, was short-lived, not legislatively productive, but was re-elected (Tables 14.1 and 14.2). The Gillard government nevertheless modeled productive federal minority government as we shall see.

Making it work—Gillard minority government (2010–13)

In Australia, legislation requires a majority vote in the lower and upper houses, with major party members bound by convention to vote with their colleagues. Minority governments seek support for their bills from their supporters, and/or the major party in opposition. The adversarial nature of Westminster parliaments creates no incentive for the two major parties to cooperate on legislation, because the opposition is attempting to replace the government. Federal minority governments also need to negotiate support with the Senate, which comprises major party, independent, and minor party senators. The marshaling of votes was complex, time consuming, and crucial during the Gillard government even with formalized support agreements and the Greens holding the balance of power in the

Senate.[6] Minority government supporters may seek to reform legislative processes, as for example in the Gillard government's 2010 *Agreement for Better Parliament*. This enhanced non-government members' engagement in debate, improved the relevance of question time, committee processes, and non-government involvement, and established a Parliamentary Budget Office to cost policy and offer advice (P&PARG 2013).

Minority government tests the negotiating skills of major party politicians with hard work required "to ensure that the business of the house is completed without mishaps" (Twomey 2018). The Gillard government never lost a vote, and was ruthlessly clear about its agenda, prioritizing it over daily distractions, in methodical fashion. Prime Minister Julia Gillard claimed that it was not possible to build alliances with the Coalition opposition, so she invested time with the independents, minor parties, and interest groups "trying to identify what was core for them and what they could negotiate," disagreeing with them, but treating them seriously and with respect (Beard 2019). At the same time, the opposition leader Tony Abbott campaigned against the government for its entire period in office, in typical Westminster adversarial fashion (Dufour, Jenson, and Saint-Martin 2011: 436). However, written agreements with government supporters (Bale and Bergman 2006) minimized his destabilization by providing stability, institutional consensus, and alliance building mechanisms (Crowley and Moore 2020). But every incentive remained for the Coalition opposition to obstruct the government.

While the Gillard government had a clear legislative pathway in both the HoR and the Senate, the Morrison government did not. This latter government dealt with its minority status by reducing sitting days in 2019, for example, to just ten prior to the May election. On average, the HoR sits for 67 days per year, and the relatively scarce sittings of the Morrison minority government have been described as the lightest workload for federal parliament since federation. The Labor opposition claimed this was running from democracy by a government that could not command the house, while the government countered that much of its business continued elsewhere (Manning 2018). By contrast, the Gillard government operated as a majority government would, on the basis that it had secured stability by way of written undertakings of formal support from independents and the Greens.

Support parties and independents—Gillard minority government (2010–13)

The particularistic agendas of the Gillard government supporters were clear in their agreements with the prime minister. These supporters had a clear aversion

---

[6] The Greens held the joint balance of power in the lower house but also held the balance of power [exclusively] in the Senate. Therefore, any legislation negotiated with the Greens in the lower house was assured passage through the Senate and into law.

to the Abbott-led Coalition opposition and strongly expressed their preference for Labor. The rural regional independents secured unprecedented funding. The Greens achieved carbon pricing, national dental care, and secured a parliamentary debate on the war on Afghanistan (Crowley and Moore 2020). The multiparty climate policy process that was achieved was a testament to the collaboration that arises under minority government circumstances. The Multi-Party Climate Change Committee, advocated by the Greens, created an institutional space for evidence-based debate about carbon pricing that curbed long-standing corporate efforts to block climate action (Crowley 2013). However, independent Andrew Wilkie, an ex-Liberal, ex-Green, and ex-intelligence officer, sought but did not receive enhanced integrity processes, Tasmanian health policy reforms, and gambling reform.

Since the 1980s, the Greens have successfully contested parliamentary seats and supported minority governments, initially at the subnational level where they have supported seven of thirteen minority governments in Tasmania and the ACT (Crowley 2003; 2012; 2017; Crowe 2018). They are more problematic for Australia's majoritarian politics than independents, stealing Labor votes and destabilizing the two-party system. Greens are also ideologically driven, with a collectivist agenda on environmental and social reform. They draw attention to neglected environmental and social justice issues, and seek to transform political, economic, and governance systems (Manning 2019). They can be dangerous supporters of Labor minority governments in jurisdictions where Greens are regarded as divisive and threatening. For these reasons, the Greens were challenging supporters for the Gillard government (Gillard 2011; Milne 2013).

Nevertheless, the independents and Greens overwhelmingly voted with the Gillard government despite relations being strained (Holmes 2013). This strain added to other pressures. Besides the Greens being seen as too radical, Prime Minister Gillard lost support for having deposed the previous popular Prime Minister Kevin Rudd (Table 14.2). There were also scandals, attacks from the opposition, and internal party tensions to deal with (Aulich 2014). Gillard endured the toughest of environments: a "largely disillusioned electorate; a hostile, often vicious press; herself burdened by scandals of others' making; pursued by allegations of her own past misdemeanors; and relentless leadership speculation that created an aura of instability around her government and raised the ire and anxiety of citizens" (Holmes 2013). Within twelve months she had already distanced herself and Labor from the Greens (Gillard 2011), and lost Wilkie's support for failing to deliver his reforms, but the rural independents remained her key supporters.

After three difficult years of attempting to placate the Greens and independents, as well as Labor members who were suspicious of them, Gillard lost the support of her own party colleagues, and was deposed as prime minister just before the 2013 election (Holmes 2013).

Minority government performance

In Australia, scant attention is paid to minority government performance, for instance to Strøm's (1990, 16) criteria of stability, durability, and legislative effectiveness (See also Field 2016: 22–31). Subnational minority governments are judged, though rarely in academic scholarship, on whether they run full term, deliver for constituents and supporters, and get re-elected.

However, closer attention has been paid to the Gillard government because it was a federal government. It ran nearly full term, and delivered in terms of policy, but Labor was not re-elected. The regional independents did not re-contest their seats; the Greens' vote dropped 3.1percent; but independent supporter Andrew Wilkie was re-elected. This was Australia's first federal minority government since the 1940s so it is wrong to generalize from it, indeed comparative experience at the subnational level and from Sweden and New Zealand shows that repeat experiences improve minority government formation, operation, and delivery (Crowley and Moore 2020). The Gillard government was "strikingly stable" and deftly managed (Kefford and Weeks 2020: 91), passing record amounts of legislation and fulfilling most of its election promises (Carson, Gibbons, and Martin 2019), as minority single-party governments tend to in Westminster systems (Naurin 2011).

However, the ability to judge its performance is compromised by leadership and popularity issues. Prime Minister Gillard was a skilled negotiator, and effective at forming and running government, but ineffective at selling her policy achievements (Carson, Gibbons, and Martin 2019: 220, 334). She was also unpopular for deposing her predecessor. This caused a 5.4 percent point swing against Labor that lost it majority government in 2010. Public support from then on was a lagging indicator, although Gillard rated well as the preferred prime minister. Poll aggregates collated by Holmes (2013) confirm that, whilst the Labor government gradually lost support, Gillard remained the preferred prime minister over the opposition leader Tony Abbott. Following his deposing of Gillard, Rudd led Labor to a significant election loss in 2013 (45.5 percent of first preference votes for the Coalition: 33.4 percent for ALP—referred to as primary votes; this translated into 53.5 percent Coalition: 46.5 percent ALP after the distributions of preference votes—see footnote 3).

The opposition benefited from the Gillard government's overall failing popularity. It traded politically on this with a misogynistic hostility[7] toward Gillard that was reflected in the media. The Greens provided secure passage for legislation in both houses, but reliance upon them agitated the government and its supporters as well as the opposition (Gillard 2011). The government did well negotiating its

---

[7] Julia Gillard was Australia's first female prime minister. See her parliamentary "misogyny speech" directed at the opposition leader—https://www.youtube.com/watch?v=ihd7ofrwQX0.

Table 14.2 Legislative record and duration, Australia, 1987–2020

Parliament	Prime minister	Government bills presented (N)	Government bills approved (N)	Government bills approved (%)	Relative duration of government (ratio)[a]
35th	Hawke	531	457	86.1	0.90
36th	Hawke	386	323	83.7	0.58
36th	Keating	273	277	101.5[b]	0.41
37th	Keating	538	482	89.6	0.99
38th	Howard	600	412	89.9	0.85
39th	Howard	715	574	80.3	1.03
40th	Howard	634	327	51.6	0.97
41st	Howard	680	649	95.4	1.05
42nd	Rudd	687	353	51.4	0.85
42nd	Gillard	0[b]	56	—	0.05
43rd	Gillard	707	504	71.3	0.95
43rd	Rudd	0[b]	62	—	0.07
44th	Abbott	467	277	59.3	0.66
44th	Turnbull	159	103	64.8	0.27
45th	Turnbull	569	274	48.2	0.71
45th	Morrison	91	51	56.0	0.24
46th[c]	Morrison	265	182	68.6	0.54
47th[c]	Albanese	nil*	nil*	nil*	Not applicable*

Notes: Shading indicates minority government.
* At the time of writing, the 47th Albanese parliament was yet to sit – due to convene 26th July 2022.
[a] Australia does not have fixed federal election dates. Constitutional provisions allow for every House of Representatives (HoR) to continue for a maximum of three years (or 1,095 days) from the first meeting of the House following a general election, but may be dissolved earlier by the governor general. Some governments may be in place longer should there be an extended period of time between the general election and the first sitting of Parliament.
[b] Bills tabled by predecessor prior to the leadership challenge but which were later debated and assented to during new PM's tenure.
[c] Current PM and government as of 31 December 2020.
Sources: Australian Government, Federal Register of Legislation [last accessed 28 November 2020]; Parliament of Australia, Bills of Previous Parliaments Database [last accessed 30 November 2020].

formation, enhancing its workability, delivering on its promises, passing a record amount of legislation, and running nearly full term, but it did not communicate its successes, rebuff opposition attacks, control its negative image, manage internal dissent or get re-elected (Aulich 2014). Labor's internal politics and its minority status were poorly regarded in the electorate at large, eclipsing any of its substantive policy achievements.

The government did indeed pass the most legislation per prime minister's days in office of any federal government (Evershed 2018). However, in a qualitative sense, much of its legislation was "routine, technical amendments," or bills "introduced under one prime minister and passed under the next" (Young 2015). The government was productive and reformist, introducing carbon pricing, national dental care, broadband, and disability insurance (Aulich 2014), but it notably failed in other domains. Policy success was at times followed by failure or dismantling, where carbon pricing and national dental care was implemented, for example, but disbanded by the next government (Crowley 2017). Policy efforts that demonstrated the difficulty of governing in minority also helped fuel adversarial politics and negative attention from the opposition and the media (Evans and McCaffrie 2014).

The Gillard government's performance nevertheless equals that of majority governments on the key criteria of stability, durability, and legislative effectiveness (see Table 14.2). It did not lose a vote in the house despite the Coalition opposition opposing 50 percent of its bills (P&PARG 2013). The key criteria of budgeting and fiscal discipline were less of a success. The government successfully negotiated a post-global financial crisis environment, but mismanaged its mining tax, its largest intended revenue raiser, and undersold carbon pricing. Deficits were not eliminated as promised, and "mismanagement," "mistaken loyalties," and "poor judgment" marginalized its achievements (Garnett and Lewis 2014: 174). Such analysis does not suggest, however, how governing in minority complicated fiscal policy, with most expecting the same performance as from a majority government. Similarly there is little acknowledgment of the procedural reforms introduced in the *Agreement for a Better Parliament* to improve parliamentary performance in the minority context (P&PARG 2013).

Conclusion

In Australia's two-party dominant Westminster system, federal minority government is rare. But when the Gillard government was reduced to a minority at the 2010 election, it drew upon the experience of minority government in the states and territories in order to lock in sufficient supporters to be able to govern in effective majority. At the subnational level, a trading of confidence and supply votes by minority government supporters in parliament in return for policy benefits has become the norm (Griffith 2010). With its supporters similarly locked in, the Gillard government ran longer than most, was legislatively the most successful, introduced major social and environmental reforms, and never lost a vote in the lower house.

While there are lessons to be learned from this experience, previous analysis has focused upon this government as an aberration, not a trend within Westminster systems (Russell 2008). However, over the next decade, the increase in Australia in support for independents and minor parties at the federal level may overwhelm two-party politics and deliver more minority governments. It is clear from the state and territory level that such governments can form, govern, deliver, and run full term, in reformist fashion. Despite the lack of federal minority governments to date in Australia, there is much to be learned from the country's subnational experience, where innovative arrangements facilitate minority government, including power sharing with government supporters, so the challenge for Australian political analysts is to begin to pay attention.[8]

References

Aulich, Chris, ed. 2014. *The Gillard Governments*. Melbourne: Melbourne University Press.
Bale, Tim, and Torbjörn Bergman. 2006. "Captives No Longer but Servants Still? Contract Parliamentarianism and the New Minority Governance in Sweden and New Zealand." *Government and Opposition* 41 (3): 422–449.
Bassi, Anna. 2016. "Policy Preferences in Coalition Formation and the Stability of Minority and Surplus Governments." *The Journal of Politics* 79 (1): 250–268.
Beard, Alison. 2019. "Life's Work: An Interview with Julia Gillard." Harvard Business Review November–December.
Bergman, Torbjörn. 1995. *Constitutional Rules and Party Goals in Coalition Government: An Analysis of Winning Majority Governments in Sweden*. Umea: Umea Universitet.
Boston, Jonathan, and David Bullock. 2010. "Multi-party Governance: Managing the Unity-Distinctiveness Dilemma in Executive Coalitions." *Party Politics* 18 (3): 349–368.
Carson, Andrea, Andrew Gibbons, and Aaron Martin. 2019. "Did the Minority Gillard Government Keep Its Promises? A Study of Promissory Representation in Australia." *Australian Journal of Political Science* 54 (2): 219–237.
Cheibub, Jose Antonio, Shane Martin, and Bjorn Erik Rasch. 2021. "Investiture Rules and Formation of Minority Governments in European Parliamentary Democracies." *Party Politics* 27 (2): 351–362.
Crowe, Shaun. 2018. *Whitlam's Children: Labor and the Greens in Australia*. Melbourne: Melbourne University Press.
Crowley, Kate. 2003. "Strained Relations: Governing in Minority in Tasmania." *Australasian Parliamentary Review* 17 (2): 55–71.
Crowley, Kate. (ed) 2012. *Minority Government: The Liberal-Green Experience in Tasmania*. Hobart, Tasmania: Australasian Study of Parliament Group (Tasmanian Chapter) [DOI: 10.13140/2.1.3404.9926].
Crowley, Kate. 2013. "Irresistible Force? Achieving Carbon Pricing in Australia." *Australian Journal of Politics and History* 59 (3): 368–381.
Crowley, Kate. 2017. "Up and Down with Climate Politics 2013–2016: The Repeal of Carbon Pricing in Australia." *Wiley Interdisciplinary Reviews: Climate Change* 8 (3): 1–13.

---

[8] My sincere thanks to Cath Hughes for her painstaking work in compiling Tables 14.1 and 14.2.

Crowley, Kate, and Sharon Moore. 2020. "Stepping Stone, Halfway House or Road to Nowhere? Green Support of Minority Government in Sweden, New Zealand and Australia." *Government and Opposition* 55 (4): 669–689.

Crowley, Kate, and Megan Tighe. 2017. "Where Greens Support Conservatives: Lessons from the Rundle Minority Government in Tasmania 1996-98." *Australian Journal of Politics & History* 63 (4): 572–587.

DPIRD. 2015. *What is Royalties for Regions?* Perth: Department of Primary industries and Regional Development. Available at: http://www.drd.wa.gov.au/rfr/whatisrfr/Pages/default.aspx.

Dufour, Pascale, Jane Jenson, and Denis Saint-Martin. 2011. "Governing Without a Majority: What Consequences in Westminster Systems?" *Commonwealth and Comparative Politics* 49 (4): 435–439.

Evans, Mark, and Brendan McCaffrie. 2014. "'Rudderless'—Perceptions of Julia Gillard's Domestic Statecraft." In *The Gillard Governments*, ed. Chris Aulich. Melbourne: Melbourne University Press, 303–321.

Evershed, Nick. 2018. "Turnbull Scores Lower than Abbott, Gillard and Rudd on Productivity in Parliament." The Guardian December 23. Available at: https://www.theguardian.com/australia-news/datablog/2018/dec/23/turnbull-scores-lower-than-abbott-gillard-and-rudd-on-productivity-in-parliament.

Field, Bonnie. 2016. *Why Minority Governments Work: Multilevel Territorial Politics in Spain* London: Palgrave Macmillan.

Garnett, Anne, and Phil Lewis. 2014. "The Economy." In *The Gillard Governments*, ed. Chris Aulich. Melbourne: Melbourne University Press, 158–176.

Gillard, Julia. 2011. *Prime Minister Julia Gillard. Gough Whitlam Oration*, March 31, Sydney. http://www.whitlam.org/__data/assets/pdf_file/0010/389197/2011_Whitlam_Oration.pdf.

Griffith, Gareth. 2010. *Minority Governments in Australia 1989–2009: Accords, Charters and Agreements*. Sydney: New South Wales Parliamentary Library Research Service.

Hazell, Robert, and Akash Paun. 2009. *Making Minority Government Work: Hung Parliaments and the Challenges for Westminster and Whitehall*. London: Institute for Government.

Holmes, Brett. 2013. Hard Days and Nights: The Final 147 Days of the Gillard Government. Research Paper. Politics and Administration. Canberra: Department of the Parliamentary Library.

Kalandrakis, Tasos. 2015. "A Theory of Minority and Majority Governments." *Political Science Research and Methods* 3 (2): 309–328.

Kefford, Glen, and Liam Weeks. 2020. "Minority Party Government and Independent MPs: A Comparative Analysis of Australia and Ireland." *Parliamentary Affairs* 73 (1): 89–107.

Liddy, Matthew. 2010. "Labor's Minority Government Explained." *ABC News*. September 8. Available at: https://www.abc.net.au/news/2010-09-08/labors-minority-government-explained/2253236.

Manning, Paddy. 2018. "Parliament Slacks Off: The Morrison Government is Grinding to a Halt". The Monthly. November 28. Available at: https://www.themonthly.com.au/today/paddy-manning/2018/28/2018/1543380026/parliament-slacks.

Manning, Paddy. 2019. *Inside the Greens: The Origins and Future of the Party, the People and the Politics*. Melbourne: Black Inc. Books.

Milne, Christine. 2013. Senator Christine Milne's address to the National Press Club, February 15. Available at: http://australianpolitics.com/2013/02/19/senator-christine-milne-npc-address.html.

Murphy, Kathryn. 2018. "Morrison Spends 200m to Nail Down Bob Katter's Support for Minority Government." November 8. Available at: https://www.theguardian.com/australia-news/2018/nov/08/morrison-spends-200m-to-nail-down-bob-katters-support-for-minority-government.

Naurin, E. 2011. *Election Promises, Party Behaviour and Voter Perception*. New York: Palgrave Macmillan.

P&PARG (Politics and Public Administration Research Group). 2013. The Hung Parliament: Procedural Changes in the House of Representatives. Research Paper Series, 2013–2014, Politics and Administration. Canberra: Department of the Parliamentary Library.

Reniu, Josep M. 2011. "'Spain is Different': Explaining Minority Governments by Diverging Party Goals." In *Puzzles of Government Formation: Coalition Theory and Deviant Cases*, ed. Rudy B. Andeweg, Lieven De Winter, and Patrick Dumont, 112–128. London: Routledge.

Russell, Peter. 2008. *Two Cheers for Minority Government: The Evolution of Canadian Parliamentary Democracy*. Toronto: Emond Montgomery Publications Limited.

Strøm, Kaare. 1990. *Minority Government and Majority Rule*. Cambridge: Cambridge University Press.

Twomey, Anne. 2018. "Explainer: What Is a Hung Parliament and How Would it Affect the Passage of Legislation". The Conversation October 21. Available at: https://theconversation.com/explainer-what-is-a-hung-parliament-and-how-would-it-affect-the-passage-of-legislation–105358.

Young, Sally. 2015. "Is Tony Abbott's Regime the Worst Federal Government Ever?" Sydney Morning Herald, August 4. Available at: https://www.smh.com.au/opinion/is-tony-abbotts-regime-the-worst-federal-government-ever-20150804-giqtnx.html.

Appendix

Table 14.1A Types of government, Australia, 1939–1987

Parliament[a]	Prime minister[b]	Start date	End date	Government party(s)	Coalition	Minority	If minority, formal/ substantive?[c]	Support parties, if any	Term length (days)[d]
15th	Robert Menzies	26-04-1939	14-03-1940	United Australia Party (UAP)	No	Yes	Substantive	Country Party (CP)	323
16th	Robert Menzies[e]	14-03-1940[f]	29-08-1941	(UAP)/(CP)	Yes	Yes	Substantive	Two independents (ind)	533
16th	Arthur Fadden	29-08-1941	07-10-1941	(UAP)/(CP)	Yes	Yes	Substantive	Lost support of two ind. & resigned as PM	40
16th	John Curtin	07-10-1941	21-08-1943	Australian Labor Party (ALP)	No	Yes	Substantive	Two ind.	684
17th	John Curtin	21-08-1943	06-07-1945[g]	ALP	No	No	—	—	684

Continued

Table 14.1A *Continued*

Parliament[a]	Prime minister[b]	Start date	End date	Government party(s)	Coalition	Minority	If minority, formal/ substantive?[c]	Support parties, if any	Term length (days)[d]
17th	Francis Forde	06-07-1945	13-07-1945	ALP	No	No	—	—	8 (*shortest term of any Australian PM*)
17th	Joseph (Ben) Chifley	13-07-1945	28-09-1946	ALP	No	No	—	—	443
18th	Joseph (Ben) Chifley	28-09-1946	19-12-1949	ALP	No	No	—	—	1,177
19th	Robert Menzies	19-12-1949	28-04-1951	LP/CP Coalition	Yes	No	—	—	496
20th	Robert Menzies	28-04-1951	29-05-1954	LP/CP Coalition	Yes	No	—	—	1,127
21st	Robert Menzies	29-05-1954	10-12-1955	LP/CP Coalition	Yes	No	—	—	560
22nd	Robert Menzies	10-12-1955	22-11-1958	LP/CP Coalition	Yes	No	—	—	1,078
23rd	Robert Menzies	22-11-1958	09-12-1961	LP/CP Coalition	Yes	No	—	—	1,113
24th	Robert Menzies	09-12-1961[h]	30-11-1963	LP/CP Coalition	Yes	No	—	—	721

25th	Robert Menzies	30-11-1963	26-1-1966	LP/CP Coalition	Yes	No	—	788
25th	Harold Holt	26-1-1966	26-11-1966	LP/CP Coalition	Yes	No	—	304
26th	Harold Holt	26-11-1966	19-12-1967[i]	LP/CP Coalition	Yes	No	—	387
26th	John McEwen[j]	19-12-1967	10-01-1968	LP/CP Coalition	Yes	No	—	23
26th	John Gorton	10-01-1968	25-10-1969	LP/CP Coalition	Yes	No	—	654
27th	John Gorton	25-10-1969	10-03-1971	LP/CP Coalition	Yes	No	—	501
27th	William McMahon	10-03-1971	05-12-1972	LP/CP Coalition	Yes	No	—	636
28th	Gough Whitlam	05-12-1972	18-05-1974	ALP	No	No	—	529
29th	Gough Whitlam	18-05-1974	11-11-1975	ALP	No	No	—	542
30th	Malcolm Fraser	11-11-1975	10-12-1977	LP/NP (formerly Country Party) Coalition	Yes	No	—	760
31st	Malcolm Fraser	10-12-1977	18-10-1980	LP/NP Coalition	Yes	No	—	1,043

Table 14.1A Continued

Parliament[a]	Prime minister[b]	Start date	End date	Government party(s)	Coalition	Minority	If minority, formal/ substantive?[c]	Support parties, if any	Term length (days)[d]
32nd	Malcolm Fraser	18-10-1980	11-03-1983	LP/NP Coalition	Yes	No	—	—	874
33rd	Robert (Bob) Hawke	11-03-1983	01-12-1984	ALP	No	No	—	—	631
34th	Robert (Bob) Hawke	01-12-1984	11-07-1987	ALP	No	No	—	—	952

Summary Statistics (1939 to 31 December 2020)

Total number of governments: 45
Total number of minority governments: 7
Percentage of minority governments: 15.5%

Notes: See also Table 14.1.

[e] Despite leading a minority government when World War 2 broke out, Prime Minister Robert Menzies did not enter into a formal UAP-Country Coalition arrangement until 14 March 1940, following the governing UAP losing a by-election to Labor. UAP/CP coalition was still in minority and needed the support of two independents.

[f] Date of by-election, which made incumbent Menzies government a minority government.

[g] John Curtin died in office. His immediate replacement, Frank Forde, was replaced by Chifley as PM one week later.

[h] The 1961 election saw both incumbent the Coalition and ALP opposition receive an equal number of seats in the House, but two of the ALP MPs represented Australia's two Territories respectively, the Northern Territory and the ACT, holding restricted voting rights in the chamber at that time.

[i] Date PM Harold Holt is presumed to have died while swimming at Portsea, Victoria.

[j] Leader of the Coalition's Country Party and Deputy PM McEwen was sworn in as caretaker PM following the disappearance of Harold Holt, and until the Liberal Party elected a new Leader.

Table 14.2A Legislative record and duration, Australia, 1939–1987

Parliament	Prime minister	Government bills presented (N)	Government bills approved (N)	Government bills approved (%)	Relative duration of government (ratio)[a]
15th	Menzies	100	87	87.0	0.29
16th	Menzies	130	126	96.9	0.49
16th	Fadden	5	2	40.0	0.04
16th	Curtin	156	140	89.7	0.62
17th	Curtin	96	74	77.1	0.63
17th	Forde	0	0	—	0.01
17th	Chifley	110	103	93.6	0.40
18th	Chifley	316	299	94.6	1.07
19th	Menzies	100	83	83.0	0.45
20th	Menzies	353	311	88.1	1.03
21st	Menzies	141	127	90.1	0.51
22nd	Menzies	333	299	89.8	0.98
23rd	Menzies	400	313	78.3	1.02
24th	Menzies	357	211	59.1	0.66
25th	Menzies	311	286	91.9	0.72
25th	Holt	99	93	93.9	0.35
26th	Holt	164	124	75.6	0.63
26th	McEwen	0	0	—	0.02
26th	Gorton	326	259	79.4	0.60
27th	Gorton	213	128	60.1	0.46
27th	McMahon	345	276	80.0	0.58
28th	Whitlam	347	240	69.2	0.48
29th	Whitlam	492	268	54.4	0.49
30th	Fraser	451	369	81.8	0.69
31st	Fraser	686	557	81.2	0.95
32nd	Fraser	483	362	74.9	0.80
33rd	Hawke	402	322	80.1	0.58
34th	Hawke	594	460	77.4	0.87

Notes: See Table 14.2.

15
Minority Governments in the United Kingdom
Nearly-Winning Minorities and Lost Majorities

Andrew Jones and Richard Whitaker

The UK's political system is often associated with single-party majority governments at Westminster.[1] Nevertheless, elections and the loss of majorities by governments while in office have led to six periods since 1974 when no party has held a majority of seats in the UK House of Commons. These minority situations have resulted in five minority governments. These periods of minority rule are worth studying because the UK is traditionally viewed as a prime example of a majoritarian system of government (Lijphart 2012). In the UK, minority situations can come about in two ways. First, there are minority governments created straight after an election, which we term post-election minority governments. Second, there are intra-term minority governments. These occur when a majority government loses sufficient seats during a parliamentary term to move from controlling a majority to a minority of seats in the House of Commons. This can result either from by-elections which take place when a legislator dies, resigns, or is recalled, or MP defections from the governing party, or some combination of these. This type of minority government has received little attention in the comparative literature. Central to understanding these governments is that the shift from majority to minority status has not seen governments simply forced from office via no-confidence votes. Instead, smaller, policy-seeking parties have offered support in exchange for policy concessions, keeping governments in office to the end (as, for example, in 1997) or almost to the end (as, for example, in 1979) of the maximum inter-electoral period.

We show that minority governments are the preferred option when minority situations occur in periods of political polarization, with policy differences limiting the number of potential coalitions. Recently, devolution has increased the likelihood of minority government through the inclusion of multilevel territorial considerations that make flexible support arrangements more attractive than

---

[1] We thank Richard Kelly for assistance with obtaining data on government bills presented and approved, and Philip Lynch for helpful advice.

Andrew Jones and Richard Whitaker, *Minority Governments in the United Kingdom*. In: *Minority Governments in Comparative Perspective*. Edited by Bonnie N. Field and Shane Martin, Oxford University Press. © Andrew Jones and Richard Whitaker (2022). DOI: 10.1093/oso/9780192871657.003.0015

formal coalitions. But deals with support parties have often broken down as a result of differences in approaches to major policy issues, namely economic policy in the 1970s and Brexit in the late 2010s. Still the legislative success of minority governments measured quantitatively is not far off that of single-party majorities, suggesting that, as in many other cases, UK minority governments are not always as ineffective as might be anticipated. Such performance has, at times, been negatively affected as much by dissent within governing parties as by differences between support parties and those in office.

The British political system

The UK is a parliamentary and bicameral system with the democratically elected House of Commons holding constitutional primacy over the mainly appointed House of Lords. While bills are considered by both chambers, governments have the power to pass bills without House of Lords approval, with the latter being able to delay but ultimately, not to veto legislation (Norton 2013: 95–96). The making and breaking of governments, however, is the sole preserve of the Commons. In the post-war period, UK governments have been dominated by either the Conservative or Labour parties. Aided by the single-member plurality (SMP) electoral system, twenty-five of the thirty-one post-war governments have been majority party cabinets (see Table 15.1). Yet from the 1970s, the UK began a trend towards multiparty politics (Quinn 2013), with several minority governments and one majority coalition.

Formation of majority governments in the UK is straightforward. Should the incumbent party win a majority, the sitting prime minister simply continues in post. When an opposition party wins a majority, the outgoing prime minister resigns, and the leader of the majority party is asked by the monarch if they can command the confidence of the Commons. By answering in the affirmative the individual is appointed prime minister and can begin to build a cabinet (Kelso 2015). In post-election minority situations, the sitting prime minister remains in office until negotiations identify the individual most likely to be able to command the confidence of the Commons. The monarch then appoints that person as prime minister.

The first test of any government comes with the speech from the throne (also known as the Queen's or King's Speech). This sees the monarch read the legislative program of the new government followed by several days of debate on a government motion. Governments need to secure simple majorities in votes on the motion, with the prime minister likely to resign should her government fail to do so. This has led some to view the House of Commons as holding ex post powers of government confirmation via positive parliamentarism (Kelso 2015). Parties with a majority of seats have few problems passing their speech from the throne. As we

Table 15.1 Types of government, United Kingdom, 1945–2019

Prime minister	Start date	End date	Government party (or parties)	Coalition	Minority	If minority: Formal or substantive	Support parties, if any
Attlee I	06-07-1945	23-02-1950	Labour	No	No		
Attlee II	24-02-1950	25-10-1951	Labour	No	No		
Churchill	26-10-1951	05-04-1955	Conservative	No	No		
Eden I	06-04-1955	26-05-1955	Conservative	No	No		
Eden II	27-05-1955	09-01-1957	Conservative	No	No		
Macmillan I	10-01-1957	08-10-1959	Conservative	No	No		
Macmillan II	09-10-1959	18-10-1963	Conservative	No	No		
Douglas-Home	19-10-1963	15-10-1964	Conservative	No	No		
Wilson I	16-10-1964	31-03-1966	Labour	No	No		
Wilson II	01-04-1966	18-06-1970	Labour	No	No		
Heath	19-06-1970	28-02-1974	Conservative	No	No		
Wilson III	01-03-1974	10-10-1974	Labour	No	Yes	Substantive	
Wilson IV	11-10-1974	05-04-1976	Labour	No	No		
Callaghan I	06-04-1976	06-04-1976	Labour	No	No		
Callaghan II	07-04-1976	03-05-1979	Labour	No	Yes	Formal (23-03-1977 – 31-07-1978)	The Liberal Party (from 23-03-1977 – 31-07-1978)
Thatcher I	04-05-1979	09-06-1983	Conservative	No	No		
Thatcher II	10-06-1983	11-06-1987	Conservative	No	No		
Thatcher III	12-06-1987	27-11-1990	Conservative	No	No		

Continued

Table 15.1 *Continued*

Prime minister	Start date	End date	Government party (or parties)	Coalition	Minority	If minority: Formal or substantive	Support parties, if any
Major I	28-11-1990	09-04-1992	Conservative	No	No		
Major II	10-04-1992	05-12-1996	Conservative	No	No		
Major III	06-12-1996	01-05-1997	Conservative	No	Yes	Substantive	
Blair I	02-05-1997	07-06-2001	Labour	No	No		
Blair II	08-06-2001	05-05-2005	Labour	No	No		
Blair III	06-05-2005	27-06-2007	Labour	No	No		
Brown	27-06-2007	11-05-2010	Labour	No	No		
Cameron I	11-05-2010	07-05-2015	Conservative, Liberal Democrats	Yes	No		
Cameron II	08-05-2015	13-07-2016	Conservative	No	No		
May I	13-07-2016	08-06-2017	Conservative	No	No		
May II	09-06-2017	24-07-2019	Conservative	No	Yes	Formal	Democratic Unionist Party
Johnson I	24-07-2019	12-12-2019	Conservative	No	Yes	Formal (but substantive after 03–09–2019)	Democratic Unionist Party
Johnson II	13-12-2019		Conservative	No	No		

Notes: Share of minority government since 1945: 16%
Share of minority government since 1990: 21%
Sources: Audickas, Cracknell, and Loft (2020) and Kelly (2019).

show below, the need for support from only a simple majority has also allowed minority governments to form with relative ease. The next section considers why minority governments have formed at particular points.

Why minority governments form

We argue that minority governments form as a result of the two larger parties pursuing the spoils of office while smaller parties are more likely to aim primarily at achieving particular policy outcomes. As we show later, UK governments maintain strong control over both procedure (Tsebelis 2002) and the committee structure (Strøm 1990), resulting in oppositions being viewed as ineffectual (Lijphart 2012). Although recent work shows opposition influence to be greater than previously thought (e.g. Russell and Gover 2017), comparisons can be made between the UK and Spain where governments employ strong agenda-setting powers during minority situations to strengthen their bargaining position (Field 2016: 123–140). Consequently, it is likely that smaller parties discount the prospect of influencing policy through such parliamentary mechanisms in their calculations of whether to support minority governments. Instead, minority government formation in the UK can be explained by smaller policy-seeking parties (Müller and Strøm 1999) taking advantage of their relative scarcity to extract the maximum policy concessions as support parties while avoiding incurring electoral costs associated with governing (Strøm 1990). Interestingly, the UK's SMP electoral system rewards parties with a stronger geographic base, meaning regional parties most often hold the balance of power when minority situations occur. This has led to territorial calculations playing a part in the formation of all post-war minority governments in the UK. This has important implications for future minority government formation in light of increased devolution within Britain over the past 25 years.

Party goals, limited options, and the costs of governing

Despite the growth of multiparty politics in elections and parliament (Quinn 2013), the Conservatives and Labour continue to dominate the executive. Participation in every post-war cabinet by one or other party has meant that they are clearly identifiable by supporters and voters as office-seekers. The growth of multiparty politics has seen greater support for smaller parties that fall into one of two categories:

1. Parties representing regions or nations, including the Scottish National Party (SNP), Plaid Cymru, and parties in Northern Ireland;

2. Parties representing single or smaller ranges of issues, namely the Green Party and UK Independence Party.

These parties seek benefits gained through influencing policy as it applies to regions, groups, or issues, and may prioritize this over participation in government. Regional parties have often held the balance of power when either of the larger parties has failed to win a majority of seats. The second group of parties listed above have not been directly involved in government formation but have an indirect effect to the extent that they take votes from the larger parties (Dennison 2015; Dennison and Goodwin 2015).

In addition to shaping the goals of parties in the UK system, the SMP electoral system also influences parties' size and position. Large "catch-all" parties (Kirchheimer 1966) able to inhabit the center of the left–right dimension are able to secure a winning coalition of voters (Green and Hobolt 2008). While single-party majority governments are returned at most elections, minority situations see an almost-winning-sized and centrally-positioned party with which smaller parties must compromise in a coalition should they wish to enter government. As Crombez (1996) shows, large and centrally located winning parties should possess strong bargaining power in relation to smaller parties. However, the effects of SMP are such that there are few potential support parties for the Conservatives or Labour in the event of a minority situation. The threat for smaller parties is that they make policy concessions to larger parties in return for few policy benefits and are then punished by voters for policy inconsistencies (Cutts and Russell 2018). An example of this is the damaging electoral consequences experienced by the Liberal Democrats after participating in a coalition government with the Conservatives in 2010–15.

So, while one of the two main parties should always enter government even in minority situations, calculations of the costs and benefits of government participation are more complex for smaller parties. However, the nature of the UK's electoral system provides an arena in which the formation of minority governments is incentivized. First, regional parties, with their stronger geographic bases, are rewarded with greater numbers of seats than other smaller parties under SMP. Since the devolution of the 1990s, these parties have been represented at both Westminster and in devolved institutions, often with split goals at the two levels. For example, the Democratic Unionist Party (DUP) arguably has office-seeking goals within the devolved institutions of Northern Ireland while holding policy-seeking objectives as a small regional party at Westminster. The electoral costs of entering government at Westminster encourage smaller parties to opt for more flexible support agreements with larger parties while remaining outside government.

The second outcome of SMP in the UK is the comparatively small number of parties in the system at the UK level. This reduces the available options for the

Conservatives and Labour when seeking to identify government partners. Smaller parties can take advantage of their scarcity by extracting the maximum policy concessions while supporting a minority government from the outside. We now examine how these dynamics have shaped how governments were formed in several minority situations in the UK. Here we concentrate on formation with more detail on majority-building and the agreements reached with support parties in a later section.

A post-election minority government: February 1974

The February 1974 election saw the first minority situation in the UK since the 1920s. Prime Minister Heath had called an election in the midst of economic unrest. Labour won a plurality of seats with fewer votes than the Conservatives (Butler and Kavanagh 1974). Attempts at government formation began with talks between the Conservatives and Liberals. These faltered over electoral reform. The Conservatives then held discussions with the Ulster Unionist Party (UUP) but they declined the offer of Conservative Party membership for seven of their MPs (Butler and Kavanagh 1974: 255). The relationship between the two parties had deteriorated as a result of the imposition of direct rule in Northern Ireland by the Heath government in 1972 and its support for the Sunningdale Agreement on power-sharing in Northern Ireland (Smith 2006). Disagreement over the latter was too great for a deal to be reached (Ziegler 2010: 438). This ended Heath's hopes of remaining in power.

Ideological differences between Labour and the Liberals (Adams et al. 2004: 597) ruled out an agreement. The sole remaining option then was a minority Labour administration. Recognizing both the electoral and financial (Godbout and Høyland 2011) costs of an immediate election, the Conservatives chose to tolerate the formation of a Labour minority government by withdrawing amendments to Labour's Queen's Speech and abstaining from the final investiture vote (Kelso 2015: 43).

Callaghan's intra-term minority government: 1976–79

The October 1974 election saw the Labour Party win a majority of three seats. By 1976 Callaghan had succeeded Wilson as prime minister with an intra-term minority beginning immediately through a by-election defeat (Haddon 2009). Labour, a primarily office-seeking party, chose to remain in office despite efforts by the Conservatives to force a motion of no confidence. Labour relied on an agreement (known as the Lib-Lab Pact) with the Liberal Party in March 1977, of which there are more details below. With little formally agreed by the parties, the pact had collapsed by July 1978. Labour then endeavored to remain in power, using its position on the center left to cultivate the support of policy-seeking regional parties, as set out below.

Major's intra-term minority government: 1996–97

Major's Conservative Party won a majority of twenty-one seats at the 1992 General Election. However, economic difficulties, deep party divisions over Europe and unpopularity with the public saw that majority lost in late 1996 (Cowley 2016). An intra-term minority government therefore began just six months before the end of a five-year term. That the Conservatives chose to soldier on provides support for Strøm's (1990) assertion that for such parties it is often better to be in office in the short run than in opposition. The UUP were able to use their position as the only viable support party to extract policy concessions and allow the Conservatives to remain in office until the end of the parliamentary term. This case shows that even when governments lose their majority late in their term, minority government can be viable.

May's post-election minority government: 2017–19

Prime Minister May's decision to seek an early election in 2017, in the polarized context of Brexit, did not go to plan with the Conservatives finishing nine seats short of a majority (Mellon et al. 2018). Policy differences with smaller parties over Brexit limited the options available after the election. Of the three smaller parties that held enough seats to give the Conservatives a majority, the largest, the SNP, could be ruled out given their anti-Brexit and pro-Scottish independence stance (Scottish National Party 2017). Likewise, the support of the Liberal Democrats for a second EU referendum precluded any alliance. This left the DUP to whom a formal coalition was offered but this was rejected. There were differences over policy on abortion and same-sex marriage (Cowley and Kavanagh 2017). However, the DUP favored Brexit and were willing to support a Conservative minority government in return for policy concessions (Tonge 2017). The Conservatives agreed to £1 billion of investment in Northern Ireland and corporation tax cuts for the province. This agreement allowed the two parties to diverge on policy issues where their supporters might have objected to compromises.

Though the aftermath of the 2017 General Election was a high point for the DUP at Westminster, the party had seen their seat share in the Northern Ireland Assembly reduced from thirty-eight to twenty-eight just three months earlier (Murphy and Evershed 2019). Any formal coalition at Westminster which might prove unpopular with the electorate, could have added to the risk of their rivals

Sinn Féin becoming the largest party. Instead, the DUP secured investment for the whole of Northern Ireland but still failed to win the 2022 Northern Ireland Assembly elections.

Minority governments in office

Minority governments in the UK have taken various different forms but securing parliamentary support has often been based around concessions to regionalist parties either informally or via a publicly available formal agreement. Nevertheless, the performance of these governments in office has sometimes been affected at least as much by governments' difficulties in building majorities within their own parties as by their relationships with others.

Minority government types

The literature distinguishes different types of minority government. Some, which Strøm (1990: 62) labels as "substantive minority governments," do not have a clear agreement with a support party or parties. In contrast, "formal" minority governments (Strøm 1990: 62) have reached agreements with support parties before being formed and can rely on a majority with this support in place. Beyond this, Bale and Bergman (2006: 424) identify contract parliamentarism as "an explicit written contract with one or more parties that remain outside the cabinet" and which is made publicly available.

In the UK, there are examples of formal and substantive minorities. The Labour government formed after the February 1974 election provides a clear example of a substantive post-election minority government. This short-lived administration had no formal agreements with support parties and instead, aimed for an election later that year (Wilson 1979: 14). Substantive intra-term minority governments also existed under Callaghan before and after the Lib-Lab Pact (March 1977–July 1978), described below. The final six months of Major's period as Prime Minister constituted an intra-term minority. Johnson's first government became a substantive minority from early September 2019 because, although the deal reached between the Conservatives and DUP (see below) was still in place, even with DUP support the government could not rely on a majority of seats. This followed the defection of a Conservative MP to the Liberal Democrats along with the government's decision to remove the whip from twenty-one of its own MPs.

Since 1945 there have been two formal minority governments, stretching to three if we include the change of Prime Minister towards the end of the 2017–19 session (see Table 15.1). Following its slim victory in October 1974, the Labour government was gradually reduced to a minority. Faced with the threat of losing a motion of confidence on March, 23 1977, Labour reached an agreement with the Liberal Party, commonly known as the Lib-Lab Pact. This meant the Liberals would "work with the government in the pursuit of economic recovery" (Callaghan and Steel 1977). The agreement established a joint consultative committee which would consider Labour and Liberal policy proposals. Arguably, this was what made the agreement attractive as it fitted with the Liberals' policy-seeking aims by giving them a chance to persuade Labour to take on policy ideas not accepted at the point of agreeing the pact (Dorey 2011: 391). While it did not explicitly mention support in votes of confidence or in budgetary matters, it referred to some specific policy areas including direct elections to the European Parliament and proposals for devolution of power to Scotland and Wales, promising free votes on both these issues. The deal meets Bale and Bergman's (2006) definition of contract parliamentarism: it was made publicly available and lasted initially until the end of the 1976–77 session and was then renewed before being abandoned in July 1978 (Haddon 2009: 23).

In 2017, the deal between the Conservatives and DUP meant the government could rely on a majority of votes in areas covered by the agreement. This confidence and supply deal constitutes contract parliamentarism (Bale and Bergman 2006). It was publicly available and set out areas where the DUP would support the government. A second document set out financial support that the UK government would provide to Northern Ireland, as part of the deal. The agreement was intended to last the length of the parliamentary term. Officially speaking it lasted into a second government (Johnson I) although it was beginning to break down during the summer of 2019. It established a coordination committee chaired by the government "to ensure the necessary support can be established by both parties to fulfil these arrangements." It committed the DUP to support the government on motions of confidence, on the Queen's Speech and legislation concerning revenue and expenditure. Crucially for the government, it also covered legislation related to Brexit, an element of the agreement that was to be put under great strain and eventually to break down.

Governments' agenda control and relations with support parties

According to Strøm (1990: 98–99) governing parties will seek to minimize the concessions they make to others in their attempts to secure majorities. In many of the cases of minority government in the UK, governing parties have been able to limit these concessions because they have often been close to holding a majority of seats. This means they have normally only needed support from primarily policy-seeking small parties. The DUP, UUP, and SNP fall into this category and fit with examples from some other European countries in being regional parties. As Field (2016: 35) points out, in this scenario, regionalist parties can provide votes for national-level policies in exchange for support to their region in some form, provided they are sufficiently ideologically close to the governing party.

Drawing on Strøm's (1990: 111–112) explanations for the variation in governments' ability to offer concessions, a high degree of government control over major infrastructure projects and over public expenditure in the UK (although much less so in Scotland in recent years) means that governments are in a fairly strong position to offer particularistic benefits to regionalist support parties.

Not only may governments get away with limited concessions, their ability to set the agenda in the UK case is enhanced by the Standing Orders of the House of Commons which give government business "precedence at every sitting" (House of Commons 2018, Standing Order 14(1)) with a few exceptions. Though these rules can be adjusted with a simple majority, the almost-winning-size of most minority governments in the UK requires opposition parties to be united if they are to make changes against the government's will.

Smaller parties face difficulties in trying to influence policy through public bill committees, which consider legislation in the Commons. Although these committees reflect the composition of the House, they can still be dominated by government under minority administrations. For instance, in 2017, May's government managed to use support from the DUP to pass motions allowing for committees with an odd number of members (the normal situation for public bill committees at that point) to have a government majority. Likewise, the minority Labour government of February to October 1974 relied on committee chairs from their own party, to rule in their favor when committee numbers were split evenly (Bartlett and Torrance 2020: 16). However, when intra-term minority governments occurred under Callaghan in 1976 and Major in 1995, both had to concede they were not entitled to a majority on public bill committees (Bartlett and Torrance 2020: 16–17). Even in these intra-term minority situations though, it can be difficult for smaller parties to achieve influence, principally because they often have just a single seat on such committees (Norton 2013: 92).

The variety of types of minority government post-1945 in the UK have seen different approaches to establishing alliances. Wilson indicated that the aim of his minority government beginning in February 1974 was to set out an agenda for dealing with the economic crisis facing the UK. He explained that "Even if much of [the legislation] could not pass into law before an election, it was important to present it to Parliament and the nation in clear legislative form" (Wilson 1979: 13). As Table 15.2 shows, the Wilson III government introduced a small number of bills commensurate with its short-lived nature. Just below 90 percent of these were passed though the government was defeated seventeen times on the floor of the Commons (Norton 2004). The government's ability to pass legislation was more likely due to the Conservatives' fear of provoking an election in the opening months of the government, at which they felt it likely they would lose even more seats, rather than due to any majority-building process. The strategy involved a mixture of either not forcing votes, despite arguing against the government in debates, or instructing their MPs to abstain (Norton 1980: 449–450). The situation changed with government defeats mainly occurring during June and July 1974 once the possibility of an election before the summer break had been removed (Norton 2004).

Labour's next period of minority government from 1976–79, as we have seen, involved an alliance with the Liberal Party for some of the time. Nevertheless, this only came to fruition on the eve of a no-confidence vote on March 23, 1977 that the government expected to lose. Labour's incentive for majority building was not simply to get the government through the vote and any future no-confidence motions. Rather, the Labour leadership's aim appears to have been to maintain themselves in office while they improved the state of the economy. The hope was to win an election under better circumstances in 1979 (Callaghan 1987: 463–465). The Labour party itself was split with forty-eight of its backbenchers signing a motion stating they did not view themselves as bound to support the pact (Callaghan 1987: 458). It came to an end partly because Liberal leader David Steel told the prime minister he wanted a period of time between the end of the deal and an election to set out a distinctive Liberal stance (Steel 1989: 144). Nevertheless, this arrangement had involved some limited procedural and policy concessions made to a small but ideologically close support party in exchange for support on confidence votes but not on budgetary issues.

For the remainder of this intra-term minority government, which lasted until a no-confidence motion forced resignation in March 1979, the SNP and Plaid Cymru gave support to Labour in return for attempts to introduce Scottish and Welsh devolution, to which the Conservatives were opposed. Labour also received support or abstentions from the UUP, despite a lack of ideological common ground, by offering commitments to increase the representation of Northern Ireland at Westminster and the devolution of powers to local government (Dorey 2016). Labour's ability to split the opposition through territorially focused incentives can be compared with Spain where parliamentary institutions allow governments to bolster their governing capacity by manipulating the territorial goals of other parties (Field 2016).

The intra-term minority government of Major survived using government policy influence and control of House of Commons committee structures and infrastructure projects to offer concessions to the UUP in return for abstentions or votes for the government. Even before its majority was lost, Major's government secured UUP support in 1993 when pushing through a programme of coal mine closures in return for the promise of an electricity interconnector cable between Scotland and Northern Ireland plus financial support for heavy electricity users (Wynn Davies 1993). In February 1997 as a substantive minority government, the Conservatives gained further UUP support by promising that Northern

Ireland farmers would be the first to escape the ban on exports of beef to the EU amid the Bovine Spongiform Encephalopathy (or "Mad Cow Disease") crisis. A month later, in return for UUP support, they enhanced the powers of the Commons' Northern Ireland Grand Committee to question ministers and scrutinize legislation (Millar 1997).

As with Labour during the Lib-Lab Pact, one of the biggest problems faced by May's formal minority Conservative government (2017–19) was majority-building within the governing party itself. One hundred and eighty Conservative MPs voted against the party line during the 2017–19 parliament and there were thirty-four government defeats on votes relating to Brexit. An inability to maintain cohesion also saw legislation passed against the government's will. Rebellious Conservative MPs achieved enough support from across the House to pass an amendment to a government motion (for which only a simple majority is required) allowing for the suspension of Standing Order 14 (Cygan, Lynch, and Whitaker 2020), meaning backbenchers were able to control the agenda temporarily. During one of the periods covered by this suspension, the Commons considered a bill requiring the government to extend Article 50 (the process by which the UK was to leave the EU). This bill was passed against the government's wishes (Cowie and Samra 2019). Another non-government bill was passed in September 2019, forcing Prime Minister Johnson to ask the EU for another extension to the negotiating period.

On crucial motions therefore, the May II and Johnson I minority governments failed to build alliances in the Commons. In the case of the UK–EU withdrawal agreement, the support of the DUP was lacking due to policy differences. In the case of legislation to extend the UK's negotiating period, the May II and Johnson I governments failed to stop bills being passed against their will due to divisions within the Conservative Party. This suggests a crucial additional element to explanations of variation in the success of legislative majority-building, namely the level of dissent in the governing party.

Minority government performance

At the subsequent election, UK minority governments have tended to lose a slightly higher vote percentage than majority governments (a mean loss of 2.6 points for minority compared to 1.5 points for majority governments). The figures for minority governments, however, are heavily affected by the eleven-point loss suffered by Prime Minister Major in 1997 suggesting that, in other cases, the pattern is not that clear. Minority governments in the UK tend to be somewhat less successful at passing legislation than majority governments. Post-election minority governments are less durable than many if not all other governments in our period of study. However, because shorter terms (especially those lasting four of a possible five years) are often associated with success, cabinet duration does not always clearly measure government performance in the UK.

Table 15.2 allows us to assess how far there are variations in the percentage of government bills approved, the relative duration of governments and the type of government in office in the UK since 1945. If we discount the Johnson I government as an outlier,[2] the range of percentages of government bills being approved is fairly small, from a maximum of all bills being passed in the final session of Major's period as prime minister to 84.3 percent in Wilson's first government (1964–66), indicating a high degree of government success in many cases.

Field (2016: 18) points out that single-party majority governments usually have greater legislative success than minorities or majority coalitions. In the case of Spain, majority governments are slightly more successful than minority ones on this measure (Field 2016: 78–79). If we look at the UK case, based on data in Table 15.2, single-party majority governments passed 93.8 percent of government bills that were introduced. The figure for minority governments of any kind is 6.5 points lower at 87.3 percent, reflecting the greater constraints facing minority compared with majority governments. These results are consistent with findings elsewhere. Nevertheless, the figures mask some variation. Differences within the substantive minority cases are bigger than those between different types of government. Among the substantive minorities, government bill success varies from 30 percent for Johnson's first government, to 100 percent for Major's last session in power. It is difficult to make inferences here as there are few examples in the UK of the different types of minority government.

There is much variation in the relative duration of governments. The ability of governments to choose the timing of election, a situation that was somewhat altered for a period of time by the Fixed Term Parliaments Act 2011 (repealed in 2022), means that shorter periods of government are sometimes related to the incumbent government's likely electoral popularity. For instance, many prime ministers have called elections four years into a potential five-year term in an attempt to capitalize on favorable poll ratings. Others have tried to stay in office as long as possible when electoral success looks unlikely, such as Major in the run up to the 1997 election. All of this means it is difficult to make judgments based on relative duration figures. Furthermore, figures for governments where a new prime minister took over within a parliamentary term complicate comparisons especially where the change of prime minister happened towards the end of the maximum five-year period between elections. Nevertheless, if we just consider those governments which began their life as a minority (Wilson III, May II) they are much shorter in relative duration than most of the other governments (with

---

[2] This was a short-lived government that spent much of its time trying to bring about an election. It was dominated by Johnson's renegotiation of the UK's Withdrawal Agreement with the European Union.

Table 15.2 Legislative record and duration, 1945–2019, United Kingdom

Prime minister	Number of government bills presented	Number of government bills approved	Percent of government bills approved	Relative duration of government
Attlee I*	212	208	98.1	0.93
Attlee II	60	58	96.7	0.30
Churchill	199	183	92.0	0.68
Eden I	—	—	—	0.11
Eden II	121	116	95.9	0.32
Macmillan I	108	107	99.1	0.83
Macmillan II	183	179	97.8	0.80
Douglas-Home	64	63	98.4	1.00
Wilson I	102	86	84.3	0.28
Wilson II	285	255	89.5	0.80
Heath	225	207	92.0	0.70
Wilson III	39	35	89.7	0.12
Wilson IV	157	145	92.4	0.30
Callaghan I	—	—	—	—
Callaghan II	153	135	88.2	0.90
Thatcher I	224	215	96.0	0.80
Thatcher II	205	197	96.1	0.78
Thatcher III	122	120	98.4	0.73
Major I	91	82	90.1	1.00
Major II	158	157	99.4	0.93
Major III	37	37	100.0	1.00
Blair I	150	139	92.7	0.80
Blair II	143	126	88.1	0.78
Blair III	92	83	90.2	0.40
Brown	81	75	92.6	1.00
Cameron I	137	121	88.3	1.00
Cameron II	26	23	88.5	0.20
May I	27	24	88.9	0.25
May II	60	51	85.0	0.40
Johnson I	10	3	30.0	0.14

Notes: 1997–98 – 2019–19 sessions: UK House of Commons Sessional Returns; 1995–96 – 1996–97 sessions: UK House of Commons Sessional Information Digest; 1979–80 – 1994–95 sessions: Guardian (2016); 1947–48 – 1978–79 sessions, Public Bills accessed via UK Parliamentary Papers.
*Figures for Attlee I are based on data from 1947–50 as data for the 1945–46 and 1946–47 sessions were not available. Data on government bills presented and approved are only available at the level of parliamentary sessions (usually, but not always, a 12-month period beginning with a speech from the throne). In cases of intra-term minority governments (e.g. Major III), and cases where a new government is brought about by a change of prime minister without an election (e.g. Major I), these session dates do not always coincide precisely with the existence of the government. Nevertheless, in most cases the dates are very close. The Eden I (one month from him taking office to dissolution) and Callaghan I (one day) governments are too short for data on government bills to be measured.

some exceptions) if we exclude those resulting from a change of prime minister within a term. Overall though, minority governments are not consistently shorter governments. Instead, either formal or informal agreements, as we have seen, often help maintain governments in office.

Conclusion

The story of governments in the UK post-1945 is mainly one of single-party majorities. Notably, when minority situations do occur, parties are short of majorities often by small amounts. The nature of the party system means that minority governments then become viable with the support of only one small, often regionalist, party needed for a government to be formed and/or to continue in office. Governing parties are able to minimize concessions if these largely take the form of particularistic benefits provided at regional level. Smaller parties can push for these benefits due to the limited options available for governing parties looking for supportive votes in the Commons. This can lead to the persistence of intra-term minorities for longer than might otherwise be the case. Often, dissent within governing parties in the UK can be as problematic for minority governments as establishing relationships with support parties. Minority governments in the UK have achieved reasonable levels of legislative success with a mixture of formal and informal agreements with others. This provides further support for the contention (e.g. Strøm 1990) that minority governments are much less of a failure than they are often thought to be.

Many questions remain unanswered. One significant question concerns the rise of the SNP to the pivotal position of third party in UK politics. Assuming continued SNP dominance of many parliamentary constituencies in Scotland and the inability of the Liberal Democrats to convert votes into seats, the SNP will hold a decisive position in minority scenarios where the largest party is fifteen or more seats short of a majority. Surprisingly little has been written about this prospect. The SNP has little in common ideologically with the Conservatives. Beyond this, the SNP has made most of its gains at Westminster in former safe Labour seats since 2015. These factors make agreement with either of the largest parties difficult. In addition, it may be challenging for the party to promote its pro-independence and anti-Westminster stance at a devolved level while being part of a coalition government in Westminster. As such, more flexible minority agreements may be more attractive to the SNP.

Future research should focus on two areas. The first is on how the differing goals of parties might interact with the UK's changing political landscape to shape government formation in future minority situations. A better understanding of this would allow the electorate to see how their votes might translate into government composition when minority situations are predicted in opinion polls. The second is a more detailed analysis of the success of past minority governments in office, assessing the quality and salience of legislation passed under them.

References

Adams, James, Michael Clark, Lawrence Ezrow, and Garrett Glasgow. 2004. "Understanding Change and Stability in Party Ideologies: Do Parties Respond to Public Opinion or to Past Election Results?" *British Journal of Political Science* 34 (4): 589–610.

Audickas, Lukas, Richard Cracknell, and Philip Loft. 2020. "UK Election Statistics: 1918–2019: A Century of Elections." House of Commons Library Briefing Paper. CBP7529.

Bale, Tim, and Torbjørn Bergman. 2006. "Captives No Longer, but Servants Still? Contract Parliamentarism and the New Minority Governance in Sweden and New Zealand." *Government and Opposition* 41 (3): 422–449.

Bartlett, Gail, and David Torrance. 2020. "The 2017–19 Government at Westminster: Governing as a minority." House of Commons Library Briefing Paper. Number 08103.

Butler, David, and Dennis Kavanagh. 1974. *The British General Election of February, 1974*. London: St. Martin's Press.

Callaghan, James. 1987. *Time and Chance*. London: Politico's.

Callaghan, James, and David Steel. 1977. "Joint Statement issued by the Prime Minister James Callaghan and David Steel." The Times, March 24, 1977.

Cowie, Graeme, and Sandip Samra. 2019. "Insight: Taking Control of the Order Paper." House of Commons Library. [online] Available at: https://commonslibrary.parliament.uk/taking-control-of-the-order-paper/ [Accessed September 1, 2020].

Cowley, Philip. 2016. "Chaos or Cohesion? Major and Conservative Parliamentary Party." In *The Major Premiership: Politics and Policies under John Major, 1990–97*, ed. Pete Dorey. London: Springer, 1–12.

Cowley, Philip, and Dennis Kavanagh. 2017. *The British General Election of 2017*. London: Springer.

Crombez, Christophe. 1996. Minority Governments, Minimal Winning Coalitions and Surplus Majorities in Parliamentary Systems." *European Journal of Political Research* 29 (1): 1–29.

Cutts, David, and Andrew Russell. 2018. "The Liberal Democrats: Green Shoots of Recovery or Still on Life Support?" *Parliamentary Affairs* 71 (1): 72–90.

Cygan, Adam, Philip Lynch, and Richard Whitaker. 2020. "UK Parliamentary Scrutiny of the EU Political and Legal Space after Brexit." *Journal of Common Market Studies* 58 (6): 1605–1620.

Dennison, James. 2015. "The Other Insurgency? The Greens and the Election." *Parliamentary Affairs* 68 (S1): 188–205.

Dennison, James, and Matthew Goodwin. 2015. "Immigration, Issue Ownership and the Rise of UKIP." *Parliamentary Affairs* 68 (S1): 168–187.

Dorey, Peter. 2011. "'A Rather Novel Constitutional Experiment': The Formation of the 1977-8 'Lib-Lab Pact'." *Parliamentary History* 30 (3): 374–394.

Dorey, Peter. 2016. "'Should I Stay or Should I Go?': James Callaghan's Decision not to Call an Autumn 1978 General Election." *British Politics* 11 (1): 95–118.

Field, Bonnie N. 2016. *Why Minority Governments Work: Multilevel Territorial Politics in Spain*. Basingstoke: Palgrave.

Godbout, Jean-François, and Bjørn Høyland. 2011. "Coalition Voting and Minority Governments in Canada." *Commonwealth and Comparative Politics* 49 (4): 457–485.

Green, Jane, and Sara Hobolt. 2008. "Owning the Issue Agenda: Party Strategies and Vote Choices in British Elections." *Electoral Studies* 27 (3): 460–476.

Guardian. 2016. "EU Referendum Bill: How Many Private Members' Bills Pass." [online] Available at: https://www.theguardian.com/news/datablog/2013/may/15/eu-referendum-bill-cameron-data [Accessed September 1, 2020].

Haddon, Catherine. 2009. "A Brief History of the Lib-Lab Pact, 1977–78." In *Making Minority Government Work*, ed. Robert Hazell and Akash Paun. London: Institute for Government, 20–24.

House of Commons. 2018. Standing Orders of the House of Commons 2018. [online] Available at: https://publications.parliament.uk/pa/cm201719/cmstords/1020/body.html [Accessed September 2, 2020].

Kelly, Richard. 2019. "Prime Ministers." House of Commons Library Briefing Paper, Number 4256.

Kelso, Alexandra. 2015. "Parliament and Government Formation in the United Kingdom: A Hidden Vote of Investiture?" In *Parliaments and Government Formation: Unpacking Investiture Rules*, ed. BjørnErik Rasch, Shane Martin, and José Antonio Cheibub. Oxford: Oxford University Press, 29–48.

Kirchheimer, Otto. 1966. "The Transformation of Western European Party Systems." In *Political Parties and Political Development*, ed. Joseph LaPalombara and Myron Weiner. Princeton, NJ: Princeton University Press, 177–200.

Lijphart, Arend. 2012. *Patterns of Democracy: Government Forms and Performance in Thirty-Six Countries*. Second Edition. New Haven: Yale University Press.

Mellon, Jonathan, Geoffrey Evans, Edward Fieldhouse, Jane Green, and Christopher Prosser. 2018. "Brexit or Corbyn? Campaign and Inter-Election Vote Switching in the 2017 UK General Election." *Parliamentary Affairs* 71 (4): 719–737.

Millar, Frank. 1997. "Unionists the Main Beneficiaries as Major Wins Vital Vote in Commons." The Irish Times. [online] Available at: https://www.irishtimes.com/news/unionists-the-main-beneficiaries-as-major-wins-vital-vote-in-commons-1.43775. [Accessed September 1, 2020].

Müller, Wolfgang C., and Kaare Strøm, eds. 1999. *Policy, Office or Votes: How Political Parties in Western Europe Make Hard Decisions*. Cambridge: Cambridge University Press.

Murphy, Mary C., and Jonathan Evershed. 2019. "Between the Devil and the DUP: The Democratic Unionist Party and the Politics of Brexit." *British Politics* 15 (4): 456–477.

Norton, Philip. 1980. *Dissension in the House of Commons 1974–1979*. Oxford: Clarendon Press.

Norton, Philip. 2004. "Parliament." In *New Labour, Old Labour: The Wilson and Callaghan Governments, 1974–79*, ed. Anthony Seldon and Kevin Hickson. Abingdon: Routledge, 190–206.

Norton, Philip. 2013. *Parliament in British Politics*. Basingstoke: Palgrave.

Quinn, Thomas. 2013. "From Two-partism to Alternating Predominance: The Changing UK Party System, 1950–2010." *Political Studies* 61 (2): 378–400.

Russell, Meg and Daniel Gover. 2017. *Legislation at Westminster. Parliamentary Actors and Influence in the Making of British Law*. Oxford: Oxford University Press.

Saalfeld, Thomas. 2008. "Institutions, Chance, and Choices: The Dynamics of Cabinet Survival." In *Cabinets and Coalition Bargaining: The Democratic Life Cycle in Western Europe*, ed. Kaare Strøm, Wolfgang C. Müller, and Torbjörn Bergman. Oxford: Oxford University Press, 327–368.

Scottish National Party. 2017. Manifesto: Stronger for Scotland. [online] Available at: https://d3n8a8pro7vhmx.cloudfront.net/thesnp/pages/9544/attachments/original/1496320559/Manifesto_06_01_17.pdf?1496320559 [Accessed September 8, 2020].

Smith, Jeremy. 2006. "'Ever Reliable Friends?' The Conservative Party and Ulster Unionism in the Twentieth Century." *English Historical Review* 121 (490): 70–103.

Steel, David. 1989. *Against Goliath: David Steel's Story*. London: Weidenfeld and Nicolson.

Strøm, Kaare. 1990. *Minority Government and Majority Rule*. Cambridge: Cambridge University Press.

Tonge, Jonathan. 2017. "Supplying Confidence or Trouble: The Deal between the Democratic Unionist Party and the Conservative Party." *Political Quarterly* 88 (3): 412–416.

Tsebelis, George. 2002. *Veto Players: How Political Institutions Work*. Princeton: Princeton University Press.

Wilson, Harold. 1979. *Final Term: The Labour Government 1974–1976*. London: Weidenfeld and Nicolson.

Wynn Davies, Patricia. 1993. "Ulster Unionist MPs 'Will Keep Major in Power.'" The Independent. [online] Available at: https://www.independent.co.uk/news/ulster-unionist-mps-will-keep-major-in-power-1484006.html [Accessed September 6, 2020].

Ziegler, Philip. 2010. *Edward Heath*. London: Harper Press.

16
Comparative Conclusions on Minority Governments

Bonnie N. Field and Shane Martin

Minority governments are no longer viewed as some kind of anomaly. But because most accounts of parliamentarism entail a government having the (at least occasionally revealed) support of a majority of the legislature, minority governments have remained something of a puzzle. And the conundrum of minority governments has challenged many of political sciences' fundamental assumptions concerning what motivates and shapes the behavior of political parties and legislators and how these preferences interact with political institutions and the "rules of the game" to shape who gets to govern, why, how, and with what consequences.

Three questions have dominated this volume: First, why do minority governments form, not least given the understanding that minimum—or minimal—winning governing coalitions are the expected outcome of legislative elections where no party wins a majority of seats? Second, reflecting a growing shift away from studying government formation in isolation from the governance stage of the parliamentary lifecycle (Bergman, Bäck, and Hellström 2021), we explored how minority governments operate once in office. Finally, and relatedly, we wanted to understand how minority governments perform, especially as they compare to periods of majority government in the respective country setting. In this concluding chapter, we summarize key findings from the thirteen cases which have formed the backbone of this volume, focusing on what we believe contributes to previously unresolved debates, unexplored or underexplored topics, and fruitful directions for further research in the study of minority governments. Many aspects of our conventional understanding of minority governments have been confirmed in the preceding chapters, but the cases also challenge many established perspectives and bring forward heretofore neglected or discounted aspects of minority government formation, operation, and performance.

Before exploring each of these themes, we briefly return to the topic of minority government frequency.

Bonnie N. Field and Shane Martin, *Comparative Conclusions on Minority Governments*. In: *Minority Governments in Comparative Perspective*. Edited by Bonnie N. Field and Shane Martin, Oxford University Press.
© Bonnie N. Field and Shane Martin (2022). DOI: 10.1093/oso/9780192871657.003.0016

Definition, frequency, and undercounting

In Chapter 1, we noted the generally accepted definition of a minority government as a government in which the party or parties that hold cabinet posts in the executive do not simultaneously hold a majority of seats in the legislature. Despite the parsimony of this definition, we also noted a number of potential challenges to operationalizing that definition, including what constitutes a majority, and, especially, what is meant by "legislature"—in a context of bicameral systems, where the government may be politically responsible to only one chamber (typically) or both (exceptionally).

We also observed, on average, a modest decrease in the number of seats held by the governing party or parties in the largest parliamentary democracies over the last decades. We noted that approximately one-third of parliamentary democracies are or are typically government by a minority cabinet. Over recent decades, Denmark has the highest proportion of minority cabinets, at 100 percent.

As we alluded to in the opening chapter, we suggested a modification to how scholars codify a change in cabinet, with consequences for how we measure the number of minority, as opposed to majority, governments. Most datasets on cabinet membership record a change in government as happening when one or more of the following conditions are met: a change in the partisan composition of the cabinet, a change of head of government, or a general election. This criterion ignores as a change in cabinet a situation where a sitting government loses its majority or gains a majority in parliament without a general election, a change in partisan composition, or a new head of government. By not recognizing such situations as a change in cabinet (instead relying on the status of the cabinet at the government formation stage), conventional counting practices likely undercount minority governments.

We remedied this in our country studies by asking the authors to classify a change in majority or minority status as constituting a new cabinet. We also asked them to determine the majority or minority status of the government in the chamber, chambers, or parliament as a whole that can hold the government responsible. This revised criterion has consequences for the number of minority governments recorded. For example, in the United Kingdom, minority governments emerge mid-term when governing-party MPs resign, are removed, or die in office, exacerbated by instances where opposition parties win the subsequent by-election. For instance, PM John Major had a majority in parliament when he took office after the April 1992 elections; however, he lost that majority in 1996, subsequently governing in minority. In Italy, for example, because a cabinet can be removed if it loses a vote of no confidence in either chamber, our counting criterion identified far more minority governments than the conventional counting rules. In the period between 1990 and 2020, 44 percent of Italian governments are minority using our rule, compared to only 16 percent using conventional datasets. One instance is the

2014 Renzi government, which had a (super) majority in the Chamber of Deputies but only a minority of seats in the Senate of the Republic. These findings suggest that minority governments cross-nationally may be undercounted.

Why?

An analysis of the thirteen country studies presented in this volume allow us to revisit why minority governments form in a minority situation. Overall, one message predominates: different parties in different countries prioritize different goals, and perhaps at different times, with regard to future electoral considerations, policy orientation, or interest in joining the cabinet with clear consequences for what types of governments form (Strøm 1990a, 1990b). However, this also illustrates and corroborates the difficulty of building a general theory based on assuming a particular fixed party goal, such as office or policy. Let's first discuss party systems.

Party system configuration

Our country studies near universally argue that characteristics of the party system shape why minority governments form. Taken together, they illustrate that distinct party system traits may lead to minority governments. However, there is no single type of party system in our set of cases that accounts for them. Comparative evidence from this volume suggests that the types of component actors in the party system, the nature of the parties or legislators themselves, may be as or more important than their number and size.

High fragmentation is not a necessary condition for minority governments. As Table 16.1 shows, minority governments form in high, moderate, and low fragmentation party systems. Even though we would expect minority governments to be less prevalent in low fragmentation party systems—since minority situations should be less frequent—minority governments are common in Canada, France, and Portugal.

We first turn to a set of explanations that focus on the weight, size, and/or distance between parties. First, there are those that rely on the strong bargaining position of a lead party to explain minority government formation (Crombez 1996; Laver and Shepsle 1996; Laver and Schofield 1998). With regard to the core party thesis, on Italy, Giannetti argues that the disappearance of a core party in the Italian Second Republic helps account for the decline in minority governments compared to the 1946 to 1992 period when the Christian Democrats were a core party. Similarly, in Sweden and India, the historically dominant and central positions of the Social Democrats and the Congress Party, respectively, were cited as

Table 16.1 Party system fragmentation and minority governments

	Party system fragmentation	Prevalence of minority government
Italy	High	Common[a]
India	High	Predominant
Norway	High	Predominant
Sweden	High	Predominant
Poland	High	Common
Ireland	Moderate	Common
Romania	Moderate	Predominant
Spain	Moderate	Predominant
Canada	Low	Common
France	Low	Common
Australia	Low	Exceptional
Portugal	Low	Common
UK	Low	Exceptional

Notes: See notes on Tables 1.1 and 1.2 of Chapter 1.
[a] Categorization changed from the case selection criterion to the counting rule developed in Chapter 1.

a factor explaining the prevalence of minority governments. However, within the same country, core and non-core parties have governed in minority, including in Canada, Portugal, and Spain.

In countries with a dominant party and/or with two-party dominant systems in which one party wins a near majority, such strong parties appear to be well positioned to resist coalitions and instead govern alone in minority. Also, in such systems, the gap between the largest party and any potential ally would likely mean a minimal presence in government, based on Gamson's Law. Thus, the costs of governing may not be worth it for such smaller parties. Moreover, since single-party government may long have been the norm, the prospect of coalescing in a multiparty government may represent something of a step too far for some political parties (as in, for example, Australia, Canada, and, until the 1980s, Ireland, as well as the Portuguese Socialists). Even in the more fragmented party system of Romania, Anghel concludes that minority government formation "is mostly the result of party system features—such as the existence of dominant parties and polarizing electoral competition."

However, even where strong, near majority parties have existed, minority governments are not always formed by a core party. As Godbout and Cochrane note regarding Canada, the core party thesis may be able to explain the formation of Liberal single-party minority governments but not Conservative ones. This similarly applies in Spain where before the 2015 change of the party system both core (the Socialists) and non-core (the conservative Popular Party) near majority parties formed single-party minority governments. Notably, the Popular Party *tried* to form a coalition with regionally-based parties in 1996. It was the latter that refused and therefore the formation of a minority government was not *because of* the former's strong bargaining position.

In other countries, our cases studies draw attention to distinct characteristics of the party system that constrain bargaining, limiting the possible governing options on the table, and in turn making minority government a likelier outcome. On Norway, Strøm suggests that minority governments result in part from two-bloc politics, a feature shared by Sweden and Denmark, which limit alliances to one side of the socialist/non socialist divide. If parties want to avoid coalitions with uncomfortable allies in their bloc, minority governments result. Nikoleyni's contribution on India points to pre-electoral alliances. Without a majority post-election, it may be potentially costly to break ranks with one's pre-electoral alliance. Thus, parliamentary arithmetic and pre-negotiated alliances constrained coalition bargaining and resulted in minority governments.

Dramatic party system change resulting in greater fragmentation, polarization, or both in countries such as Ireland and Spain, yet with the persistence of minority governments, suggest that the types of parties (or MPs) in the party systems may matter as much or more than their number and weight. This of course relates to party goals discussed previously. But, the case studies demonstrate that the relevance of some party families in the government formation process fosters or facilitates minority governments. This seems particularly true of (regionally-based) nationalist parties, which appear to be more resistant to joining national cabinets (e.g. in Canada, Ireland, and Spain). And there are a variety of parties willing to let minority governments form in exchange for policy or pork concessions and/or to avoid the costs of governing. This includes the nationalist parties mentioned previously, as well as independents in Ireland and Australia, regional parties in India and the UK, and ethno-regional parties and rogue parliamentarians in Romania. Notably, all of these parties (or independents) are not at the fringes of the party systems—for example some regionally-based parties in Spain or independents in Ireland are located ideologically in the center. Radical parties may be excluded from government (e.g. the populist radical right in Sweden), as uncomfortable allies, or exclude themselves (the radical left in Portugal). Though others have been included or demanded inclusion, such as the radical left in Spain or the radical right in Norway. Therefore, it does not appear that the relevance of radical left or right parties, at least in the period examined here, provides much of a firm guide to the type of government formed in a particular country context.

Thus, it is clear that the party system shapes the formation of minority governments. But, it does not appear that one type of party system accounts for them. We now turn to institutions.

Parliamentary investiture rules

Investiture consists of a vote in parliament to demonstrate that an about to be formed or already formed government has legislative support (Rasch, Martin, and Cheibub 2015). Many of our case studies appear to confirm earlier work that the absence of a formal investiture vote (or one with a negative form) works to *facilitate* the emergence of minority governments (Bergman 1993; Strøm 1990b). As Bäck and Hellström note in their chapter, the investiture vote in Sweden is negatively formulated—the person nominated by the speaker to be prime minister is only blocked from office if half of all legislators vote against the nominee. Sweden represents an example of *negative parliamentarism*—government must only be tolerated by the parliament, and does not need to have the support of a majority of its members in order for a government to form. And minority governments form often. In India, where minority governments are also predominant, confidence confirming votes do happen, but not always, and with reduced frequency over time.

But, several countries where minority governments are predominant or common show that stronger investiture requirements do not prevent minority governments. In Spain, a formal investiture vote in the Congress of Deputies is required for a government to be formed. In Ireland, a double-investiture vote is required for the cabinet composition to be confirmed. In Romania, the government needs the support of the absolute majority of the deputies and senators. Hence, while investiture votes in parliament represent a hurdle to the formation of a minority government, they are just that: an obstacle that can be and often is overcome. Thus the correlation between minority government and lower hurdles for investiture is far from perfect, as Table 16.2 shows.

Beyond how investiture rules shape the prevalence of minority governments, our country studies reveal two significant insights. First, investiture rules and the formation of minority governments interact in particular national contexts, and often in unexpected ways. While Poland has an investiture rule for initial government formation, minority governments at times form after an incumbent cabinet breaks down and moves into minority status. At that time, Zubek notes, no new investiture vote is required, thus allowing a sitting government to simply continue. The situation in the United Kingdom is similar, with no immediate requirement for re-investiture allowing the emergence of a mid-term minority government, as Jones and Whitaker note.[1] In France, Rozenberg cites the absence of a compulsory investiture vote in the National Assembly as a significant reason for the existence of minority governments—a presidential decree is sufficient to confirm a new government. This has allowed several one-month minority governments to

---

[1] The vote on the Queen's Speech at the opening of each parliamentary term acts as an ex post investiture vote.

Table 16.2 Government formation rules and minority governments

	Formation hurdle	Prevalence of minority government
India	Lower	Predominant
Norway	Lower	Predominant
Sweden	Lower	Predominant
Canada	Lower	Common
France	Lower	Common
Portugal	Lower	Common
Australia	Lower	Exceptional
Poland	Higher[a]	Common
Ireland	Higher	Common
Romania	Higher	Predominant
Spain	Higher	Predominant
UK	Higher	Exceptional
Italy	Higher	Common[b]

Notes: See notes on Tables 1.1 and 1.3 of Chapter 1.
[a] An investiture vote is not required if a sitting prime minister reshuffles the cabinet or loses their majority. See Zubek, this volume.
[b] Based on the counting rule developed in Chapter 1, this volume.

form when the opposition wins the presidential election and while parliament is in recess to campaign for the upcoming parliamentary elections.

Second, while most research has examined how investiture rules impact the types of government that form, our country studies show that institutions are in some cases endogenous. For two of our younger democracies, Spain and Portugal, Field and Fernandes, respectively, argue that investiture rules were designed at the constitution-shaping stage to facilitate minority government formation (and governance in Spain). In Portugal, this meant no formal investiture vote, which would permit the Portuguese Socialists to govern without allying with parties to its left. In Spain, investiture rules were written with a minority government in power, and allowed the possibility of a government being selected with a lower, simple-majority rule in a second-round investiture vote in Spain, and with an eye to strengthening governments. Thus, the causal arrow can go in the other direction.

Legislative organization and opposition influence

By some conventional accounts (Strøm 1990b), the presence of strong committees within the legislature provides an opportunity for parties outside government to influence public policy. Strong committees thus create incentives for parties (or parties interested in policy) to remain outside government, potentially increasing

Table 16.3 Opposition influence in parliament and minority governments

	Opposition influence	Prevalence of minority government
Italy	Strong	Common[a]
Romania	Strong	Predominant
Poland	Average (Above)	Common
Portugal	Average (Above)	Common
Sweden	Average (Above)	Predominant
France[b]	Average	Common
Ireland	Average (Below)	Common
UK	Average (Below)	Exceptional
Norway	Average (Below)	Predominant
Canada	Weak	Common
Australia	Weak	Exceptional
Spain	Weak	Predominant
India	Weak	Predominant

Notes: See notes on Tables 1.1 and 1.3 of Chapter 1. Opposition influence categorized by the authors based on Wegmann (2022). This table breaks the *average* category into two subcategories, *above* and *below* average. *Above* refers to those cases that are within one standard deviation above the average in the Wegmann study; *below* refers to cases within one standard deviation below the average. France falls at the cross-national average (0.588), with a score of 0.59.
[a] Based on the counting ruled developed in Chapter 1.
[b] Based on the authors' coding.

the propensity for minority governments to form. To our knowledge, this has not been tested quantitatively in cross-national studies. Particularly outside of the Scandinavian cases, we found little evidence in our country case studies that the strength of the legislature's committee system impacts minority government formation. Additionally, Table 16.3 shows little correlation between the parliamentary opposition's influence, measured in terms of institutional features, and the prevalence of minority governments.

Two potential reasons for this are that parties are less policy-oriented than heretofore considered, or committees within the legislature do not provide the alternative avenues to policy influence that some expected. And here, the Italian case may be most illuminating, as Giannetti suggests that "committees have ceased to work as a privileged setting for negotiation over policy among governing and opposition parties but have increasingly become a bargaining arena for the members of governing coalitions." In Portugal, committees are weak and provide few avenues for opposition, with the budget process serving as an alternative focal point for the opposition to attempt to influence policy.

However, we suspect that strong committees are but one way to institutionalize influence over public policy for parties that remain outside of government, and are therefore not necessary to assure it. Contracts, other agreements, and non-cabinet offices, which we discuss further ahead, also affect parties' calculations about policy influence.

Further illustrating the challenges of endogeneity, Nikolenyi argues, the shift to minority governments in India led to a strengthening of committees in the *Lok Sabha*. As with investiture rules, this questions the direction of causality between strong committees within the legislature and the formation of minority governments in some cases.

Feedback loops

Jointly the country analyses also suggest that experiences with minority or other types of government feed back into formation decisions. Where single-party governments have been the norm, parties in Australia and Canada view them as the default whether they are in a majority or not, as noted by Crowley, and Godbout and Cochrane, respectively. On Spain, Field notes that a prior history of unstable coalition government in the Second Republic led many political actors to prefer single-party governments, even if in minority. On Portugal, Fernandes suggests that minority government success in delivering public policy, in part, creates enduring incentives for their formation. If such reasoning is correct, the generally strong performance of minority government that we discuss later becomes potentially very important for helping to account for their prevalence.

How?

The country studies presented in this volume also allow us to reach a number of conclusions about how minority governments govern. We first turn to the types of minority government.

Types of minority government

It is common, and often useful, to distinguish between minority governments that have an explicit agreement with a political party or parties in parliament that is negotiated prior to government formation, provides more than a short-term commitment to the government's agenda and survival, and brings the government's support to a majority; and those that do not, that is, Strøm's (1990b) formal and substantive categories. However, the country studies make several additional contributions.

First, this distinction can mask a great deal of variation that is significant for understanding how minority governments operate. Romanian parties, for example, tend to rely on informal support arrangements between party leaders and vague commitments, as Anghel notes. Some support agreements were formalized after the government formed, and therefore would not meet Strøm's (1990b) criteria, and most are not comprehensive. Yet, half of the minority governments in Romania relied on at least one explicit agreement. In Ireland, where substantive minority governments are most common, Weeks notes that formal relationships between (potential) external supporters and minority governments have entailed a vote for investiture without a commitment beyond the government formation, and negotiated deals that imply an ongoing commitment. However, the latter are not often made public. The same occurs in Spain. Even when formal minority governments were in power there in the 1990s, the agreements upon which they relied were not comprehensive and they co-existed with the possibility of opposition from support parties. Field's chapter on Spain also draws our attention to the difficulty of determining what should qualify as a support agreement and indeed as a support party. In sum, the country studies show it may at times be useful to relax the substantive versus formal minority government dichotomy.

Second, among our rich selection of cases, there is little evidence of a general trend to date toward contract parliamentarism (Bale and Bergman 2006). This is a governing arrangement where relations between the minority government and support parties are so highly institutionalized that it resembles majority government. In many countries where minority governments predominate or are common, formal minority government, let alone contract parliamentarism, is not prevalent. In Canada, Norway, Poland, and Portugal, ad hoc majority building in parliament is most common. In Romania, most parties prefer informal support arrangements. In Spain, formal minority governments are far less common than substantive ones and the latter have been more recent.[2]

This does not mean that contracts or contract parliamentarism are irrelevant. As mentioned previously, they are one important way to attempt to ensure cooperation and policy influence. Contract parliamentarism became common in post-1990s Sweden, in contrast to more ad hoc arrangements previously, as Bäck and Hellström note. Nikolenyi shows the gradual development of contract parliamentarism in India, which meant establishing progressively more formal and sophisticated practices to lock in minority coalition members and support parties. Linking the *how* and the *how well*—to which we return later—several authors attribute better minority government performance to formalized support agreements, including in Portugal (Costa, 2015–19), Australia (Gillard, 2010–13), Romania, and India, which is in line with quantitative research that associates them with durability and legislative success (Thürk 2021; Krauss and Thürk 2022).

[2] We know from research on multiparty government that coalition agreements are important documents, dictating the agreed coalition compromise and adding structure to how multiparty governments govern. This line of research could be expanded to explore the substance, shape, and length of agreements between minority governments and support parties.

In sum, our chapters provide evidence of the strategic use of a complex array of arrangements and relationships with parties in parliament, along the lines of Boston and Bullock (2012), rather than a trend toward a particular arrangement.

Motivations and majority-building arrangements

The chapters illustrate the complex mix of multiple goals (and across different combinations of parties) that can lead to distinct majority-building arrangements. While very difficult to do methodologically, this is an area where further comparative research is needed. Many of the chapters reveal the motivations behind distinct majority-building arrangements. Notably, Strøm argues that the few center-right formal minority governments in Norway reflect the weakness of the governing parties, whereas Labor minority governments have felt relatively secure in their ability to secure support ad hoc. In Romania, Anghel notes that the scarcity of formalized agreements is a sign of parties' disinterest in the implementation of specific policies and short-term strategies. In Poland, where formal agreements are also scarce, support parties are often wary of openly supporting governments tainted by corruption scandals.

In Portugal, coalescing difficulties between left-wing parties creates incentives for minority governments on the left, generally, and substantive ones, particularly. However, specific electoral and policy motivations led to a formalized agreement among left parties in Portugal in 2015. In Canada too, the same incentives for the formation of minority governments also encourage substantive minority governments. The party system, with national and regional parties, facilitates ad hoc voting alliances in part because a majority can always be built on at least two types of issues: left–right ideological and center–periphery regional.

While explicit agreements are the product of negotiation and interparty (or party–MP) commitments, the chapters show an array of reasons why parties may opt for ad hoc arrangements. This suggest there may be greater variation among substantive minority governments when it comes to performance and other outcomes.

Territorial politics

Since much of the early work on minority governments focused on parliamentary systems in unitary or more centralized states, less attention was paid to how multilevel and/or territorial politics affect how minority governments work (Field 2016). More recent research demonstrates that we need to pay attention to territorial politics in many countries (Godbout and Høyland 2011; Sridharan 2012; Field 2014). Our country studies further this understanding.

In several countries, territorial politics and national identity divisions affect parties' goals (Field 2016, 141–156; Reniu 2002). As mentioned previously, several regionally-based parties are reluctant or opposed to entering a central government as a coalition partner. This includes parties such as the nationalist Bloc Québécois in Canada, the Catalan and Basque nationalist parties in Spain and the Democratic Unionist Party (DUP) and Scottish National Party in the United Kingdom, as well as several regional parties in India. But, these same parties often opt to support minority governments from the outside in exchange for concessions. This dynamic in Spain outlasted a change to a more fragmented party system and indeed the greater polarization of parties on the center–periphery dimension of party competition. A frequent ally of the minority coalition government of the Socialists and United We Can government (2020-) there is the Republican Left of Catalonia, a party that supported the unilateral (though unsuccessful) declaration of independence in Catalonia in 2017.

A strong center–periphery cleavage and the presence of regional (and, in some cases, nationalist) parties allows governments to make deals on issues pertaining to at least two policy dimensions, the center–periphery and the left–right. This also impacts concessions. For example, in the UK, the 2017 May Conservative minority government signed an agreement to provide additional financial support to Northern Ireland in exchange for the DUP's support. In Spain, parties governing in minority governments at the national level often provide support to regional parties to govern at the subnational level, where they are office seeking.

Regional parties are not important in federal Australia. Nonetheless, Crowley argues that the Labor minority government of PM Gillard (2010–13) built on the experience of minority government in the states and territories, including the use of formal support agreements with the policy-seeking Greens and independents. While this volume focuses on national government, this shows that governing dynamics in the subnational arena are potentially important, whether regional and national governance are linked or not (Downs 1998; Ştefuriuc 2009, 2013).

Support parties and support MPs

Regarding support parties and MPs, the country studies reaffirm the importance of distinct goals, including office, policy, and electoral (Bergman 1995; Strøm 1990a, b; Ganghof and Bräuninger 2006), not only for understanding why parties opt to stay out of government, but also the types of support they are willing to provide externally, if any, and the concessions they demand.

Two observation are important. First, primarily policy-seeking parties, which make up a large share of support parties, come from a variety of party families. This includes ethno-regional parties in Romania, radical left and communist parties in Portugal and France, regional-nationalist parties in Spain and Canada, Greens in Australia, and regional parties in India and the UK.

Second, there are some parallels between MPs in candidate-centered electoral systems, such as in Australia, Ireland, and France, and regional parties. Australia and Ireland show that a similar goal-centered framework can be used to analyze independent MPs. For example, independents in Ireland often have a precarious hold on their seat; therefore, constituency-specific concessions can help bolster the electoral chances. This makes concessions to independents in Ireland, from the perspective of a minority government, less costly than might be the case for parties. However, this should not be overstated—regional parties often have both particularistic and ideologically-oriented policy goals.

Concessions to support parties and other allies

As implied by the previous discussion, concessions to support parties and allies vary greatly. For policy, Strøm's (1990b: 98–99) range from general policy concessions on one end to particularlistic benefits, often referred to as pork-barrel politics, on the other remains relevant. Detailed policy agreements, such as those found in Sweden, thus, would fall on one end of the spectrum. Somewhere in the middle, we see central government regionalized investment concessions to regional support parties in the UK. At the other end, we see potentially corrupt benefits to individuals in Romania. In Ireland and France, individual opposition parliamentarians are also targeted with constituency-oriented spending in return for supporting the government.

An important take away from this volume is that office concessions are also important. While Strøm also referred to potential subcabinet office concessions, the literature since has paid less attention to office concessions (though see Field 2016). In Poland, for example, office concessions in the form of seats on boards of state-owned enterprises and jobs for activists in public agencies acted as an important inducement for new populist and radical parties that sought office spoils as a means to reward supporters and expand their party networks. In Sweden, support parties have been given non-cabinet appointments in the government, further indication of the existence of contract parliamentarism. In Spain, national minority governments often facilitate governance for regional parties in their regions. Support parties there have also attained posts on state regulatory boards. In Italy, office concessions have taken the form of parliamentary positions, such as rapporteur or important committee chairs. As discussed previously, we believe office concessions, contracts, and strong committees serve as a variety of mechanisms through which policy influence can be secured.

Intraparty politics

An area that has received less attention in the study of minority governments is intraparty politics. A relevant exception is Field (2016: 167–172), who argues that interparty agreements in Spain are possible in part because political parties are disciplined. Horizontal party discipline is important to secure parliamentary agreements, and vertical party discipline to ensure that multilevel agreements that link national and regional governance are carried out. Our country studies provide additional insights. On the UK, Jones and Whitaker argue that dissent within single-party minority governments was at times as problematic as establishing relationships with support parties. In contrast, party switching in Romania has at times undermined and at other times shored up minority governments. Personal ambitions led party leaders and individual members of parliament to switch parties at key moments, at times ensuring the continuation of individual payoffs or greater ones. This indicates that further research is necessary to understand better how intraparty politics impacts the functioning of a minority government.

In sum, our country studies have provided additional insight into how minority governments in distinct national contexts govern. We now turn to how well minority governments govern once in office.

How well?

Of course, governments govern not in their interest but, at least in theory, to make and implement good public policy. Our final task assigned to our country study authors was to explore how well minority governments governed, and to see if meaningful contrasts and comparisons could be made with periods of majority government within the country. Any such quest to assess a minority government's performance could include almost limitless litmus tests of success, including citizens' satisfaction, good governance indicators, democracy measures, quality of life indices, anti-corruption measures, and a whole raft of economic tests. We asked the country experts to consider, where possible and useful, three often-used indicators: the volume of legislation produced (as a proxy for policy innovation and the capacity of the minority government to produce new public policy), the amount of time the government was able to survive in office (perhaps the most primeval measure of a government's "success"), and/or how the electorate subsequently rewarded or punished governing parties at the subsequent election. We also encouraged them to go beyond standard indicators where fruitful to contextualize performance. We note two main conclusions: (a) minority governments generally and often perform well, and (b) some perform better than others in the same country.

Minority governments, generally and often, perform well

Despite the wide variety of country cases in the volume, the general picture that emerges is that minority governments perform pretty well. It is particularly interesting that comparisons between minority and majority government *in the same country* generally conclude that minority governments tend to perform comparably to majority governments. On Ireland, Weeks finds that minority governments are generally as productive, survive as long, and are no less electorally unsuccessful as majority counterparts. On Italy, Giannetti finds that minority cabinets do not differ greatly from their majority counterparts in terms of duration and legislative effectiveness. On Portugal, Fernandes presents evidence that minority governments perform (at least) as well as majority governments. On Romania, Anghel argues that while minority cabinets are among the most and least durable, they are similar to majority cabinets in terms of legislative success. On Spain, Field argues minority governments have often performed as well as their majority counterparts. On Sweden, Bäck and Hellström find no systematic difference between how minority and majority governments perform in Sweden.

There are (partial) exceptions. In Canada, minority governments survive less long and are always less productive than majority governments. However, Godbout and Cochrane also show they provide more opportunities for opposition party members to influence the legislative process and are more responsive to public opinion. Zubek suggests that Polish minority cabinets have had a mixed record in legislative performance. Majority governments outperform minority cabinets overall by a small margin, though some minority governments perform on a par with those having a majority status.

Minority governments are not always equally successful across our standard measures. In the Irish case, minority governments are actually more productive (controlling for length of time in office), and lose fewer votes at the subsequent election than majority governments, but majority governments last considerably longer. Rozenberg goes so far as to characterize the longer-lasting minority government in France as having been particularly successful in terms of public policy (but not the volume legislation), but he notes a major contrast between policy achievement and the electoral outputs: the governing Socialists experienced what was at that time their worst electoral defeat in the 1993 parliamentary elections. Fernandes concludes that in Portugal minority governments deliver on as many pledges and pass as many laws as majority governments, but they are less stable and more prone to early termination.

Some perform better than others

We do observe within-country variation in terms of minority government performance, suggesting that not all minority governments are equal to one another in terms of performance. Our country studies suggest that there may be multiple and alternative conditions for success: a strong partisan bargaining position (such as a core party in government), formalized agreements (such as contract parliamentarism), and/or government-strengthening institutions (such as strong agenda control).

In some countries, governments with a strong partisan bargaining position performed better than those that were in a weaker position. For example, in Spain, while minority governments have often performed as well as majority governments, minority governments since 2015 have tended to perform less well, which Field attributes in part to post-2016 minority governments controlling far fewer seats. In India, minority governments that control over 40 percent of legislative seats actually outperform single-party governments, but minority governments further away from having a majority of seats were significantly less stable, less durable, and less productive in terms of bill passage. In the Polish case, Zubek argues "minority cabinets formed by a core party and those formed by non-core parties with external support perform better than unsupported cabinets formed by non-core parties." However, a core position did not guarantee high performance if the PM's party was not disciplined.

Others find that formal minority governments, contract parliamentarism or some type of formalized agreement between the government and support parties bolster performance vis-à-vis those that do not, in line with recent quantitative cross-national studies (Thürk 2021; Krauss and Thürk 2022). In addition to Poland, this includes the exceptional formal minority governments of PM Costa in Portugal and PM Gillard in Australia, minority governments in Romania that rely on agreements (even if they do not bring the government to a majority), and contract parliamentarism in India.

Others draw attention to the importance of government-strengthening institutions for minority government performance (Field 2016), in contrast to accounts that posit the importance of parliament- or opposition-favoring institutions for minority government formation. On Spain, Field argues that partisan bargaining circumstances, the reconcilability of party goals and political institutions affect performance. Regarding the latter, governments have agenda-setting advantages, can carry budgets over into a new year and issue executive decree laws, and cannot be removed unless there is a constructive vote of no confidence (in other words, an alternative must be identified and supported simultaneously). In France, Rozenberg argues that the government has a diversity of tools under rationalized parliamentarism that helped minority governments last. Notable is the ability to pass legislation without an assembly vote. And no-confidence votes require an absolute majority, again making it difficult to remove the incumbent government because abstentions and no votes favor the government. As Zubek notes in his chapter on Poland, perhaps as consequential for the duration of minority cabinets, the government can only be removed if the Sejm passes a constructive no-confidence vote, two-thirds of all MPs support early elections, or the government loses a confidence vote it has called.

In addition to these variables, some chapters suggest that scholars may have underestimated the importance of leadership skill and political culture for making minority governments work. In her chapter on Australia, Crowley notes that "minority government tests the negotiating skills of major party politicians." PM Gillard was methodical about the government's agenda. Though she was a skilled negotiator and highly effective at running the government, she was unable to effectively sell its achievements to the public. For Rozenberg, strong performance in France was attributable to institutional, political (accommodating partners in parliament) and managerial variables. Regarding the latter, he draws our attention to the governing team's extensive knowledge of parliament and its members.

Finally, on Norway, Strøm argues that a political culture that counts on high levels of interpersonal trust "allows party leaders to take longer-term views of their political interests and avoid more conflictual forms of political contestation."

Conclusion

This volume has examined minority governments in countries where they are predominant, common, and exceptional, in party systems with different numbers, sizes, ranges, and types of political parties, and in political systems with a variety of institutional arrangements. The contributors were thus able to address the why, how, and how well of minority governments in distinct national contexts. Comparatively, we highlight several key conclusions:

1. Minority governments cross-nationally have likely been undercounted. We offer a modified counting rule on cabinet change to remedy this, where solely switching from a majority to minority status, or vice versa constitutes a new cabinet (even without a change of prime minister, general election, or change in partisan composition of the cabinet).
2. Party systems clearly shape the formation and functioning of minority governments. Nonetheless, no particular party system appears necessary for either. The comparative evidence from this volume suggests that the types

of component actors in the party system may be as or more important than the number and size of the parties in the system.
3. While investiture rules present a hurdle to the formation of a minority government, they are just that—a hurdle that can and often is overcome.
4. Strong parliamentary committees may certainly affect parties' calculations about governing formulas. However, among our cases, there is little evidence outside of the Scandinavian democracies that this helps explain cross-national patterns of minority government formation.
5. Instead, strong committees are one way to institutionalize influence over public policy for parties that stay out of government—others include contracts and agreements and the allocation of non-cabinet offices to support parties.
6. Institutions are at times endogenous. Investiture rules and committee strength sometimes result from the existence of a minority government, and not the reverse.
7. There does not appear to be a trend toward contract parliamentarism. Instead, a wide variety of minority government arrangements continue to characterize the relationship between minority governments and (potential) allies.
8. The territorial dimension of politics matters for understanding minority governments in a wide variety of countries. This includes regional parties, multilevel state exchanges, and multidimensional competition/cooperation.
9. Office concessions to supporters are important, including subcabinet offices in governments, regional offices, positions on state regulatory boards or on boards of state enterprises, and (non-cabinet) parliamentary megaseats.
10. Minority governments, generally and often, work well or comparably to majority governments in the same country. This is striking given the diversity of countries covered in this volume. This provides further evidence—as Strøm noted decades ago—that they are a rational cabinet solution, which, we think, feeds back into their formation.
11. Our country studies suggest that there may be multiple and alternative conditions for success: a strong partisan bargaining position (such as a core party in government), formalized agreements (such as contract parliamentarism), and/or government-strengthening institutions (such as strong agenda control).

Cumulatively, the volume demonstrates that there is no one path to minority government or to one performing well.

References

Bale, Tim, and Torbjörn Bergman. 2006. "Captives No Longer, but Servants Still? Contract Parliamentarism and the New Minority Governance in Sweden and New Zealand." *Government and Opposition* 41 (3): 422–449.
Bergman, Torbjörn. 1993. "Formation Rules and Minority Governments." *European Journal of Political Research* 23 (1): 55–66.
Bergman, Torbjörn. 1995. *Constitutional Rules and Party Goals in Coalition Formation: An Analysis of Winning Minority Governments in Sweden.* Umeå: Umeå Universitet.
Bergman, Torbjörn, Hanna Bäck, and Johan Hellström, eds. 2021. *Coalition Governance in Western Europe.* Oxford: Oxford University Press.
Boston, Jonathan, and David Bullock. 2012. "Multi-party Governance: Managing the Unity-Distinctiveness Dilemma in Executive Coalitions." *Party Politics* 18 (3): 349–368.
Crombez, Christophe. 1996. "Minority Governments, Minimal Winning Coalitions and Surplus Majorities in Parliamentary Systems." *European Journal of Political Research* 29 (1): 1–29.
Downs, William M. 1998. *Coalition Government Subnational Style.* Columbus: Ohio State University Press.
Field, Bonnie N. 2014. "Minority Parliamentary Government and Multilevel Politics: Spain's System of Mutual Back Scratching." *Comparative Politics* 46 (3): 293–312.
Field, Bonnie N. 2016. *Why Minority Governments Work: Multilevel Territorial Politics in Spain.* New York: Palgrave Macmillan.
Ganghof, Steffen, and Thomas Bräuninger. 2006. "Government Status and Legislative Behaviour: Partisan Veto Players in Australia, Denmark, Finland and Germany." *Party Politics* 12 (4): 521–539.
Godbout, Jean-François, and Bjørn Høyland. 2011. "Coalition Voting and Minority Governments in Canada." *Commonwealth & Comparative Politics* 49 (4): 457–485.
Krauss, Svenja, and Maria Thürk. 2022. "Stability of Minority Governments and the Role of Support Agreements." *West European Politics* 45 (4): 767–792.
Laver, Michael, and Norman Schofield. 1998. *Multiparty Government: The Politics of Coalition in Europe.* Ann Arbor: University of Michigan Press.
Laver, Michael, and Kenneth A. Shepsle. 1996. *Making and Breaking Governments: Cabinets and Legislatures in Parliamentary Democracies.* Cambridge: Cambridge University Press.
Rasch, Bjørn Erik, Shane Martin, and José Antonio Cheibub, eds. 2015. *Parliaments and Government Formation: Unpacking Investiture Rules.* Oxford: Oxford University Press.
Reniu, Josep M. 2002. *La formación de gobiernos minoritarios en España, 1977–1996.* Madrid: Centro de Investigaciones Sociológicas.
Sridharan, E. 2012. "Why are Multi-party Minority Governments Viable in India? Theory and Comparison." *Commonwealth & Comparative Politics* 50 (3): 314–343.
Ștefuriuc, Irina. 2009. "Introduction: Government Coalitions in Multi-level Settings—Institutional Determinants and Party Strategy." *Regional & Federal Studies* 19 (1): 1–12.
Ștefuriuc, Irina. 2013. *Government Formation in Multi-Level Settings: Party Strategy and Institutional Constraints.* New York: Palgrave Macmillan.

Strøm, Kaare. 1990a. "A Behavioral Theory of Competitive Political Parties." *American Journal of Political Science* 34 (2): 565–598.

Strøm, Kaare. 1990b. *Minority Government and Majority Rule*. Cambridge: Cambridge University Press.

Thürk, Maria. 2022. "Small in Size but Powerful in Parliament? The Legislative Performance of Minority Governments." *Legislative Studies Quarterly* 47 (1): 193– 224.

Wegmann, Simone. 2022. "Policy-making Power of Opposition Players: A Comparative Institutional Perspective." *The Journal of Legislative Studies* 28 (1):1–25.

Index

Abbott, T. 286t, 293–4, 295, 296t
absolute majority 6–7
  Australia 284
  France 170, 173, 341
  Portugal 271
  Romania 90, 92, 330
  Spain 112, 114–15
ad hoc coalitions 32, 241, 251, 252, 254, 334
ad hoc majorities 25, 334
ad hoc management 200, 202
ad hoc support
  Australia 33, 292
  France 185
  India 55, 62
  Norway 77, 80, 334, 335
  Sweden 136–7
ad hoc voting alliances 31, 156, 159–61, 164, 167, 334, 335
agenda control 340, 342
Ahern, B. 192t, 202, 203t
Albanese, A. 287t, 296t
alliance-building 337
  France 178
  Portugal 270–1, 277
  Romania 96, 98–9
  Spain 118, 119, 125
  United Kingdom 316
Amato, G. 211t, 213t, 221, 224
Andreotti, G. 223, 235–7t, 239–40t
Anghel, V. 30, 328, 334, 335, 339
Askim, J. 79
Attlee, C. 308t, 320t
Australia 3, 5, 13, 14, 15, 29, 283–98, 301–5
  absolute majority 284
  ad hoc support 33, 292
  Agreement for a Better Parliament (Gillard) 293, 297
  Australian Labor Party (ALP) 32, 283–5, 286t, 287t, 288–9, 291–6, 301–4t
  caretaker governments 288
  Coalition (Liberal and National parties) 32, 33, 283–4, 285, 286–7t, 288–90, 291–5, 297
  confidence votes 284
  conservative governments 285
  constitution 284

contract parliamentarism 289, 291
Country Party (CP) 301–3t
Democrats 290
durability 295, 297
duration of minority governments 296t, 305t
efficacy 285
federal level 283–4
feedback loops 333
formal minority governments 286t
formal support agreements 334, 336
formation of governments 21, 285, 288–91, 331t
  minor parties and independents 290–1
  power sharing, resistance to 289–90
  two-party system 288–9
  types of government 286–7t
fragmentation of party systems 15t, 328t
functioning 26
governor general 284, 288
Greens Party (AG) 33, 285, 288–95, 336, 337
House of Representatives 284, 288, 293
independents 33, 283, 285, 288–9, 290–4, 295, 297, 301t, 329, 336
institutional variation 16t
interest groups 293
Katter Australia Party 290
Labor 336
legislative effectiveness 295, 296t, 297, 305t
Liberal Party (LP) 290, 302–4t
majoritarian system 283, 284, 291, 294, 297
minority governments in office 291–4
  Gillard government 292–4
  support parties and independents 293–4
  types of government 291–2
minor parties 288–93, 297
Multi-Party Climate Change Committee 294
National Party (NP) 290, 303–4t
near-majority 33
opposition influence 332t
Parliamentary Budget Office 293
parliamentary democracy 284
party system configuration 328
performance 295–7, 340, 341
policy-seeking 288, 289
political system 284–5
power sharing, resistance to 289–90

Australia (*Continued*)
  preferential voting 285, 288
  prevalence of minority governments 15*t*
  proportional representation 284
  proportion of seats held by governments 12*f*
  rate of minority governments 9*f*
  rightist parties 289
  Senate 284, 292–3
  single-party 32, 291, 295
  stability 285, 295, 297
  subnational level 27 n.6, 33, 283, 285, 288, 290–2, 294–5, 297–8, 336
  substantive minority governments 287*t*, 301*t*
  supply votes 284
  support parties 293–4
  testing the will of the house 284
  Two-Party Preferred (TPP) voting 285 n.3, 288
  two-party system 288–9, 297
  types of government 286–7*t*, 291–2, 301–4*t*
  United Australia Party (UAP) 301*t*
  West Australian National Party 290–1
  Westminster-type system 283–4, 285, 288, 292–3, 295, 297
Austria 9*f*, 12*f*, 23, 133
Ayrault, J.-M. 172*t*
Aznar, J.M. 110*t*, 121*t*

Bäck, H. 31, 330, 334, 339
Bale, T. 25, 136, 251, 270, 314, 315
Balsemão, F.B. 265*t*, 273*t*, 275*t*
Banks, J. 290
bargaining power 23, 28
Barros, D. 267
Barroso, J.M. 265*t*, 273*t*, 275*t*
Băsescu, T. 93, 95, 96, 103
Bassi, A. 21–2
Batasuna, H. 123
Belgium 9*f*, 12*f*, 133
Belka, M.M. 242*t*, 248–9, 252, 253*t*, 257, 257*t*, 261*t*
Bérégovoy, P.E. 172*t*, 176, 184
Bergman, T. 22–3, 25, 114–15, 134, 136, 137 n.3, 244, 251, 270, 314, 315
Berlusconi, S. 209, 211*t*, 213–15*t*, 221, 225 n.18, 228
bicameral systems 6, 326
  France 171 n.2
  Italy 209
  Poland 241
  Romania 90
  Spain 109
  United Kingdom 307
Bildt, C. 132*t*, 142*t*

Blair, T. 309*t*, 320*t*
Blaney, N. 195*t*
Boc, E. 88*t*, 95, 98–9, 100, 102*t*
Bondevik, K.M. 68*t*, 71 n.4, 73, 77 n.9, 79, 80, 81
Borten, P. 66, 67*t*
Boston, J. 25, 251, 335
Botswana 9, 9*f*, 12*f*
Bratteli, T.M. 67*t*
Bräuninger, T. 25
Brenton, S. 27 n.6
Brown, G. 309*t*, 320*t*
Brundtland, G.H. 67*t*, 68*t*, 81
Bruton, J. 192*t*, 203*t*
Bullock, D. 25, 251, 335
Buzek, J.K. 242*t*, 245–6, 248, 252, 253*t*, 254, 257, 257*t*, 261*t*
Byng, Lord J. 155 n.4

Callaghan, J. 308*t*, 312–13, 314, 316, 320*t*
Calvo-Sotelo, J. 109, 110*t*, 112, 121*t*
Cameron, D. 309*t*, 320*t*
Canada 5, 13, 14, 15, 29, 41, 151–67
  ad hoc voting alliances 31, 156, 159–61, 164, 167, 334, 335
  bargaining theories 163
  Bloc Québécois 153–4, 158, 160, 161, 163, 166–7, 336
  Canadian Alliance (formerly Reform Party) 154
  CCF 160, 163
  center-left 153
  center-periphery regional issues 31, 159, 335
  center-right 153
  coalition agreements 158–9
  confidence votes 155, 158–9
  Conservatives 151, 153–4, 155 n.3, 156, 157*t*, 158–63, 166–7
  Constitution 154
  duration of governments 8, 164, 165*t*, 167
  efficacy 167
  Election Data Act (2007) 159 n.7
  electoral incentives 160
  executive dominance 166
  executive oversight 166
  federalism 151, 167
  feedback loops 333
  formation of governments 152–3, 156–60, 167, 331*t*
    and institutions 156, 158–9
    party system 159–60
    types of government 157*t*
  fragmentation of party systems 15*t*, 328*t*
  frequency of minority governments 8
  functioning of minority governments 26

governor general 152, 155
House of Commons 151–2, 160, 166
hung parliament 154–6, 158, 159, 160, 161, 162, 164–7
ideological proximity of parties 160, 163, 167
institutional variation 16t
investiture vote 155, 158
left-right ideological issues 31, 159, 335
Liberals 151, 152 n.2, 153–4, 155 n.3, 156, 157t, 158–63, 166–7, 328
majority building 161–2
majority governments in office 151, 154, 160–4, 166, 167
minority governments in office
　types of government and majority building 161–2
　voting alliances 162–4
monarchy 152
multiparty system 153
nationalist parties 31, 329, 335, 337
negative parliamentarism 156
New Democratic Party (NDP) 153–4, 158, 159–60, 161, 163, 166–7
opposition influence 332t
party system 153–4, 159–60, 167, 327, 328
performance 28, 164–6, 339
plurality voting system 151–3, 156, 160, 166
political system 152–6, 167
　formation rules 154–5
　general description 152–3
　party system 153–4
　types of government 156
positive parliamentarism 158
prevalence 15t
procedural tools 162
Progressives 153
proportion of seats held by government 12f
proximal voting alliances 163
Queen's Speech 155–6
rate of minority governments 9f
Reform 153–4, 160
regional conflicts 151, 160, 163, 167
regional parties 31, 151, 153, 159–60, 166, 335, 337
single-party 31, 151, 153, 156, 158–9, 164, 167
Social Crédit 160, 161, 163
substantive minority governments 156, 157t, 161, 335
supply agreements 158–9
types of government 156, 157t, 161–2
United Farmers 153
voting alliances 161–4
Westminster-style parliamentary system 152, 154–5, 158–9

Cancela, F. 268 n.3
Capo Giol, J. 114
Carcassonne, G. 178, 180–2
Carlsson, I. 132t, 140 n.6, 142t, 144
Carneiro, F. 265t, 273t, 275t
Carroll (independent, Ireland) 195t
Cavaco Silva, A. 264, 267, 276
center-periphery 14, 22, 336
　Canada 31, 159, 335
　Norway 74, 80
　Spain 108, 124, 126, 336
Cheibub, J.A. 8, 23, 115, 155, 156
Chifley, J. (Ben) 302t, 305t
Chrétien, J. 157t, 165t
Christiansen, F.J. 25
Churchill, W. 308t, 320t
Ciampi, C.A. 211t
Cioloș, D. 89t, 101, 102t
Ciorbea, V. 87t, 93, 102t
Cîtu, F. 89t
Clark, C.J. 157t, 165t
coalition agreements 138, 158–9, 334 n.2
coalition bargaining 24
coalitions 5, 8, 10, 25, 27, 325
　India 42, 43, 44, 54, 56–7, 58, 61, 62, 190, 193, 196, 200
　Italy 23, 209, 210, 218–20, 221, 222, 228
　Norway 23, 30, 66, 69, 69t, 77, 78–80, 83
　Poland 244–5, 246–7, 247f
　Portugal 263, 264, 274
　Spain 108, 114, 126
　United Kingdom 307, 311
Cochrane, C. 31, 328, 333, 339
Colombo, E. 235t
committee systems 24, 332–3
communist parties 14
comparative conclusions 325–42
　definition, frequency and undercounting 326–7
　formation 327–33
　　feedback loops 333
　　formation rules 331t
　　investiture rules 330–1
　　legislative organization and opposition influence 331–3, 332t
　　party system configuration 327–9
　　party system fragmentation 328t
　functioning of minority governments 333–8
　　intraparty politics 338
　　motivations and majority-building arrangements 335
　　support parties and allies, concessions to 337
　　support parties and support MPs 336–7

comparative conclusions (*Continued*)
    territorial politics 335-6
    types of government 333-5
    performance 338-41
confidence votes
    India 42, 44, 53-4
    Ireland 190
    Italy 226
    Portugal 264, 267-8
    Romania 90
    Spain 114
consistent membership 25
Conte, G. 217*t*
contract parliamentarism 25, 334, 340, 342
    Australia 289, 291
    India 29, 42, 54-8, 62, 334
    Portugal 28, 270, 276
    Spain 118
    Sweden 31, 129, 136, 144, 334, 337
    United Kingdom 314-15
contracts 337
core parties 244, 256-7, 327, 328, 329, 340, 342
Cosgrave, W.T. 191*t*, 203*t*
Cossiga, F. 237*t*
Costa, A. 3, 32, 262, 264, 265*t*, 268 n.3, 270-1, 273*t*, 275, 275*t*, 340
Costello, J.A. 191*t*, 203*t*
counting rules 29, 341
country studies 14-16
Cowen, B. 192*t*, 203*t*
Craxi, B. 225 n.18, 238*t*
Cresson, E. 172*t*, 176
Crombez, C. 134, 159-60, 220, 311
Crowley, K. 32, 333, 336, 341
Cunha, C. 269
Curtin, J. 219 n.9, 283, 301*t*, 305*t*
Cyprus 95
Czech Republic 9*f*, 12*f*

D'Alema, M. 212-13*t*, 221, 224
Damgaard, E. 25
Dăncilă, V. 89*t*, 94, 98-9, 102*t*
da Silva, A.M. 265*t*, 273*t*, 275*t*
definitions 5-8, 326-7
De Gasperi, A. 232*t*
De Gaulle, C. 171
De Giorgi, E. 268 n.3, 272
De Mita, C. 239*t*
democratization 13
Denmark 3, 9, 9*f*, 12*f*, 23-5, 28, 72, 80, 129, 133, 326, 329
Deptner, Q. 160
Desai, M. 60*t*, 65*t*
De Valera, É 191*t*, 203*t*

Diefenbaker, J. 157*t*, 163, 165*t*
Dillon, J. 195*t*
Dini, L. 212*t*
dominant parties 328
Douglas-Home, A. 308*t*, 320*t*
Dukes, A. 199
duration of governments 28
    Canada 8, 164, 165*t*, 167
    India 30, 59, 61*t*
    Ireland 203-4, 203*t*
    Italy 208, 225, 229
    Norway 81
    Romania 98, 100-1, 102*t*
    United Kingdom 319, 320*t*

Eanes, A.R. 272 n.6
Eden, A. 308*t*, 320*t*
electoral costs 21, 41, 54, 83, 94, 218
Erlander, T. 131*t*, 133, 141*t*, 143
Ersson, S. 22
ethnic parties 16, 26
European Union 13, 14

Fadden, A. 301*t*, 305*t*
Fälldin, T. 131-2*t*, 141-2*t*, 143
Fanfani, A. 232-4*t*, 238*t*
federalism 14, 151, 167
feedback loops 333
Fernandes, J.M. 28, 32, 263, 275 n.7, 331, 333, 339
Field, B.N. 139, 315-16, 319, 331, 334, 339, 340
Fini, G. 221
Finland 9, 9*f*, 12*f*, 24
first-past-the-post 42
FitzGerald, G.D. 191*t*, 203*t*
Forde, F. 302*t*, 305*t*
Forlani, A. 237*t*
formalized agreements 340, 342
formal minority governments 24-5, 333-4, 340
    India 45*t*, 46*t*, 47*t*, 48*t*, 49*t*, 50*t*, 51*t*, 61
    Italy 212*t*, 221, 223, 232-7*t*
    Norway 68*t*, 335
    Portugal 265*t*, 270, 271, 277
    Romania 97
    Spain 28, 110*t*, 118-19, 334
    Sweden 132*t*, 136
    United Kingdom 308-9*t*, 314, 318
formal support agreements
    India 334
    Portugal 334
    Romania 334
formation of minority governments 4, 5, 13, 16, 19-24, 325, 331*t*, 341-2
    India 41, 44-54, 62

INDEX 349

Foxe (independent, Ireland) 195*t*
fragmentation of party systems 15*t*, 22, 327, 328, 328*t*, 329, 336
  Canada 15*t*, 328*t*
  India 41, 43, 44, 62, 328*t*
  Ireland 189–90, 193, 328*t*, 329
  Italy 15*t*, 328*t*
  Norway 15*t*, 328*t*
  Poland 328*t*
  Portugal 15*t*, 328*t*
France 5, 9*f*, 12*f*, 14, 15, 15*t*, 16*t*, 29, 95, 170–86
  absolute majority 170, 173, 341
  ad hoc support 185
  alliances 178
  Article 49.3 provision 177, 178*f*, 184–5
  bicameralism 171 n.2
  blocked votes 177
  Center Party 172*t*
  center-right parties 172*t*, 173, 179
  centrists 174, 175*t*, 176, 177, 178, 179, 180, 181–2, 182*t*, 184
  Communist Party 173–4, 175*t*, 176–82, 182*t*, 337
  constituency-oriented particularism 31
  Constitution 170, 171, 172, 175 n.5, 177
  decree of nomination of the ministers 172
  divided governments 172
  duality 170
  emergency procedure 184
  extreme left parties 173
  Fifth Republic 170, 174, 176, 184
  formation of governments 171–5, 331*t*
  Fourth Republic 170 n.1, 171
  fragmentation of party systems 328*t*
  Gaullists 172*t*, 174, 179, 184
  good relations 31, 180
  greens 172*t*
  inquiry committee 184
  institutional factors 176
  investiture votes 173
  irregular minority governments 174, 182
  left-wing parties 173, 178, 184, 185
  Leftwing Radicals 176 n.6
  legislative procedure 171, 182–3
  managerial factors 176
  National Assembly 171–2, 175, 176–7, 182, 184, 330
  non-confidence vote 170 n.1, 172, 173, 175, 176–7, 178, 341
  office-seeking 175*t*, 182*t*
  one-month governments 31, 170, 183
  opposition influence 332*t*
  oversight of governments 171
  party system 31, 327
  PCF 178–9
  performance 339, 341
  polarization 179, 185
  policies vs. public opinion 182–5
  policy-seeking 174, 175*t*, 182*t*
  political limitation 172
  political system 171–3, 172*t*
  pork 180–2, 185–6
  presidential decree 173
  radical left parties 337
  radical parties 172*t*
  rationalized parliamentarianism 31, 176–8, 185, 340
  reformist movement 176
  regular minority governments 31, 170, 173, 185
  rightist parties 173, 174 n.3, 176, 178, 184, 185
  semi-presidential system 170–1, 185
  Senate 171, 176, 182–3, 184
  Socialists 172*t*, 173–4, 175*t*, 176, 179, 182, 183–4, 339
  stereo majority 178–9
  strategic choices 173
  support party concessions 337
  survival of minority governments 176–82
    Article 49.3 178*f*
    pork 180–2
    rationalized parliamentarianism 176–8
    stereo majority 178–9
  swing groups 178–9
  Third Republic 170 n.1
  UDC 178–9
  UDF 179, 182
  Union of the Center 178 n.8
  veto points 179
  vote-seeking 174, 175*t*, 182*t*
Franco, F. 113–14
Fraser, M. 303–4*t*, 305*t*
Freire, A. 264
frequency of minority governments 8–10, 325, 326–7
functioning of minority governments 4, 5, 13, 19, 24–6, 325, 341–2

Gamson's Law 328
Gandhi, I. 59, 60*t*, 61, 65*t*
Gandhi, R. 60*t*, 61, 65*t*
Gandhi, S. 58
Ganghof, S. 25
Gentiloni, P. 217*t*
Gerhardsen, E.H. 67*t*, 73 n.7
Germany 3, 9, 9*f*, 10, 12*f*, 19, 27 n.6, 114, 133
Gervais, M. 161

Gianetti, D. 32, 222 n.13, 327, 332, 339
Gildea, T. 195t
Gillard, J. 33, 283, 285, 286t, 289–90, 291–5, 296t, 297, 336, 340, 341
Giscard d'Estaing, V. 179
Godbout, J.-F. 26, 31, 328, 333, 339
Golder, M. 23
Golder, S.N. 23
González, F. 110t, 121t, 122t, 123
Gorbachev, M. 179
Goria, G. 239t
Gorton, J. 303t, 305t
government-strengthening institutions 340, 342
Gowda, H.D. 45t, 53, 55–7, 60t
Greece 9f, 12f, 13
green parties 14, 26
Green-Pedersen, C. 271
Gregory, T. 195t, 201–2
Grindeanu, S. 89t, 101, 102t
Gujral, I.K. 45t, 53, 60t
Guterres, A. 265t, 267, 272, 273t, 274, 275t, 276

Hansson, P.A. 131t, 141t
Hareide, K.A. 74
Harper, S. 166
Haughey, C. 191–2t, 202, 203t
Hawke, R. (Bob) 286t, 296t, 304t, 305t
Healey-Rae, M. 195t
Heath, E. 308t, 312, 320t
Hellström, J. 22, 31, 179, 330, 334, 339
Herman, V. 5
Hjermitslev, I.B. 144
Hobolt, S.B. 28
Holger, D. 179
Holt, H. 303t, 305t
Homes, B. 295
Howard, J. 286t, 296t
how minority governments govern *see* functioning of minority governments
how well minority governments perform *see* performance of minority governments
Høyland, B. 26
Høyland, H. 163
Huber, J. 185
Hungary 13
hung parliaments 41
  Canada 154–6, 158, 159, 160, 161, 162, 164–7
  India 43, 44
Hyest, J.-J. 178

Iceland 24
ideologically-oriented goals 337
Iliescu, I. 92

India 5, 6, 13, 14, 15, 15t, 16, 16t, 29–30, 41–62, 65
ABLTC 47t, 48t, 49t
AC 46t
AD 51t, 52t
ad hoc support 55, 62
AD(S) 52t
AGP 45t
AIADMK 46t, 52t, 65t
AIDMK 46t
AIFB 45t
AIMIM 49t, 50t, 51t
AINRC 51t, 52t
AJSU 52t
alliances 57
AUDF 50t, 51t
Bharatiya Janata Party (BJP) 43, 45t, 46t, 47t, 48t, 49t, 51t, 52t, 53, 55, 57, 58, 62
bi-polar party system 53
BJD 46t, 47t, 48t, 49t
BJE 47t
BPF 50t, 51t
BSMC 46t
BSP 49t, 50t, 51t
BVA 50t, 51t
CCF 46t
centrally-positioned party 30, 41–2, 62
coalitions 42, 43, 44, 54, 56–7, 58, 61, 62
Common Minimum Programme (CMP) 56–8
confidence votes 42, 44, 53–4
Congress Party 42, 45t, 53, 55–8, 61, 62, 65t, 327
contract parliamentarism 29, 42, 54–8, 62, 334
Coordinating Committee (CC) 57
Council of State (Rajya Sabha) 42
counting rule 44
CPI 45t, 65t
CPI(M) 45t, 55–6, 65t
C(T) 45t
decentralization 56
Departmentally-Related Standing Committees (DRSCs) 54
DMK 45t, 47t, 48t, 49t, 50t, 51t
DPI 45t
durability of minority governments 61
duration of minority governments 30, 59, 61t
effective number of parties 43, 43f
electoral costs 41, 54
Emergency Rule 59
federalization 42, 53, 56, 62
first-past-the-post 42

INDEX 351

formal minority governments 45*t*, 46*t*, 47*t*, 48*t*, 49*t*, 50*t*, 51*t*, 61
formal support agreements 334
formation of minority governments 41, 44–54, 62, 331*t*
fragmentation of party systems 41, 43, 44, 62, 328*t*
Group of Ministers (GoM) 57–8
HLD 46*t*
hung parliaments 43, 44
HVC 47*t*, 48*t*, 49*t*
HVP 46*t*
IFDP 47*t*, 48*t*, 49*t*
INC 49*t*, 50*t*, 51*t*
IND 52*t*
independents 46*t*, 47*t*, 48*t*, 49*t*, 50*t*, 51*t*
INLD 47*t*, 48*t*, 49*t*
investiture rules 330
IUML 50*t*, 51*t*
Janata Dal 45*t*
Janata Party 65*t*
JD(S) 50*t*, 51*t*
JD(U) 47*t*, 48*t*, 49*t*, 52*t*
JKPDP 49*t*, 50*t*
JMM 49*t*, 50*t*, 51*t*
JUML 49*t*
JVM(P) 50*t*, 51*t*
KC 49*t*, 50*t*, 51*t*
law production 30, 59, 61, 61*t*
Left Front 45*t*, 49*t*, 50*t*, 55, 57–8, 62
legislative committees 42, 54
LJP 49*t*, 50*t*, 51*t*, 52*t*
Lok Sabha (House of the People) 42–3, 55, 56, 57, 333
LS 46*t*
MADMK 47*t*, 48*t*, 49*t*
majorities 59, 61*t*
MDMK 46*t*, 47*t*, 48*t*, 49*t*, 50*t*
MGP 45*t*
MSCP 46*t*, 47*t*, 48*t*, 49*t*
multilevel politics 42
multi-party coalitions 62
multiple bipolarities 53
National Advisory Committee (NAC) 58
National Agenda for Governance (NAG) 57
National Front 55
NC 46*t*, 47*t*, 48*t*, 50*t*, 51*t*
NCP 49*t*, 50*t*, 51*t*
NDA 53, 57
NDPP 52*t*
near-majority 29–30, 42, 44, 55, 58–9, 61*t*, 62
negative parliamentarism 41, 44, 53
no confidence votes 42
NPF 50*t*, 51*t*, 52*t*

NPP 51*t*, 52*t*
opposition influence 332*t*
parliamentary committees 44
partisan blocs and alliances 43
performance of minority governments 41, 58–62, 60*t*, 62, 340
plurality electoral system 53
PMK 46*t*, 47*t*, 48*t*, 49*t*, 50*t*, 51*t*, 52*t*
policy benefits 41
political system 42–4
pre-electoral alliances 43, 44, 53, 62, 329
PSP 65*t*
regional parties 29, 42, 55, 56, 62, 329, 336, 337
RJD 49*t*, 50*t*, 51*t*
RJP 46*t*
RLD 48*t*
RLP 52*t*
RLSP 51*t*, 52*t*
RPI(A) 51*t*, 52*t*
RSP 45*t*
SAD 45*t*, 46*t*, 47*t*, 48*t*, 49*t*, 51*t*, 52*t*, 65*t*
SDF 46*t*, 47*t*, 48*t*, 49*t*, 50*t*, 51*t*
secularism 55, 56, 58
SHS 45*t*, 46*t*, 47*t*, 48*t*, 49*t*, 51*t*, 52*t*
single-party minority governments 30, 55, 58, 59, 340
single transferable vote system 42
SJP 45*t*
small minorities 59, 61, 61*t*
SMT 46*t*
SP 45*t*, 49*t*, 50*t*, 51*t*, 52*t*
stability 59
Standing Committee 56
state assemblies (Vidhan Sabha) 42
state-level committees 57
state parties 55, 56, 62
Steering Committee 56
substantive minority governments 45*t*, 61, 65*t*
TDP 45*t*, 46*t*, 47*t*, 48*t*, 49*t*, 51*t*, 52*t*
TMC 45*t*
TRS 49*t*, 50*t*
two-party systems 53
types of government 45–52*t*, 65*t*
United Front 55–7
 Steering Committee 57
UPA 53, 57–8
 Coordination Committee 58
 Government-Left Coordination Committee (UPLCC) 58
VCK 50*t*, 51*t*
WBTC 46*t*, 50*t*, 51*t*
WBTMC 47*t*, 49*t*, 50*t*

informal support 95–7, 334
Ingvaldsen, B. 71 n.3
institutional structure 24
institutional variation 16*t*
interconnected questions 29–33
intraparty politics 338
investiture procedure 23, 330–1, 342
  Canada 155, 158
  France 173
  India 330
  Ireland 201–2, 330, 334
  Italy 209, 221–2, 223
  Poland 244, 246, 248, 330
  Romania 90, 92
  Spain 112, 114–15, 118, 330, 331
  Sweden 130, 133, 134, 135–7
  United Kingdom 330
investiture rules, positive 243–5, 258
Iohannis, K. 95
Ireland 5, 9*f*, 12*f*, 14, 15, 15*t*, 16*t*, 26, 29, 41, 189–206
  ad hoc management 200, 202
  center-left parties 190
  centrist parties 194, 197
  Clann na Poblachta 195*t*
  Clann na Talmhan 195*t*
  coalitions 190, 193, 196, 200
  committee system 193
  confidence votes 190
  constituency-oriented particularism 32
  Dáil (House of Representatives) 190, 193–4, 196–7, 199, 202, 204
  Democrats 192*t*
  double-investiture vote 330
  dualistic party system 196
  duration of governments 203–4, 203*t*
  electoral performance 204
  ethno-nationalism 190
  extra-parliamentary organizations 193
  far-left parties 196, 197
  Fianna Fáil 190, 192*t*, 193, 195*t*, 196–200, 201 n.1, 202, 204, 206
  Fine Gael 190, 192*t*, 195*t*, 196–202, 204
  formal rules 190
  formateurs 190
  formation of governments 193–8, 331*t*
    independents 194*f*, 195*t*
    institutions 193–4, 196
    party system 196–7
  fractionalization 31
  fragmentation of party system 189–90, 193, 328*t*, 329
  Green Party 192*t*, 195*t*, 201 n.1, 205 n.2
  'Gregory Deal' 202

  Independent Alliance 195*t*, 201
  independents 189–90, 193–4, 195*t*, 196–7, 198, 200–2, 204, 205–6, 329, 337
  informal rules 190
  informateurs 190
  institutional factors 193, 205
  interest groups (social partners) 193
  investiture votes 201–2, 334
  Irish Republican Army (IRA) 196
  Labour Party 190, 192*t*, 195*t*, 197, 199–200, 202
  left-wing parties 189
  legislative record 203–4, 203*t*
  minority governments in office 199–202
    ad hoc management 200
    in government 201
    investiture vote 201–2
    negotiated deals 202
  nationalist parties 329
  National Labour 195*t*
  negotiated deals 202
  no confidence votes 199
  office-seeking 197–8
  Oireachtas 190
  opposition influence 332*t*
  party competition 193, 205
  party goals 198
  party system configuration 328
  patronage agreements 194, 195*t*, 198
  performance 202–5, 339
    legislative record and duration 203*t*
  polarization 329
  policy goals 197–8
  political system 190, 193
  pork 194, 198
  Progressive Democrats 190, 192*t*, 195*t*
  regional parties 3, 337
  'reservation price' 197
  Senate (Seanad) 190
  single transferable vote 193, 205
  Sinn Féin 190, 196–7, 199
  Socialist Party 197
  Socialist Workers Party 197
  Solidarity party 197
  substantive minority governments 192*t*, 334
  support parties 199–200, 337
  Taoiseach (prime minister) 190, 201
  tripartite agreements 193
  two and a half party system 189–90
  types of government 191–2*t*
  voting goals 197–8
  Westminster style of government 189
irregular minority governments 174, 182
Isărescu, M. 88*t*, 102*t*

INDEX 353

Israel 8–9, 9f, 12f
Italy 5, 6–7, 14–15, 29, 32, 208–29, 232–40, 326–7
   bipolar pattern of party competition 209, 219
   caretaker governments 221
   CCD 211t, 213–14t
   CD 216–17t
   CDU 213–14t
   center-left parties 210, 221, 223, 228
   center-right parties 209, 210, 221, 228
   centrist parties 223
   Chamber of Deputies 209–10, 218, 221, 222 n.12, 223, 224, 228, 327
   Christian Democratic Party (DC) 209–10, 211–12t, 218–20, 223, 225, 226, 232–40t, 327
   closed party lists 209–10
   coalitions 23, 209, 210, 218–20, 221, 222, 228
   committee system 218, 224, 228
   Communist Party (PCI) 209, 221 n.11, 223, 224, 237t
   Communist Refoundation party (PRC) 212t, 214–15t, 221, 221 n.11, 223
   confidence votes 226
   congruence dimension 222
   consensualism 224
   Constitution 209, 226 n.19
   Constitutional Court 227 n.20
   core parties 327
   corruption 209
   cost-benefit calculus 208
   counting rule 218 n.6
   Daisy 210
   decentralized procedure 224, 227
   democracy 209
   Democratic Party of the Left (PDS) 210
   Democratic Party (PD) 210, 215–17t
   DINI-RI 212–13t
   dual responsibility 210
   duration of governments 208, 225, 229
   electoral costs 218
   electoral rules 228
   electoral success 225
   electoral volatility 225
   emergency decrees 226–7
   empty core 219, 220, 220f
   ex ante agreements 223–4
   executive and legislative level 222
   ex post governance 224
   extreme left parties 210, 221, 223
   FdV 212–15t
   FI 209, 211t, 213–15t
   First Republic 209, 218, 223–4, 225
   Five Star Movement (M5S) 210, 217t
   formal minority governments 212t, 221, 223, 232–7t
   formation of governments 218–22, 331t
   fragmentation of party systems 15t, 328t
   frequency of minority governments 10
   Future and Freedom for Italy (Fli) 215t, 221
   Go Italy 209
   IdV 214–15t
   Iniziativa Responsabile 221
   institutional conditions 220
   institutional features 218
   institutional variation 16t
   institutions 218–22
   inter-electoral governments 220, 224
   internal party politics 220
   intra-party politics 218, 220
   investiture rules/vote 209, 221–2, 223
   IR 215t
   law-decrees 227
   Left Democrats (DS) 210, 213–14t
   left-wing parties 209, 219, 223
   legislative activity 227, 227t
   legislative effectiveness 208, 225, 229
   legislative organization and opposition influence 332
   Legislature I 226
   Legislature V 224
   Legislature VI 226
   Legislature X 224, 226
   Legislature XII 226
   Legislature XIII 227, 227t
   Legislature XIV 227t
   Legislature XV 227t
   Legislature XVI 224, 227t
   Legislature XVII 227, 227t
   LeU 217t
   LN 211t, 213–15t, 217t
   majority summits 224
   megaseats 224
   minimal winning coalitions (MWC) 210, 211t, 218, 225
   minority governments in office 222–4
   mixed-member majoritarian (MMM) electoral system 209–10, 220
   MpA 215t
   MSI 209, 233t
   multiparty systems 210, 219
   National Alliance (AN) 209, 211t, 213–14t
   national solidarity phase 223
   NCD 216t, 217t
   negative responsiveness 225
   no confidence votes 209, 326
   non-empty core 219f
   Northern League (NL) 209, 220

Italy (*Continued*)
  north-south/institutional policy
    dimension 209
  NPSI 213–14*t*
  office-seeking 218
  open-list proportional representation
    (PR) 209
  opposition influence 332*t*
  Partido Democratico della Sinistra
    (PDS) 211*t*, 221 n.11
  Partito dei Comunisti Italiani (PdCI) 212–15*t*,
    221
  party policy positions and seats 219*f*, 220*f*
  party system 228
  People of Freedom (PDL) 210, 215–16*t*, 221
  performance of minority governments 225–8,
    229, 339
  PLI 211*t*, 217*t*, 232–3*t*, 236–40*t*
  plurality 209
  PNM 232–4*t*
  polarization 219
  policy benefits 218, 224
  policy influence differential 218
  policy-seeking 208, 218
  policy stability 225–6
  political system 209–10, 218
  Popular Party (PPI) 210, 212–13*t*
  populist parties 210
  positive parliamentarism 209
  post-electoral governments 224
  prevalence of minority governments 15*t*
  PRI 213–14*t*, 223, 232–9*t*
  proportional representation (PR) 210
  proportion of seats held by governments 12*f*
  PSD 232–40*t*
  PSDI 211*t*
  PSI 211*t*, 233–40*t*
  PSU 235*t*
  R 215*t*
  rate of minority governments 9*f*
  Red Brigade 223 n.15
  regionalist parties 209
  right-wing parties 209, 219, 223
  RnP 214*t*
  SC 216*t*
  SD 215*t*
  SDI 212–13*t*
  Second Republic 209, 218–20, 223–4, 225,
    327
  Senate 209–10, 221, 222, 223, 228, 327
  simple majority 209
  single-member districts (SMD) 209
  single-party 210, 219, 225
  Socialist party 223
  substantive minority governments 223, 232*t*,
    235*t*, 237–8*t*
  Sud Tiroler Volkspartei (VP) 223
  support agreements/parties 223, 337
  surplus coalitions 210, 218, 221, 225
  surplus majority 211–17*t*, 228, 232*t*, 234–40*t*
  SVP 213–17*t*
  symmetric bicameralism 209
  types of government 211–17*t*, 232–40*t*
  UDC 211*t*, 216*t*, 217*t*
  UDEUR 214–15*t*
  UDR 212–13*t*
  Ulivo 221

Jagland, T. 68*t*
Jalali, C. 263
Jamaica 9, 9*f*, 12*f*
Japan 9*f*, 10, 12*f*
Johnson, B. 7, 309*t*, 314–15, 318–19, 320*t*
Jones, A. 33, 330, 338
Juan Carlos I, King 113

Kaczyński, L. 242*t*, 249, 250–1, 251 n.6, 252,
  253*t*, 254, 257, 257*t*, 261*t*
Kalandrakis, T. 22
Keating, P. 286*t*, 296*t*
Kefford, G. 26
Kemmy, J. 195*t*, 200
Kenny, E. 190, 192*t*, 193, 203*t*
Kesri, S. 56
Klein, E. 98
Klüver, H. 28
Koehl, E. 182
Kopacz (Poland) 242*t*
Korvald, L. 67*t*, 73, 75
Kristersson, U. 135

Lajoinie, A. 180
Lange, A. 72 n.6
Latvia 86
Laver, M. 92, 218, 219 n.7, 225–6
leftist parties 14
legislative committees 16, 42, 54, 244
legislative organization and opposition
  influence 331–3, 332*t*
legislative success 27–8, 139–40, 256
Lemass, S. 191*t*, 203*t*
Leneghan (independent, Ireland) 195*t*
Leone, G. 234–5*t*
Letta, E. 216*t*
liberal-conservative regimes 14
libertarian-authoritarian regimes 14
Lijphart, A. 108
Lindvall, J. 143

INDEX 355

Linz, J.J. 266
Lithuania 9f, 12f
Löfven, S. 132t, 135–6, 139, 142t
logrolling strategy 25
lower chamber 6–7
Lowry (Ireland) 195t
Luxembourg 9, 9f, 10, 12f
Lynch, J. 191t, 203t
Lyng, J. 67t, 78

McClean, C.T. 225
McEwen, J. 303t, 305t
McGrath, M. 195t
Mackenzie-King, W.L. 155 n.4, 157t, 165t
McMahon, W. 303t, 305t
McMillan, A. 53
Macmillan, H. 308t, 320t
Macron (France) 172t
Madison, J. 70
Magalhães, P.C. 28, 270
majoritarian system
 Australia 283, 284, 291, 294, 297
 United Kingdom 306–7
majority-building 25, 79–80, 335
majority governments
 India 59, 61t
 Norway 67t, 81, 81t, 82
 Poland 247, 255–6, 258
 Portugal 263, 273–4, 275, 277
 Spain 121–2t, 123
 Sweden 140, 143, 144
Major, J. 309t, 313, 314, 316–17, 318–19, 320t, 326
Malta 9, 9f, 10, 12f
Marangoni, F. 224, 228 n.21
Marcinkiewicz, K. 242t, 254, 255, 255t, 257, 257t, 261t
Martin, M. 192t, 203t
Martin, P. 157t, 161, 165t
Martin, S. 23, 115, 155, 156, 197
Matthieß, T. 27 n.6
Mauritius 9, 9f, 12f
Mauroy, P. 172t
May, T. 3, 213–14, 309t, 316, 318–19, 320t, 336
Mehaignerie, P. 179, 180
Menzies, R. 301t, 302–3t, 305t
Mershon, C. 226
Migneault, P.-L. 164
Miller, L. 242t, 246–8, 249, 253t, 254, 257, 257t, 261t
minimum winning coalitions (MWC)
 Italy 210, 211t, 218, 225
 Norway 67t, 68t, 69t
 Romania 100

Mitchell, P. 193, 200, 204
Mitterand, F. 174, 176, 180, 184
Modi, N. 51–2t
Monti, M. 216t, 221
Morawiecki (Poland) 242t
Moro, A. 223 n.15, 234t, 236t
Morrison, S. 287t, 289, 290, 296t
motivations of political parties 21, 335
Moury, C. 274
Mulroney, B. 157t, 165t
multidimensional competition/cooperation 342
multilevel state 342
multiparty system 5, 41, 62, 130, 153, 210, 219, 307

Narud, H.M. 78
Năstase, A. 88t, 96, 97, 100, 102t, 103
nationalist parties 336
Naughten (independent, Ireland) 195t
Naurin, E. 143
near-majority 33, 328
 India 29–30, 42, 44, 55, 58–9, 61t, 62
negative parliamentarism 23
 Canada 156
 India 41, 44, 53
 Portugal 264, 267
 Spain 115
 Sweden 129, 133, 134, 144, 330
Nehru, J. 60t, 65t
Netherlands 9f, 11–12, 12f, 23
new left parties 14
New Zealand 9f, 12f, 25, 136, 295
Nikolenyi, C. 29, 329, 333, 334
no confidence vote, France 170 n.1, 172, 173, 175, 176–7, 178, 341
no confidence votes 7, 23
 India 42
 Ireland 199
 Italy 209, 326
 Norway 71–2
 Poland 243–4, 251 n.6, 341
 Portugal 268
 Romania 94, 98, 99, 101
 Spain 109, 112, 114, 117, 124, 125
 United Kingdom 317
non-core parties 244–5, 256–8, 328, 329, 340
Nordic countries 22
 see also Denmark; Finland; Iceland; Norway; Sweden
Nordli, O. 67t
Norway 5, 14–15, 29, 66–84, 208
 ad hoc support 77, 80, 334, 335
 adverse incumbency effect 82
 Agrarian (later Center) Party 72

Norway (*Continued*)
 alliances 79–80
 Article 15 71
 budget process 80
 cabinet conferences 77–8
 cabinet record 66, 69
 Cabinet Rules 77 n.8
 cabinets by composition and majority status 69*t*
 center-left parties 73, 74
 Center Party (SP) 66, 67*t*, 68*t*, 72, 73, 74–5
 center-periphery axis 74, 80
 center-right parties 73, 74, 77, 80, 83, 335
 center-right Sundvolden negotiations 71
 Christian Democrat Party (KRF) 67*t*, 68*t*, 71 n.4, 72, 73, 74, 79–80
 coalition advisor 79 n.11
 coalitions 23, 30, 66, 69, 69*t*, 77, 78–80, 83
 Communist Party (NKP) 72
 conflict resolution 78
 consensus culture 75–6, 83
 Conservatives (H) 67*t*, 68*t*, 71 n.4, 72, 73, 74, 77, 80
 Constitution 69, 70–2, 77 n.8, 83
 Cooperation Agreement 79
 Council of State meetings 77
 cross-partisan appointees (CPA) 79
 duration of governments 81
 electoral costs 83
 electoral gains and losses 82
 electoral volatility 75, 83
 fixed parliamentary terms 72
 'flank' parties 75
 formal minority governments 68*t*, 335
 formation of governments 20, 24, 69–76, 331*t*
  consensus culture 75–6
  institutional setting 70–5
  party system and two-bloc politics 72–5
 fraction meetings 79
 fragmentation of party systems 15*t*, 328*t*
 free-style bargaining 71
 frequency of minority governments 10
 fringe parties 83
 functioning of minority governments 25
 Green (Environmentalist) party (MDG) 72–3
 inclusiveness 75, 83
 institutional setting 69–75
 institutional variation 16*t*
 interpersonal trust 66, 70, 76, 341
 intra-cabinet committees 78
 junior ministers 79, 84
 King's Council 70
 Labor Party (A or DNA) 66, 67*t*, 68*t*, 72, 73, 74–5, 80, 82, 335
 late deciders 75
 Left Socialists (SV) 66, 68*t*, 72, 73, 75, 80, 83
 legislative productivity 81
 liaison officer 79 n.11
 Liberal Party (V) 67*t*, 68*t*, 71, 72, 73, 74–5, 79
 limited governments 70
 majority building 79–80
 majority coalitions 81, 81*t*, 82
 majority single-party 67*t*
 Marxist-Leninist Party (aka Red Party) 72–3
 minimum winning coalition 67*t*, 68*t*, 69*t*
 ministerial responsibility 71
 minority governments 67*t*, 68*t*, 69*t*, 81, 81*t*, 82
 minority governments in office 77–80
  alliances and majority building 79–80
  coalition agreements 78–80
 no confidence vote 71–2
 non-socialists 66, 73–4, 80
 opposition influence 332*t*
 parliamentary committees 76
 parliamentary democracy 66, 69–71
 parliamentary group meetings 79
 party system 69–70, 72–5
 performance of minority governments 81–3, 81*t*, 341
 political appointees 79 n.11
 prevalence of minority governments 15*t*
 private members' bills 81
 Progress Party (FRP) 68*t*, 72, 73, 74–5, 77, 80, 83
 proportional representation 72
 proportion of seats held by governments 12*f*
 radical right parties 329
 rate of minority governments 9*f*
 red-green coalition 66, 71, 73, 83
 separation-of-powers 70, 83
 single-party minority governments 30, 66, 67*t*, 68*t*, 69, 69*t*, 73, 81, 82
 slalom method 80
 Socialist People's Party 72, 73
 socialists 73, 80
 Soria Moria agreement 71
 Storting 66, 72, 79
 sub-committees 78
 surplus majorities 67*t*, 69, 69*t*
 two-bloc politics 72–5, 83, 329
 types of government 67–8*t*
 urban-rural dimension 74–5
 watchdog minister 79 n.10
numerical requirement 6

OECD countries 143
office-seeking goals 20, 336, 337, 342

France 175t, 182t
Poland 254, 258
Portugal 269, 272
Romania 94–5, 99
United Kingdom 310, 311, 312
opposition influence 332t
Orban (Romania) 89t, 95, 99, 102t
oversight 7

Palme, O. 131–2t, 141–2t
Pambuccian, V. 100
parliamentarianism, rationalized 31, 176–8, 185, 340
parliamentarism 7, 23, 325
  see also contract parliamentarism; negative parliamentarism; postitive parliamentarism; Westminster style of parliamentarism
parliamentary committees 21, 44, 76, 123, 342
parliamentary democracies 6, 7–8, 20, 326
particularistic-oriented goals 337
partisan bargaining position 340, 342
party goals 22, 115–17, 198, 310–12, 340
party organizations 24
party systems 20 n.2, 21, 24
  configuration 327–9
  fragmentation 15t, 328t
  Ireland 328
  Italy 228
  Norway 69–70, 72–5
  Portugal 327, 328
  Romania 30, 86, 92–4, 328
  Spain 114, 126, 328–9
  Sweden 328
  see also two-party systems
Passos Coelho, P. 264, 265t, 273t, 275t
Pearson, L. 157t, 161, 163, 165t
Pedrazzani, A. 222 n.13
Pella, G. 232t
performance of minority governments 4, 5, 13, 19, 26–8, 325
  India 41, 58–62, 60t, 62, 340
  Italy 225–8, 229, 339
  Norway 81–3, 81t, 341
  Poland 256–7, 339
  Spain 120, 121–2t, 123–6, 339, 340
  Sweden 26, 28, 139–40, 141–2t, 143–4, 339
  United Kingdom 318–19, 321
Persson, T. 132t, 137–8, 142t, 144
Philippe, E. 172t, 183
Pickering, H. 27 n.6
Pickup, M. 28
Pinto, A.C. 266
Pinto, L. 219 n.9, 222 n.13

Poland 5, 13, 14, 15, 15t, 16, 16t, 29, 241–58, 261
  ad hoc coalitions 32, 241, 251, 252, 254, 334
  AWS 242t, 243, 245–6, 252, 254
  bicameral parliament 241
  bipolarity 243
  Civic Platform (PO) 242t, 243, 247, 249, 251 n.6, 252, 253t, 254, 255t
  coalitions 244–5, 246–7, 247f
  communists 243
  conservatives 243
  constitution 243, 246
  core parties 244, 256–7, 340
  corruption 243, 248, 252, 335
  executive coalition 255
  external support 254–5, 340
  FKP 252
  formal coalitions 252
  formation of governments 244–55, 331t
    Belka 248–9
    Buzek 245–6
    Kaczyński 250–1
    Miller 246–8
    post-2005 elections 249–50
    winning coalitions 246f, 247f, 249f
  fragmentation of party systems 328t
  gate-keeping 244
  government bills and approval rates 261t
  institutional factors 244
  instrumental motives 251
  inter-party policy differences 245
  investiture rules 244, 246, 248, 330
  Law and Justice party (PiS) 242t, 243, 247, 249–50, 251, 253t, 254, 255
  left parties 243
  legislative committees 244
  legislative success 256
  liberal parties 243
  LPR 242t, 247, 250–2, 253t, 254, 255, 255t
  majority governments 247, 255–6, 258
  majority requirement 243 n.1
  minority governments in office 251–2, 254
    ad hoc coalitions 252, 254
    external support 254–5
    party support 253t, 255t
  negative investiture provisions 244
  no confidence votes 243–4, 251 n.6, 341
  non-core parties 244–5, 256–8, 340
  office motivations 244
  office payoffs 32
  office-seeking 254, 258
  opposition influence 332t
  party support 253t, 255t
  performance of minority governments 256–7, 339

Poland (*Continued*)
    polarization 243, 249
    policy cycling 256
    policy-seeking motives 244, 251, 258
    political system 241–4
    populist parties 247, 254, 258, 337
    positive investiture rules 243–5, 258
    PSL 242*t*, 245, 247, 248, 251, 252, 253*t*, 254, 255*t*
    radical parties 258, 337
    rightist parties 243
    rolls and defeats 256–7, 257*t*
    ROP 245, 253*t*
    Rywin affair 248
    Samoobrone (SO) 242*t*, 247, 250, 253*t*, 254, 255, 255*t*
    SdPL 248, 252
    Sejm 241, 243–4, 341
    semi-presidential system 241
    Senat 241
    simple majority 243 n.1
    SLD 242*t*, 243, 246–8, 249*f*, 251, 252, 253*t*, 254, 255*t*, 257
    Solidarity 243, 245
    speakership 244
    stabilization pact 255
    sub-committees 254
    support parties 242*t*, 251–2, 256–7, 335, 337
    types of government 242*t*
    unsupported minority governments 242*t*, 256–8, 340
    UP 242*t*, 246–8, 252, 254
    UW 242*t*, 245–6, 252, 253*t*, 254
    winning coalitions 246*f*, 247*f*, 249, 249*f*
polarization 22
    France 179, 185
    Ireland 329
    Italy 219
    Poland 243, 249
    Portugal 266, 271–2
    Spain 125, 126, 336
    Sweden 135
    United Kingdom 306
policy concessions 329, 337
policy disagreement 22
policy-seeking goals 21, 336–7
    Australia 288, 289
    France 174, 175*t*, 182*t*
    Italy 208, 218
    Poland 244, 251, 258
    Portugal 262, 266, 269–70, 271, 272
    Romania 94–5, 99
    United Kingdom 306, 310, 311, 313
policy success 28

political decentralization 14
politics of minority governments 3–17
    changing contexts 12–14
    country studies 14–16
    definition 5–8
    frequency 8–10
    undercounting 10–12
Ponta, V. 89*t*, 94, 98–9, 101, 102*t*, 103
Pope, J. 5
Popescu-Tăriceanu, C. 88*t*, 95–6, 98–9, 100–1, 102*t*, 103
populist radical right parties 16
pork-barrel politics 180–2, 185–6, 194, 198, 329, 337
Portugal 5, 13–14, 15, 16, 29, 32, 95, 262–77
    absolute majority 271
    ad hoc majority building 334
    agenda-setting 264
    alliances 270–1, 277
    anti-system parties 264, 268–9, 270, 277
    Assembleia da República 263, 272
    center-right parties 263 n.1
    Christian Democrats (CDS) 263–4, 265*t*, 266, 268, 271–2
    closed-list proportional representation 263
    coalitions 263, 264, 274
    committee system 269
    communist parties 337
    Communist Party (PCP) 263, 264, 266–7, 268–9, 270, 271–2, 277
    competition structure 264, 268, 270
    confidence votes 264, 267–8
    Constitution 267, 277
    contract parliamentarism 28, 270, 276
    corruption 269
    democratic legitimacy 266
    dual legitimacy 266
    duration and survival of governments 272, 273, 273*t*
    election pledge fulfillment 274
    Enough (*Chega*) 263
    extreme left parties 266, 268, 276, 277
    feedback loops 333
    formal minority governments 265*t*, 270, 271, 277
    formal support agreements 334
    formateur 264, 267
    formation of governments 266–70, 331*t*
    fragmentation of party systems 15*t*, 328*t*
    Free (*Livre*) 263
    gross domestic product (GDP) growth 274–6, 275*t*
    ideological purity 269
    informateur 264, 267

institutional design 268
institutional peril 263
institutional solution to historical legacies 266, 267, 277
institutional variation 16t
intra-party politics 270, 277
law-making success 273t
Left Bloc (BE) 263, 264, 265t, 268–9, 270, 271–2, 277
left-wing parties 262, 264, 266, 270, 271, 277, 335
legislative debate about the government program 267
Liberal Initiative 263
majority building 270–1
majority governments 263, 273–4, 275, 277
minority governments in office 270–2
negative parliamentarism 264, 267
no confidence votes 268
office-seeking goals 269, 272
opposition influence 332t
Pactos MFA-Partido 266
party competition 266
party factions 277
party system configuration 327, 328
patronage 269
PCP 265t
performance 272–6, 277, 339, 340
 indicators 274, 275t
 law-making success and duration 273t
PEV 265t
polarization 266, 271–2
policy-seeking goals 262, 266, 269–70, 271, 272
political system 263–4, 266
PP 265t
PPM 265t
prevalence of minority governments 15t
proportion of seats held by governments 12f
pro-system parties 268–9
public deficit 274, 275t, 276
radical left parties 329, 337
rate of minority governments 9f
revolutionary legitimacy 266
rightist parties 264, 266–7, 268, 270–1
semi-presidentialism 263
single-party 262, 264, 274
Social Democrats (PSD) 263–4, 265t, 266, 268, 271–2
social expenditures 274–5, 275t
Socialist Party (PS) 3, 262, 263–4, 265t, 266–7, 268–9, 270–1, 272, 274, 277
Socialists 328, 331

substantive minority governments 265t, 270–1, 335
support parties 270–1
types of government 265t
unemployment 274–6, 275t
positive parliamentarism 23, 90, 92, 115, 158, 209
Potrafke, N. 21 n.3, 143–4
preferential voting 285, 288
presidential systems 7–8
 see also semi-presidential systems
prevalence of minority governments 15t, 29
Prodi, R. 212t, 214–15t, 220–1, 223, 224, 225, 228
proportional representation 72, 90, 113, 209, 210, 263, 284
proportion of seats held by governments 10f, 11f, 12f
public support 27
Pujol, J. 115, 116
pure parliamentary systems 9

radical parties 22–3, 329
 left 14, 16, 22
 right 14, 23
Rajoy, M. 110–11t, 112, 117, 119, 120, 121t, 123, 124–5
Rao (India) 45t, 53, 54, 55, 56, 58–9, 60t, 61, 62
Rasch, B.E. 22, 23–4, 115, 155, 156
Rasmussen, L.L. 3
rationalized parliamentarianism 31, 176–8, 185, 340
rational theory of formation 21
regional parties 14, 16, 24, 26, 336, 342
regular minority governments 31, 170, 173, 185
Reinfeldt, J.F. 132t, 142t
Reniu, J.M. 22
Renzi, M. 216t, 327
responsibility requirement 7, 20
Reynolds, A. 192t, 203t
rightist parties 22
Rocard, M. 171, 172t, 176, 178, 179–80, 182–4
Rodríguez Zapatero, J.L. 110t, 119, 121t
Romania 5, 7, 14, 15, 15t, 16, 16t, 29, 86–104
 absolute majority 90, 92, 330
 alliance-building 96, 98–9
 Alliance of Liberals and Democrats (ALDE) 89t, 91, 94, 98
 anti-corruption 101
 Arter, D. 94
 bicameralism, equal (or symmetric) 90
 center-left parties 91, 93, 99
 center-right parties 91, 93, 95, 99

Romania (*Continued*)
  Chamber of Deputies 90–1, 100, 103
  clientelism 86, 92, 96, 104
  coalitions 30, 93, 97, 98, 99
  Communist Party (PCR) 91
  confidence votes 90
  Conservative Party (PC) 88*t*, 89*t*, 96
  Constitution 90
  Constitutional Court 90
  corruption 86, 92, 96–7, 99, 103, 104, 337
  Democratic Alliance of Hungarians in Romania (UDMR) 87*t*, 88*t*, 89*t*, 91, 93–9, 103
  duration of governments 98, 100–1, 102*t*
  electoral competition 94
  electoral costs 94
  ethno-regional parties 99–100, 329, 337
  explicit agreement 96, 334
  FDSN 87*t*
  formal institutions 95–7
  formal minority governments 97
  formal support agreements 334
  formateur 90
  formation of governments 91–7, 331*t*
    formal and informal institutions 95–7
    office, policy and vote goals 94–5
    party system attributes 92–4
  fragmentation of party systems 328*t*
  government bills 103
  hinge party strategy 93–4
  Humanist Party/Conservative Party (PUR/PC) 91
  independents 93
  informal institutions 95–7
  informal support 334
  institutionalization 30, 91
  investiture rules 92
  investiture vote, ex-post 90
  issue-based bloc alignment 93
  junior coalition partners 94
  legislative record 102*t*
  Liberal Democratic Party (PDL) 87*t*, 88*t*, 89*t*, 91, 93–4, 98
  mainstream parties 99
  majority-building 335
  MER 87*t*
  minimum winning coalitions 100
  minority governments in office 97–100
    alliance-building 98–9
    cabinet duration 100–1
    electoral and policy performance 101, 103
    government performance 100–3
    support parties 99–100
    types of government 97–8
  National Anti-corruption Agency 96
  National Liberal Party (PNL) 87*t*, 88*t*, 89*t*, 91, 94, 98, 101
  National Minority Caucus (NMC) 88*t*, 89*t*, 91, 93–5, 98, 99–100
  National Salvation Front (FSN) 87*t*, 91, 92
  National Unity Party (PUNR) 87*t*, 91, 92–3, 94
  no confidence votes 94, 98, 99, 101
  non-partisan parties 89*t*
  office-seeking goals 94–5, 99
  opposition influence 332*t*
  PAR 87*t*
  party switching 96, 98–9, 104, 338
  party system 30, 86
    attributes 92–4
    configuration 328
  PD 87*t*, 88*t*
  PDAR 87*t*
  PDSR 87*t*, 97–8
  performance of governments 98, 100–3, 339, 340
  personalization 91
  PL 87*t*
  PLR 89*t*
  PNLCD 87*t*
  PNTCD 87*t*, 88*t*
  policy performance 101, 103
  policy-seeking goals 94–5, 99
  political system 90–1
  Popular Movement Party (PMP) 89*t*, 94
  positive parliamentarism 90, 92
  power-sharing 96
  presidential activism 95
  PRM 87*t*
  proportional representation 90
  Pro-Romania (PRO) 94
  PSD 88*t*, 89*t*, 92–3, 98, 101, 103
  PSDR 87*t*, 88*t*
  PSM 87*t*
  rogue parliamentarians 329
  Save Romania Union (USR) 89*t*, 94
  semi-presidential regime 86, 90, 95
  Senate 90
  single-party 86, 90, 92, 98
  Social Democratic Party (PSD) 91, 95, 96
  Social Liberal Union (USL) 93
  state capture 96
  support agreements/parties 94, 97–8, 99–100, 101
  surplus winning coalitions 100
  temporary agreements 99
  Truth and Justice Alliance 96

INDEX   361

types of minority government 87–9t, 97–8, 333–4
Union for the Progress of Romania (UNPR) 88t, 89t, 91, 93–4, 98
voter polarization 93–4
voting goals 94–5
Roman, P. 87t, 92
Rozenberg, O. 31, 330–1, 339, 340, 341
Rudd, K. 285, 286t, 290, 294, 295, 296t
Rumor, M. 235–6t
Russell, P.H. 164
Russo, F. 272
Rutte, M. 11

Saalfeld, T. 151
Sánchez, P. 3, 109, 111t, 112, 117, 119, 120, 121–2t, 124–5
Santana Lopes, P. 265t, 273t, 275t
Santana-Pereira, J. 28, 270
Savage, L.M. 245
Scandinavia 3, 13, 22
    see also Denmark; Norway; Sweden scel
Scandinavian model of minority governments 125
Scelba, M. 233t
Schlesinger, J. 98
Schofield, N. 92, 218–19, 244
Segni, A. 233t
semi-presidential systems 8, 9, 13, 86, 90, 95, 241, 263
Sened, I. 244
Shastri, L.B. (India) 60t, 65t
Shekhar, C. 45t, 53, 60t
Shepsle, K.A. 225–6
Sheridan, R.B. 195t
Sherwin, F. 195t
shifting majorities 25
Siegel, D.A. 23
simple majorities 6, 114, 209, 243 n.1, 316
Singh, C. 60t, 61, 65t
Singh, M. 44, 49–51t, 58–9, 60t, 62
Singh, V.P. 45t, 55, 60t
single-member plurality (SMP) 307, 310, 311
single-party minority governments 5, 8, 10, 27, 41, 328, 333
    Australia 32, 291, 295
    Canada 31, 151, 153, 156, 158–9, 164, 167
    India 30, 55, 58, 59, 340
    Italy 210, 219, 225
    Norway 30, 66, 67t, 68t, 69, 69t, 73, 81, 82
    Portugal 262, 264, 274
    Romania 86, 90, 92, 98
    Spain 25, 28, 30, 108, 109, 112, 114–15, 117
    Sweden 129, 133, 134, 137

United Kingdom 306–7, 311, 319, 321, 338
single transferable vote system 42, 193, 205
Skjeie, H. 78
Slovenia 9f, 12f
small minorities 59, 61, 61t
Soares, M. 264, 265t, 273t, 275, 275t
social democratic parties 14
Sócrates, J. 262, 264, 265t, 272, 273t, 275t
Soisson, J.-P. 179, 181
Solberg, E. 68t, 74, 77, 78, 79, 80, 81, 83
Spadolini, G. 238t
Spain 5, 7, 13–15, 29, 108–26, 133, 310, 317, 319
    absolute majority 112, 114–15
    alliance building 118, 119, 125
    Aragonese Regionalist Party (PAR) 110t
    Aragonese Union (CHA) 110t
    Asturias Forum (Foro) 111t
    Basque Nationalist Party (PNV) 110t, 111t, 113, 116, 117, 125, 126
    Basque nationalists 116, 124, 336
    bicameralism 109
    Canary Coalition (CC) 110t, 111t, 116, 124
    caretaker governments 121t
    Catalan Democratic Union Party (PDeCAT) 116 n.8
    Catalan nationalists 113, 116, 117, 124–5, 126, 336
    Catalan Republican Left (ERC) 110t, 119
    center-left parties 109
    center-periphery 108, 124, 126, 336
    center-right parties 109, 116
    Citizens party 109, 111t, 117, 125
    coalitions 108, 114, 126
    Commitment for the Valencian Country (CPV) 111t
    Communist Party (PCE) 113
    confidence votes 114
    Congress of Deputies 109, 112–13, 115, 124, 125, 330
    constitution 108, 112, 113, 114, 115, 116
    contextual factors 108, 112, 115
    contract parliamentarism 118
    Convergence and Union (CiU) 110t, 115, 116, 117
    core parties 329
    decentralization 26, 108–9, 116, 125–6
    Democratic Coalition (CD) 110t
    Democratic Convergence of Catalonia (CDC) 116 n.8
    democratic transition 113
    EH Bildu 119
    executives-parties dimension 108
    formal minority governments 28, 110t, 118–19, 334

Spain (*Continued*)
 formation of governments 22, 112–18, 331*t*
  formation post-2015 117–18
  political context and institutional design 112–15
  regional parties and party goals 115–17
 fragmentation of party systems 15*t*, 328*t*, 329, 336
 Galician Nationalist Block (BNG) 110*t*, 111*t*
 historical legacies 108, 112
 institutional variation 16*t*
 intra-party politics 338
 investiture procedure 112, 114–15, 118, 330, 331
 left-wing parties 113, 116, 124
 legislature or parliamentary term pact 118
 majority governments 121–2*t*, 123
 minority coalitions 112
 minority governments in office 118–20
 More Country (MP) 111*t*
 multilevel exchanges 118, 120, 126
 nationalist parties 3, 109, 116, 329, 337
 negative parliamentarism 115
 New Canaries (NC) 111*t*
 no confidence votes 109, 112, 114, 117, 124, 125
 non-core parties 329
 office concessions 118, 120
 opposition influence 332*t*
 Organic Laws 123
 parliamentary committees 123
 partisan bargaining 31, 113, 123, 124, 125
 party goals 31, 115–17, 123, 125
 party system 114, 126, 328–9
 PDC 116
 performance of minority governments 120, 121–2*t*, 123–6, 339, 340
 polarization 125, 126, 336
 policy concessions 120
 political instability 114
 political institutions 31, 114, 123, 126
 political system 109, 112
 Popular Alliance (AP) 113, 113 n.4, 116
 Popular Party (PP) 109, 110*t*, 111*t*, 113 n.4, 116, 117, 120, 124–5, 329
 positive parliamentarism 115
 prevalence of minority governments 15*t*
 proportional representation 113
 proportion of seats held by governments 12*f*
 radical left parties 3, 329
 radical right parties 109
 rate of minority governments 9*f*
 regional parties 108–9, 112, 113, 115–20, 124–6, 329, 337

Republican Left of Catalonia 336
right-wing parties 109, 113, 124
Second Republic 114, 333
Senate 109
simple majorities 114
single-party 25, 28, 30, 108, 109, 112, 114–15, 117
Socialist Party of Andalusia (PSA) 110*t*
Socialists 3, 113, 120, 329, 336
Socialist-United 7
Socialist Workers' Party (PSOE) 109, 110*t*, 111*t*, 113, 114, 116, 117, 119, 124–6
subnational level 336
substantive minority governments 25, 28, 110–11*t*, 118–19, 334
support parties 118, 119, 120, 334
Teruel Exists (TE) 111*t*
Together for Catalonia (JxCat) 116 n.8
types of government 110–11*t*, 126
Union of the Democratic Center (UCD) 109, 110*t*, 112–17
Union of the Navarre People (UPN) 110*t*, 111*t*
United Left (IU) 110*t*, 118
United We Can (UP) 111*t*, 118, 119, 125–6, 336
Vox 109, 117
We Can (Podemos) 109, 111*t*, 117–18, 125
Sridharan, E. 62
standing committees 23
Steel, D. 317
Stepan, A. 266
St-Laurent, L. 157*t*, 165*t*
Stolojan, T. 87*t*
Stoltenberg, J. 68*t*, 77 n.9, 83
Strøm, K.W. 3 n.1, 4, 6–7, 13, 20–1, 23–5, 27, 30, 44, 54, 61, 78, 97, 118–19, 134, 136, 151, 202, 208, 218, 222–5, 227–8, 251, 269, 295, 313–16, 329, 333–5, 337, 341–2
strong committees 331, 337
Suárez, A. 109, 110*t*, 112–15, 121*t*
substantive minority governments 24–5, 333–4
 Australia 287*t*, 301*t*
 Canada 156, 157*t*, 161, 335
 India 45*t*, 61, 65*t*
 Ireland 192*t*, 334
 Italy 223, 232*t*, 235*t*, 237–8*t*
 Portugal 265*t*, 270–1, 335
 Spain 25, 28, 110–11*t*, 118–19, 334
 Sweden 131–2*t*
 United Kingdom 308–9*t*, 314, 317, 319
super majorities 6
support agreements/parties 24–6, 336–7, 340
 Australia 293–4

Italy 223, 337
Poland 242t, 251–2, 256–7, 335, 337
Romania 94, 97–8, 99–100, 101
Spain 118, 119, 120, 334
Sweden 129, 136–9, 144–5, 337
United Kingdom 307, 310, 314, 315–18, 321, 337, 338
surplus coalitions 100, 210, 218, 221, 225
surplus majorities 12
Italy 211–17t, 228, 232t, 234–40t
Norway 67t, 69, 69t
Sweden 5, 14–16, 29, 72, 129–45, 295
ad hoc agreements/support 136–7
Alliance parties 135, 137, 139, 143–4
Centre Party (Agrarian party) (C) 130, 131–2t, 133, 135, 137–8
centre-right parties 133, 137
Christian Democrats (KD) 130, 132t, 133, 139
coalition agreements 138
coalition bargaining 135, 145
committee system 133
constitution 134, 140
contract parliamentarism 31, 129, 136, 144, 334, 337
coordination group 138
December agreement 139
extremist parties 135
fiscal performance 143
formal minority governments 132t, 136
formation of governments 24, 130, 133–6, 331t
fragmentation of party systems 15t, 328t
functioning of minority governments 25
Green party (MP) 130, 133, 135, 137–9
Greens (G) 132t
'hinge party' 137
informateur 130
institutional variations 16t
Instrument of Government (1809) 130
Instrument of Government (1975) 130, 140–1
investiture requirements/vote 130, 133, 134, 135–7
Left party (V) 130, 131–2t, 133, 135, 136–9
left-right alignment 134, 144–5
left to center-left bloc 133
legislative success/effectiveness 139–40
Liberal Party (L) 130, 131–2t, 133, 135, 138–9
majority governments 140, 143, 144
minority governments in office 136–9
Moderate Party (M) 130, 131–2t, 133, 135
multiparty system 130
negative parliamentarism 129, 133, 134, 144, 330

New Democracy 137
non-socialist parties 133, 135
opposition influence 332t
party system configuration 328
performance of minority governments 26, 28, 139–40, 141–2t, 143–4, 339
pledge fulfillment 143
polarization 135
political system 130, 133
populist right parties 137, 329
prevalence of minority governments 15t
proportion of seats held by governments 12f
rate of minority governments 9f
right-wing parties 133
Riksdag 130, 134, 138, 140, 143
single-party 129, 133, 134, 137
Social Democrats (S) 31, 129–30, 131t, 132t, 133–8, 143–5, 327
socialist parties 133
Speaker of Parliament 130
Standing committees 134, 140
substantive minority governments 131–2t
support parties 129, 136–9, 144–5, 337
Sweden Democrats (SD) 130, 133, 134–5, 137, 139, 145
trust in governments 144
two-bloc politics 329
two-dimensional system 130
types of government 131–2t
Syse, J.P. 68t
Szydlo, B.M. 242t

Tambroni, F.T. 233t
Teles, M.G. 277
temporal trends 9
territorial dimension of politics 24, 335–6, 342
Thatcher, M. 308t, 320t
Thomas, P.E.J. 28
Thürk, M. 22, 179
Torp (Norway) 67t
Trudeau, J. 157t, 167
Trudeau, P. 157t, 162, 165t
Tudose, M. 89t, 102t
Turnbull, M. 287t, 290, 296t
Tusk, D. 242t, 249, 257t, 261t
two-bloc politics 72–5, 83, 329
two-party systems 20 n.2, 53, 288–9, 297, 328
types of minority government 333–5
Australia 286–7t, 291–2, 301–4t
Canada 156, 157t, 161–2
India 45–52t, 65t
Ireland 191–2t
Italy 211–17t, 232–40t
Norway 67–8t

types of minority government (*Continued*)
    Poland 242*t*
    Portugal 265*t*
    Romania 87–9*t*, 97–8, 333–4
    Spain 110–11*t*, 126
    Sweden 131–2*t*
    United Kingdom 308–9*t*, 314–15, 319

Ullsten, O. 131*t*, 142*t*
undercounting 10–12, 326–7, 341
Ungureanu, M.R. 89*t*, 93–4, 98–9, 102*t*
United Kingdom 3, 5, 6, 14–15, 29, 33, 306–22, 326
    agenda control 310, 315–18
    alliances 316
    bicameral system 307
    coalitions 307, 311
    committee structure 310, 317
    Conservatives 3, 7, 307, 308–9*t*, 310–18, 321, 336
    contract parliamentarism 314–15
    coordination committee 315
    Democratic Unionist Party (DUP) 309*t*, 311, 313–16, 318, 336
    devolution 310–11, 317
    duration of governments 319, 320*t*
    Fixed Term Parliaments Act (2011) 319
    formal minority governments 308–9*t*, 314, 318
    formation of governments 310–14, 331*t*
        Callaghan intra-term government (1976-9) 312–13
        Major intra-term government 313
        May post-election government 213–14
        party goals, limited options and costs of governing 310–12
        post-election minority government (1974) 312
    fragmentation of party systems 15*t*, 328*t*
    Green Party 311
    House of Commons 7, 306–7, 317, 318, 321
    House of Lords 7, 307
    Independence Party 311
    institutional variation 16*t*
    intra-term minority governments 306, 314, 316–17, 321
    investiture rules 330
    joint consultative committee 315
    Labour 307, 308–9*t*, 310–18, 321
    legislative record 320*t*
    Liberal Democrats 308*t*, 309*t*, 311, 312, 313, 315, 317, 321
    Lib-Lab Pact 312–15, 318

    majoritarian system 306–7
    minority governments in office 314–18
        agenda control and support parties 315–18
        types of government 314–15
    multiparty politics 307
    no confidence votes 317
    Northern Ireland Grand Committee 318
    office-seeking goals 310, 311, 312
    opposition influence 332*t*
    parliamentary system 307
    performance of minority governments 318–19, 321
    Plaid Cymru 310, 317
    polarization 306
    policy-seeking goals 306, 310, 311, 313
    political system 307, 310
    post-election minority governments 306, 307, 318
    prevalence of minority governments 15*t*
    proportion of seats held by governments 12*f*
    public bill committees 316
    Queen's Speech 307, 312, 330 n.1
    rate of minority governments 9*f*
    regional parties 310–11, 314, 315–16, 321, 329, 337
    Scottish National Party (SNP) 310, 313, 315, 317, 321, 336
    simple majorities 316
    single-member plurality (SMP) 307, 310, 311
    single-party 306–7, 311, 319, 321, 338
    Standing Orders of the House of Commons 316, 318
    substantive minority governments 308–9*t*, 314, 317, 319
    Sunningdale Agreement on power-sharing in Northern Ireland 312
    support parties 307, 310, 314, 315–18, 321, 337, 338
    types of government 308–9*t*, 314–15, 319
    Ulster Unionist Party (UUP) 312–13, 315, 317–18
    Withdrawal Agreement 319 n.2
upper chamber 6

Văcăriou, N. 87*t*, 92–3, 94, 98, 100–1
Vajpayee, A.B. 44, 45*t*, 46–7*t*, 48–9*t*, 57, 58, 60*t*, 61, 62
Valera, É. de 204
Varadkar, L. 192*t*, 203*t*
Vasile, R. 87–8*t*, 102*t*
Vercesi, M. 224
veto points 22, 179
Vizcaya Retana, M. 116

Voiculescu, D. 96
vote-seeking parties 21, 174, 175*t*, 182*t*
voting system plurality 151–3, 156, 160, 166

Weeks, L. 26, 31–2, 205, 334, 338
Westminster-style parliamentary system 70, 152, 154–5, 158–9, 189
Whitaker, R. 33, 330, 338
Whitlam, G. 303*t*, 305*t*

why minority governments form *see* formation of minority governments
Wilkie, A. 289–90, 294, 295
Willoch, K. 68*t*, 77, 78
Wilson, H. 308*t*, 312, 316, 319, 320*t*
winner takes all 20 n.2

Zappone, K. 195*t*
Zoli, A. 233*t*
Zubek, R. 28, 32, 330, 339, 340, 341